The Russian Quest for Peace and Democracy

The Russian Quest for Peace and Democracy

Metta Spencer

Professor Emeritus
University of Toronto

LEXINGTON BOOKS
Lanham • Boulder • New York • Toronto • Plymouth, UK

Published by Lexington Books
A wholly owned subsidary of The Rowman & Littlefield Publishing Group, Inc.
4501 Forbes Boulevard, Suite 200, Lanham, Maryland 20706
http://www.lexingtonbooks.com

Estover Road, Plymouth PL6 7PY, United Kingdom

British Library Cataloguing in Publication Information Available

Library of Congress Cataloging-in-Publication Data

The hardback edition of this book was previously catalogued by the Library of Congress
as follows:

Spencer, Metta, 1931–
The Russian Quest for Peace and Democracy / Metta Spencer.
    p. cm.
  Includes bibliographical references and index.
  1. Soviet Union—Politics and government—1985–1991. 2. Democracy—Soviet
Union—History. 3. Peace movements—Soviet Union—History. 4. Civil society—
Soviet Union—History. 5. Transnationalism—Social aspects—Soviet Union—History.
6. Russia (Federation)—Politics and government—1991– 7. Democracy—Russia
(Federation) 8. Peace movements—Russia (Federation) 9. Civil society—Russia
(Federation) 10. Transnationalism—Social aspects—Russia (Federation) I. Title.
  DK288.S7246 2010
  320.947—dc22
  [B]   2010021541

ISBN 978-0-7391-4472-5 (cloth : alk. paper)
ISBN 978-0-7391-4473-2 (paper : alk. paper)

Printed in the United States of America

Table of Contents

Introduction

They have built a museum in the Kremlin, but it displays only ancient things. You have to discover the new things for yourself. Fortunately, outside the fortress walls many changes are obvious: The traffic, for example, is too clogged with Mercedes and Lexus cars to move, but when it does move, they all race fiercely.

There are subtle changes too, such as the vibrations. If you know where to look, you can go dig up quartz crystals that liberal "New Age" Russians have buried in strategic spots around the Kremlin, hoping to counteract the vibes of tyranny. But I don't know where to look, and if you find any, please leave them alone. The fortress needs all the purification my democratic friends can give it.

I can tell you a bit about the political intrigues inside the Kremlin, but I am more fascinated by the political orientations of the people living outside its walls. Their changes I will describe in this book.

My account is based on hundreds of interviews spanning twenty-eight years, from my first visit to Moscow in 1982 until 2010. I have interviewed quite a few people six or eight times. Long ago I lost count of my trips to Russia. I used to go once or twice a year, but there were two interruptions—once for four years after I was expelled for associating with dissidents, and again later for health reasons. When I could not go there, I continued interviewing Soviets and then Russians at conferences and by phone.

This is not an ethnography; instead, I have some political theories to disprove. One of my professors, Karl Popper, insisted that science doesn't progress by proving certain theories true, but rather by proving other theories false and thereby eliminating them from the list of possible explanations. Political sociology progresses in the same way.

There are three main theories that I intend to refute here; all of them are widespread and influential. I wish I could absolutely eliminate them from our shared worldview, for doing so would alter the way we conduct international affairs. These three assumptions are as follows:

First, there's the false belief *the West won the Cold War by "containing" Communism and spending more on weapons than the Soviets could match, until finally Gorbachev "blinked."* (The truth: We all lost the Cold War, and nobody

1

imposed democracy and disarmament on Gorbachev. He and his advisers had been seeking democratic and anti-militaristic innovations of Western origin for years. Far more advanced than Reagan, he adopted innovative proposals eagerly and, after Communism faltered in 1989, encouraged the third great global wave of democratization.)

Second, there's the false belief that, *at best, only a country's own population can influence its policies. Indeed, in an authoritarian regime, even the citizens have virtually no say, and certainly foreigners who lack a vote or corporate power can have no impact.* (The truth: Democracy, human rights, and nonviolence are rarely re-invented independently by local citizens. Usually they are imported from abroad and spread by personal contacts in international civil society, not by diplomats or rulers. That was the way it happened in the Soviet Union. This book will describe how certain back-channel relationships with foreign peace researchers and activists influenced that country's brief democratization, its foreign policy, and its military doctrine.) As political scientist John Sigler noted in a lecture at the University of Toronto just before the USSR dissolved,

> In our present preoccupation with the failures of the Soviet system, we may be neglecting one very positive contribution of the Gorbachev era: "New Thinking" about international politics. This may be one of the greatest ironies of recent changes in world politics because the ideas espoused and practiced recently by the Soviet Union do not derive from Soviet think tanks, nor in the imitation of the practices and ideas of the Western foreign policy establishment. They come from Western critics of defense and security policy over the past thirty years.
>
> John Steinbrenner of the Brookings Institution in Washington recently pointed out that Gorbachev and his original foreign policy team had borrowed their "New Thinking" from the Western peace research movement. One of the key figures in that borrowing was Alexander Yakovlev, for ten years the Soviet Ambassador in Ottawa, who read widely in this literature in peace research—particularly the ideas of this college's own peace studies mentor, Anatol Rapoport, himself an immigrant to North America from Russia. The irony is that the peace research movement appears to have had very little influence on the Western governmental establishments.[1]

Third, there's *the false belief that peace and democracy are two different matters that should be addressed separately. It makes sense for liberal democracies to work for peace when dealing with other countries, but whether those other countries are democratic or authoritarian is nobody's business except their own. No country should try to promote democracy in another state.* (The truth: Dictatorships use weapons against their own people and other nations alike, whereas democracies treat other democracies nonviolently. When any two states are at war against each other, you can be sure that one or both is authoritarian. Establishing democracy in every country will eliminate international warfare and most internal repression as well. In Russia, as elsewhere, the project of peacebuilding is inseparable from the project of democratization.)

I hope to dispel these three false myths by telling a single story about the political changes that occurred in the Soviet Union/Russia between the early 1980s and 2010. Understanding these ups and downs will suggest useful foreign policies—especially the crucial importance of transnational civil society, which we should revitalize today.

I was a part of that international network. I started visiting Russia as a peace activist, and a peace activist I remain. Yet my approach has expanded as I came to cherish my relationships with a growing number of Russian friends. I visit there, time after time, because I enjoy the many remarkable, intelligent, perceptive people I meet there. Our conversations always are about significant ideas, not idle chit-chat. It's a rich culture.

Yet even as my personal relationships continue to grow, I also worry about Russians, sensing the precariousness of their post-totalitarian society. This book is a study of their progress toward peace and democracy, but equally it is a reminder that vigilance is required for the prevention of totalitarian rule. Some conditions remain present, one must acknowledge, for the loss of peace and freedom. In every society, but perhaps most in Russia, there are social traps that jeopardize democracy. The memory of Stalinism stands as a warning, yet not all Russians notice their vulnerability. Thus my motive has become this: to show how they were acquiring democracy for a short time, what endangers it now, and how Russians and the rest of the world may protect it.

Gorbachev's advancement of democracy and peaceful foreign relations was fostered by private conversations in international civil society. And yet peaceable democracy didn't take root in Russia; it still fluctuates in sync with varying foreign civil society contacts. My conclusion will offer one main suggestion: that the prospects for peace and democracy can be enhanced most by facilitating personal encounters between Russians and foreigners who are addressing global problems. Fortunately, this is technologically easy to do.

The advocates of freedom everywhere—especially in Russia—now regard civil society as essential for democratizing societies. When people participate together in voluntary groups—stamp collectors' clubs, trade unions, Bible study groups, or senior citizens' gardening societies—they create new social networks and develop new personal capacities. They learn how to organize collective events and mobilize groups to oppose a public policy or support a political candidate.

But if civil society is a necessary precondition for the development of democracy, not all such independent groupings are equally conducive to democracy. I'll show that *transnational* civil society organizations are the most helpful, for they create heterogeneous relationships that inform and strengthen individuals who, in an authoritarian setting, face heavy pressures to conform.

As the sociologist Robert Putnam has shown,[2] civil society organizations can have two different, sometimes even contradictory, effects: by either "bonding" or "bridging" their members. Groups whose members have similar attitudes tend to generate internal bonds of *in-group* solidarity. On the other hand, civil society organizations with heterogeneous memberships tend to *bridge* the society's disparate elements. An evangelical church is mainly a bonding civil society organization, whereas an Internet chat group is more a bridging one. It is primarily these latter, bridging, groups that have democratizing effects, largely by exposing citizens to ideas that may be proscribed by their rulers, and thereby challenging facile group consensus.

The bridges created within transnational civil society organizations influenced the liberalization of policies in Moscow for a time. For example, Soviet scientists—including even weapons designers—had opportunities to meet their Western counterparts abroad and discuss military policies during the 1980s in a context of civility. Such personal back-channel dialogues influenced the substance of treaties that were negotiated to end the Cold War.

Not all of these democratizing and peace-building reforms were fulfilled, however. The Soviet Union broke apart in 1991 with a turn toward capitalism, and for several years the changes yielded more chaos than progress, mainly because of the deficiency of trust and social capital in Russian society.

But lessons can be learned by studying those failures, which were the direct effect of a prolonged polarization within the pro-democracy movement. There had long been two mutually hostile (albeit mostly hidden) networks in Soviet civil society. These communities hated each other—irrationally so, for they actually shared compatible liberal goals. The gap between them widened until at last Gorbachev's centrist base abandoned him. As a result the Soviet Union disintegrated, and Russia fell back into an authoritarian system of governance. This is the substance of the story that I'll tell, before reflecting on the possibilities for democracy and peace that remain alive in 2010 and beyond.

The issues and dynamics that form the plot of this drama were not limited to the unique circumstances of Soviet and post-Soviet Russia, but occur in various societies again and again. Insofar as we learn from the recent Russian experience, we will acquire insights that will help meet challenges in other societies that face similar issues, now and in the future.

Metta Spencer
Toronto
RussianPeaceAndDemocracy.com

Notes

1. John Sigler, "The Search for Peace" (lecture, Science for Peace, Toronto, April 1991).

2. Robert D. Putnam, Robert Leonardi, and Raffaella Y. Nanetti, *Making Democracy Work: Civic Traditions in Modern Italy* (Princeton: Princeton University Press, 1994).

Chapter 1: Termites and Barking Dogs

In an authoritarian regime, most people favor (or pretend to favor) whatever the state decrees—regardless of what they truly believe or wish for in their hearts. We can call them "Yea-sayers" or even "SHEEP." But Yea-sayers are not all alike. Some are truly fervent supporters of the state's policies, while others don't know what to believe, but assent only from habit or to protect themselves.

Besides Yea-sayers, there exist some critical people—"Naythinkers"—who harbor political opposition to official state policies, which they may or may not express aloud. Most histories of the Soviet Union describe its collapse as resulting from conflict between the "Yea" and "Nay" groups—those who favored and those who opposed the regime. But there is more to the story than that.

Naythinkers too are not all alike. Some are like termites, toiling silently within the structure of the state that they dislike. Others are like barking dogs—noisily challenging the political status quo. And, unlike other histories of the Soviet Union, this book will argue that the Soviet downfall primarily resulted from the conflict between these two mutually antagonistic groups of its Naythinkers—its TERMITES and its BARKING DOGS. Let me describe how I came to see that hostility, which would have grave implications.

* * *

In October Moscow had already been dusted with snow when I first visited in 1982. The Cold War was even frostier. The Soviet Union and the United States were installing nuclear missiles, but the Soviets were gruffly offering to stop if their adversary would do likewise, whereas the Americans were not even pausing. Perhaps that is why the Soviets had invited us, in a forlorn hope that we Canadians would talk some sense into our American neighbors' heads.

But I was an American myself at that time and not especially friendly. The border guard stared at my U.S. passport, compared its photo to my eyes, my mouth, my hair, and wordlessly waved me through without smiling. We both coldly disliked each other, though I had come to build bridges if I could, and eventually I succeeded.

Our delegation of peaceniks from Canada did not expect Brezhnev to die within weeks and be succeeded by a more intelligent but ailing Yury Andropov,

5

who would crack open the frozen society slightly. Andropov and his successor Chernenko would each last only about a year, eventually making way for an enlightened new general secretary, Mikhail Gorbachev. Had I known what lay ahead, I would have smiled at the dour young border guard; indeed, we might have laughed together.

Our delegation of about a dozen had been invited, all expenses paid, to participate in a "dialogue" with Soviet policymakers about the escalating nuclear showdown. Indeed, I would be invited again and again to similar meetings, mostly in Moscow, some in Vienna, and once in Prague. Always we would transit Moscow and stay a day or two before proceeding to our final Eastern European destination. Later, captivated by the country, I would continue visiting, but paying my own way.

Initially I expected most of the Canadian guests to be Communists, but this was not so. The organizers, led by Mac Makarchuk, a former Ontario parliamentarian and stalwart of the New Democratic Party, had stopped rewarding the Communist faithful with free junkets and now chose cross-sections of Canadian activists. I was probably invited because, as a sociology professor at the University of Toronto, I taught peace studies and had organized a clearinghouse for disarmament groups, with its monthly tabloid paper, which would become *Peace Magazine*. (I am still its editor.)

The Official Communist Peace Movements

Nobody told us who was paying the bills, but it was easy to guess: the Soviet Committee for the Defense of Peace (SCDP—usually known as Soviet Peace Committee). Millions of Soviet citizens regularly donated money to the Soviet Peace Fund at their workplace. As one woman explained, there was hardly anything in shops worth buying anyway, so she regularly contributed a big part of her earnings to the fund, which never had to give a public accounting of its income or expenditures, nor was it governed by any elected board of directors. The fund supported not only the SCDP but also other related bureaucracies, such as international student organizations and women's committees, each of which had parallel structures in every Eastern-bloc country, to promote various "peace-loving" policies. The Peace Fund also covered about three-quarters of the expenditures of the World Peace Council (WPC), based on Helsinki. It and the SCDP were founded in 1949 as official Party agencies, staffed by bureaucrats.

For several years there also existed something called the "International Liaison Forum" (ILF), which was created to be a front for the World Peace Council. Many reputable Westerners accepted invitations to its events who would not have accepted a WPC invitation. The Soviet Peace Fund also supported it.

Though the WPC and the Soviet peace and international friendship bureaucracies claimed not to be agencies of the state, their officers were appointed by the Central Committee of the Communist Party of the Soviet Union (CPSU), which also determined their policies. There were no parallels between these official agencies and the protest groups of independent Western activists. The chairperson of the SCDP was always a high-ranking party official. For example, when I first attended conferences of the SCDP, its president was Yury Zhukov, the hard-line journalist at *Pravda*. His successor during the Gorbachev era was Genrikh Borovik, a famous journalist, who loosened control periodically.

For years the World Peace Council functioned as the global Communist peace movement. It had a staff of about sixty in Helsinki and some 140 member organizations worldwide.[1] Originally it tried to attract prominent Europeans such as Einstein, but he and many others refused the tainted organization. When the French and Italian Communists considered it too tied to Soviet policy, they quit, leaving it an official Soviet tool with little sway in Europe. China withdrew in 1966 because of the Sino-Soviet split, reducing the organization's credibility with Western Maoists, the "New Left" of the day.

But an Indian Communist, Romesh Chandra, became WPC leader in 1966 and devoted his attention to the Third World, with much success. The Third World wanted ties with Moscow but such connections irritated Americans, the British, and the French, with whom they also wanted ties. Their solution was to forge links with Moscow—not directly, but through the WPC. Third World countries considered Moscow the friend of the anti-imperialist movement.[2]

Chandra organized Third World opposition to the U.S.'s war in Vietnam. It was easy to vilify the United States. However, the Soviet invasion of Czechoslovakia in 1968 was a problem for the WPC, since the Third World opposed it. Still, Chandra's approach worked well until the Soviets invaded Afghanistan in 1979, an action that the WPC supported but Third World countries did not.

In the early 1980s a new peace movement emerged in Europe that, like the U.S. movement in opposition to the Vietnam War, was completely beyond WPC influence. Western activists wanted cuts in both the Warsaw Pact and NATO; we criticized NATO's decision to put tactical (mid-range) nuclear weapons such as the U.S. cruise missile in Europe, and also criticized the deployment of the Soviet SS-20 mid-range missiles. The WPC antagonism to this Western movement caused an internal crisis in the Socialist camp. Several Eastern European Peace Committees (East Germans, then Hungarians and Czechoslovaks) broke with the WPC and developed independent contacts with the West.

By 1986, even the SCDP would be making its own contacts in Europe and North America rather than working through the WPC. The type of command-style bureaucrat who worked at the WPC was inept in dealing with West German or Canadian peace activists, whereas the Eastern European committees could do so. Responding to the need for more flexible leaders, the SCDP briefly chose Andrei Melville as their secretary, and the Czechoslovakians chose a remarkable man, Ivan Fiala. An open-minded American, Robert Prince, joined the WPC in Helsinki. Reflecting regretfully on that period, Prince told me in 1995,

> Not only did we need contacts with peace movements outside [the Soviet Union], we also needed contacts with peace movements *inside* it: unofficial movements. But that's where the Peace Committees drew the line. Otherwise, though, these committees were able to reach out. The SCDP dropped its [foreign] Communist Party contacts like a hot potato and went for the new U.S. think tanks—organizations like the Center for Defense Information—and a new circle who tended not to be poor people but white, well-do-do people.

But this period of reform ended quickly. It was a form of liberalization but *glasnost* required real *democratization*—quite a different thing. The WPC and the Soviet Peace Committee saw that this liberalization had gotten out of their hands. They[3] rejoined forces with Chandra and put an end to the reform with a purge in 1990. The WPC is still there but cannot become democratic.[4]

I saw Romesh Chandra speaking a couple of times while he headed the WPC—most memorably in the University of Toronto's Convocation Hall in the mid-1980s. I was sitting in the back of the room where I could see outside. During the question period a man in the audience challenged Chandra in a manner that is normal in democracies. About ten men sprang up, dragged the questioner from the hall, and beat him mercilessly on the stone steps. I had never seen such behavior in an American or Canadian meeting. No police were present to intervene. Chandra paused fleetingly but then continued serenely without commenting on the event we had just seen. I don't know what happened afterward.

When the Soviet Union ended, the WPC continued in a much reduced level. According to a Finnish newspaper in November 1991, the organization was surviving on the interest from a fund established by a one time donation from the SCDP. The annual interest amounted to U.S. $220,000. Only ten of the member organizations had paid their dues for 1991, as contrasted with 140 in the good old days. It is now based in Athens, under a charter that was revised in 1996. It held a congress in Venezuela in 2008 and organized demonstrations in 2010 to support the Nuclear Non-Proliferation Treaty Review Conference in New York.

* * *

The Soviet Peace Committee (SPDC), my host at the official dialogues to which I was invited, occupied in 1983 a building located on Prospekt Mira (Peace Street) in Moscow. As with other Soviet buildings, an elderly person behind a desk guarded the entrance. One needed an appointment to get inside. On the main floor was an elegant lunchroom with smartly dressed waiters. (After the dissolution of the Soviet Union it would be occupied by an Italian restaurant.) A spiral staircase of marble led up to the conference hall, where large international peace meetings were held. The head interpreter told me that he was engaged in at least one such meeting per week in Moscow or abroad, often in Vienna.

During the period when the SCDP was letting non-Communists such as Mac Makarchuk choose whom to invite, he brought in a diverse bunch: the rector of a Catholic university; a Congressman; Pierre Godfroy, the Gaullist MP; members of the British peace group CND; senators, parliamentarians from Australia;[5] and even Jesse Jackson. And he brought me.

I doubted that these dialogues could have an impact. We Canadian women kept our knitting needles clicking away, sitting at a table opposite high Soviet officials, who listened patiently for two days straight. I couldn't imagine why they wanted to hear my thoughts. Officials in neither the Canadian nor U.S. governments had any interest in my opinions, so why should these Soviet guys?

But I did express them—politely. I said that because Western arms control negotiators understand that Soviet dissidents are punished harshly for criticizing government policies, this probably worsens the prospects of the negotiations. In Toronto I had often argued angrily about the links among human rights, democracy, and nuclear disarmament, but here I chose my words carefully, half expecting abusive shouts in reply. But no. I got the canned response, the usual party line denying the problem, but it was offered in friendly tones.

My real surprise came during the coffee break. My interlocutor, a SCDP official named Vladislav Kornilov, approached with a smile. "I am so glad you brought up that subject," he said. "It's very important and you expressed it so well! We need to hear this point of view more often. Please keep talking about human rights and democracy every time you have a chance."

This was the first, but not the last, time when I would see the disparity between the official Party line and the actual opinions of Soviet mandarins speaking "backstage." A few Canadian colleagues described similar experiences.[6] There was a way of signaling approval without words, by using the eyes. As we passed in the hallway, an official would gaze at us and pointedly prolong an expression of gentleness, almost endearment. We apparently shared a secret understanding—but about what? I was puzzled by these new allies—the people whom I would come to call TERMITES.

I doubt that major policy issues were significantly influenced by the official dialogues. The real exchanges of opinion took place in different settings, such as at meetings of eminent scientists (Pugwash) and European Nuclear Disarmament (END) where both sides could debate frankly and openly. I do know, however, that these SCDP-orchestrated dialogues were taken seriously. There was simultaneous translation and the tapes were transcribed and kept. An official of the organization always wrote a summary report of the meeting, which was widely circulated in the top levels of the Party. According to the research director of the SCDP, "all these memos were sent to people at the Central Committee, the Foreign Ministry, the Ministry of Defense. All these were analyzed."[7] The backstage interactions between Western activists and Soviet officials were often meaningful, though the written reports probably influenced no one.

But—gosh!—they certainly listened attentively to us. I mentioned a mathematical model by a Romanian man named Bereanu for estimating the odds of inadvertently launching a nuclear war. A white-haired strategic analyst named Lev Semeiko joined me at the exit and shook my hand gratefully, assuring me that my intervention would be studied intently by the ranking military staff.

Certainly, the SCDP or WPC bureaucratic staff had little influence on policies. I once asked Georgi Arbatov, the man who brought the most Western ideas to Gorbachev's attention, whether Soviet peace organizations had been influential and he said no.[8] Their roles were scripted; they rarely had independent ideas.

But I know of one exception. Tair Tairov was Secretary of the WPC from 1980–85. Dealing with European activists, he soon become a dove and was quoted in the Western press criticizing the Soviet approach. In 1988 Tairov told *Peace Magazine*,

> I myself sent a cable to Moscow saying, "Please, for God's sake, make an oath not to test [nuclear weapons] for half a year. We can't lose."

I was reprimanded by the Soviet Peace Committee. They told me, "It's none of your business. No, we will not stop unilaterally."

So I said, if you won't stop, at least don't test in August 1985. Every year we test on Hiroshima and Nagasaki days.

They said, "Tair, forget the unilateral moratorium, but we promise we won't test at the beginning of August."[9]

I sent another cable. "Please, thousands of people from Australia to Canada are waiting. Bruce Kent, Daniel Ellsberg, CND, SPAS are waiting." I sent this two weeks before the moratorium was declared and I know it was read by all the top people—the Ministry of Defense, Gorbachev. When I read in the paper that Gorbachev had announced the moratorium, I felt that I was lucky that day.[10]

Tairov also wrote a twenty-page letter to Gorbachev explaining what was wrong with the World Peace Council. His superiors in the system recalled him to Moscow from his post in Helsinki and did not allow him to return there, even to move his household. Later he had an occasion to see his letter, which had reached Gorbachev. An order had been written on it: "Check into this and get back to me with whatever you find out." Tairov's negative assessment of WPC may have influenced its subsequent loss of much Soviet support.[11]

But Tair Tairov would be above average in courage and candor, no matter what society he might live in. Few people in the West speak their minds so frankly, and even fewer in the Soviet Union. Almost every Russian I met in those days complied, at least superficially, with authority.

However, the population was by no means unified. Two areas of disagreement were especially significant. First was the question of *loyalty to the regime.* The overwhelming majority of the Soviet population either genuinely favored the existing Soviet state or at least acquiesced to it consistently. We can call them "Yeasayers," or SHEEP. On the other side were people who actively opposed the existing regime and were committed to reforming it, openly or not. One might call them "Naythinkers," but they were not all alike, except that they all shared an attitude of habitual skepticism toward officially approved ideas.

Only among these "Naythinkers" was the second disagreement salient. It concerned whether reforms would come from "above" or "below." Those who believed that change must be conferred from above by an enlightened ruler were mostly Party members. They never challenged authority openly, but "backstage" they discussed possible reforms and planned for a new era, mainly one with a democratic socialist form of government. I came to call these people TERMITES, for they burrowed silently within the Soviet state, secretly preparing for change.

I never hid my own views. My new Russian friends knew that I was anything but a Communist, that I disliked their form of government and preferred democracy—but then, so did they. And as for the other issue— whether change would come from above or below—I never took a position. What seemed more important was the reformers' opportunity to participate in "civil society."

Indeed, other writers who have explained the emergence of democracy, from Alexis de Tocqueville until today's Robert Putnam, have usually depicted civil society as crucial to its development. Probably most dictators intuitively realize that fact too, for they invariably try to prohibit independent groups of citizens from forming. Probably the most consistent attribute of totalitarianism or authoritarianism is the intent of the dictators to suppress civil society. Independent social groups generate "social capital"— the personal capacities of their members to work effectively in public activism and to build personal networks that can be marshaled against a repressive government.

Not all independent organizations are equal in stimulating democratization. The crucial ones are the *transnational groups*, for they create "bridging" relationships that inform and bolster individuals who, in an authoritarian country, face heavy pressures to conform.

As the sociologist Robert Putnam has shown,[12] civil society organizations can be divided into two types, which predominantly "bond" or "bridge" their membership. Groups whose members have *similar* orientations (e.g. common ethnic or religious backgrounds) "bond" within themselves, augmenting in-group solidarity. On the other hand, civil society organizations of great *diversity* tend to "bridge" the society's disparate elements. It is primarily these bridging groups that have democratizing effects in autocracies, largely by exposing members to ideas that may be opposed to their rulers and that break the public's consensus. The bridges created by *transnational* civil society organizations during the 1980s would encourage democratic policies in Moscow, but then fail.

I placed all my bets on the spread of civil society, not taking a stand as to whether change would come from above or below. I believed that wherever civil society flourishes "below," among ordinary citizens, they acquire the capacity to challenge authority. Moreover, if an elite group is to create new reformist ideas "from above," its members must also be able to meet, discuss, and coordinate plans independently from the state. As I met people from both camps—those endorsing the "above" or "below" approaches to freedom—I found that each group actually constituted a distinct, separate civil society, despite the Party's opposition to both. Hence reform might come from either direction or from both.

Unfortunately, I did not immediately realize that these two communities hated each other. Instead of working together toward goals that they both shared, they were enemies, and remained so. Internally they were both "bonding" groups, but almost the only "bridges" linking them were foreigners in the international peace movement, who had friendly relationships with both sides.[13]

We were insufficient. These two communities should have been allies, for their goals were absolutely compatible, but the mutual hostility that arose from their disagreement about the "from above" versus "from below" issue would keep the groups from cooperating throughout most of the Gorbachev years. Indeed, it would doom the new democratic state that they both wanted. I will tell that part of the story later. For now, let me describe four diverging "schools of thought," whom I call the SHEEP, the TERMITES, the BARKING DOGS, and the DINOSAURS. See Figure 1 for a typology of these categories of public opinion in the years just preceding and following Gorbachev's elevation to power.

Perhaps I should apologize for the names I have given these political orientations. I don't want to offend, and I realize that classifying people as animals may seem rude. Still, I have met perfectly lovely sheep, dogs, and maybe even termites in my time, as well as first-rate human beings who remind me of these creatures. Some of my best friends are dinosaurs. I have chosen these animals because they so vividly symbolize particular political tendencies and help me keep track of the characters in my story.

	Favor existing state	Oppose existing state
Believe change comes from above	• SHEEP (est. 257 million) • KGB • DINOSAURS (~19 million?)	TERMITES (Est. 1 million)
Believe change comes from below	None	BARKING DOGS (a few hundred)

Figure 1. Soviet Attitudes & Civil Society Groups, 1982.

Sheep

Publicly, the population of the Soviet Union in 1982 seemed compliant and satisfied with the regime. There were no protest marches demanding policy changes. But even on my first day in Moscow, I encountered latent opposition to the government among people who publicly gave their assent. A plumber arrived at my hotel room to repair a non-existent problem, and asked my help to escape from "this horrible place." How unusual was this man? Did most other people secretly loathe the regime? It was impossible to guess, for even dissatisfied plumbers did nothing to challenge the rulers visibly.

Acquiescence varied from enthusiastic support of the regime to fatalistic resignation, in proportions that I cannot estimate. There were about 270 million Soviet citizens at the time, of whom 20 million belonged to the CPSU. Many Party members had simply joined to advance their careers. But they and almost all other 250 million Soviet citizens assented overtly as (to be blunt) SHEEP or hardline DINOSAURS.

Grudging compliance is understandable; everyone wants to survive and sometimes the only way is simply to obey. But for many, their outer conformity was matched by unquestioning inner faith. As I got acquainted with Muscovites, I sometimes asked them when they had ceased trusting Stalin, for example, and for some this was still an upsetting question. A retired engineer told me about his panic and despair at the time of Stalin's death. He had scrambled over roofs and crossed the city's back alleys to get near the front of the queue and view the corpse. The dictator's death meant the end of his world. But until I questioned him, fifty years later, he had never discussed with anyone the flaws of his old idol. Our conversation was so stressful that he could not sleep that night because of heart palpitations and anxiety. His compliance had run too deep. And yet this SHEEP had always shown an independent streak, for when his daughters were adolescents he had taught them to find the BBC, the Voice of America, and Radio Liberty on the dial and keep up with the news about Russian dissidents.

The same contradictions existed in the hearts of independent-minded persons. For example, in his *Memoirs*, written late in life, Andrei Sakharov recalled the same period—Stalin's death—when he had written to his first wife, Klava,

I wrote, "I am under the influence of a great man's death. I am thinking of his humanity."

Very soon I would be blushing every time I recalled these sentiments of mine. I can't fully explain it—after all, I knew quite enough about the horrible crimes that had been committed . . . .

In the face of all I had seen, I still believed that the Soviet state represented a breakthrough into the future, a prototype (though not as yet a fully realized one) for all other countries to imitate. That shows the hypnotic power of mass ideology.[14]

Dinosaurs

Not only did Soviet SHEEP spend their lives obeying CPSU officials, but most of the officials themselves adhered inflexibly to the Party line. There were approximately 20 million Party members during the 1980s. Initially the Party members had been zealous Marxist-Leninists, but failures had become apparent over time, and most of them must have harbored hidden doubts about Communism's long-term invincibility. If so, they never said so, but overtly recited the pre-packaged doctrines when speaking to each other and certainly to foreigners.

In many cases their membership in the Party was only a strategic career move, since promotions to high rank were awarded only to members. Nevertheless, these officials rigidly imposed the obsolete doctrines and prescribed forms of behavior on every SHEEP, and on each other. For this officiousness and inflexibility, I mentally named the hard-line Party members "DINOSAURS."

But there are other DINOSAURS in today's world who are not Party members. Indeed, from 2000 onward, Russia would be governed by President Putin's entourage, many of whom had belonged to the KGB, as had he. Though Communism no longer rules Russia, authoritarian ways still prevail, with heavy-handed enforcers administering Putin's policies. They are a strange new species of capitalist DINOSAUR.

Termites

Initially, my Western peacenik colleagues and I were astonished at East-West dialogues when SCDP officials urged us "back-stage" to politely continue our "on-stage" criticism of Soviet human rights abuses. What they couldn't say in public themselves, they encouraged Westerners to say. And there seemed to be quite a few of these anti-Communist Communists—the friendly TERMITE officials—but just how many?

Since the 1970s or even earlier, approximately one million of the 20 million Party members had belonged to networks of TERMITE reformers who knew and supported each other. Before Gorbachev came to power in 1985, a group of consultants—all TERMITES—had already been advising Andropov and serving on the Central Committee staff. They included Georgi Arbatov, Oleg Bogomolov, Alexander Bovin, Fyodor Burlatsky, Karen Brutents, Anatoly Chernyayev, Gennady Gerasimov, and Georgi Shakhnazarov.[15]

Western political scientists would not have classified these people as members of "civil society" because that term is defined specifically as the voluntary, private sector of society between the government and the family. It includes such groups as churches, clubs, professional associations, trade unions, and organizations devoted to music, say, or sports or social problems. In the Soviet Union of 1982, however, such a limited definition was misleading, for the TERMITE Party officials interacted precisely as a civil society behind the scenes. And they changed their society for the better.

Perhaps the most useful graph of TERMITE society from about 1985 would be a series of concentric circles. I'll mention only the two innermost circles. The center consisted of Gorbachev and his closest advisers, who funneled ideas—"New Political Thinking"—to him from Western political scientists and peace scholars, especially those developing less hard-line military doctrines. (I'll give examples in subsequent chapters.) The innermost circle in the 1980s included Georgi Arbatov, Yevgeny Chazov, Anatoly Chernyayev, Ivan Frolov, Vadim Medvedev, Yevgeny Primakov, Roald Sagdeev, Eduard Shevardnadze, Georgi Shakhnazarov, Yevgeny Velikhov, and Alexander Yakovlev.[16]

In the second circle from the center of Gorbachev's TERMITE advisers there were others whose liberalizing ideas sometimes had influence. On the basis of reputation, I would place here Gennady Gerasimov and several civilian analysts of military policy: Alexei Arbatov (Georgi's son), Sergei Blagovolin, Fyodor Burlatsky, Lev Deliusin, Sergei Karaganov, Andrei Kokoshin, two brothers, Andrei and Sergei Kortunov, Anatoly Lukyanov, Vladimir Petrovsky, Nodari Simonia, and Vitaly Zhurkin. In earlier years, Lev Mendelevich had belonged in that second circle.[17] And in circles further out, there were about a million others.

TERMITES met in certain places. For example, in the 1970s and 1980s, there were certain library rooms that scholars could enter only with special permission, to study books forbidden to the general public. People working there often became acquainted and discussed their research and their political opinions too.

Then there were the restricted books—not the forbidden *samizdat* books that were circulated in manuscript form, but politically sensitive foreign books published by Soviet publishing houses, especially Progress Books.[18] Two categories of such books were published until the late 1980s. The first series, which had a run of 3,000 to 5,000 copies, were by respected foreign authors. Access to them was very limited but, nevertheless, the intelligentsia had some possibility to read them. For example, one series, "Western Economic Thought," included classical works by John Stuart Mill, Joseph Schumpeter, and Max Weber.

The second category consisted of a series of numbered books with white covers. Every Soviet company had an office called the "first department" that was staffed by the secret police. At Progress Books, the "first department" was in charge of preparing this series, which was restricted to a smaller list authorized by the office of the ideological secretary of the party's Central Committee. It included members and candidate members of the Politburo, a few members of the Party Central Committee, a few directors of science institutes.

Mainly these were political books by renowned Western Sovietologists, translated into Russian.[19] Progress often got a special order to translate a particular book. They contributed to the evolution of elite perception of the world. Some of their translators came to doubt that Soviet propaganda was truthful.

Though everyone on the list had to sign when receiving one of the white books, some of their subordinates managed to read them furtively and discuss them at social gatherings.[20] Forbidden fruit is especially delicious. As the Moscow political scientist William Smirnov told me,

> The outcome was the opposite of what the apparatchiks intended. These special books were "injected" into the society and read by intellectuals, predominantly in the largest cities. Mostly they would never reach into small cities—except for books such as Solzhenitsyn, who became so famous that his books had a much wider circulation. . . .People would try by all means to read them, which was somewhat risky. But I have a speculation that in most cases, the KGB crowd knew who read them, who discussed them, but in general their policy was not to prevent it. What they tried to prevent were books written and published about Soviet events—even books, like those by Zamiatin and Avtorkhanov,[21] that had been written and published much earlier. . .

In addition to these books and special libraries, there were "TERMITE nests" in a number of academic research institutes. I will mention only three. One was "Academic City" in Novosibirsk, a place remote from the close scrutiny of Moscow. Quite a few social scientists there produced original ideas—notably the economist Abel Aganbegyan, who became Gorbachev's chief economic adviser during his first years as general secretary,[22] and the economic sociologist Tat'iana Zaslavskaia.[23] However, the remoteness meant that scholars in Siberia had little contact with foreigners—a circumstance that hampered their work. As we shall see, contact with foreign intellectuals is almost essential for independent-minded scholars. Perhaps for that reason, Gorbachev's economic policies never equaled the innovativeness of his foreign and military policies.

In Moscow the most influential center for bold research was the Institute for USA and Canada studies (ISKRAN; also called the USA/Canada Institute), headed by Georgi Arbatov. He was probably the most influential scholar importing Western ideas and explaining them to Gorbachev. He had a staff of hundreds, many of whom I interviewed there.

Finally, on the outskirts of Moscow is a high-rise building called the Institute for World Economy and International Relations (IMEMO), which at its peak had about 1,000 researchers.[24] Many of my interviews were at IMEMO.

In later chapters I will introduce you to other notable TERMITES, but now I want to turn to their opponents, the dissidents—my friends the BARKING DOGS.

The Barking Dogs

In sharp contrast to the Party members who kept hoping and even planning quietly for a more democratic and less militaristic Soviet Union, there were a few brave (some say foolhardy) individuals who stood up publicly for their principles, even when they knew they would pay dearly for doing so. I call them BARKING DOGS because not all of them liked to be called "dissidents." Besides, even though they lacked political power (they could not "bite" anyone) they deliberately made enough noise to wake everyone up.

I considered these brave people the real counterparts of our Western peace and human rights activists, though (thank God!) we never had to endure the penalties they underwent for speaking their minds truthfully. Dissidents are extraordinary (sometimes cantankerous) human beings of vast integrity. As one of them said, "If you want to be trusted you have to tell the truth. And if you always tell the truth, other people *have* to trust you, whether they want to or not."

Even during the totalitarian years preceding Khrushchev's 1953 denunciation of Stalin, there had been a few dissidents, especially among suppressed religious groups and national minorities. Some of them were pacifists.

In the 1970s, two new groups of dissidents had formed: "refusenik" Jews who sought to emigrate and the Moscow Helsinki Group.

We should distinguish among three kinds of dissent: (a) protests, mainly on the part of Jews ("refuseniks"), for having been refused permission to emigrate; (b) demands for human rights (notably by the Moscow Helsinki Group) and (c) peace activists' desire for less militaristic policies (notably by the Trustbuilders Group). Each group developed its own agenda, specializing in one of these three concerns. Some individuals participated in two or all three of these categories of dissent. I will discuss the Refuseniks and the Helsinki Group together first.

* * *

In 1975 the Conference on Security and Cooperation in Europe was held with the intention of improving relations between the Communist bloc and the West. It ended in Helsinki, Finland, by issuing an important new document, the Final Act of the Helsinki Accords,[25] which was signed by thirty-five states: the United States, Canada, and all European states except Andorra and Albania. Surprisingly, Leonid Brezhnev's Soviet Union also signed, triumphant at having obtained an important concession.[26]

Each side of the Cold War gained something and had to sacrifice something. From Brezhnev's viewpoint, he was gaining a promise that the borders of states would remain inviolate and could only be changed by peaceful means. He expected to use this concession by the West to end their continuing objections to the forced incorporation of Lithuania, Latvia, and Estonia into the Soviet Union at the end of World War II.

But Brezhnev miscalculated. In signing the Helsinki Final Act, the Soviet Union was promising to respect human rights and fundamental freedoms, including freedom of thought, conscience, and religion or belief. And, for their part, few Westerners realized how much this document would mean to those living in repressed Eastern bloc societies.

Within months a new movement was created to monitor whether the Communist states were fulfilling their new promises. The Moscow Helsinki Group is a non-governmental organization that met first in the apartment of Andrei Sakharov and was convened by the physicist Yuri Orlov.[27]

Though the Moscow group arose first, there soon followed similar organizations across the Warsaw Pact region. For example, Charter 77 was founded in 1977 in Czechoslovakia. In time, all these Helsinki Watch monitoring groups would form a transnational NGO, the International Helsinki Federation.

The Helsinki Final Act, Principle VII, declares that individuals have the right to know and act upon their rights and duties. This promise was certainly not kept in the Eastern bloc countries. Some of the Moscow Group members were hoping to emigrate, and according to the new treaty were entitled to do so, but instead they were beaten and kept in police custody.

The Helsinki Watch organization exposed the mis-use of psychiatry as a means of political repression.[28] For this they incurred great penalties.[29]

During the 1970s and '80s, perhaps 500 political prisoners were directly subjected to psychiatric abuse. Human rights activists feared mental hospitals far more than prison camps. For one thing, a prison sentence had a known duration, whereas one might be kept in a mental hospital indefinitely, even forever, unless one recanted.[30] Even when it did not bring release, recanting usually brought relief from the worst mistreatments.[31]

Most other inmates were actually mentally ill and social life in the hospitals was unpleasant. Moreover, the usual treatment for those diagnosed as having "sluggish schizophrenia" (the most common label for political prisoners) involved drugs that produced excruciating pain, sulfazin, and sometimes insulin shock therapy, combined at times with wrapping the patient in wet sheeting or strapping him or her to the bed for a week or more.[32]

The Helsinki organization collected proof of these abuses, appealed to the international community of psychiatrists, and confronted the leading Soviet psychiatrists responsible for them.[33] A few years later, while the World Psychiatric Association prepared to condemn their Soviet members, the latter group quit.[34]

The DINOSAURS' abuse of psychiatry was eventually greatly reduced, if not eliminated, through influence from abroad. The international professional network of psychiatry played an important role, as did national organizations, such as the American profession, which sent a delegation of inspectors to look into the problem. Other networks, such as Amnesty International and the Helsinki movement, also contributed a great deal. It would be hard to overestimate the usefulness of transnational networks in putting pressure on the Soviet Union that led to the reforms of the late 1980s. The Moscow Helsinki Group led the way.

* * *

All these brave "BARKING DOGS" constituted an independent civil society, though their incarceration and forced exile limited their opportunities for contact. There were virtually no direct contacts between networks of human rights activists in other countries, though they all heard of each other through international visitors or foreign radio broadcasts. The founder of the Moscow Helsinki Group, the physicist Yuri Orlov, says there had been no contact between Helsinki Watch and Eastern European groups such as Charter 77, but later Václav Havel had told him that Charter 77 had been organized under the influence of the Helsinki Movement in Russia. "And Bujak!" exclaimed Orlov. "When I came to Warsaw [after being deported to the U.S. during the Gorbachev years] we hugged as if we knew each other."

The Moscow Helsinki Group became famous. They sent abroad their papers, which were read aloud over foreign radio stations that covered the Soviet

Union. Orlov told me, "You cannot imagine how many people traveled to Moscow from the countryside to find dissidents. Every day! Usually by the night train. I couldn't get any sleep. They had heard about human rights groups."[35]

Orlov was arrested in 1977 and not released until 1986. Part of that time was spent in labor camps in the Urals, the rest in a Siberian work camp. In Siberia he found that even Yakutian hunters recognized his name. One woman told him that in high school she and her girlfriends had secretly read his articles in the washroom. The men would take a radio out onto the lake where they could secretly listen to foreign broadcasts. They asked him to explain what they heard about Sakharov, whom they respected. "They asked me, 'Who is Sakharov? Who is Solzhenitsyn? What do you want?' All the workers were interested."

Ongoing persecutions continued to reduce the group's membership. In 1982 the Moscow Helsinki Group was forced to dissolve, but in 1989, when *glasnost* was flourishing, nine of the original activists re-established it. The group continues to function. Its conditions under Putin are much improved over Soviet days but still deplorable. In 2008 I interviewed Lev Ponomarov, a current leader of the Russian human rights movement, who continues to demonstrate publicly. My friends had seen him being beaten in the streets two weeks before.

* * *

Throughout the 1970s, many thousands of Jews applied for permission to emigrate on the only official grounds: to be reunited with family members in Israel. Most of them did not go to Israel; they just wanted to leave the Soviet Union.

Application to emigrate was considered a disloyal act and immediately led to the loss of status. The applicant would lose his professional job and have to do menial work while waiting indefinitely for permission to leave. Or the applicant might even be sent to the camps, then given the requested exit permit. In a classic "catch-22" situation, one might be dismissed from one's job for applying to emigrate—and then charged as a parasite for being unemployed.

Those who were free to do so gathered outside the synagogue every week to keep up with their network. The would-be emigrants tried to spend their time in useful and stimulating ways. For example, scientists who could no longer hold professional jobs organized scientific seminars and invited scholars from abroad. The authorities tried to block these initiatives, though not always successfully.[36]

At first, most refuseniks kept their distance from the human rights BARKING DOGS. Ludmilla Alexeyeva explained that this is the way they thought: "I do not want to have anything to do with this country. I want to leave, and to achieve this I must avoid quarrels with the authorities. After all, permission to leave depends on them, not on the dissidents. So the further away one is from the dissidents, the better."[37] When the first person who was both a refusenik and a BARKING DOG actually got his emigration papers quicker than anyone else, the refuseniks began to change their minds and, over time, the two networks drew closer together. The Helsinki Accords also drew them together, for unlike Soviet law, it requires signatory countries to permit the reuniting of families.

All BARKING DOGS could expect to be charged with similar crimes and jailed for anti-Soviet slander, or agitation, or malicious hooliganism, or parasitism. The most prominent of these "criminals" was an active member of the Moscow Helsinki Group, a refusenik and a peace activist: Anatoly Shcharansky, who was arrested in 1973. His wife worked for his release, turning his legal case over to a Canadian lawyer, Irwin Cotler.

In 1979 Cotler attended an international political science conference in the Soviet Union. After he had been present for ten days, he was seized by the police and swiftly deported to London. This expulsion received world-wide publicity and made Cotler famous as a human rights lawyer, but he was not able to return to the Soviet Union until 1988. In the interval, however, Cotler did all he could for Shcharansky and other BARKING DOGS. After one of his trips to Vienna on their behalf in 1986, he returned to Canada with the first positive news from the Soviets on the subject of human rights. Several BARKING DOGS were present, having just been released. According to Cotler, "What Shevardnadze[38] said in his opening speech to the plenary was nothing short of revolutionary, because he spoke of the Helsinki Final Act as being the basis for the development of a civil society and the protection of human rights."

Mr. Shevardnadze, in promising Soviet compliance with the Helsinki Final Act, had indicated that human rights was the basis of international peace and that family reunification was essential. Though many in the audience doubted Soviet intentions, Shevardnadze invited all the signatory countries to a human rights conference in Moscow in September 1991. Cotler dates the human rights revolution in the Soviet Union to that Vienna meeting in November 1986.[39]

A smaller breakthrough had already taken place, however, when Cotler had met in Geneva with Soviet authorities about Shcharansky, who was released as part of an East-West trade.[40]

Gorbachev's team kept their word about living up to the Helsinki Final Act. They did allow emigration to increase—not just of Jews but also of other Soviet citizens. They did hold the Human Rights Conference in Moscow in 1991 and the whole array of delegations did attend, recognizing the advances that had taken place in Soviet practices. Yet the circumstances were unexpected: The conference immediately followed the attempted coup.

Much of Gorbachev's difficulty stemmed from the resurgence of nationalism and anti-Semitism, for which no one was prepared. It would no longer be just a matter of letting Jews emigrate; the challenge would be to keep the Soviet Union from coming apart. In this matter, the BARKING DOGS were not his allies.

* * *

Human rights BARKING DOGS and refuseniks were alike in two important respects. First, initially they were not totally opposed to militarism on principle. In fact, some of them even favored the West's keeping up strong military pressure against the Soviet state, which they considered brutal and expansionist.

This attitude also prevailed during the same early period among human rights activists, for whom the human rights issue seemed less a problem to be solved than a weapon for right-wing Cold Warriors to use in attacking communism. Briefly, the main human rights activist, Andrei Sakharov, even urged the

U.S. to continue its nuclear buildup so as to keep his own government in check.[41]

However, the Helsinki Final Act clarified the interdependence of peace and human rights, and because this document was so important to all BARKING DOGS, they tended to recognize the connection more than before. Certain Western European peace activists took the initiative to contact their human rights counterparts in Warsaw Bloc, and the dialogue between them was fruitful.

A second common aspect of human rights and refusenik groups is that they accepted the nationalistic position that ethnic "self-determination" is a human right. (This implies that every ethnic group has a right to a sovereign homeland if it chooses to secede.) During the Brezhnev years, nationalistic groups had been subdued inside the Soviet Union, except for a few riots in Central Asia.

The Holocaust and the experience of anti-Semitism in the Soviet Union disposed Jews to favor the notion of national homelands, but the human rights movement had not unequivocally taken the side of nationalism until the Baltics demanded independence during Gorbachev's time. Since they had been illegally annexed, their case for secession was the strongest of any of the republics; it was also the thin end of a wedge that forced open opportunities for other separatists.

Andrei Sakharov, who led the human rights movement for a whole generation, favored protecting the rights of national minorities, but never urged the proliferation of independence movements that might break up the union. His attention was focused on revising the constitution to eliminate the entrenched special role of the Communist Party. He died in 1989, before the separatist movements gained full strength. Then his widow, Yelena Bonner, who had sometimes taken positions that seemed inconsistent with his,[42] became engaged in nationalist causes, especially that of the Armenians of Nagorno-Karabakh.

Unlike refuseniks, human rights BARKING DOGS expected to live permanently inside the borders of their country. They were loyal to their society, though not to its political elite. They stood proudly outside the establishment.

But theirs is an honorable role. They were unwilling to forget the past of Stalinism. Alexander Solzhenitsyn took on the task of remembering faithfully, recording his memories and appealing for help when a name or date escaped him. In those days, the Soviet citizens revered him, though they supposed he was a bit fanatical or even politically dangerous. Evidently they were right. Who else could be a Slavophile[43] in the 1990s? In 1994, on Solzhenitsyn's return to Russia from exile in America, he would be considered an anachronistic crank.

A new generation of witnesses would take on Solzhenitsyn's work of witnessing and recording. Many were not young. Sergei Grigoryants, for example, was in his fifties when I visited him in 1992. He carried his memories austerely, respectfully. In his apartment on the outskirts of Moscow there hung paintings by numerous friends, all dead. He still published a newsletter in English every day, reporting accurate details of new atrocities perpetrated, not in camps, but in provincial towns by militias or nationalists.

Grigoryants denied that totalitarianism was over, claiming that although fewer prisoners inhabited camps, there were more deaths than ever. I read his items from Kishinev and Tskinval about current skirmishes and old mass graves, but he often filled space with complaints about taxes and the price of butter.

Memorial is an organization dedicated to remembering. It occupies one of the rare separate houses still standing in the center of Moscow, and its shelves rise all the way to the high ceilings, holding cardboard boxes of letters, computer records, and even tapes of singers in the Gulag.[44] There is not enough storage space, so members take boxes home and live with them.

One member is Victor Bulgakov, who had been sent to a camp while he was young, where he organized prisoners' resistance. In 1953–55 his organization conducted a census of the camps that took two years to complete. According to Mr. Bulgakov, "at the end of 1954, there were no less than 24 million prisoners in this country—more than one-tenth of the population at that time."[45] Robert Johnson, a demographic historian I consulted who was making new calculations, believes that a more accurate figure might be 20 percent as high as that. What a waste, suffering so much to remember a mistaken estimate!

To remember is not to forgive. The guilty try not to remember, and perhaps they succeed. Besides, who can forgive on behalf of dead victims? The dead must be presumed implacable. Only the cycle of death and birth, bringing a generation of innocents who have neither perpetrated nor witnessed the deeds, who are neither victims nor guilty, can allow a society to start afresh. Yet such new generational moments arise only with the cyclical turning of personal memories into the impersonal detritus of history and culture. The BARKING DOGS of Memorial have pledged to resist that cycle, to prevent the ebbing of memory, as if they could bronze each leaf to honor what it used to be. Who could wish them to fail? Yet who could wish them to succeed?

BARKING DOGS guard watchfully, remembering and expecting new instances of whatever they have witnessed. Self-preservation is not a priority. They are not easily discouraged by failure to set the world right. They take risks and are uncompromising and unforgiving. They do not have much fun and evidently don't miss it. They are overwhelmingly devoted to political action, yet, lacking any talent for compromise or pragmatic exchanges, they do not make good elected politicians. For their intransigence, they bear much of the responsibility for the failure of Gorbachev's reforms.

Still, BARKING DOGS have other qualities for which they are loved. They are moral exemplars and are loyal to each other. Without them, there could be no shining characters to look back upon during the long and ugly totalitarian period. If BARKING DOGS are admired only ambivalently by those who saved their own skins and don't want to be reminded of that fact, they will be admired extravagantly by later generations. Their tales need to be preserved, for they are as important as the stories of the victims whose records are kept at Memorial. Their tragedy is that they cannot claim to have left, as a legacy of their courage, either a functioning Soviet Union or a flourishing civic culture.

* * *

Now I want to turn to my good friends, the independent peace activists known as "Trustbuilders" or the "Trust Group," whom I always used to visit.

In June 1982, a circle of Moscow intellectuals invited the press to the founding meeting of the "Group to Establish Trust Between the USSR and the USA." Only Western reporters attended the gathering, which took place in the two-room apartment of a young Moscow artist, Sergei Batovrin. From the first meeting, it was clear that the group would encounter obstacles; a black Volga with two antennae (a clue that it belonged to the KGB) had parked in the flower bed in front of Batovrin's building, blocking the entrance. During the press conference, the KGB barged in and tried to break up the meeting. This was a mistake because the Western journalists immediately demanded some explanation: "How can it be against the interests of the Soviet state for people to display posters about peace?" The KGB operatives, who were not accustomed to explaining themselves when they carried out their physical assaults, found the whole occasion embarrassing. The foreign journalists reported the event widely abroad, especially since by chance the press conference happened on the same day that Daniel Ellsberg, the American dissident,[46] had appeared in the Leningrad harbor with other protesters, insisting that the Soviets immediately cease testing nuclear weapons. The two stories were run side by side, and of course Ellsberg's group was immediately thrown out of the country.[47]

The new group denied that they were dissidents. Initially they took only uncontroversial positions that in no way contradicted Soviet policies. It was not so much *what they stood for* that made the Trustbuilders into pariahs; rather, it was the fact that they dared to use their own judgment as if they had a perfect right to do so. Such independence was a threat to the system. Soviet citizens could not undertake militant actions of the kind that Western citizens carried out. Anyone, for example, who tried to blockade a Soviet military installation or go over its fence to demonstrate inside, would instantly have been killed. Moreover, Soviet citizens had no military information about the number of missiles and launchers, or other technical facts about the arms race. Unlike some Western peaceniks, they could not have debated the strategic basis of Warsaw Pact plans.

For these reasons, the Trustbuilders limited themselves initially to proposals to improve people-to-people relationships between Soviet and American citizens. They noted that "a disarmament formula is important, but it is not the starting point. Weapons alone do not kill; it is people who press the triggers, who are killers. Let us start by abolishing the image of enemies in respect of people and nations in the 'opposite camp.'"[48] They produced an initial list of twenty-seven suggestions, some of which seem naïve. I'll list only a few. Notice, however, the similarity between some of these and my proposals in chapter 15.

> Develop a program for an exchange of children (for instance, during school vacations) between Soviet and American families, including the families of government leaders and those in positions of authority.
>
> Broadcast regular joint Soviet-American TV discussions (simultaneously in the USSR and the USA) with high ranking political figures and scientific and cultural leaders from one of the countries answering telephone questions by viewers from the other country.
>
> Develop joint proposals for propagating peace in school books.

Create Soviet and U.S. cultural centers in the USSR and the USA.

Create a Soviet-American marriage bureau to increase the number of marriages between Soviet and American citizens.

Create Soviet-American medical centers in the USSR and the USA, in which physicians of both nations would use the most advanced methods and equipment, treating patients of both countries.

Create in both countries a bureau for promoting correspondence and meetings between citizens of both countries.

Develop a program of regular joint space explorations (for instance using a long-term Soviet-American space station).

A program for mutual aid to neutral developing nations.

Create a non-governmental public opinion research commission to survey the populations of both countries on questions of bilateral relations, to develop recommendations to both governments.

Forbid war games among children.

Organize public discussions of film and art to put forward anti-war ideas and ideas which restore trust between the U.S. and USSR.

The first cohort of Trustbuilders were all intellectuals. Many were "Refusenik" Jews who had applied to emigrate but had not received permission to do so. This fact made the group vulnerable to the accusation that its members' hidden motive was to get thrown out of the country, having failed to secure exit visas in the ordinary way. In order to overcome this label, the group later sought to diversify its membership. They recruited from other disaffected communities, such as the physically handicapped, stigmatized religious groups (e.g. Baptists), and nonconformist youths who preferred alternative cultures.

In any case, many of the core members *were* expelled from the country. Others were subjected to brutal repression. For example, Sergei Batovrin was committed to a mental hospital and subjected to drugs that caused great physical pain. The group publicized these abuses in the Western press, which emphasized the negative stories even more than the group's positive suggestions. While the Trustbuilders had mixed feelings about this negative news, they did benefit from it. Members who were incarcerated seemed to be released sooner than would otherwise have been the case. The Trustbuilders were generally more successful than the Helsinki Group; Olga Medvedkov attributes their "luck" to the much greater support they obtained from Western public opinion. Instead of trying to prevent KGB infiltration, the Trustbuilders simply let their activities be known without hiding anything. As a result, they received more foreign publicity than the Helsinki Group, and were somewhat protected from the worst abuses by support from their foreign friends. I'll review outsiders' influence later.

At first the Trustbuilders tried to keep a proper membership list, showing everyone's address, phone number, and profession. After a week or two they had a list of 1,000 and the movement was snowballing. However, the KGB confiscated some copies and used the list to facilitate their own searches and interrogations. The group therefore abandoned the whole business of official membership, which had been more useful to the KGB than to themselves. They decided that what counted was not signing a paper but rather taking action. True members were those who contributed through their own efforts and initiatives toward peace, without expecting any guidance. Unlike the top-down SCDP, the Trustbuilders were a grass-roots movement without leaders issuing commands.

Soon groups first began to form in Leningrad, Novosibirsk, Odessa, and Kiev, and, a year or so later, in the capital cities of the Baltic region, in Moldavia, and even in Gorky.[49] Communication was difficult between the groups in different areas, though the Leningrad and Moscow groups managed to stay in touch. The Estonian groups chose to communicate with other Trustbuilders in English instead of Russian, a preference that foreshadowed the separatism that would lead to the break-up of the Soviet Union.[50]

Every week the group had a planning meeting in a member's apartment, without regularly choosing any one home. The group studied various issues and delivered lectures to each other and to a constant flow of Western visitors. However, there were few visits from activists from other Eastern bloc countries. Any communication between these movements was facilitated by the Western visitors or by the foreign press, especially radio services such as Radio Liberty, the Voice of America, or the BBC. Every statement that it issued was immediately read, without comment, by Radio Liberty, which broadcast across the Soviet Union, reaching an estimated 20 million listeners. Some of the group's coordinating committee (which included non-Jews) could be reached at every weekly service of the Moscow synagogue, a well-known meeting place for contact with the public, since members of the group had been deprived of phone and mail service. A large portion of the Soviet population became aware of the Trustbuilders and to some extent their counterparts throughout the East—especially Dialog in Hungary, Charter 77 in Czechoslovakia, Freedom and Peace in Poland, and the Swords into Ploughshares movement in East Germany.

If some of the group's papers and proposals seemed amateurish in the context of a well-informed Western peace movement, others were scholarly—and all were audacious for Soviet citizens of that day. They dared not mention the words "Afghanistan" or "human rights." However, in one seminar Yuri Medvedkov analyzed the legacy of the Yalta Agreements (about which the Soviet public had been deliberately misinformed) and sent the paper to a conference in Berlin. Another member, economist Lev Dudkin concentrated on proposals for converting from a military to a civilian economy and putting the savings into jointly funded projects to benefit humankind. They conducted a seminar on the Nuclear Winter theory. They asked their numerous pacifist visitors from the West to educate the group by offering seminars on nonviolence and the teachings of Gandhi, Martin Luther King, and even their countryman, Leo Tolstoy.

They also went beyond analysis. On Hiroshima Day the group held an art exhibition especially to display Batovrin's anti-war paintings (which were immediately confiscated and never returned) and later several street exhibits of children's drawings on peace. Upon receiving packets of flower seeds from the Fellowship of Reconciliation, they planted a "peace garden" in front of a police station, which sprouted and briefly proclaimed the slogan "Ban the Bomb" in both English and Russian until it was dug up.[51]

The group called for a "four-sided dialogue" in which the four sides were the two governments, U.S. and USSR, and the two groups of citizens belonging respectively to those societies. Eventually the group changed its name and enlarged its ambitions from a bilateral one, as the "Group for Establishing Trust between the USSR and the USA," toward a more inclusive project as the "Group for the Establishment of Trust Between East and West." Olga Medvedkova[52] says nearly 1,000 American visitors had come to her apartment while she was involved with the group,[53] and there were more British than American visitors. The group's first response from one of their Western counterparts was from European Nuclear Disarmament (END), led by Edward P. Thompson, and in 1983, a British support network was founded, "The UK Trustbuilders."

Sometimes the presence of foreigners provided a little protection for the group, as when two Englishwomen from the Greenham Common Peace Camp went with the group to stick up anti-nuclear posters on trees around Moscow. The KGB plainclothesmen who were watching did not interfere with that action. The group distributed leaflets, gave speeches, and answered questions. Whereas any Soviet citizen who attempted such an action normally would be arrested in a minute or two, this demonstration went on without any interference for fully two hours. Evidently the KGB didn't want to clamp down on Western peace activists or even display their repressive tactics with Western witnesses present.

However, there were limits to the DINOSAURS' tolerance of BARKING DOGS. Among Olga Medvedkova's Greenham Common friends were two who had come to a Moscow conference organized by the Soviet Peace Committee. Olga accompanied them into the building without being challenged. She sat quietly while her friends spoke, and then took a turn herself, surprising the officials with her perfect Russian and by describing the activities of the Trustbuilders. Almost immediately the meeting became pandemonium, as a furious Grigory Lokshin berated her, saying that he would not sit at the same table with her. The Soviet officials—all DINOSAURS, of course—began banging on the table to make it impossible for others to hear her speech. Oleg Kharkhardin, the highest official present, shouted that he was the boss of the building and ordered the interpreter to stop translating her speech for the benefit of the foreigners.[54] The episode was reported on foreign radio programs beamed to the Soviets.

Medvedkova's intrusion was evidently too bold to go unpunished. Soon thereafter, she was arrested on the false charge of having assaulted a police officer after having attended the political trial of another Trustbuilder. This event had taken place when I first visited the Medvedkovs; they had depicted it as merely one in a long series of harassments. After my return to Canada, however, the matter grew more serious and it seemed that Olga was likely to be sent to a labor camp, despite her pregnancy. Several Western embassies sent observers to her trial; they were not allowed in, but showed their support in the street outside. Her lawyer proved that the policeman whom she was alleged to have struck was not even on duty that day, and she—for the first time of any dissident—was given a "suspended sentence." I saw her release as the first sign that during Gorbachev's period, dissidents might face less repression than before.

Nevertheless, it took another two years for that trend to become unmistakable. During that period, Trustbuilders continued to be assaulted on the street, jailed for "hooliganism," and dismissed from their jobs. The Medvedkovs were called before a meeting of their colleagues, who were asked to condemn them for their political misbehavior by revoking their doctoral degrees. When the vote came, Olga watched her co-workers, without exception, lower their eyes in shame while raising their hands to vote against her. Fortunately, she and especially her husband were prominent geographers. (Yuri had served as chief ecologist for the World Health Organization and had been awarded honorary doctorates in the U.S.) Their foreign colleagues threatened to retaliate by excluding the Soviet Union from various international organizations if they were stripped of their credentials. This aspect of the campaign succeeded, though without saving their jobs or keeping Yuri from being jailed as a "hooligan."

Some members of the group believed that they had sympathizers in the top levels of the government, even before Gorbachev took office in 1985. As one exiled member, Mark Reitman, speculated, the Trust Group could not have survived "if it did not have supporters in the top ranks of the Soviet hierarchy."[55]

If this was so, those supporters must have been weak or inhibited. Even after Gorbachev came to power, he had to introduce changes a little at a time, and for the first year or so there was little change with respect to civil liberties.

Take, for example, Larissa Chukaeva, a twenty-three-year-old nurse whose husband was in prison for his activism. She was charged with forgery, deprived of the custody of their child, and sentenced to two years in a concentration camp.[56]

Nikolai Khramov, a twenty-five-year-old journalist, was expelled from Moscow State University for participating in the Trust Group. Though exempt from the draft because of poor eyesight, he was shipped off with conscripts to the Far East. There he went on a hunger strike and was put into a military psychiatric ward. An international campaign was organized to support him. After four months he was released and became prominent again in the Trust Group.

The cardiologist Vladimir Brodsky was convicted of assaulting two police aides and was sent to a labor camp. His wife Dina Zisserman and Olga Medvedkova were both mothers. Wearing T-shirts that demanded the release of their husbands from jail, they paraded together in the streets of Moscow, carrying their infants. Dina was beaten on one occasion by the police.

Such events were publicized widely through the Western press—especially the radio—and became well known throughout the Soviet Union. The publicity was probably essential in protecting the group and eventually securing their freedom. However, the Trustbuilders had mixed feelings about these stories. The Western press would always publicize the accounts of their persecution, but they wanted to be a positive force, not merely a group of victims. And they believed that they did have a positive impact, sometimes unobtrusively so.

Their apartments were always "bugged," and after they became famous, it seemed that the Soviet Peace Committee (SCDP) sometimes started "borrowing" ideas that they had discussed privately, such as a proposal to exchange the photographs of Eastern and Western families. The "official peace movement" also began using private apartments as discussion clubs, giving ordinary Soviet citizens a chance to meet foreign guests in a way that made surveillance possible, yet seemed freer and more informal than meetings in bureaucratic settings.[57]

Sometimes Trustbuilders were even able to do constructive work without being much impeded. This was especially true at the time of the Chernobyl disaster. Already they had been visited for a week by several West German Greens, who had participated in seminars and had left behind a number of publications criticizing the so-called "peaceful atom." This was the first time certain members of the Trust Group had become quite aware of the dangers of nuclear energy, and the information prepared them to react swiftly a month later, when the catastrophe occurred in Ukraine.[58]

The accident took place on the night of April 25–26, 1985, only a few weeks after Gorbachev had become general secretary. Two days later the Swedes raised the alarm because of unusual levels of radiation. That evening, Soviet TV announced a "minor breakdown" at Chernobyl but said it was back to normal. By that time, the Trust Group activists were on an emergency timetable, contacting experts and seeking the necessary information. Certain members of the group were actually employed in making computations for the Chernobyl plant and could tell the others about the inept management they had seen there.

By May 5, the Trust Group had developed suggestions for minimizing casualties. They phoned the reporters of Western press agencies simultaneously from many pay phones and read their statement. That night, millions of Soviet citizens were able to hear the Russian text. The Medvedkovs also visited the Moscow correspondent of *U.S. News and World Report.* Eventually the Soviet authorities adopted practically all of the Trust Group's proposals, except one: the Group urged that people be given or sold simple radiometers so they could check their own food and water for radiation.[59] To permit such independence must have seemed threatening to officials accustomed to being in command.

It was a year later before the Trust Group was able to successfully carry out a street demonstration calling for a change in nuclear energy policy. In May, 1986, two Trustbuilder mothers went to Gorky Park with their children, carrying signs and petitions. Many people eagerly signed their petition. In half an hour they collected about 200 signatures, and were then arrested. The usual KGB way of intimidating them was to make an example of one member with a severe punishment for any street action. In this case it was Serge Svetushkin, who spent a year in an exceptionally horrible prison cell as revenge for this demonstration.

A few months later, the group received visitors from New York who joined them in distributing leaflets and waving a big poster that read, "No More Hiroshima—No More Chernobyl." The four-page leaflets offered vital information on how to avoid radiation from food or water. This time the KGB did not interfere, and some of the police slipped leaflets into their own pockets. When additional leaflets arrived from abroad, the group repeated their action with the same success outside the Moscow Zoo. Again, no one was arrested.[60]

Between the summer of 1985, when I was expelled from the Soviet Union, and the summer of 1990, I did not try to return. Nevertheless, the Trustbuilders were an important part of my life. I kept getting messages from them through others. Moreover, gradually almost all of the first cohort of members were expelled, or at least given an exit visa and strongly advised to use it.

The Trust Group continued to be supported by several other groups of peace activists in Britain and the East Coast of the United States. Several anarchist groups were especially interested in their fate.

Canadian peace activists who visited Moscow in the second half of the eighties usually tried to visit the Trust Group and I reported the news in *Peace Magazine*. In the summer of 1986, for example, there were several large peace gatherings in Moscow. A historian friend, John Bacher, attended a youth conference there, and two physicists, Eric Fawcett and Derek Paul, attended gatherings of scientists, then visited the Medvedkovs. Yuri had just been released after a fifteen-day stint in jail. There they met Daniel Ellsberg, who had just come from Nevada, where he had been over the fence in a civil disobedience protest, and the Boston psychiatrist Margaret Brenman.

The Trust Group's gatherings were the most stimulating place in Moscow, Derek Paul enthused. To illustrate, he mentioned Medvedkov's suggestion that all around the world, the daily weather reports on television and the newspapers ought to include reports on the amount of radiation in the atmosphere. Eric Fawcett added that Yuri had been informed that the tapes of their apartment were being transcribed and conveyed to people in the Party hierarchy. Fawcett noted that, in a well-organized society, Medvedkov would be part of a committee taking action on the problems following the Chernobyl disaster.[61]

Still, long-time Trustbuilders were finding the stress wearing. Having already been demoted, the Medvedkovs at last lost their jobs. Apart from the financial implications, there was another problem: it was illegal for an able-bodied Soviet male to remain unemployed. When we heard the news, there were long-distance phone calls among their professional colleagues and previous visitors, who discussed how best to support them. It became clear that the time had come for the family to emigrate. With their two children and Olga's retired parents, they moved to Ohio in 1987 and took academic jobs as geographers.

Almost all the early Trustbuilders were living in the United States by 1988. For every immigrant, the first years are stressful. Although these immigrants were almost all intellectuals, they were not all well-prepared for life in America. Some spoke no English, others found that their technical education did not match the requirements for the jobs they wanted. Some arrived with serious health problems. Some took academic posts, some published a magazine for Russian émigrés, while still others became salesmen or drove taxis.

None of them became activists in the American peace movement.[62] Most of the Trustbuilders harbored resentment toward the American peace movement, which they perceived as unjustly ready to compromise with the Soviet regime and overlook the abuses of everyday Soviet life. There was some truth in this perception, but it was not a correct appraisal of all, or even most, Western peaceniks, as they surely knew from the days when they had received us in their homes. The Trustbuilders did not stay in contact with each other after immigrating to the U.S., and still less did they stay in contact with Western peaceniks.

Besides, the Soviet Union was changing quickly. Most Soviet émigrés had endured incarceration and public humiliation, and they were amazed that others now could participate in the Trust Group with total impunity. Moreover, the

Trustbuilders, as they existed in Moscow, were becoming only one group among thousands, no longer uniquely important.

* * *

The cleavages in political opinion in Soviet society were intense all along. The primary dividing line was between the docile SHEEP (who were satisfied with the Soviet regime as ruled by the CPSU's DINOSAURS) and the BARKING DOGS and TERMITES, who loathed it and were preparing for radical reforms. The SHEEP acquiesced to the commands of the Party leaders. Had they wanted to oppose the regime, they lacked any way of doing so, for they could not easily meet privately to share their misgivings or mobilize any kind of activism.

There was almost no civil society, as the term is usually defined. To organize even a group of musicians to play together, authorization was required. Every group had to be registered and was open to inspection by the state. Moreover, there were no coffee shops where people could simply sit and talk. I used to stay with a Moscow family (illegally, for I had to pay to get fake papers for registration with the local authorities). They arranged my appointments, transported me to interviews, and translated, when necessary. A family member often had a couple of hours free in the center of the city before the next appointment, but there was no place to wait. In Toronto I would have bought a newspaper and dawdled over tea in a coffee shop, but no such places existed in Moscow. Later McDonald's and Pizza Hut came to Moscow and won my respect for giving Russian SHEEP public places to create civil society.

Yet somehow opponents of the regime were not wholly lacking in "underground" civil societies. The TERMITES met with virtual impunity, but it was more difficult for the BARKING DOGS, who were followed and whose apartments were bugged. Sometimes when talking at home with a guest, they would pause and write a sensitive sentence on a children's toy—a sheet of plastic on a sticky black background. They'd write, display it, then lift the plastic to erase the sentence. And when it came to circulating forbidden books—"samizdat" literature—they'd re-type the whole manuscript with five layers of carbon paper and deliver copies to their friends. Yet they persevered.

Regrettably, the groups who opposed the regime also opposed each other. Their civil societies were wonderful—but separate. Each was a "bonding" type without any "bridging" members allied to the other side. The mutual contempt was palpable. In my interview with her, one eminent BARKING DOG referred to the other group as "whores." For their part, TERMITES often dismissed dissidents as uninformed and naïve. (That was partly true, for citizens could only obtain adequate information if they held important posts in the Party apparatus—and even that was often not enough.) Yet the main goals of both civil societies were the same. They should have been firm allies.

Although a certain amount of secrecy was necessary in order to carry out dissident activities, a key objective of BARKING DOGS was to live much as if they were free, thereby setting a public example for others and, by making conspicuous the abuse heaped on them, show that the state held power by violence, not by the glad consent of the governed. Instead of keeping their activities secret, BARKING DOGS sought publicity and got it, with the help of the Western press. Their network was extensive, despite the efforts of the state to limit it.

A few people, especially artists and writers, served as bridges linking the networks of top TERMITES and the BARKING DOGS. For example, members of both groups attended Yuri Lyubimov's Taganka Theater and knew its director and the most popular actor, Vladimir Vysotsky. Moreover, most mainstream scholars and intellectuals in major cities could count one or more dissidents among their acquaintances or friends, from whom they may have kept a cautious distance.

And as we have seen, BARKING DOGS expressed utter contempt toward TERMITES, who compromised with a system they did not believe in. However, they too had friends who assisted them in various ways without greatly jeopardizing their own security. In fact, without the support of such friends, they could not have performed their own highly visible functions in Soviet society. When they were jailed, for example, they could be sure that a kind neighbor would take care of their children and receive messages on their behalf. The neighbor would receive a visit and a warning from the KGB, but probably nothing more serious would come of it.

Later I will describe the contacts that the regime's critics (mainly TERMITES) made with foreigners, and the significance of those conversations in shaping public policy.

Notes

1. Robert Prince, in discussion with the author, 1992. See his article, "The Ghost Ship of Lonnrotinkatu: The Catabolism of the World Peace Council, Part I," *Peace Magazine* 8, no. 3 (May–June 1992): 16–17. Prince cites an article by Tapio Kari in the Nov. 1, 1991 weekend edition of *Kansan Uutiset,* the newspaper of the Finnish Communist Party.

2. Robert Prince's interview is my main source for the WPC history.

3. Notably Genrikh Borovik, Oleg Kharkhardin, Grigory Lokshin, and Vladimir Oryol.

4. Prince, in discussion with the author, 1995, Toronto.

5. Mac Makarchuk, in discussion with the author, 1990, Prague.

6. Toronto psychiatrist Dr. Frank Sommers had several such experiences, especially after he had made critical statements about Soviet policies.

7. Alexander Povolovsky, in discussion with the author, August 1990, Washington DC.

8. Georgi Arbatov, in discussion with the author, 1992, Moscow.

9. Genrikh Borovik also mentioned in our interview that he too had appealed to Gorbachev's assistant not to schedule the tests at the time of Hiroshima Day.

10. Tair Tairov, interview by Jane Mayes, July 1, 1988, Lund, Sweden, published in *Peace Magazine* 4, no. 6 (December 1988–January 1989): 30–31.

11. Discussions with Tair Tairov in Moscow and Nova Scotia.

12. Robert D. Putnam, Robert Leonardi, and Raffaella Y. Nanetti, *Making Democracy Work: Civic Traditions in Modern Italy* (Princeton: Princeton University Press, 1994). See also Robert D. Putnam, *Bowling Alone* (New York: Simon and Schuster, 2000).

13. Concerning the attitudes of the SPDC on this and other issues, see Lawrence Wittner, *Toward Nuclear Abolition* (Stanford, CA: Stanford University Press, 2003), especially chapter 15.

14. Andrei Sakharov, *Memoirs* (New York: Vintage, 1992), 164.

15. I interviewed Arbatov, Burlatsky, Gerasimov, and Shakhnazarov.

16. I interviewed Arbatov, Burlatsky, Petrovsky, Shakhnazarov, and Velikhov.

17. I draw mainly on my interviews with Blagovolin, Deliusin, Gerasimov, Karaganov, Andrei Kortunov, Simonia, and Sheinis. For another discussion of Gorbachev's team and their intellectual backgrounds, see Robert D. English, *Russia and the Idea of the West: Gorbachev, Intellectuals & the End of the Cold War.* (New York: Columbia University Press, 2000).

18. I interviewed Boris Oryeshene, editor of Progress Books, who explained these details to me.

19. Oryeshene kindly provided us with a list of the titles published in these numbered editions. Many of them are anthologies of articles, but some are books that many readers will have read. Between 1984–1990, the series included the following titles:

- Martin Anderson, *Revolution* (New York: Harcourt Brace Jovanovich, 1988)
- Seweryn Bialer and Michael Mandelbaum, *Gorbachev's Russia and American Foreign Policy* (Boulder: Westview, 1988).
- Lenni Brenner, *Zionism in the Age of the Dictators* (London: Croom Helm, 1983).
- Zbigniew K. Brzezinski, *Game Plan: A Geostrategic Framework for the Conduct of the U.S. Soviet Contest* (New York: Atlantic Monthly Press, 1986).
- E. H. Carr, *What is History?* (New York: Knopf, 1962).
- Fidel Castro, *Fidel and Religion: Castro Talks on Revolution and Religion with Frei Betto* (New York: Simon and Schuster, 1987).
- John B. Dunlop, *The New Russian Nationalism.* (New York: Praeger, 1985).
- Martin Ebon, *The Soviet Propaganda Machine* (New York: McGraw-Hill, 1987).
- Marceau Felden, *La Guerre Dans l'Espace: Armes et Technologies Nouvelles* (Paris: Berger-Levrault, 1984).
- Dietrich Fischer, *Preventing War in the Nuclear Age* (Totowa, NJ: Rowman and Allanheld, 1984).
- Daniel F. Ford, *The Cult of the Atom: The Secret Papers of the Atomic Energy Commission* (New York: Simon and Schuster, 1982).
- Tom Gervasi, *The Myth of Soviet Military Supremacy* (New York: Harper and Row, 1986).
- Marshall Goldman, *Gorbachev's Challenge: Economic Reform in the Age of High Technology* (New York: Norton, 1987).
- Stephen Green, *Taking Sides: America's Secret Relations with a Militant Israel* (New York: W. Morrow, 1984).
- Alexander Meigs Haig, *Caveat: Realism, Reagan, and Foreign Policy* (New York: Macmillan, 1984).
- Friedrich August von Hayek, *The Road to Serfdom.*
- Barukh Hazan, *Soviet Impregnational Propaganda* (Ann Arbor: Ardis, 1982).
- David Holloway, *The Soviet Union and the Arms Race* (New Haven: Yale University Press, 1983).
- Nicholas Lampert, *Whistleblowing in the Soviet Union: A Study of Complaints and Abuses under State Socialism* (New York: Schocken, 1985).

- Herbert M. Levine, *The Nuclear Arms Race Debates* (New York: McGraw-Hill, 1986).
- Robert S. McNamara, *Blundering Into Disaster: Surviving the First Century of the Nuclear Age* (New York: Pantheon, 1986).
- Daniel Patrick Moynihan, *Came the Revolution: Argument in the Reagan Era* (New York: Harcourt Brace Jovanovich, 1988).
- George Orwell, *Nineteen Eighty-Four* (New York: Harcourt Brace Jovanovich, 1977).
- Juho Kusti Paasikivi, *Diaries* (Porvoo: W. Svderstrom, 1991).
- Bruce Parrott, ed. *Trade, Technology, and Soviet-American Relations.* (Bloomington: Indiana University Press, 1985).
- Peace Pilgrim, *Peace Pilgrim: Her Life and Work in Her Own Words* (Ocean Tree Books, 1983).
- Richard F. Staar, ed. *Public Diplomacy: USA Versus USSR* (Stanford: Hoover Institution Press, 1986).
- David Stockman, *The Triumph of Politics: How the Reagan Revolution Failed* (New York: Harper and Row, 1986).
- Michel Tatu, *Eux et Nous: Les Relations Est-Ouest Entre Deux Détentes* (Paris: Fayard, 1985).
- Françoise Thom, *The Gorbachev Phenomenon: A History of Perestroika* Trans. Jenny Marshall. (London: J. Spiers, 1989).
- Peter Ustinov, *My Russia* (Boston: Little, Brown, 1983).

20. In post-Soviet days I was given one of these numbered white books: Yves Lecerf and Edward Parker, *The Chernobyl Affair* (Paris: Presses Universitaires de France, 1987).

21. Abdurakhman Avtorkhanov, *Stalin and the Soviet Communist Party: A Study in the Technology of Power.* (Hyperion, 1975). Avtorkhanov adduces evidence that Stalin may have been murdered—an opinion that is not shared by many informed people today. Yevgeny I. Zamiatin's book was *We*, trans. Mirra Ginsburg (New York: Viking: 1972).

22. Abel Aganbegyan's proposals, which seemed radical for only a short period, included joint enterprises with foreign firms and a strong emphasis upon democratization. See his book, *Inside Perestroika: The Future of the Soviet Economy* (New York: Harper and Row, 1980).

23. Tat'iana Zaslavskaia, *A Voice of Reform* (Armonk, NY: M.E. Sharpe, 1989).

24. I interviewed Sergei Blagovolin, Nodari Simonia, Victor Sumsky, Yevgeny Rashkovsky, and Ida Kuklina there.

25. In an uncharacteristic move, the Brezhnev government had published in Soviet newspapers the text of the Helsinki Final Act in 1975. Perhaps the Party leaders were boasting about their triumph.

26. Robert M. Gates, who had been director of the CIA, has noted that President Ford was strongly criticized for entering into this agreement, which Westerners widely considered at the time as only an irrelevant document paid for by legitimizing Soviet domination of East Central Europe. Actually, it turned out to be a great asset to the West. See Gates's memoirs, *From the Shadows: The Ultimate's Story of Five Presidents and How They Won the Cold War* (New York: Simon and Schuster, 1996).

27. Other founders included Ludmilla Alexeyeva, Mikhail Bernshtam, Yelena Bonner, Alexander Ginzburg, Pyotr Grigorenko, Alexander Korchak, Malva Landa, Anatoly Marchenko, Gregory Rosenstein, Vitalin Rubin, and Anatoly Shcharansky. Ten other people joined later. Sakharov himself was already being persecuted, and Sergei Kovalev, who would become a stalwart of the organization, was already serving time in labor camps and would not be released until 1986.

28. For a period around the time of the revolution, Soviet psychiatrists had expressed opposition to governmental policies and their support for fundamental political reforms. They attributed many cases of mental disorder to the socio-political problems and violence prevailing before the revolution. Soon their profession had become radicalized, and was pressuring its members to say that they all favored the psychological benefits of activism. The profession censored itself and promoted the revolution, making life difficult for those members whose political convictions ran in the other direction. See Julie V. Brown, "Revolution and Psychosis: The Mixing of Science and Politics in Russian Psychiatric Medicine, 1905–13." *The Russian Review* 46 (1987): 283–302. The consequences of this professional pressure were to become visible only gradually.

29. Dr. Anatoly Koryagin, himself a psychiatrist, spoke against such abuses in the Soviet Union and was given a twelve-year sentence in 1981 and later exiled.

30. Sidney Bloch and Peter Reddaway, *Soviet Psychiatric Abuse: The Shadow Over World Psychiatry* (Boulder: Westview Press, 1985).

31. Vladimir Bukovsky and Semyon Gluzman, "A Dissident's Guide to Psychiatry," in *A Chronicle of Human Rights in the USSR* 13 (1975): 31–57.

32. Stephen Faraone, "Psychiatry and Political Repression in the Soviet Union," *The American Psychologist* 37, no. 10 (Occtober. 1982): 1105–08.

32. Especially one Andrei Snezhnevsky.

33. Improvements took place under Gorbachev (reportedly because of the intervention of Alexander Yakovlev) but as late as 1991, a Soviet reformist psychiatrist expressed concern that the Soviet Ministry of Health still had not disseminated the relevant UN documents condemning the practice of torture with psychiatric medications. See Semyon F. Gluzman, "Abuse of Psychiatry: Analysis of the Guilt of Medical Personnel," *Journal of Medical Ethics* 17 (1991): 19–20.

34. The issue of psychiatric abuse was to prove significant during the campaign against the nuclear arms race in the mid-eighties. One of the most influential organizations in that campaign was the International Physicians for the Prevention of Nuclear War (IPPNW), founded jointly by Soviet and American physicians. The organization would win a Nobel Peace Prize for its campaigns, and generally deserves the respect it enjoys in the West. Some Soviet human rights activists, on the other hand, held generally negative views of IPPNW, for several different reasons, not least of which is the leading role played by a Soviet psychiatrist, Dr. Marat Vartanyan, in the peace work. Vartanyan was described by several investigative teams as head of the main institution responsible for the psychiatric abuse of political prisoners. See Peter Reddaway, "Soviet Psychiatry: An End to Political Abuse?" *Survey* 29 (Oct. 1988): 31. When confronted about the matter, Vartanyan defended all existing practices. I asked the co-founder of IPPNW, Dr. Bernard Lown, about Vartanyan. He claimed it was a mistake, since Vartanyan was doing research with rats, not clinical work. Still, Lown acknowledged that Vartanyan was an apologist.

35. Yuri Orlov, in discussion with the author, 1994. Orlov had emigrated to the U.S., where he is still doing physics research at Cornell University.

36. Mark Yakovlevich Azbel, *Refusenik: Trapped in the Soviet Union*, ed. Grace Pierce Forbes (Boston: Houghton Mifflin, 1981), 467–70. Azbel notes that, when the KGB failed to prevent the seminar from taking place, they took over the restaurant where the participants went for a final dinner and stocked it with every lavish delicacy for the occasion to prevent the foreigners from seeing the usual conditions in Moscow restaurants. Eric Fawcett also described these meetings to me in 1991.

37. Ludmilla Alexeyeva, *Soviet Dissent*, trans. Carol Pearce and John Glad (Middletown, CT: Wesleyan University Press, 1985), 186.

38. Eduard Shevardnadze was then the Foreign Minister of the Soviet Union.

39. Irwin Cotler, in telephone discussion with the author, 1992.

40. He and his wife now live in Israel. He changed his name to Natan Sharansky, and is a prominent right-wing politician there.

41. See Andrei Sakharov, "The Danger of Thermonuclear War," in *Memoirs* (New York: Vintage, 1992): 664–70.

42. In our interview, Irwin Cotler mentioned such an occasion, when Bonner inexplicably reversed the position that she and her husband had taken earlier when they asserted that, according to the best evidence, Raoul Wallenberg had not died in 1947, as the Soviet government had pretended.

43. For a long period of Russian history there were strong conflicts between the intelligentsia who wished to become more Western and more modern and the "Slavophiles," who believed that Russian traditions were superior to anything found abroad and particularly that Russian spirituality was deeper than other forms of Christianity.

44. Thanks to a tour and interview with Dr. Yelena Rusakova.

45. Victor Bulgakov, in discussion with the author, 1992, Moscow.

46. Ellsberg had been an analyst at the RAND Corporation during the Vietnam War. He gained fame for publishing the "Pentagon Papers," classified documents that had established the duplicity of the U.S. government in that war.

47. Olga Medvedkov, "Uncontrolled Grass-Roots Movement in the Soviet Union: The Moscow Trust Group," 85-page mimeo, about 1987, with numerous appended documents generated by the group, p. 4. Medvedkov later published much the same information in an entire issue of the *Mershon Center Quarterly*, the newsletter of a research institute in Columbus, Ohio at Ohio State University, where she and her husband Yuri began working after their immigration to the United States in 1987.

48. Medvedkov, 12.

49. Medvedkov, 19.

50. Medvedkov, 19.

51. Gale Warner, *Invisible Threads: Independent Soviets Working for Global Awareness and Social Transformation*, (Washington, DC: Seven Locks Press, 1991), 81.

52. Upon immigrating to the United States, Medvedkova adapted to Western ways by dropping the final "a" from her married name. This seemed to be a necessary way of reducing the confusion of their American acquaintances, who often tried to resolve the inconsistency by adding an "a" to her husband Yuri's surname.

53. Medvedkov, 31.

54. Medvedkov, 62.

55. Mark Reitman, as quoted by John Bacher, "The Independent Peace Movements in Eastern Europe," *Peace Magazine* 1, no. 11 (December 1985): 9.

56. Medvedkov, 53.

57. Medvedkov, 42.

58. Medvedkov, 39–40.

59. Medvedkov, 52–53.

60. Medvedkov, 54–55.

61. Eric Fawcett and Derek Paul, in discussion with the author, 1986.

62. Catherine Fitzpatrick, in dicusssion with the author, 1993, New York. Fitzpatrick was for several years the Soviet observer at Helsinki Watch in the United States, and was more familiar with the Trustbuilders than any other American. She has since served as interpreter for several high level Soviet figures and has translated the memoirs of Yegor Ligachev, Eduard Shevardnadze, and Alexander Yakovlev.

Chapter 2: Social Capital and Ideology

Since the collapse of communism, democratic reformers and political theorists alike have promoted civil society organizations as the chief support for democracy and peace. Authoritarian rulers, on the other hand, have continued trying to suppress such independent organizations, which they recognize as undermining their control over the populace. Yet it may not be self-evident how civil society can have such beneficial political and social effects. In this chapter I'll explain: It's about social capital.

Democracy requires and supports civil society, which creates what is now called "social capital." A totalitarian state, on the other hand, suppresses social capital by enforcing unquestioning conformity and preventing the formation of independent groups that would challenge the state's authority or ideology.

To be sure, ideologies abound even in democratic countries, where they are, however, endorsed voluntarily. Many religious communities, for example, require their members to believe and obey their teachings, but in a free society one is able to quit such a group without being burned at the stake or sent to the Gulag. Moreover, in a democracy, one may join all kinds of independent groups that discuss controversial issues and increase dissent.

Authoritarian rulers underestimate the price to be paid for enforcing their own ideology. Whenever free communication is suppressed, the effectiveness of the whole society is reduced, for problems may not be recognized and addressed in a timely fashion. Obedient workers in any economy are uncreative workers—people whose intelligence cannot be applied where it is needed. Let me give two regrettably typical examples.

Once I attended a peace conference as one of a thousand Western guests in Estonia, which was still part of the Soviet Union. Our breakfast queue stretched around the building and down the street for two blocks. Each guest waited over one hour to reach the serving area, where there was plenty of food and a dispenser that dribbled out kefir at a rate of about two tablespoonfuls per minute. That dispenser was holding up a thousand hungry people. I could see a solution to the problem immediately. There were several empty tables available, which I could easily rearrange to create two or three speedy queues. Why had none of the staff seen the problem or the solution? I suggested to the other Westerners around me that we offer our services, but they explained that this would be considered rude. Because the kitchen crew was not allowed to exercise independent initiative, they would have been offended, had we used our own.

Another example: In the late Soviet period a highly qualified young physician visited me in Toronto from Ukraine, where he worked in a hospital emergency room. I learned that lately there was such a severe shortage of syringes and needles that my young friend could not send any off to be sterilized, but had to keep re-using the same hypodermics throughout the day. Everyone realized that this practice would spread HIV, but he saw no alternative. In Toronto there is a needle exchange facility for drug users precisely to prevent HIV transmission, so I took him down to meet the nurse there, who showed him how to kill HIV viruses by cleaning needles and syringes with alcohol—or in a pinch, even with vodka. She gave him a photocopy of a medical journal article attesting to the effectiveness of the procedure. Although he was deeply grateful for the information, he said he could not apply it. The head physician always told him what to do and if he used his own professional judgment, he would certainly be fired. He intended to go on using contaminated syringes and needles until he was ordered to do otherwise.

Soviet cafeteria workers and physicians were as intelligent as anyone needs to be. They were suffering from a deficit, not of sound neurons, but of democracy. They were prisoners of ideology, which prohibited the use of their own common sense.

Of course, the official Soviet ideology, Marxism-Leninism, had nothing to say about how to organize an efficient cafeteria or how to sterilize hypodermic equipment. Nevertheless, the heavy-handed enforcement of that political doctrine had a "stupidifying" effect on society. Sociologists understand that *any* ideology, if imposed forcibly on individuals, undermines their capacity for independent problem-solving. Their resulting incompetence is a manifestation of a lack of social capital—a concept that will recur throughout this book.

In later chapters I will show how social capital was enhanced by face-to-face contacts in international organizations. In this chapter, however, I will simply try to illustrate how the society was deprived of vital skills and knowledge by requiring Soviet people to give their uncritical assent to pre-determined, politically enforced, ideologies.

Dogmatism has been widespread throughout human history. People don't need a dictator to keep their minds closed—though it helps. But old-fashioned dictators lacked one thing that all communist regimes had: state-appointed officials who were in charge of policing the minds of the population. And one of their methods was to quash independent voluntary organizations—civil society —thereby destroying social capital.

Social capital refers to the networks of trusting relationships among the members of a society. The more social capital there is, the better—both for the individuals themselves and for the collectivity. To have lots of friends and acquaintances is a valuable personal resource—at least if the quality of those relationships is good. Mutual trust is an essential factor. If you have a thick, full address book but the people listed in it distrust each other, you cannot expect them to accomplish much together. To coordinate a project in which they are engaged will require close monitoring and supervision, for they may be unable to discuss and solve ordinary problems by themselves.

Another term—*human capital*—is associated with social capital. Human capital is the stock of skills and knowledge that allow workers to produce economic value. Economists often use these concepts to emphasize that one can invest capital in human beings to make them more competent producers, just as one can invest capital in machinery or raw materials. Education and on-the-job training are the main factors that increase human capital. However, voluntary associations also augment human capital, for people develop skills and knowledge in free, cooperative activities. Social capital is a source of human capital.

(Personally, I consider the word "capital" misleading here. I prefer the term "capacity-building" since, to me, capital is inherently limited. If I give you some of my money, I have less of it left. But if I give you some information or expertise, I have as much as before, and you have it too. The second law of thermodynamics does not apply to knowledge or to human relationships, as it does to physical things. Still, we must use the terms that are in common currency.)

Soviet society had plenty of certain kinds of human capital. The quality and levels of education there had become quite good by the 1970s, but could not always be applied effectively or creatively because of prevailing ideological constraints.

Soviet citizens did participate in group activities, but these were organized by the state and participation was obligatory. No independently organized groups were allowed. Even stamp collectors were required to register with the state and pay fees; in 1922 the secret service arrested some Moscow philatelists for exchanging stamps. Ideologically, this hobby was suspected of involving speculation—an economic crime.[1] Totalitarian groups, created and managed by the state, have effects exactly opposite to the groups of civil society: They don't build initiative and mutuality.

Social capital was impaired by pervasive lack of trust. This climate of mistrust did not originate with the CPSU, but instead involved an institution, the *poruka* (peer-keep) system, that dated back to Muscovite times, perhaps the fourteenth century. Soldiers entering the army in those days had to promise not to run away, and if they did, their peers were punished for not tipping off the officers.[2] Likewise, in Soviet times a person might be punished for failing to denounce to the authorities any acquaintance who seemed intent on violating the rules. This institution was also employed in other totalitarian systems, and it made people guarded about trusting their peers.

Nevertheless, most people managed to develop warm friendships. There is no reason to conclude that Soviet people were deprived of a fulfilling social life. About 40 percent of the population had dachas—cottages in the countryside where they spent weekends and vacations in the summer, gardening and socializing with neighbors. Even so, the state encouraged people to spy on their own family members; one "heroic boy," Pavlik Morozov, still has a street named after him in Moscow for having denounced his father to Stalin's secret police. Fortunately, such disloyalty among family members never became widespread.

Nevertheless, family ties and private friendships are not aspects of civil society. It is self-organized, purposive public groups that count.

If weak social capital can limit the spread of vital new ideas, strong social capital can stimulate them. Creativity results from exposure to *diversity*. A historian, Frederick J. Teggart, studied the circumstances under which cultural innovations took place in the past.[3] He attributed periods of remarkable development to "intrusions" that occurred whenever a group's routines were interrupted by (often unwanted) contact with foreigners. This was especially common when there had been great migrations that forced strangers to interact. The contact unsettled them all, demonstrating alternative ways of cooking, say, or building temples, embalming corpses, or keeping time. Although such contacts were mainly unwelcome, they forced people to think in new ways and innovate.

Today, Richard Florida is also attempting to explain why creative workers tend to gravitate to certain cities and not others. His answer is similar to Teggart's: they crave and are stimulated by diversity and unfamiliar ideas.[4] Where there are lots of foreign-born immigrants living in a city, where there are lots of gays, lots of university graduates, and a "cool" district with musicians, artists, and a lively night life, talented workers will come. Thus social capital is enhanced by diversity, and in turn it enhances human capital. The worst place for a creative worker to live is in an isolated rural area.

Several large Soviet cities were culturally diverse, attracting people of varied nationality and ethnicity. They should have been centers of innovation, and to some extent they were. As we shall see, what held them back was the largely the imposition of a fixed ideology on everyone: Marxism-Leninism.

* * *

When the Bolsheviks won the October Revolution and the subsequent civil war, they foisted their version of Marxist ideology onto the entire population. Later, as the CPSU, they reduced access to diverse ideas by suppressing contacts with alternatives. Moreover, the Communists took a position on every possible topic, including art, science, and philosophy, and imposed it on the populace—even when it was not relevant to Marxism-Leninism.

Take Lysenkoism,[5] for example. Between the late 1920s and the early 1960s evolutionary biology, genetics, and agronomy were subordinated to the control of a charlatan, Trofim Lysenko (1898–1976) who insisted that acquired traits can become hereditary. Many genuine scientists such as the eminent plant breeder Nikolai Vavilov were imprisoned for dissenting from his doctrine. Not only Stalin but also Khrushchev believed in Lysenko, whose theory was displaced only after Khrushchev's ouster.

Lysenkoism was the most egregious example of political control over science, but there were many others. Government officials who were accustomed to giving orders did not stop respectfully at the limits of their scientific expertise, but seemed to expect even the laws of nature to obey their commands. Thus even Andrei Sakharov, while he was working to develop nuclear weapons, was forced to abandon what he regarded as a more promising line of investigation (his "third idea"—key to the hydrogen bomb) in favor of an official's alternative preference. When one of Sakharov's team objected, he was given a severe Party reprimand for "anti-state behavior."[6]

Since it destroys ordinary human trust, totalitarianism depends on institutional controls, such as mandatory identity cards and agencies capable of monitoring the movement of vast numbers of citizens.

Marxism was not inherently manipulative. Indeed, Karl Marx, who had worked as a journalist, strongly defended freedom of the press, which he regarded as "the ubiquitous vigilant eye of a people's soul,"[7] a view that he carried so far as to oppose all censorship. His close associate, Friedrich Engels, also claimed that press laws were disgraceful, since the workers' movement was "fighting to establish the environment necessary for its existence, for the air it needs to breathe."[8] Nor was Marx's view of ideology favorable; he invariably portrayed it as a deception perpetrated upon working people. In *The German Ideology,* he introduced the idea of ideological subjection, claiming that as social classes are generated by the division of labor, "one dominates all the others."[9]

Ideological repression was Lenin's invention, not Marx's. Before coming to power, Lenin had personally drafted a clause of his party's platform calling for freedom of the press; it was adopted unanimously by his party. However, on the second day after coming to power (and against some opposition within his own party) Lenin introduced a law authorizing the monopoly of the Bolshevik press.[10] This was only one of many ominous signs. By 1920, Lenin's wife, Krupskaya, was purging Soviet public libraries, removing from the shelves vast numbers of books that seemed "counter-revolutionary" or "harmful." This tradition of secrecy continued throughout the Soviet period. In 1987 the Lenin Library in Moscow was accused of concealing at least 1.5 million Russian-language books from the readers' catalogue.

Yet ideology was not equally repressive throughout the entire Soviet period. There were two periods of comparative freedom: during the New Economic Program (NEP) of 1921–28 and during a "thaw" in Khrushchev's period from the mid-1950s to the early 1960s, when censorship was considerably relaxed. I'll review the cultural history briefly here.

Between the end of the Civil War and the beginning of agricultural collectivization and industrialization was the period of market socialism, NEP, when small private businesses were permitted, along with considerable cultural freedom. At first, the Party was reluctant to dictate to artists, but the intellectuals and artists often disagreed among themselves and petitioned the Party leaders to function as arbiters of their disputes, a practice that would lead to more heavy-handed political control over time.

Many of the leading cultural figures, such as Lenin's friend, Maxim Gorky, a playwright and novelist, went into exile. The most creative artists—Prokofiev, Stravinsky—also left, though some of them, like Gorky and the novelist Ilya Ehrenburg, returned later and learned to live with Stalinism. Others were deported,[11] while still others, such as Boris Pasternak and Osip Mandelshtam, never left Russia, though paying dearly for their fidelity to their homeland. (Pasternak's prose was never published in his country during his lifetime.)[12]

Nevertheless, it remained possible for intellectuals to produce novel ideas during the NEP. For example, Eisenstein made his great films; "avant-garde" painting flourished; and Stanislavski's Moscow Art Theater thrived. The playwright and novelist Mikhail Bulgakov stayed,[13] though not until the 1960s were five of his finest works from the first half of the century published, including his great novel *The Master and Margarita*.

Lenin had died in January 1924, probably of a stroke, though he also suffered from syphilis. There followed several years of palace intrigue until Stalin gained decisive control of the country. In 1928 he decided to industrialize and collectivize agriculture. This spelled the end of NEP and the rise of a more totalitarian CPSU.

Soon the Soviet Union was at war against Hitler, losing about 26.6 million souls in that struggle. Moreover, the persecutions of Soviet citizens by other Soviet citizens defy comprehension. About three million persons died in the Gulag prison camps between the time Lenin established them and Stalin's death in 1953. Social capital—trusting relationships—declined to almost zero. Only close family members could speak confidently to each other.

At last, in a sensational speech to the Twentieth Party Congress in 1956, Nikita Khrushchev denounced Stalin's crimes. His revelation was the sign that a new period of relative liberalization was about to begin: the "thaw."

During the heady days of the thaw, intellectuals were able to speak frankly to each other. Ideological controls were lenient and even the term *glasnost* (openness) came into use. Idea-workers began to assemble regularly in private apartments in groups called *kompanii*; they danced, drank, listened to jazz, and talked throughout the night. As Ludmilla Alexeyeva recalls, *"Kompanii* emerged in a flash in the mid-1950s, stayed vibrant for a decade, then faded away."[14]

Although these social gatherings were stimulating and personally enriching, they were not "civil society"—not organizations with particular objectives. The only purposive organizations were those created and managed by the state, in which people were required to participate. Nevertheless, throughout the Soviet period, most people maintained vibrant social lives with a circle of close friends. In the postcommunist period, researchers have found that civil society in the former Soviet Union is weaker than in countries that previously had been either democratic or authoritarian. One explanation seems to be that people hated having to participate in state-run organizations and now resist all purposeful groups—even self-organized ones.[15]

The generation of liberal intelligentsia who experienced the thaw identified themselves permanently as the "children of the Twentieth Party Congress," or the "sixty-niks" (*shestidesyatniks*). By the time Stalin's body was removed from Lenin's mausoleum in 1961, bold literary works had appeared in print by, for example, the historian Roy Medvedev,[16] the poet Yevgeny Yevtushenko,[17] the novelist Vladimir Dudinstsev,[18] and a group of intellectuals connected with the thick journal *Novy Mir*, which in 1962 even published Solzhenitsyn's novella about life in a Gulag camp, *One Day in the Life of Ivan Denisovich*. This work had even more influence on public awareness of Stalinism than the author's massive later work, *The Gulag Archipelago*.[19] A few theaters in Moscow—notably the Contemporary Theater and later Yury Lyubimov's Taganka Theater—were staging provocative plays.

The thaw was an intoxicating period for the intelligentsia, resembling in some respects the sixties in the West. Mikhail Gorbachev and Raisa Maksimovna Titorenko just missed this open cultural renaissance in Moscow; they became students at Moscow State University in 1950 and 1949 respectively.[20] They married in 1953, the year of Stalin's death, when they and almost everyone else were Stalinists (at least in public), and moved away to Stavropol in 1955—too early to participate fully in the public cultural liberalization in the capital. In fact, Gorbachev behaved during his university years as a properly strict leader of the CPSU's youth wing, the Komsomol, even kicking out other members for breaking the rules.[21]

Nevertheless, he showed a bold streak too, as for example during a wave of anti-Semitism that swept through the university after Stalin accused a group of Jewish doctors of assassination under the guise of medical treatment. One student began to smear a Jewish fellow. Mikhail Gorbachev leapt to his feet and defended his friend, fiercely berating the anti-Semite for being a "spineless beast."[22] Gorbachev's roommate, Rudolf Kolchanov, recalls private conversations in the dormitory for which they all could have been jailed.[23]

Many of these university friends would later become prominent "sixty-nik" social critics. For example, Merab Mamardashvili and Yuri Levada were both especially close friends of the Gorbachevs[24] and both of them married girls who were roommates of Raisa. Mamardashvili would later gain world fame as a philosopher,[25] but would run into so much political opposition that he would move to Georgia, where cultural life remained somewhat freer than in Russia.[26] Gorbachev lost touch with him, but Raisa continued to read his works[27] until his death in 1990. In her memoirs she praises his attempts to cool nationalistic passions in Georgia.[28]

Levada became the most eminent sociologist in Russia, specializing in public opinion research, but he too experienced intellectual repression at first hand during the early 1970s. As head of the department of Social Change at the Institute of Sociology, he was criticized for being too open, and his department staff were fired, along with the other scholars at the institute who were acquainted with Western sociology.[29]

Only much later in life would these "sixty-nik" TERMITES attain enough power to apply their ideals openly, after careers in a culture that froze over again almost as soon as it had thawed.

Although Khrushchev was more tolerant than his predecessors or his successor Brezhnev, he was a rough, uneducated man who embarrassed the TERMITES who worked for him. And his tolerance was limited. For example, when he attended an exhibit of art in 1962 that included abstract works, he called the paintings "shit" and the painters "homosexuals." This uncouthness annoyed the more sophisticated and democratic Russians. When in 1964 he was deposed by two Politburo rivals, Leonid I. Brezhnev and Nikolai V. Podgorny, his liberal advisers mainly felt relieved, expecting that society would become more open under the new leaders.[30] They were wrong.

The Shaping of Public Opinion

Long before the 1917 Russian Revolution, an authoritarian tendency had been apparent in the traditional Russian peasantry, fostered by the hierarchical social structures: the monarchy, serfdom, and Russian Orthodox traditions;[31] the Communist regime then reinforced it by the rule of "democratic centralism"—the principle that criticism by a minority was not legitimate after a political decision had been reached.

The Soviets also carried out campaigns of persuasion.[32] Under the direction of the party's chief ideologist, frequent and often mandatory "educational" courses were taught in workplaces throughout the country. Armed with righteousness, these "agitprop" instructors were free to put pressure on anyone who refused to be persuaded. The result, of course, was that the regime deprived itself of feedback from its intimidated citizens and lost the necessary mechanisms for detecting and correcting its own mistakes.[33]

How effective were these ideological manipulations? Most people apparently did think along officially approved lines. The pollster Nikolai Popov writes,

> It is a mentality of slaves, born in slavery, who loved their cage and their guards, of those who would hail—not with gloomy desperation, but with sincere joy and adoration, "Caesar, we who are about to die salute you!"[34]

Over time public opinion would become less unanimous, but the "slave mentality" would remain. Around the time of the breakup of the Soviet Union, Popov's polls found that the majority of his respondents agreed, for example, that "a few strong leaders can do more for our country than all the laws and rhetoric."[35]

"Double-thinking" became a common means of self-preservation. In 1989 sociologist Yury Levada conducted a survey of 2,700 Soviet citizens, asking employees what they did when their boss gave them a stupid order; 21 percent said they pretend to obey; 16 percent fulfill the stupid order without objecting, 11 percent try to avoid doing it, and only 29 percent tell the boss that his order is wrong.[36] When social networks in the workplace lack mutual trust, economic productivity is reduced.

One resulting trait was a tendency to turn away from the dark or tragic sides of life. Levada's respondents reported that only 28 percent of their families had ever discussed the Stalinist repressions. Only 11 percent could remember talks with their parents about death; talks about sex could be recalled by only 4 percent of the respondents; and only 2 percent could recall talks of suicide.[37] I learned when visiting with Soviet physicians that they never disclosed to a patient that he was dying.

The first post-World War II Russian emigrés to the West were not entirely opposed to the Soviet system. A large Harvard study showed that, although they detested the secret police, collective farming, and the intrusion of the state into personal affairs, they liked many other aspects of socialism, including state control over heavy industry, transportation, and communications systems. Over 86 percent favored state ownership of heavy industry, free education and health care, and guarantees of job security.[38] The ideal economy, in the opinion of the majority, was the mixed NEP system of the 1920s, when banking, most industry, and foreign trade had been managed by the state.

The Harvard study found significant differences of opinion among these respondents, with the younger, better educated ones being most favorable toward the socialist regime. The researchers concluded that at that time the Soviet state seemed to be successfully socializing the population to accept political values congruent with its declared objectives. Nothing suggested the likelihood of a counter-revolution or any significant opposition to the Stalinist regime.

However, a later study of emigrés in the 1980s, the "Soviet Interview Project," interviewed 2,793 Russians and emigrants from other Soviet republics,[39] revealing some difference in public opinion. Previously the well-educated and prosperous had been most supportive of the Soviet regime. That was no longer true of the later emigrés. Political Scientist Brian D. Silver then predicted that, as education increases, new demands would be placed on the Soviet state.[40]

In the late 1980s, Yury Levada claimed that, "According to the data collected in the last few months, the ardent advocates of the old system made up 10–12 percent of the population. . . . There are reasons to believe that such people had never made up a majority or significant minority of the population."[41]

Perhaps so, but there is evidence that Soviet citizens believed much of what they were told. The state was particularly careful to keep the public from hearing sympathetic accounts of grievances in their "satellite states." According to sociologist Elizabeth Teague, who studied relations between the Soviet Union and the Solidarność movement, by the time martial law was declared in the 1981 crackdown on Solidarność, the great majority of Soviet citizens held hostile views of their Polish neighbors' aspirations.[42]

So did the regime, of course. Although Western radio broadcasts had not been jammed since 1973, the authorities re-imposed jamming ten days after the outbreak of strikes in Gdansk in 1980.[43] The better-educated Moscow residents were the most sympathetic toward the Poles in those days, but according to a nation-wide sample survey, even they (especially Slavic respondents) were predominantly negative toward the strikers. They envied the Poles who, though they were better off than Soviet citizens, could still demand more.[44]

Thus before Gorbachev came to power the vast majority of people were (in the classification scheme I'll use) SHEEP. They complied overtly, but the party had not completely succeeded in controlling public opinion through propaganda. Support for the regime (and especially for Stalin) had been intense at certain points, especially during World War II, but had declined after Khrushchev had revealed the dictator's worst crimes. Workers' and farmers' chief grievance was the shortage of consumer goods, but they were not well enough informed to make meaningful comparisons between situations at home and abroad.

The intelligentsia, especially those who were young, constituted a growing class who were well informed and whose discontent was clearly increasing. Some of them were gaining social capital by organizing quasi-civil society groups in private. These TERMITES were so few and furtive, however, that pollster Nikolai Popov concluded: "The system was stable. Its decay, stagnation, and growing absurdity could have lasted for many more years. There were no signs of self-disintegration."[45]

But along came Gorbachev.

Ideology and the Social Capital of TERMITES

TERMITES did not start off as full-blown reformists. Only gradually, as one reform after another proved insufficient, did Gorbachev and his advisers become more radical. Some of the reformers had previously enforced the Party's rule, or had even participated in repressing true dissidents.

They never repented, nor will they ever admire the BARKING DOGS; their basic assumptions are too different. Whereas dissidents believed that totalitarianism could only be abolished by the refusal of ordinary citizens to cooperate with their oppressors, the TERMITES believed that only a "revolution from the top" was possible. As one prominent TERMITE, Fyodor Burlatsky, insisted, "No, I don't think you can say that our dissidents prepared the way for *perestroika*. *Perestroika* was prepared by people *within the system* who continued to speak out for revolutionary structural reforms. . ."[46]

Most TERMITES enjoyed considerable social capital from early life, having come from relatively privileged backgrounds. Some were the sons of old Bolshevik intellectuals who had been true believers in the ideology, not pragmatic opportunists. Charles H. Fairbanks has argued that they were very different from the corrupt cronies of the none-too-bright Brezhnev.[47] He believes that Gorbachev and his reformers were utopians who initially wanted to revive the revolutionary spirit by inspiring people, giving them back a worthy ideology.

Fairbanks traced this network of reformers back as far as the late thirties, to a circle of intellectuals around A. A. Zhdanov who promoted what they called "*perestroika*," "*glasnost*," and "democratization."[48] Ironically, their patron, Zhdanov, was an altogether different kind of person: dogmatic and ideological. He held the second highest position in the Soviet hierarchy (just below Stalin), actively participated in the Great Terror, and was responsible for ideological and cultural matters. Famous for abusing artists who showed spiritual independence, such as the poet Anna Akhmatova, the best that can be said of Zhdanov is that some people in the Party were even worse. It was Zhdanov who decided that foreign Communist Parties must conform to Soviet policies.[49]

When Zhdanov died in 1948, two of his rivals, Lavrenti Beria and Georgi Malenkov, fabricated a criminal case against his many protégés, probably with Stalin's approval. Although it is unclear exactly what the charges were, nearly five hundred people were implicated and several were executed in what came to be called the "Leningrad Case." This virtually eliminated Zhdanov's faction, leaving Beria and Malenkov uncontested as favorites of Stalin.[50] Nevertheless,

Malenkov lost power soon after the death of Stalin. Khrushchev came to power and executed Beria.

Fairbanks points out the surprising network links between Zhdanov and three men whose views were opposed to his own. We might consider them "proto-TERMITES." They were Otto Kuusinen, Yury Andropov, and Aleksei Rumyantsev. Kuusinen and Andropov had been members of Zhdanov's circle[51] and all three created a group of critics who would become key figures during the Gorbachev years.[52]

Stalin promoted all three men to high positions. Rumyantsev became head of the Science and Culture department of the Central Committee, and his deputy was Aleksandr Yakovlev, who one day would be the most influential designer of *perestroika*. Thus Kuusinen, Andropov, Rumyantsev, and Yakovlev were working together as early as the fifties and sixties. They were the core members of an early network that Fairbanks identifies as "reformers" and that I call TERMITES.

After Stalin's death a new textbook on Marxism-Leninism was needed to replace the Stalinist ones. Kuusinen, a Finnish labor specialist, brought together a group of young experts to work collaboratively on this book, *Fundamentals of Marxism-Leninism*. The team worked well together and went on to serve as Andropov's consultants and on the Central Committee staff. The consultants included Fyodor Burlatsky, Georgi Arbatov, Georgi Shakhnazarov, Anatoly Chernyayev, Gennady Gerasimov, Karen Brutents, Aleksandr Bovin, and Oleg Bogomolov. When Rumyantsev created the journal *Problems of Peace and Socialism* members of this group became its first editors and later, under Gorbachev, would become key figures responsible for developing *perestroika*. Until that opportunity opened up, however, they carried on their work under considerable risk. The regime was authoritarian; for writing ideologically unacceptable ideas one could be sacked or even imprisoned.

During the Brezhnev years social researchers discussed the growing problems of Soviet society and proposed solutions, many of which could not then be published. Everyone with unorthodox ideas was vulnerable, as I discovered while interviewing Sergei Kapitza, Victor Sheinis, Sergei Blagovolin, Nodari Simonia, and Lev Deliusin. All of them were TERMITES—unusually bold ones— and some of them had paid a penalty for their scholarly honesty. Occupying high positions, they had built up substantial social capital, which nevertheless had not been enough to protect them from the attacks of ideologues.

* * *

Sergei Kapitza is probably the scientist most familiar to the Soviet/Russian public, for he has long been appearing regularly on Soviet/Russian television to explain scientific matters. He is the son of the late Nobel laureate Peter Kapitza, and his physics laboratory occupies his father's old buildings in a wooded area beside the golden-topped high-rise Academy of Sciences building.

The first time I visited him there was in 1992. He was proofreading an article, "Lessons of Chernobyl," which he intended to deliver the following month at a Pugwash conference in Korea. He gave me a copy of the paper, which pessimistically analyzed the social and psychological factors behind the nuclear catastrophe. It pointed out that the Soviet nuclear projects had been marred from the beginning by a disregard for human life and hampered by the emphasis on secrecy. Kapitza had written,

> Most, if not all, of the construction work for the nuclear industry was conducted by slave labor of the Gulag. Often those who were engaged in building the most secret and sensitive "installations," as they were called in the newspeak of the industry, were later sent to camps to be isolated for life, as witnessed by Sakharov in his *Memoirs*.[53]

Despite the secrecy imposed by the director of the project, Lavrenti Beria, who headed Stalin's secret police, the first decade of Soviet nuclear power was conducted efficiently. Thereafter, however, a mediocre generation of scientists came in, chosen not for their scientific excellence but for their unquestionable political loyalty. The number of radiation accidents increased. Kapitza wrote, "The compartmentalization of society not only for demands of misguided secrecy, but for reasons of retaining control and preserving the power of the central authority, did contribute to the general deterioration of the educational level of engineers. . . "[54]

To summarize Kapitza's argument: As a means of controlling the society, the Party leaders reduced the social capital of the nuclear power industry, which in turn reduced its human capital and made the management of the Soviet nuclear power industry so incompetent that the outcome was the catastrophe at Chernobyl.

* * *

Victor Sheinis, a short man then in his sixties, greeted my research assistant, Julia Kalinina, and me across a huge vase of peonies on his desk in the Russian White House, where in early post-Soviet days he was a member of parliament. (He would quit before it was shelled by the army in 1993.) I asked about what had happened to him in 1956.

As a graduate student at Leningrad State University, it seems he had written an article criticizing the Soviet invasion of Hungary. A KGB agent had captured it before many people had read it, and Sheinis was expelled from the university and any teaching post. He worked for six years as a metal-worker in Leningrad but then another TERMITE professor helped him return to academe. In 1975 some Party informants attended his lectures on modern capitalism, denounced him for his ideological "unreliability," and he was forced to leave the university.

Nevertheless, Sheinis had published a lot by then, so he was invited to the prestigious Institute of World Economy and International Relations (IMEMO) in Moscow. Whereas Leningrad State University had been an institution for promoting Communist ideology, IMEMO had been tasked by the Central Committee with a legitimate research function: to keep the Committee abreast of real information rather than propaganda. Sheinis said that IMEMO was therefore staffed by what might be described as "politically unreliable" people. Because the Party also controlled IMEMO, this sometimes led to conflicting objectives.

For example, at the end of the '60s IMEMO was supposed to generate predictions about world development until the year 2000. These predictions were top-secret. One day a high-level party commission visited IMEMO, looked at the predictions, and issued a denunciation: "Revisionists are working in IMEMO! They predict that in the year 2000 capitalism will still exist!" IMEMO was too liberal an institution to suit Party propagandists and ideologues because it was distributing real information about foreign countries, which undermined their job.[55]

One of the issues that Sheinis studied at IMEMO was the Soviet oil industry. Sheinis worried about the de-industrialization of exports. At a time when well-developed countries were exporting machine tools, the Soviet Union was exporting raw materials—especially oil, which accounted for over half of the country's exports. Worse yet, the oil production was done in what Sheinis called a "barbarian" way. The holes were filled with water to obtain the upper level of oil, making it impossible to pump out what was left. He said,

It depleted nonrenewable resources, spoiled the environment, and plundered the national wealth. Moreover, the earned money was used to import grain and custom goods—things that could have been produced in the USSR if industry had not been oriented toward military production. I tried to propagate these views and the need for economic reforms, but this information couldn't get into the open media. My articles were read by only a few thousand scholars. I stated candidly that the USSR had lost in competition with capitalism.[56]

IMEMO was producing real information for the Central Committee International Department. In the same building was their worst enemy, the Central Committee Ideological Department, which distributed propaganda. Led by the powerful Party ideologist, Mikhail Suslov, that group sought ways of striking at IMEMO, which nevertheless supported the honest scholarship of its staff, including Sheinis.

* * *

Alexander Yakovlev was the USSR's ambassador to Canada for just over a decade, starting in 1972. In 1983 Mikhail Gorbachev, then the official in charge of Soviet agriculture, came to Canada and toured the country with Yakovlev. The two men, who had known each other slightly long before, became fast friends. Later that year, Andropov recalled Yakovlev to the Soviet Union at Gorbachev's request, and appointed him director of IMEMO.

Gorbachev, who wasn't yet the general secretary, was in a struggle with rivals for the number two position in the Party and admitted to Yakovlev that he was almost illiterate professionally with regard to security problems. Indeed, he knew that the military leaders, not wanting disarmament, would "cook" the statistics to make them seem to support their own views, so he asked Yakovlev for help: "Show me what is really happening. What is the real balance of power? What is the real size and scale of the military buildup?" He did not trust the information from the Soviet military leaders, who seemed to be exaggerating the military threat from the West.

Yakovlev gave this secret assignment to Sergei Blagovolin, whom I interviewed in 1993 at IMEMO, where he headed a department dealing with military problems.

At first Blagovolin and his team were not allowed to see Soviet data, but they had access to American data, which were extremely accurate. The figures had been published in the reports of some Congressional hearings. Over the next couple of years, Blagovolin had started assembling his own country's comparable figures, albeit unofficially, from Soviet military sources.

In late 1985, after Gorbachev had taken over from Chernenko as general secretary of the CPSU, he asked Yakovlev's successor at IMEMO, Yevgeny Primakov, to write up the Blagovolin team's findings for him, describing the true security situation.

Blagovolin's big assignment took place on a weekend when the institute was nearly empty. Because of the top-secret nature of the report being written, Primakov locked Blagovolin in a room with two other co-authors and stood guard outside. They made only one copy. Then Primakov and Blagovolin brought it to Yakovlev—not in his office, but in his car—for him to deliver personally to Gorbachev.

I was surprised by Blagovolin's dramatic account of this event and asked him skeptically whether there had been any reason for anxiety. He replied,

> Absolutely! For Gorbachev, and for us, it was the first time when we tried to formulate a new concept of relations with the Western world. In it we *declared openly that we faced no military threat from the West!* It was absolutely explosive. . . . Later, in 1987, we prepared a first blueprint of military reform. Of course it was not for the newspapers, but by then we were not forced to do it in a locked room.[57]

* * *

Nodari Simonia was Deputy Director of IMEMO when I interviewed him there in June 1992. A tall Georgian man of boundless energy, he sprinkled his English sentences with colloquialisms. He had formerly worked for the Central Committee's Department of International Affairs, where he had built considerable social capital—trusted friends—who would help later when he got into arguments with powerful Party ideologists. As Simonia explained with a laugh, "My character is that I am the enemy of myself."

His troubles began when he published his doctoral dissertation in 1975, a huge book, half of which was a critical review of Marxism-Leninism, of Russian history, and of the history of the Party. He criticized socialist political economy, the whole idea of socialism, and concluded that socialism had never been built in the USSR. It had failed when the NEP failed. This perspective did not win any applause.

> The reviews called me an opportunist, an anti-Marxist and that kind of stuff. It was a struggle in '75, '76, '77. I was sitting with my wife in the kitchen think-

ing about what I would do when I got fired, but this never happened because my liberal and progressive [co-workers], Zagladin and Brutents defended me, though not always openly. I was just thrown off the staff of one scientific magazine. They still tried to publish my articles, but I was not listed on the masthead.

But Simonia was irrepressible and by 1986 he was in trouble for opposing the Soviet war in Afghanistan. The next year, in May 1987, he published articles in foreign newspapers calling for troop withdrawal. Behind closed doors at his institute he criticized other scholars for failing to speak up frankly about what they actually thought.

> I am not a specialist on Afghanistan, but it was evident what was happening there. And they *are* specialists but were not sending papers to the government, not proposing anything. Some of them even went as advisers to Afghanistan for six or eight months. I asked them: for what? For the coordination of the war or what? Even then, nothing happened to me. This meant that there were doubts about the policy in the highest leadership.

* * *

Lev Deliusin is a stubbornly independent-minded sinologist who has engaged in political battles throughout his career. In 1973 he became head of the Institute of Information on Social Sciences (INION), which tracked Western social science and summarized such publications for the use of scholars and government officials. He accepted the post only on condition that he could hire whomever he wished and work in his own way. He would, in fact, use this freedom with rare valor.

Ludmilla Alexeyeva, one of the leading BARKING DOGS, in her history of the Soviet dissident movement, praised Deliusin's loyalty—a source of social capital to her. This is one of the unusual cases where a TERMITE and a dissident supported and admired each other. For her political activities, Alexeyeva had been dismissed from her job as an editor and was blacklisted for other "intelligent" jobs, but Deliusin helped her.

> His institute found an ingenious way to hire me. First, I was brought in as a typist. After two years of being unemployed, I was glad to take any job. I did my typing at home, didn't show up at the institute, and told no one that I was working again. As soon as my trial period was over, I was promoted to editor and could once again go in to the office when convenient.
>
> At about that time, Deliusin noticed that his personnel department had begun to get involved in hiring decisions and that high-placed officials were starting to offer unsolicited guidance. According to institute lore, Deliusin said simply: "Either I work the way I want to or I don't work." His resignation was accepted.
>
> Before he left his prestigious job, his fine salary, and his chauffeured car, Deliusin transferred me to the Department of Scientific Communism, which was headed by his personal friend Yakov Berger. Despite its hideous name, the department tracked the writings of Herbert Marcuse and Jean-Paul Sartre and

the latest pronouncements of Western Sovietologists. These were the sort of materials I would otherwise have read in *samizdat*.[58]

For twenty years Deliusin was involved in clashes with another institute. Andropov appointed him, as a specialist on China, to head the China Department of the Institute of Oriental Studies (IVAN), one of two institutes dealing with Asian affairs. The other was the Institute of the Far East (IDV) which was less a place for critical research than for ideologues and bureaucrats.

The relations between scholars at two institutes bordered on hatred, for they generated information that served very different purposes—scientific knowledge and ideologically based foreign policy.[59] Some of the "bureaucrats" at IDV were in a position to read others' manuscripts and block the publication of ones that were not "strictly governed by Marxist-Leninist methodology."[60]

Deliusin wrote a number of articles on China that he was unable to publish, even during the first years of Gorbachev's leadership. Sometimes he published in an Estonian journal because he could not get his work published in Moscow or elsewhere.[61] For example, he and the eminent journalist Alexander Bovin tried to publish an article in *Izvestia* describing the successful Chinese agricultural reforms, but the Central Committee refused permission. By 1986 or 1987 they could publish it but, even so, such information did not necessarily reach Gorbachev. Deliusin told me,

> The people who were against *perestroika* wanted to diminish the success of China's reforms. We, however, wanted to say much more about the positive aspects of China's reforms in agriculture. . . . But nevertheless, Mr. Gorbachev and some other decision-makers believed their sources of information, not [ours].
> It was not just a problem of agricultural reforms, but a problem of the relations between the Soviet Union and China. Those who opposed *perestroika* also opposed normalization of relations with China and criticized the reforms in China, arguing that it might restore capitalism to China. . . . At that time, the bureaucrats wanted to convince our leadership that China was not going in the socialist way; they were revisionists.[62]

Theoretical and methodological conflicts are common among social scientists in all societies. Such a fight as this between sinologists might seem familiar to scholars in Europe or America. Yet in this case it was not just a matter of scholars debating against other scholars, but rather of scholars fighting against Party bureaucrats—and for a long time the bureaucrats won. Gorbachev did not receive an accurate assessment of the remarkable reforms going on in Chinese agriculture. The ideologists' abhorrence of capitalism won the day.

* * *

The interviews and anecdotes that I have recounted show that many intellectuals had been unable to offer constructive, much-needed criticism. Admittedly, however, these stories prove little, since the information was given to me well *after* the reforms had begun, when it was no longer dangerous to speak out against the old system. Also, these stories are not sample surveys of opinion, so I wanted some way of determining how widespread such criticism must have been within the intelligentsia. Victor Sheinis directed my attention to a secret study of the opinions of leading experts in which he had been involved much earlier. He had helped formulate the questions.

This research was carried out in the late 1970s by the Leningrad sociologist Andrei Alekseev, who asked a sample of several dozen top specialists whether they expected changes in social and economic life. The survey consisted of open-ended questionnaires, which I had an opportunity to read and reproduce. Virtually all of the respondents expressed anxiety about a looming crisis and confirmed the necessity of social and economic changes. All of them were working in academic institutions (humanities) or in the university, except for a few artists, journalists, or actors. The survey was entirely anonymous, and the researchers did not know who wrote what. Here are three typical excerpts from these lengthy transcripts.

> **Expert 1:** Sooner or later, [the regime] will be forced, because of objective economic or political circumstances, to resign itself to some elements of Western-type democracy (as, for example, to the expression of opposition views in the media or even to a multiparty system). If changes occur, they will be executed, not from below, but mainly by the ruling group.
> **Expert 2:** The most constructive idea is that of convergence: One has to take from socialism ideas of equality, social welfare, free education, elimination of great fortunes. But much has been done in these respects in the West.
> **Expert 3:** The development of contemporary industrial society is impossible without positive changes within the system. This society is gravitating toward the Western, industrial, type of development.

The experts whose opinions I have reported here had been working in top-ranking institutes, where they nevertheless were unable to publish or publicly express their true opinions. This survey shows that even in the 1970s there was substantial hidden support for reform among the most qualified experts, TERMITES, who in fact considered their society to be in a virtual state of crisis.

While such support was a *necessary* condition for radical change, it was not a *sufficient* condition. The desire for reform should have been matched by practical, systematic planning for reform. This was not possible. Therefore, when the opportunity for change presented itself, Soviet social capital was inadequate to the task. To be sure, there were relationships among the intellectuals, scientists, and government decision-makers—but too few of them were *trusting* relationships to support much collaborative work. Soviet human capital—the access to crucial new information—was blocked by the state's official ideologues.

* * *

Soviet society had no shortage of human capital—intelligent, thoughtful men and women who produced useful insights. Collectively, the experts were probably as capable as their counterparts in any other country on earth. Nevertheless, the intelligentsia, however eager for change they had been privately, were unable to prepare for it adequately.

The Soviet Union reforms might have succeeded, had the scholars whom I have named been able to publicize their research. Sergei Kapitza knew how scientific work should be organized. Had his critique been made public in time, the Chernobyl disaster might have been averted. Had Victor Sheinis's analysis of the faulty exploitation of oil resources been heeded, the Russian economy today would be in better condition. Had Blagovolin been given access to the true Soviet military data instead of having to use the CIA estimates, his research might been more precise; had his research findings about Soviet offensive weaponry become public knowledge earlier, the vital military reforms that he proposed might have been adopted then. Had Simonia's suggestions been publicized when he urged the Soviets to leave Afghanistan, many lives might have been saved and the Cold War might have ended sooner. Had Lev Deliusin's recommendations been heeded that the Soviet reformers consider emulating the Chinese reforms, *perestroika* might even have worked and the Soviet economy might have started growing at the rate of 10 percent per year, as the Chinese economy often does nowadays.

When *perestroika* began, these honest researchers were expected to produce critiques and plans instantaneously. But too much time had been lost. For haste and confusion there is a high price. For years to come Russian society will pay that price.

I have told here the stories of TERMITES—habitually cautious people. Nevertheless, some of them were courageous to the point of recklessness. Simonia, for example, published in foreign newspapers his reasons for opposing the Soviet war in Afghanistan. Deliusin resigned from a high managerial post rather than acquiesce when Party ideologists began interfering with his professional work and his social capital. My typology—TERMITE versus BARKING DOG—is perhaps too reductive, not calling attention to the TERMITES of this chapter who incurred penalties for opposing official ideology. A degree of security was available only to SHEEP—the category that interests us least of all.

Although my two terms for progressives do not always capture the most important qualities, I will continue to use them anyway, for one main reason: As *perestroika* proceeded, polarization would intensify between TERMITES and BARKING DOGS. They would despise each other more and more instead of finding common ground and working together toward the political objectives that, on the whole, they really did share. We must distinguish sharply between them.

* * *

Finally, I must qualify my comments about ideology hindering responsible decision-making and creativity. It does—and yet it's not the *ideas* themselves that constrict people so seriously. Many of the TERMITES and perhaps even more of the SHEEP had lost any faith in Marxism-Leninism long before the system fell apart. It did not reflect their thinking. They were simply afraid to express any objection to those ideas because they feared what others would say or do. As long as they believed that others truly upheld the official ideology, they felt trapped into following along. As Tolstoy wrote, there are "no conditions of life to which a man cannot get accustomed, especially if he sees them accepted by *everyone* around him."

Apparent unanimity was the problem.

Notes

1. Jonathan Grant, "The Socialist Construction of Philately in the Early Soviet Era," *Comparative Studies in Society and History* 37, no. 3 (1995), 483–94.

2. Helju Aulik Bennett, "Institutions and Political Terminology for a Well-Tethered Society: Foundations of Continuity in Russian Political Tradition," paper, American Association for the Advancement of Slavic Studies, November 20, 2008.

3. Frederick J. Teggart, *The Processes of History* (New Haven: Yale University Press, 1918), 148–64.

4. Richard Florida, *Cities and the Creative Class* (New York: Routledge, 2005).

5. Helena Sheehan, "Who was Lysenko? What was Lysenkoism?," http://webpages.dcu.ie/~sheehanh/lysenko.htm (accessed April 26, 2010).

6. Andrei Sakharov, *Memoirs*, trans. Richard Lourie (New York: Vintage, 1992), 183.

7. Karl Marx and Friedrich Engels, *Collected Works,* trans. Emile Burns and Clemens Dutt, ed. Tatyana Chikileva, vol. 1 (New York: International Publishers, 1975), 164.

8. Karl Marx and Friedrich Engels, *Collected Works* trans. Emile Burns and Clemens Dutt, ed. Tatyana Chikileva, vol. 20 (New York: International Publishers, 1975), 78.

9. Karl Marx, *The German Ideology* ed. and trans. C. J. Arthur (New York: International Publishers. 1970).

10. Yuri Akhapkin, comp., *First Decrees of Soviet Power* (London: Lawrence and Wishart, 1970), 29–30. See also Robin Blick, *The Seeds of Evil: Lenin and the Origins of Bolshevik Elitism* (London: Ferrington, 1993), 55.

11. Michael Kort, *The Soviet Colossus: History and Aftermath* (Armonk, NY: M.E. Sharpe, 2001), 146.

12. Kort, 148.

13. Kort, 148.

14. Ludmilla Alexeyeva and Paul Goldberg, *The Thaw Generation: Coming of Age in the Post-Stalin Era* (Boston: Little, Brown, 1990), 83–84. Literally, the word *kompaniya* simply refers to any group of people, but it seemed to mean more than that to Alexeyeva and her friends.

15. Marc Morje Howard, "Postcommunist Civil Society in Comparative Perspective," *Demokratizatsiya* 10, no. 3 (Summer 2002): 285.

16. Medvedev and his brother Zhores published several volumes of commentaries over a period of years under the title "Political Diary" (*Politichesky dnevnik*).

17. Yevtushenko's poem *Babi Yar* was published in 1961 in *Literturnaya Gazeta.*

18. Vladimir Dudintsev, *Not by Bread Alone*, trans. Edith Bone (London: Hutchinson, 1957).

19. At least this is the contention of Boris Kagarlitsky, *The Thinking Reed: Intellectuals and the Soviet State from 1917 to the Present*, trans. Brian Pearce (London: Verso, 1988), 177.

20. For an account of their university years, see Raisa Gorbachev, *I Hope: Reminiscences and Reflections*, trans. David Floyd (New York: HarperCollins 1991), chapter 3.

21. Gail Sheehy, *The Man Who Changed the World: The Lives of Mikhail S. Gorbachev* (New York: HarperCollins, 1990), 65. Sheehy's chapter is based on interviews with his former classmates.

22. Sheehy, 75.

23. Sheehy, 76.

24. Among the other friends of the Gorbachevs during their university years were Rudolf Kolshanov, Natasha Rimashevskaya, and Dimitri Golovanov. Rudolf Kolchanov would become editor of *Trud*, a newspaper for trade unions with the largest circulation of any Soviet paper. Rimashevskaya, a member of Gorbachev's four-person study group, would become director of a Moscow institute that studies socioeconomic conditions. Golovanov would become for a time the producer of the most important television program in the Soviet Union, the nightly *Vremya*, and be consulted regularly by Gorbachev as an opinion-maker. Raisa's memoirs also list some of the famous professors with whom they studied at Moscow State University: Valentin Ferdinandovich Asmus, a philosopher whose publications included work on Kant and theory of history; Abramovich Leontiev, who wrote a textbook on Marxian economics; A. R. Luria, a developmental psychologist who studied how children learn speech; and I. S. Narskii, a philosopher whose publications include work on dialectical materialism, theory of logic, positivism, and Marxism and existentialism. She does not mention that she also studied with Alexander Zinoviev, a philosopher who later emigrated to the West and wrote a satirical book called *Homo Sovieticus*, trans. Charles Janson (London: Gollancz, 1985). This scathing description of the "flexible" character traits required for a careerist's success in the Soviet establishment, was among the books most severely repressed by the KGB. He also wrote an unflattering book called *Gorbachevism*, trans. Charles Janson (London: Claridge Press, 1989).

25. Mamardashvili's works address problems of rationalism, consciousness, language, and symbolism.

26. Marina Pavlovna Pavlova-Silvanskaya, in discussion with the author, March 1993, Moscow.

27. "Interview with the First and Last President of the USSR," *Komsomolskaya Pravda*, December 25, 1991.

28. Raisa Gorbachev, *I Hope*, 49.

29. Boris Oreshene, in discussion with the author, July 1992, Moscow.

30. Nikita Sergeevich Khrushchev, *Khrushchev Remembers*, with an introduction, commentary, and notes by Edward Crankshaw, trans. and ed. Strobe Talbott (Boston: Little Brown, 1970).

31. Nikolai Popov, *The People of Russia at the Crossroads* (Syracuse, NY: Syracuse University Press, 1994), chapter 5.

32. David Wedgwood Benn, *Persuasion and Soviet Politics* (New York: Blackwell, 1989), 21–22, 37.

33. Benn, 124.

34. Popov, chapter 2.

35. Popov, Table 5.6.

36. Yury Levada, "The Disappearing Model? Homo Sovieticus: The Preliminary Results," *Znamya* no. 6 (1992): 203–4.

37. Levada, 205.

38. Alex Inkeles and Raymond Bauer, *The Soviet Citizen* (Cambridge, MA: Harvard University Press, 1959), 236.

39. James R. Millar, "History, Method, and the Problem of Bias," in *Politics, Work, and Daily Life in the USSR*, ed. James R. Millar. (Cambridge: Cambridge University Press, 1987), 16–17.

40. Brian D. Silver, "Political Beliefs of the Soviet Citizen," in *Politics, Work, and Daily Life,* 132–33.

41. Levada, 203.

42. Elizabeth Teague, *Solidarity and the Soviet Worker: The Impact of the Polish Events of 1980 on Soviet Internal Politics* (London: Croom Helm, 1988), 138. Ludmilla Alexeyeva also reports on two other surveys conducted during that period that found only a little over 20 percent of the Soviet respondents approved of Solidarity. See Alexeyeva, 455–56.

43. Teague, 143.

44. Teague, 150.

45. Popov, chapter 1.

46. Fyodor Burlatsky, "Democratization is a Long March," in *Voices of Glasnost: Interviews with Gorbachev's Reformers,* ed. Stephen Cohen and Katrina vanden Heuvel (New York: Norton, 1989), 179–80.

47. Charles H. Fairbanks, "The Nature of the Beast," in *The National Interest* no. 31 (Spring 1993): 46–49. Actually, Fairbanks seems to think more highly of these old Bolshevik ideologues than of the Brezhnev-era bumpkins. Given the history of Bolshevik totalitarianism, we can hardly imagine that, on the whole, they were morally superior to Brezhnev's stupid crooks.

48. Fairbanks, 48–49.

49. Jerry Hough, "Debates About the Postwar World," in *The Impact of World War II on the Soviet Union,* ed. Susan J. Linz (Totowa, NJ: Rowman and Allenheld, 1985).

50. Amy Knight, *Beria: Stalin's First Lieutenant* (Princeton: Princeton University Press, 1993), 150–51.

51. Even if they were employed by him, their open-mindedness does not necessarily reflect favorably on Zhdanov, who may not have known his subordinates' views.

52. This alleged intellectual genealogy is not acknowledged by everyone. For example, when I asked Fyodor Burlatsky about Kuusinen's connection to Zhdanov, he replied, "Zhdanov was a very dogmatic and pro-Stalinist man. [There was a] Leningrad group, yes, but I don't think that Kuusinen was very close to them."

53. S. P. Kapitza, "Lessons of Chernobyl: Psychological and Social Aspects," photocopy of a paper presented in Seoul, August 1992.

54. Kapitza, "Lessons of Chernobyl."

55. Victor Sheinis, in discussion with the author, 1993, Moscow.

56. Sheinis discussion.

57. Sergei Blagovolin, in discussion with the author, 1993, Moscow.

58. Ludmilla Alexeyeva and Paul Goldberg, *The Thaw Generation,* 236.

59. For an analysis of the differences between these two groups, see Gilbert Rozman, *A Mirror For Socialism: Soviet Criticisms of China* (Princeton: Princeton University Press, 1985).

60. Rozman, 52.

61. Lev Deliusin and Gilbert Rozman, in discussions with the author, 1992.

62. Deliusin discussion.

Chapter 3: Two Scientists, Two Paths

Each Soviet intellectual or scientist had to find his own response to the limitations imposed by the Party's ideologists, the "thought police" who defined the range of conclusions that might be drawn from research. Here I will contrast the contradictory paths taken by two outstanding, principled scientists. One became a TERMITE, the other a BARKING DOG. Both of them were nevertheless vulnerable to persecution. Both of them were deprived of an opportunity to build the kind of social capital that might have supported them successfully in their struggle against ideological constraints.

In the previous chapter you met Sergei Kapitza, the scientist whose regular TV show reaches all across Russia, teaching viewers about current scientific research. Now meet his father, Peter.

Peter Kapitza

Peter Kapitza (1894–1984) had been on the threshold of a career in physics when the revolution broke out in 1917. Tragically, within a few short years his wife and both children died of Spanish influenza during the famine and epidemic. However, Kapitza received a fellowship to study at Cambridge with the great Ernest Rutherford, and he took the opportunity. There he studied low temperatures in magnetic fields, married again, and stayed for thirteen years. But in 1935, he was asked to come home; his Soviet exit visa was revoked and for the next thirty-two years he was not allowed to travel to the West.[1]

Kapitza became director of a new institute in Moscow just before the Great Terror, and soon his students and colleagues began to be arrested. He was, despite everything, a true socialist and a loyal Soviet citizen. In a way that today seems almost touchingly guileless, he would write a letter of protest to a powerful figure in government whenever one of his acquaintances suffered an injustice. He never spoke out against the regime in a public way, but kept his letters entirely confidential. Inexplicably, he got away with this.

Alexander Rubinin, who was Kapitza's assistant for almost thirty years, was still working in Kapitza's laboratory (by then headed by Peter's son Sergei) when I interviewed him in 1992. In our interview, Rubinin recalled that Peter Kapitza "wrote to Stalin, Molotov, Malenkov, and so on, trying to influence them. These were not only requests, but concerned science and the universities. They were sometimes ten to fifteen pages long, like real articles. He wrote three or four versions before sending one. His wife usually typed the letter and took it personally to the Central Committee. Copies are in the archive. Some of them deal with the destinies of arrested scientists whom he was trying to rescue."

He wrote to Stalin in 1937 when the physicist Vladimir Fok was arrested; a week later, Fok was actually freed. He also tried to protect Lev Landau, a Nobel Prize winner, like Kapitza himself, who headed a department of theoretical physics. He wrote a letter on the day Landau was arrested—April 28, 1938—but Stalin did not react and Landau spent a whole year in prison, practically dying. After a year Kapitza wrote to Molotov and in a few days Landau was liberated.

Kapitza was always trying in his letters to explain fundamental science, which he thought was underestimated. He wrote forty-five letters to Stalin, seventy-one to Molotov, sixty-three to Malenkov, twenty-six to Khrushchev. He wrote only one or two letters to Brezhnev because he understood immediately that it would be useless. He had the naïve idea that he could re-educate others. The letters were sincere, without any hypocrisy, which is probably why the officials liked them. Most other people's letters contained mainly grievances or praise. Rubinin said,

> In 1980 he wrote Andropov to protect Sakharov. I typed it (he did not even trust the typist) and took it to the KGB. Kapitza wanted to help him and [Yuri] Orlov, who was in jail. Sakharov didn't know about the letter and the dissidents wanted Kapitza to appear publicly. Kapitza couldn't do it. He had a different approach. If he communicated with power, it must be tête-à-tête. He considered that in our country something could be changed only with the help of power. He turned out to be right. Gorbachev understood that something must be changed and he changed it. . . .
>
> Kapitza had an inner independence. He was a member of the committee to develop a nuclear bomb, and the chairman of that committee was Beria. Kapitza could not work with him. He wrote two letters to Stalin criticizing him. For that he was fired, and for years he did not leave his dacha, for he was permanently in danger of being arrested or killed. A car could have run over him, as happened to Mikhoels, the actor.
>
> General Khrulev, who had been present at a conversation between Beria and Stalin, said that Beria had wanted to arrest him, but Stalin said it was impossible because Kapitza was too famous in the West. Stalin said, "I'll fire him, but you may not touch him." Probably Stalin liked Kapitza.
>
> But he did not have good relations with Khrushchev and was allowed to travel only to the socialist countries. Khrushchev didn't like the fact that he opposed Lysenko. But he appreciated Khrushchev highly, especially his report on agriculture in 1954. Kapitza was convinced that socialism was more progressive and reasonable than capitalism, and he believed that in our country, power might change by itself if the officials understood that changes were needed.
>
> He respected Sakharov highly, but he always acted in the way that he considered right. Kapitza never condemned him for attending trials, protecting dissidents, and writing letters, but he could not behave the same way. He was also acquainted with Solzhenitsyn and respected him highly. Kapitza was always aware of the dissidents' activities. He worried about Orlov and Brodsky[2]. . . .

Some painters were not allowed to exhibit their art in galleries, but Kapitza hung their paintings in our institution where everyone could come and see them. The officials didn't like it but they couldn't do anything.

He didn't always succeed with everything. In 1976 there was an accident in an American nuclear power station. A worker was testing something with a candle and set the station on fire. Nobody could find the phone number of the fire team and when they came, they didn't know how to extinguish the fire. When Kapitza read about it, he realized that the same situation could happen in our nuclear stations. He wrote a report and wanted to publish it in *Science and Life*, which has a print run of three million copies. But they refused, certainly on the directive of the Central Committee. "No need to make people nervous." Who knows? If the article had been published or if the party officials had paid attention to the problem, the Chernobyl disaster might not have happened.[3]

Despite his socialist convictions, Kapitza managed to run his own institution in a sensible, but un-socialist manner. He paid people what they were worth. For example, he was displeased with the unkempt appearance of the grounds, which three maintenance men were employed to keep clean. Kapitza dismissed two of them and paid all three wages to the remaining man—who actually had to work to earn it. Such a rational practice was not permitted anywhere else.[4]

After 1946, when Peter Kapitza was fired and went to live in the countryside, he improvised homemade apparatuses and continued experimenting as best he could. He remained in solitary seclusion for almost ten years of his life.[5] After Beria's death, he resumed his position as director of his institute, but could travel only to socialist countries. In the year after Khrushchev's forced resignation, he traveled to the West for the first time. Thereafter, he was not isolated again; he participated actively in the Pugwash Conferences on Science and World Affairs, the organization of scientists formed in response to Bertrand Russell and Albert Einstein's 1955 manifesto urging nuclear abolition.

* * *

Kapitza's later work in the area of nuclear weaponry was contradictory. On one hand, during his years in seclusion, he began to consider how to defeat nuclear weapons, and conceived the idea of using high-intensity beams of microwaves to intercept incoming missiles. This was one of the first anti-ballistic missile (ABM) proposals, and a precursor to the much later "Star Wars" technology.

As early as 1950, he wrote about the idea to Malenkov, who suggested that he write to Stalin. Stalin was too sick to carry the idea forward, but Khrushchev did so in 1954, putting Kapitza back in charge of his old institute and urging him to develop his microwave defense system speedily.[6] The proposal was impractical and hundreds of millions of rubles were spent on it without result. Only later, with the development of lasers, could the beam idea become at all realistic.[7]

While he was working on a precursor to ABM, Kapitza was also arguing against it. He may have been the first person to attain the insight that opponents of Reagan's Strategic Defense Initiative would make many years later: that a defense system can actually heighten the danger of war. If a would-be aggressor has an excellent defensive weapon in addition to offensive ones, he will feel tempted to start the fight before the other side does so. Until then, no one had noted that a defensive weapon might increase the risk of war.[8]

There is no evidence that Kapitza experienced cognitive dissonance over the fact that he was working (however ineffectively) on the very type of weapon system that he was arguing against. Perhaps he reconciled the inconsistency by assuming that his own country would never be the aggressor.

But of course his country *was* an aggressor sometimes with conventional weapons—a fact that also seems not to have troubled him much. Roald Sagdeev, one of the Soviet weapons scientists who would play an important role later in cooling down the nuclear arms race, recounts in his memoirs a pleasant day that he spent in Paris with Kapitza just after the Soviets had invaded Czechoslovakia. Kapitza said, "I'm not going to apologize before our Western colleagues at the Pugwash conference. Both sides, from time to time, do shameful things."

Sagdeev was disappointed in his friend and concluded that "the most important message for me was that Kapitza was indeed too philosophical, and apparently too unwilling, to identify himself with the historic challenge to our national self-consciousness. At that moment, for the first time in Soviet history, a new breed of people, younger than Kapitza, represented the consciousness of the nation. These people were emerging as keepers of the flame of the free-spirited old Russian intelligentsia. It was the time for Sakharov and his friends."[9]

Andrei Sakharov
That accolade, "keeper of the flame," was well-earned. Andrei Sakharov (1921–1989), the man who had played such a big part in developing Soviet nuclear weaponry, would gradually become wholly dedicated to controlling the threat that it posed. Speaking truthfully about his principles, whatever it cost him, and defending the rights of others, by the time he died in 1989, he would be lionized as the "conscience of the nation." Yet, as Peter Kapitza described him in a secret letter appealing to Andropov for his freedom, Sakharov had a "difficult character," and, one might add, an even more difficult wife, Yelena Bonner. Together, the two of them, with their fierce principles, inspired and exasperated their countrymen, often at the same time.

* * *

As a young man during World War II Andrei Sakharov had to become a scientist-weaponeer in a hurry. In his memoirs he mentions his inventive research in a munitions factory from those early years. By 1950, he was involved in top-secret work on thermonuclear weapons and related research at the "Installation"—a secret city for people working on atomic and thermonuclear weapons. He worked there until his clearance was revoked in 1968.[10] In 1955 he became the "father of the hydrogen bomb" when his "Third Idea" became the working model for the first such Soviet bomb that was successfully tested. (The first American hydrogen device had been tested in 1952.)

Immediately, numerous thermonuclear devices began to be tested (all in the atmosphere) and Sakharov worried about the biological effects. As early as 1957, he published an estimate as to how many cancers would ultimately result from the genetic damage being caused by nuclear tests.[11] Nearly fifty megatons of nuclear explosive power had been released by those weapons, which he projected would create 500,000 casualties. Another article, pointing to the moral implications, was one factor that led to the Soviet unilateral moratorium on testing in 1958, though he believed his writings were not noticed in the West.[12]

Already Sakharov had begun interceding for victims of repression—initially on behalf of a physician who had been imprisoned for gossiping about Khrushchev's rumored romance with the first female minister of culture. However, his major preoccupation was his growing conviction that testing in the atmosphere was a crime against humanity. When a colleague insisted on trying out a device that was redundant for research purposes, he shouted, "Zhenya, what are you doing? This is tantamount to murder!"[13] He called Khrushchev to try to prevent the test and when he failed, he put his head down on his desk and wept.

Sakharov did not quit his weapons research (very few scientists in either bloc of the Cold War went *that* far) but he decided to devote himself to ending biologically harmful tests. "That was the main reason I didn't carry out my threat to quit the Installation. Later, after the Moscow Limited Test Ban Treaty was signed, I found other grounds for postponing my resignation."[14]

That 1963 treaty was one of the few nuclear decisions in which Sakharov played a significant role. It did nothing to slow down the nuclear arms race, but it did put testing underground. There had been objections to it, however: notably the difficulty of monitoring underground tests from a distance, especially if a country deliberately deceives the other side by exploding its tests in a large underground chamber. Still, Sakharov kept pushing the idea until, finally, a colleague phoned to tell him, "there's a great deal of interest at the top in your proposal, and probably some steps will shortly be taken on our side." Indeed, the USSR soon proposed to ban testing in the atmosphere, underwater, and in outer space. Sakharov was glad he had contributed to the Moscow Treaty.[15]

Scientifically, the Installation was an enthralling place in the sixties, and Sakharov stayed on there, though his attention was focused more and more on ethical issues. Advances in missile technology prompted all the scientists of the period to consider the possibility of a ban on anti-ballistic missile systems (ABMs).[16] He wrote,

> 1. An effective ABM defense is not possible if the potential adversary can mobilize comparable technical and economic resources for military purposes. A way can always be found to neutralize an ABM defense system—and at considerably less expense than the cost of deploying it.
> 2. Over and above the burdensome cost, deployment of an ABM system is dangerous since it can upset the strategic balance. If both sides were to possess powerful ABM defenses, the main result would be to raise the threshold of strategic stability, or in somewhat simplified terms, increase the minimum number of nuclear weapons needed for mutual assured destruction.[17]

Here Sakharov distinguishes between two arguments—and rightly so, since they do not necessarily go together. Many opponents of ABM systems, and of nuclear weapons, accept the first argument while rejecting the second—the appeal to strategic balance and stability based on mutual assured destruction.

Although he mentions only two arguments here, there are at least two other stronger ones than the one based on balance: (a) the high cost and, ultimately, the ineffectiveness of ABM systems relative to the simple decoys and chaff that could defeat them;[18] and especially (b) the temptation to strike preemptively when one has a combination of both superior offensive and defensive capability.

Yet Sakharov would hold onto the belief that strategic balance was essential. It was not a radical idea; quite the contrary. Indeed, the belief in balance was a conservative theory shared by hawks and many ardent doves around the world—people who wanted to end the nuclear arms race by negotiations between two sides, always keeping parity while the weaponry was being reduced.

The emphasis on balance always defeated disarmament. When Gorbachev would later make his remarkable advances in ending the arms race, these would largely come from ridding himself of the policy of strategic balance.

Throughout the sixties, Sakharov grew ever more critical. In 1966 he signed a letter opposing the posthumous rehabilitation of Stalin and took part in a street demonstration. He lost his post as department head and took a pay cut. By 1968, he published a book proposing liberalization and an end to the Cold War, *Reflections on Progress, Peaceful Coexistence, and Intellectual Freedom*.[19] It was, of course, highly controversial, and the following year, he was sacked from the Installation and given a smaller post at an institution where he had done his graduate work. In that same year, his first wife, Klava, died of cancer.

In the course of his increasing human rights activism, he met Yelena Bonner, a physician who became his second wife and fierce partner in the escalating confrontations with government and numerous personal acquaintances.

In 1973 Sakharov's opponents multiplied after the broadcast in Sweden of his radio interview about global problems in general and the wretched conditions in his own country. Although the tone was overwhelmingly negative, he held out a faint chance of improvement. "Within the Soviet Union certainly some kind of process is going on, but so far it is so imperceptible and hidden that it's [almost impossible] to anticipate any positive, general changes. . . . I am skeptical about socialism in general."

His interviewer asked why he continued protesting, in view of his pessimism about the possibility of improving the system. Sakharov replied,

> Well, there is a need to create ideals even when you can't see any way to achieve them, because if there are no ideals then there can be no hope and then one would be left completely in the dark, in a hopeless blind alley.
> Moreover, we can't know whether there is some kind of possibility of cooperation between our country and the outside world. If no signals about our unhappy situation are sent out, then there would be no way to make use of any possibility which might exist. We wouldn't know what needs changing or how to change it.
> Then there is another consideration—that the history of our country should serve as a warning. It should deter the West and the developing countries from committing mistakes on the scale we have during our historical development.

Therefore, if a man speaks out, it does not mean that he hopes necessarily to achieve something. He may hope for nothing but nonetheless speak because he cannot remain silent. We really have no hope, and unfortunately, experience shows we are right. Our actions don't lead to positive results.[20]

After this interview was publicized, a campaign was organized to show that the intelligentsia disagreed with Sakharov. Scientists had to sign letters of condemnation. On the other side, however, support increased. Aleksandr Solzhenitsyn proposed Sakharov for a Nobel Peace Prize and two years later, in 1975, it was awarded, though Sakharov could not go to Oslo to receive it.

In 1980, Sakharov was arrested and sent to Gorky, where he and Bonner were kept under house arrest. His scientific manuscripts were not touched, but the KGB stole his diaries and other private papers. Their health worsened and after Bonner had a heart attack in 1984 Sakharov frightened his supporters by a hunger strike, trying to force the authorities to give her proper treatment.

Writing in 1986, Sakharov responded brusquely to some of Solzhenitsyn's writings, especially to an effusive but inaccurate portrayal of himself in *The Oak and the Calf*.[21] Among other points, Solzhenitsyn had said that it had become only too evident to Sakharov that work on nuclear weapons served aggressive purposes. Surprisingly, Sakharov retorted, "I reject such a categorical judgment on my weapons work; as I never tire of repeating, life is a complicated thing."[22] This was perhaps the most elaborate justification that Sakharov offered in his memoirs for his weapons research: "Life is a complicated thing."

In December 1986, a phone was installed unexpectedly in the Sakharov apartment in Gorky. The next day, Mikhail Gorbachev rang up to tell Sakharov he was free. Sakharov was curt, immediately demanding the release of all other prisoners of conscience. Then he impolitely ended the conversation. In recounting it he seemed proud of his tone. If Gorbachev expected to enlist the Sakharovs' support for *his* reforms, he was wrong. That would never be their role.

* * *

Upon returning to Moscow, Sakharov was everywhere, participating in every possible meeting, always playing moral critic in the fast-paced development of *perestroika*. He was elected to the new Congress of People's Deputies and played the same role there in a group of parliamentarians, the Inter-regional Group of People's Deputies, who thought that changes were coming too slowly.

He assigned top priority to the abolition of Article 6 of the Soviet constitution—the clause that specified that the Communist Party should play the leading role in the political life of the nation. Gorbachev either was, or pretended to be, opposed to eliminating that stipulation at that time. (I personally believe the latter, for tactical reasons.) To eliminate Article 6 would have created a multi-party system, as in pluralistic, democratic societies, and the effort would probably have provoked the DINOSAURS to undertake desperate maneuvers to save their jobs. In fact they later did so on the eve of adoption of the Novo-Ogarevo Treaty, which made no provision for the Party bureaucracy.

On the last day of his life Sakharov addressed the independent deputies, and was preparing for an even more dramatic battle the next day. He wanted to form an opposition party and challenge Gorbachev, whom he defied by refusing to step down after using up his allotted time at the podium. Around the world, TV viewers watched the two titans in a petty exchange. The deputies opposed Sakharov, but Gorbachev nevertheless appeared to lack magnanimity.

After his death, even more than during his last years back in Moscow, Sakharov became an icon of integrity and true reform. His funeral was a day of mourning for the entire society, and the "radical democrats" in particular took up his banner and extolled him as a martyr. By contrast, Gorbachev and the other reformists in power seemed reactionary.

In death Sakharov was able to mobilize far more opposition to Gorbachev and the TERMITES than while he was alive. Soon it was impossible for the government to resist his followers' demands that Article 6 be revoked. The deceased Sakharov's BARKING DOG faction was winning over the populace—not only the ordinary citizens but even many of Gorbachev's own staff of TERMITES. Almost every day a prominent political figure would announce his resignation from the Communist Party. There were, of course, still many DINOSAURS, both in government and in the wider society, but the BARKING DOGS had claimed the moral high ground, and the others appeared cowardly by comparison.

Soon Yelena Bonner, along with almost all other BARKING DOGS, was expressing admiration of Boris Yeltsin. By then, of course, it was questionable whether anyone could properly be called a dissident, since all penalties for criticizing the government had been abolished, and possibly a majority of Soviet citizens were demanding that the reforms be speeded up and that hard-liners be ejected from all important roles and forced to fend for themselves. These were the radical positions that had been previously maintained only by BARKING DOGS. Yeltsin had no stronger supporter than Sakharov's widow, whose moral authority swayed many other citizens to identify with the causes she promoted. She joined his defenders against the coup at the White House in 1991.

Thus Andrei Sakharov posthumously won his battle against Gorbachev. Nevertheless, one could maintain with some justification (as some astute Pugwashites believed) that[23] the BARKING DOGS' victory was a "gift to the rightist forces," since it undermined Gorbachev's tactical defenses against the still-powerful DINOSAURS. At any rate, Bonner herself would reject Yeltsin after he came to power and waged war against the Chechens.

Sakharov never knew who his true allies were. He spurned the support of his scientific colleagues and attacked many of the people who tried to help his cause. Finally his zeal reversed much of the work of Gorbachev, whose own objective—democratization—was evidently similar to his own. How, one may ask, did a brilliant and morally committed man such as Sakharov come to carry on such a counterproductive vendetta? One factor in the explanation must be the isolation that he experienced as an outsider in the Soviet establishment.

* * *

Neither Kapitza nor Sakharov had much opportunity to travel abroad or to meet foreign scientists during their most productive years. Kapitza attended one Pugwash meeting during the group's first decade. Sakharov was unable to attend Pugwash until his return from exile in Gorky.[24] Bonner had long grumbled about this on his behalf, specifically mentioning his exclusion from Pugwash. How much difference did this make in his way of functioning? I can only speculate.

International meetings have several different useful outcomes, the most conspicuous one being the opportunity to become informed about the opinions of foreigners. Only slightly less important, however, is a second outcome that is rarely noted: the opportunity to see one's peers and colleagues interact with foreigners—how they present their views and how the foreigners perceive them.

This way of understanding one's own countrymen and colleagues can add an important extra dimension to existing relationships. My conjecture cannot be based on much evidence, since I never met Sakharov, but his writings suggest that his relationships with some of his colleagues could have benefited greatly from experiencing them in the presence of respected foreigners. Kapitza may not have been deprived as much by his lengthy isolation (such opportunities had been open to him during his formative period as a scientist) but Sakharov's perceptions were probably limited by isolation. He distrusted many people who were his allies, who were supporting him without his knowledge.

This is suggested by the observations he records in his memoirs. He seems not to have known that there were, in his own backyard, several scientists and even government officials who were quietly working toward objectives that he cherished. For example, although he had known Lev Artsimovitch since 1951 or earlier,[25] and though Artsimovitch had personally complimented him on his controversial book, *Reflections*, Sakharov does not seem to have recognized him as a potential ally in opposing ABM defenses. As we shall see, had he witnessed at first hand Artsimovitch grappling with this issue at Pugwash conferences abroad, he might have seen his colleague in a different light.

The same goes for Mikhail Millionshchikov, another Pugwash participant who came to oppose ABM. The only mention that Sakharov makes of him has a hostile tone, referring to having appealed unsuccessfully to Millionshchikov for help in saving some skyjackers from the death penalty.[26] In another context, Sakharov mentions Vladimir Petrovsky, who makes the public announcement that Bonner and Sakharov are to be allowed to return to Moscow. From his description one might suppose that Petrovsky was a simple apparatchik, carrying out his orders in a craven way. In fact, the generous-spirited Petrovsky should be counted among the most influential people in the Soviet Union when it came to promoting humane values and nuclear disarmament. Sakharov probably did not know that fact, much to his loss, because of his isolation from the variety of other contexts in which people were acting constructively.

Notes

1. The accounts of his return to Russia vary. Sagdeev makes it sound involuntary; Sakharov makes it sound negotiated. See Roald Sagdeev, *The Making of a Soviet Scien-*

tist (New York: Wiley, 1994), 85, and Andrei Sakharov, *Memoirs* (New York: Vintage, 1992), 301.

2. Joseph Brodsky was a poet who was arrested and in 1964 charged with parasitism.

3. Alexander Rubinin, in discussion with my assistant Julia Kalinina, 1992.

4. Mark Azbel, *Refusenik: Trapped in the Soviet Union* (Boston: Houghton Mifflin, 1981), 122.

5. Roald Sagdeev, *The Making of a Soviet Scientist* (New York, Wiley, 1994), 95.

6. Sagdeev, 95–96.

7. Sagdeev, 99, 139.

8. Matthew Evangelista, "Soviet Scientists as Arms Control Advisers: The Case of ABM," Paper prepared for the Fourth World Congress for Soviet and East European Studies, July 1990, 10. Evangelista cites Peter Kapitza, "The Paramount Task," *New Times* no. 39, Sept. 1956, 10–11. See also Evangelista's book, *Unarmed Forces* (Ithaca: Cornell University Press, 1999).

9. Sagdeev, 132.

10. Sakharov, 101.

11. Sakharov, 200.

12. Sakharov, 202–03, 206.

13. Sakharov, 227.

14. Sakharov, 229.

15. Sakharov, 230–31.

16. This was long before Reagan would announce his "Strategic Defense Initiative," or "Star Wars," a more sophisticated technological approach to ABM defense.

17. Sakharov, 268. His argument against ABM was not published at the time, but circulated in samizdat without his knowledge, according to Matthew Evangelista, *Unarmed Forces*, 207–08.

18. Demonstrations of cheap means of outwitting ABMs would later be proposed by Richard Garwin of IBM and would be developed further by the Committee of Soviet Scientists, which would persuade Gorbachev not to respond in kind to the Strategic Defense Initiative. Frank von Hippel, "Nongovernmental Arms Control Research: The New Soviet Connection," in *Citizen Scientist*, ed. Frank von Hippel (New York: Simon and Schuster, 1991), 89.

19. Andrei Sakharov, *Reflections on Progress, Peaceful Coexistence, and Intellectual Freedom* (New York: Norton, 1968).

20. Sakharov, *Reflections*, 626–72, appendix A.

21. Aleksandr Solzhenitsyn, *The Oak and the Calf* (New York: Harper and Row, 1980), 367–368.

22. Sakharov, *Reflections*, 400.

23. Vitaly Goldansky, in discussion with the author, May 1993, Moscow.

24. But there was correspondence between Sakharov and Pugwashites. At a meeting in Cambridge, Massachusetts, a year or so before his death Sakharov participated in a debate over nuclear energy. Though this was well after the Chernobyl accident, according to Rotblat, "He was in favor of nuclear reactors. But he had this very strange idea of putting it underground. He thought it would be safe [that way]—and that they wouldn't be safe if they were above ground." (Joseph Rotblat, in discusson with the author, July 1994, Pugwash, Nova Scotia.)

25. Sakharov, 142.

26. Sakharov, 324.

Chapter 4: Foreign Communists

Diversity cracks open closed minds and lets the light in. Diversity is the source of inventive new notions. Yet diversity comes in many varieties. Among Communists, even the opinions of foreign comrades differed enough to challenge a stagnant ideology. And indeed, initially it was foreign Communists who, more than any other outsiders, and more than native intellectuals, cracked open settled Soviet minds. Thank God for foreigners.

In this chapter we will explore some early foreign contacts that took place from the late 1950s until about 1990, right within high echelons of the Communist Party. It was here that a quasi-civil society emerged, and here that the first groups of TERMITES began to discuss possible reforms.

I have a special motive for devoting extra attention to these early reformists. In Russia, to this day, one encounters many people who believe that Gorbachev and his closest advisers never intended to abandon Communism, but only to "tweak" it in minor ways to make it more acceptable. This belief is mistaken.

To be sure, throughout his term as leader of the country, Gorbachev did not try to abolish the party, but his goal was to transform the "stagnant" system he inherited (which he continued to call "totalitarian") into democratic socialism.[1] Most TERMITES around him shared the same intention. I want to show, therefore, that contacts between reformist Soviets and their democratic-minded counterparts abroad were immensely significant at the time, and that *every step of perestroika* was devised to move the Soviet Union toward changes that became increasingly liberal from the time of Gorbachev's conventional youth.

TERMITES spent their careers weakening the totalitarian system from within—eventually with success. One example is Len Karpinsky, the son of a top Stalinist official, who became a CPSU cadre and called himself a "half-dissident." In a 1989 interview he explained such Party members as himself.

> Party cadres who understood the need for change . . . knew they had to wait until their time came, remain in the apparatus, develop their ideas, seek out like-minded people, and be ready when their hour struck. They are the ones who began *perestroika*. . . . They needed patience and maybe cunning to survive with such views. But if you consider that the Communist Party now has 20

million members, I can imagine that a million party members or more were getting ready for *perestroika* in one way or another.[2]

How did this invisible movement emerge within the Party? Initially, *it did so mainly as a result of foreign Communist influences.* I want to trace the movement of ideas through the international networks of Party officials.

The communist movement was organized internationally. Some prominent members of European Communist Parties were treated as weighty comrades in the Soviet Union, even when they criticized Soviet policies. Among these foreign TERMITE Communists, the most important were the Western Europeans known as "Eurocommunists" (mainly in Italy and Spain), and in the East certain Czechs and Slovaks whose reforms were known as the "Prague Spring." After 1968, however, the Czechoslovak innovators could no longer be called "insiders," for they were expelled from the Communist Party and treated as pariahs.

Nevertheless, their economic and political proposals continued to be discussed after they themselves had become outsider dissidents. Thus, when Gorbachev pronounced a policy that his witty press secretary called the "Sinatra doctrine," he was not expressing a new idea. For a whole generation, the Eurocommunists and Eastern European reformers had insisted that each country should be allowed to "do it their way." Indeed, Gorbachev has affirmed that some of his deepest convictions—such as his belief in democracy—came directly from Eurocommunists. We even know who his teachers were.

This chapter will tell three stories. First, I want to discuss the methods by which Soviet officialdom attempted to insulate ordinary citizens from contact with foreigners whose knowledge might have contradicted the narratives they were telling. One such quarantine was in the Institute of Social Sciences in Moscow. Second, I will consider the impact on Soviet policies of various Eastern European reformers, especially in Czechoslovakia, and Eurocommunists in the West. The most important Czech character in this story was Zdeněk Mlynář, Gorbachev's closest longtime friend—and a dissident. The third story in this chapter is about a group of Soviet intellectuals who worked in Prague at the main journal of the world Communist movement, meeting strangers from all countries and discussing their ideas freely. These people returned to Moscow as TERMITES who would unintentionally bring down the whole Communist edifice.

Critical consciousness is a network phenomenon, the product of dialogue. As we shall see, some individuals became "contaminated" by contact with deviant ideas. So apparent was this danger to Party leaders that they prohibited foreign contact whenever possible, and made sure that all who had to be exposed to it were chosen for their doctrinal reliability. International networks had to be sealed off. Even zealous Party members from abroad were kept from fraternizing with the general population.

Still, despite all precautions, foreign contact had its effects among the diplomatic corps.[3] Those officials working in the International Department of the CPSU were especially likely to become TERMITES. Even KGB officers who traveled abroad or met foreigners were not immune to the influence of dialogue.[4] And in some educational institutions Soviet students met foreign students, with predictable results. This was the case with Gorbachev himself, the dormitory mate of a Czech intellectual who became a reformer and later a dissident.

Isolation in The Institute of Social Sciences
Until the end of the 1980s, the Central Committee of the CPSU maintained the Institute of Social Sciences as a top-secret training center for foreign party cadres, who were invited to live there as guests of the Soviet government for periods ranging between six months and three years, studying to become political functionaries in their home countries.

Though many of the students at the Institute were from Third World countries, this organization cannot be compared, say, to Lumumba University, the plebeian university in Moscow for ordinary Third World students. The Institute for Social Sciences was a luxurious place for elites, who lived in sequestered splendor, enjoying their own secret shops, their swimming pool, and their movie theater. Normal contacts with ordinary Soviet citizens were prohibited. They inhabited well-guarded but anonymous-looking buildings that were objects of curiosity to the CIA but not to Muscovites. There were good grounds for CIA curiosity, since some overseas students living there were trained not only in Marxist-Leninist theory but also in technologies uniquely useful to insurgents.

Yury Skvirsky was not a true DINOSAUR Party official, yet at the beginning of *perestroika* one could not have called him a TERMITE either. When I met him in 1992 at the Gorbachev Foundation in its original location he was on the staff, but before that he had taught in the same building, which had housed the Institute of Social Sciences until its collapse, and he had behaved there as a committed Communist. (A bolder scholar, who had been punished for expressing his convictions, told me that Skvirsky had passed up every chance to speak out on his behalf. In this regard he cannot be considered unusual; there would have been penalties. The affable Skvirsky did not claim to have been daring or even to have harbored unusual doubts during the pre-Gorbachev years.)

Because the Institute had been a stimulating place to work as a professor, it had attracted a worldly-wise staff. Party members from Europe had stopped coming to study there in the sixties, but Third World Communists came, and some of the students were general secretaries of the Party in their own countries. Although these Communist guest-students unwittingly influenced the DINOSAUR staff by apprising them about the world outside, they had not *tried* to spread critical ideas. On the contrary, the foreign students had opposed *perestroika* when it began, and had wanted to hear nothing about it.

"We had to deal with foreigners who knew the world much better than we did," Skvirsky recalled. "We couldn't simply deceive them, telling them nonsense. We had to adjust our lectures to reality, more or less, and not just base them on textbooks and manuals published in Moscow. . . . Most of the people in this building lived in two worlds—the official world that was recognized and supported by the Party, and our small private world, where we could see things as they really existed, and speak to each other frankly and sincerely."

Skvirsky taught a course on the international labor movement, which was harder to explain to foreign students than to Soviet students, who just tried to repeat whatever the lecturer told them. The foreigners often knew too much for that.

"A student from our country couldn't come to this building, which was like a special world," Skvirsky said. "Nobody knew what was here and very few people know even now. It was segregation. We had a special textbook. Often people from the Central Committee, from the International Department, came here and briefed us about what was going on in the world and how to explain it."

For any totalitarian system to persist as long as the Soviet Union lasted, while justifying its policies on an ideology, it was necessary to curtail contacts between ordinary people and alien visitors who knew certain "inconvenient facts." Indeed, one of the main challenges for the international communist movement was to manage the relations between various Communist Parties in the world, for controversies could always arise that might split the movement.

It may be useful here to review briefly the historic changes among the various worldwide communist movements.

The International Communist Movement and Eurocommunism
The ideas behind Gorbachev's reform of socialism had been discussed for a long time in Europe, where the Communist Parties had divided, nation by nation, into two camps: a "monistic" one that remained loyal to Moscow through thick and thin, and a pluralist one that came to accept the name "Eurocommunist." This latter group opposed the solidarity bloc organization of the international socialist movement, which had gone through three previous incarnations.

The First Socialist-Communist International, the "Communist League" formed in 1864 but fell apart because of a split between Marxists and anarchists. Karl Marx argued that the socialist movement should aim to *seize* state power (which would only later "wither away"), whereas the anarchists, led by Mikhail Bakunin, intended instead to *destroy* state power. After this dispute sundered the movement the Marxists formed the Second International (1889), a group of revolutionary parties that remained united until 1914, when it also divided; one wing supported and another wing opposed their countries' participation in World War I. Lenin called the former group "socialists" and the latter group "communists."[5] Today a Socialist International still functions, comprising social democratic parties; it is the successor to that Second Socialist International

The Third Communist International (or "Comintern") was formed in 1919. It served Stalin well. Between 1929 and 1934 the Comintern concentrated on opposing capitalist parties more than fascist ones. By 1939 Stalin entered into a pact with Hitler, thereby recovering Russian territories that had been lost after World War I. Though quietly abhorring this alliance, the international communist movement officially stood by the Soviet leader.

At the insistence of the United States, then a Soviet ally, Stalin formally dissolved the Comintern during World War II, though a new organization, the "Cominform," actually continued to promote Stalin's foreign policy. Its unity was broken only in 1948, when Tito took Yugoslavia on an autonomous path toward socialism, for which he was vilified as heretical. Other communist states, including China, were still in Stalin's camp when he died in 1953.

In 1955 Khrushchev opened a new option. He visited Tito in Belgrade and issued with him a joint statement accepting the policy of "many roads to social-ism." Shortly afterward Khrushchev dissolved the Cominform and denounced the crimes of Stalin in a secret speech to the XXth Congress of the CPSU. The de-Stalinization of that autumn, 1956, brought upheavals to Poland and Hungary. The turbulence in Poland was dramatic but bloodless, returning to power Władysław Gomułka, a Communist leader who had been jailed in a Stalinist purge. Gomułka launched several reforms, most notably by abandoning the col-lectivization of agriculture in favor of peasant smallholders, and briefly won considerable popular legitimacy for his variant of Communism.[6]

The Hungarian changes were influenced by Yugoslavia. During its brief pe-riod in power (Oct.-Nov. 1956) the new government of Hungary withdrew from the Warsaw Pact, granted freedom to form political parties, and established workers' councils. However, Soviet troops invaded in November 1956, pro-nouncing the uprising a "counter-revolution" and blaming it on supposed agents of Western imperialism. The leader, Imre Nagy, was executed and replaced by János Kádár, who, despite the absence of democracy, won a measure of popular acceptance over the years by introducing moderate economic reforms of his own.[7] These innovations would gradually present a model that Gorbachev's team took into account when designing their own *perestroika*.

However, in 1956 most European Communist Parties (CPs) followed Mos-cow's line, accepting the assault on Hungary and, as a result, suffering sharp losses of membership. Some Western CPs, on the other hand, took advantage of de-Stalinization by expanding their autonomy. Indeed, Palmiro Togliatti, leader of the Italian Communist Party (PCI), despite having supported the invasion of Hungary, turned pluralistic, proposing what he called "polycentrism," a policy by which Communist Parties would share their leadership in the transition to socialism with social democrats and anti-colonial movements. Togliatti privately called on the Soviets to allow civil liberties—free expression and debate—though he failed to persuade them. After 1964, it became apparent that even the limited liberalization that Khrushchev had launched in the Soviet Union would be reversed by those who ousted him.

However, the trend toward Eurocommunism would not be reversed. Those Communist Parties that stayed independent of Moscow saw their support in-crease in elections. Paramount in this trend was the rise of the PCI, which (apart from a drop after it supported the invasion of Hungary) always won the largest share in the popular vote of any Western Communist Party. Also important were the Spanish Communists, under the influence of Santiago Carrillo, whose book *Eurocommunism and the State*[8] was a major theoretical text for the movement.

The Western Eurocommunists markedly influenced their comrades in the Eastern states, who were split right up to the level of the Politburo. When West-ern Marxists traveled to the East, they brought books that were otherwise banned. For example, the East German Marxist theorist Rudolf Bahro recalls that it was Westerners who exposed him to writings by Trotsky and Bukharin.

Many Soviet officials were alarmed by the liberal trends of CPs abroad. In December 1957 they convened a meeting in Moscow of all foreign Communist

Parties. The statement adopted by that meeting seemed in some ways to represent a reversion to the Stalinist monistic international movement. Titoism was disparaged as "revisionism" and Yugoslavia did not endorse the statement. Otherwise, however, the document conferred legitimacy on Communist Parties that wanted more autonomy, at least within limits set by Moscow. This show of flexibility restored bloc unity for a time and renewed international solidarity.[9] The Eurocommunists remained within the world communist movement.

Globally, Eurocommunism eventually comprised the CPs of Japan, Australia, Spain, Sweden, Italy, Belgium, Netherlands, Great Britain, and Finland. The CPs that remained loyal to Moscow until the end of the Cold War were Ireland, Norway, Denmark, Switzerland, Luxembourg, Portugal, West Germany, Austria, and France—although the French had been on the Eurocommunist side until 1968, when they supported the invasion of Czechoslovakia.[10] And indeed, Czechoslovak reformers were allies of the early Eurocommunists of Western Europe. Their role requires a special review, for they and their Italian allies probably deserve the most credit of any foreign parties for influencing Gorbachev and his team to become, in effect, Eurocommunists.

* * *

Czechoslovakia had suffered less devastation during World War II than some of its neighboring countries. The Soviet troops liberated the country, but soon left instead of occupying it. President Beneš, trying to keep good relations with the Soviet Union to avoid a Communist coup, formed a coalition government that was only gradually taken over by Communists.

The real shift toward Stalinism began in 1948 when one-party rule by the Czechoslovak Communist Party was instituted legally, within the constitutional framework.[11] It was followed by fierce political repression, in which many political leaders were jailed and thirteen were executed. An estimated 100,000 political prisoners were held in concentration camps. Even Stalin's death did not bring immediate relief; the severe repression continued until 1963.[12]

At that point, the reformist Communists themselves began to make extensive plans for re-introducing democracy and elements of a market system. Unlike the 1956 uprising in Hungary, the Prague reforms were thought out in advance over a period of five years and articulated by writers and expert economists. A prolonged, rousing period of intellectual ferment preceded the Prague Spring. Displaying gumption, people formed political discussion clubs. In 1967, at a writers' congress, speakers openly called the existing regime a failure.

The Prague Spring began in 1968. After an intra-party struggle, Alexander Dubček, a Slovak, was chosen as the new leader of the Communist Party and launched the overt changes outlined in the Party's "Action Program."[13] As many as 6,000 citizens came together in political meetings.[14] Censorship was abolished, and the history of purges and repression was discussed openly. Numerous political prisoners wrongly jailed in the past appealed for retrials and were rehabilitated. Open political participation became possible, though the proposed reforms could not be called pluralist democracy of the Western sort.

Of all the changes, the Soviet Union objected most to the weakening of the "leading role of the Communist Party," for the Action Program stated that the Party must *deserve* to play such a leading role, rather than enforcing its primacy.[15] However, the people were not opposing socialism on principle in those days, but only the way it had been bungled.

Viewed thirty years later, the Action Program did not seem radical to the economist Rudolf Zukal. He said,

> Many economic ideas in the Prague Spring were normal, rational ideas, such as to eliminate the state monopoly in the foreign trade; to allow competition; to allow some unemployment; to introduce currency convertibility; and to dismiss some slackers. . . . The Action Program was worked out by the best brains available then. Now I have to laugh that I was naïve. It was not feasible to preserve most of the state enterprises. Today I know that. State companies are administered by bureaucracies and are not flexible. If you ask me whether the Prague Spring would have been successful or not, I cannot answer with certainty. But 80 percent of the nation supported these ideas. It was incredible! You can see it in the economic figures, in the collection for the state treasury, when people were giving money and gold, when people were going to voluntary work. I believe it should have succeeded, but it would have had to pass into private ownership.[16]

According to Dr. Čestmír Císař, who had been the Secretary of the Czechoslovak Central Committee during the Prague Spring, the economic benefits of the reforms immediately became noticeable. He said, "In 1968 the production rose by 11 percent and even in 1969 it was still by 9 percent. Only in 1970 did it go down, because they returned the old system and killed the reform. Then they were worried when it decreased and decided there had been something good in it, but it was too late."[17]

According to Dubček's memoirs, the Soviet ambassador did not comprehend much and, when he came to call, asked stupid questions. He evidently told Brezhnev that the Prague reforms constituted a "counter-revolution."[18]

On August 20, 1968, the armies of the Soviet Union, Poland, East Germany, Hungary, and Bulgaria invaded Czechoslovakia without the prior knowledge of Dubček's government. Two days later, Dubček was arrested and taken to Moscow, along with his Presidium. The President of the Republic voluntarily took other officials to Moscow to try to intervene and prevent bloodshed. Dubček's aide, Zdeněk Mlynář (who had been Gorbachev's university friend), arrived and reported that passive resistance was going on back at home in Prague.

To prevent a bloodbath, all the kidnapped Czechoslovak officials except František Kriegel signed an "agreement" with the Soviets—the "Moscow Protocol"—which sanctioned the occupation. Dubček hoped that its terms would give him a little room to maneuver.[19] In fact, it simply slowed by a few months the transition back to a repressive regime, the long period called "normalization." Dubček himself then had to take a job as a mechanic on the outskirts of Bratislava, where he remained under police surveillance throughout his working career, forbidden even to converse about politics.

A leading intellectual during the Prague Spring was Eduard Goldstücker, head of the Writers' Union and editor of a large literary magazine. He had been taken political prisoner and tortured during the Stalinist terror of 1948–49, until after ten months he confessed to acts that he had not committed. He was in prison four years, the first quarter of it in solitary confinement, with nothing to read or write. When he was hunted again in 1968, he fled to England until 1990.[20] I asked Professor Goldstücker how many people the Soviets had arrested and killed after the invasion. He replied, "Immediately they arrested hardly anybody. They tried to maintain the 'brotherly help' attitude. But in the process of occupation they killed about seventy people who got in the way of the tanks."[21]

Though the Czechoslovak reformers became pariahs, certain Soviet thinkers retained a quiet interest in their ideas. For their part, some of the Czechs continued trying to wield influence in the Soviet Union. The Soviets could never reply openly. Still, I heard several comments about such dealings in my interviews with Czech and Slovak reform leaders of the 1968 period. These included Jaroslav Šabata, Vanek Silhan, Miloš Hájek, and Čestmír Císař. Šabata told me,

> Of course the Prague Spring had an influence on *perestroika*! Any Russian reformist will tell you that the main source of their thoughts was really the documents from the Prague Spring, the Action Program. . . . In the '80s there were meetings between [Soviet] people and [Czechoslovak economist] Ota Šik. After Gorbachev got to power, these contacts were renewed and the Soviet authors undoubtedly knew Šik. Not only economists had an influence in this direction but the key influence in this area may have been the Czech ex-Communists in exile, headed by Jiří Pelikan,[22] editor of *Listy*.[23]

Miloš Hájek said,

> The Russian economists, at least the more progressive ones, knew all the Czechoslovak economic materials from the '60s. . . . Many intellectuals knew the documents of the Prague Spring. When Karel Kouba arrived in Moscow, a number of people there literally apologized to him. . . .
>
> In a speech in the summer of 1986, Gorbachev used the word "democratize," which had been taboo so far. Democratization had been one of our objectives, and so people began saying, "This is already the Prague Spring!"

It was far too dangerous for a Soviet to interact with Czech dissidents. However, it was much less dangerous to deal with the Western Eurocommunists, who were still "insiders," even though their Parties had tried to protect the Czechs from Soviet wrath about the Prague Spring reforms. The Italians, unlike Soviet Party members, fearlessly associated with the Czechoslovak reformers.

Gorbachev himself developed relations with a number of European Party members as early as 1966. It was almost unheard of, in that period, for Soviet officials to be permitted to travel abroad independently and meet whomever they wished. Remarkably, Gorbachev took his wife along when he went with a group of Soviets to France as the guest of a leftist French businessman. He and Raisa then took a 5,000 kilometer car trip as tourists in the country. The next year they vacationed in Italy, where they visited Sicily, Rome, Turin, Florence, and San Gimignano.[24] The privilege of being a private, unsupervised tourist could only have been conferred on Gorbachev by an extremely high-level person—perhaps Mikhail Suslov, the CPSU's head ideologist.

According to Fyodor Burlatsky, the Italian Communist Party leader Enrico Berlinguer had a big influence on Gorbachev—a fact that Gorbachev confirms in his memoirs, though it seems he never met Berlinguer in person. Burlatsky told me, "When Berlinguer died in 1984 Gorbachev was head of the delegation there, and said very important words at the burial: 'Enrico, we will never forget your advice about democracy in the Soviet Union.' It was the first time when I personally took much note of Mr. Gorbachev. It was published in the Italian newspapers, but never published in Russian."[25]

* * *

Zdeněk Mlynář was a Czech whom Gorbachev met while they were both studying law at Moscow State University in the early 1950s. For the rest of their lives they would be close friends, though for twenty-two years there would be no contact between them. (Forty years later, Gorbachev would nevertheless tell a journalist, "Zdeněk is probably the person I'm closest to. He always has been."[26])

They took the same examinations and belonged to the same study group. Gorbachev is even said once to have mended Mlynář's pants.[27] Later Mlynář visited the Soviet Union several times and visited Gorbachev in Stavropol as late as 1967. Zhores Medvedev, in a biography of Gorbachev, points out how rare such foreign contacts were in that period. He wrote, "This personal contact with the culture and attitudes of a traditionally Western nation must have almost had the effect of a lengthy stay abroad in the early 1950s."[28]

As youths, both Gorbachev and Mlynář were doctrinaire Communists. In 1956, for example, when Soviets crushed the Hungarian uprising, neither of them opposed the attack. Yet Khrushchev's denunciation of Stalin took place the same year, raising questions in their minds that would lead them toward reform.

Soon Zdeněk Mlynář was a dissident. Upon completing his studies and returning to Prague, he was appointed assistant to the General Procurator of Czechoslovakia, and by 1967 he became a secretary of the Central Committee of the Czechoslovak Party. He was a leader of the Prague Spring[29]—indeed, the main author of the Action Program. The Soviet invasion was, as he told Gorbachev much later, "the collapse of my political world." Mlynář was dismissed from his high post and forbidden to work as a lawyer. Instead he worked in the museum as an entomologist,[30] deliberately withdrawing from political life for five years. He was expelled from the Czechoslovak Communist Party.

Although Dubček was kept from meeting his old allies, Mlynář visited him and they had a few long conversations in the middle of a lake, treading water.[31]

In 1976 Mlynář was one of the initiators of Charter 77, a platform of civil liberties and human rights. Many of the signatories were arrested. Mlynář was dismissed from his job at the museum and placed under house arrest, but the next year he was allowed to emigrate to Vienna, where he worked as a political scientist for the next twenty years.

Gorbachev made two official visits to Prague. Few people know about the first one, in 1969, when he was part of a delegation of Soviets surveying the effects of the recent invasion and the ongoing "normalization" process. By then, his friend Mlynář was no longer working in government and Gorbachev was not allowed to meet him. Strangely, Gorbachev believed at that point that the Soviet invasion had been justified as a way of defending socialism. He refused to consider Mlynář a counter-revolutionary. Yet the trip shocked him. "With my own eyes I saw that the people did not accept what had happened in August 1968. . . People turned their backs on us; they didn't want to speak with us. . . . From that time on I began to think more and more about our own situation and I came to rather unconsoling conclusions—that something wasn't right among us."[32]

Gorbachev's second visit to Prague was an extremely public event that must be regarded as tragic. He came in the spring of 1987, when his *perestroika* was fully underway. The Czechoslovak people greeted him warmly—a mood that Gorbachev spoiled by his own words. I heard about this mistake from several sources, including Dubček's good friend, Václav Slavik, and also from Čestmír Císař, who had been Secretary of the Party's Central Committee in 1968. Jaroslav Šabata told me,

> Gorbachev actually undermined all the opposition or freedom-oriented forces here in this country, to their great disappointment. I swear, he was not forced to make such a move. . . . In the streets downtown, when people were depending on every sign and word, Gorbachev had given three or four sentences that were understood by those who had been involved in 1968 as supporting the position of Husak [the leader of the totalitarian regime that had crushed the Prague Spring]. Even today, as I am speaking about it, I don't feel well. . . . Afterward, instead of having the sympathy of 90 percent of the Czechoslovak population, he had the support of only 10 percent. It was an unbelievably hard consequence. It deeply influenced the Czechoslovakians' shift to the right here, the tendency to support capitalism. And I am saying this as a representative of the Czech left.[33]

Gorbachev and Mlynář renewed their friendship in person in 1989, after twenty-two years without contact. Thereafter they talked often. Eventually they began to tape record their conversations, which were edited and published after Mlynář's death as a book, *Conversations with Gorbachev*. It is a remarkable record of the political transformation of two men who started and ended thinking alike, but who arrived at their late opinions by very different routes. The two old friends speak frankly and warmly, but Mlynář is harsh in challenging most of the important decisions that Gorbachev made as leader of his country. Naturally, he also criticized "Misha" for having supported the crushing of Prague Spring. Yet, oddly, it is Mlynář, the flagrant dissident and counter-revolutionary, who appears to be the more old-fashioned, militant Communist. For example, he asks why Gorbachev did not use armed force on several occasions, citing the example of Abraham Lincoln to make his point.[34] It is Gorbachev who reminds him of the suffering caused by the American Civil War.

Yet throughout their long conversations, they both agree that what they want now is democratic socialism. Mlynář presses Gorbachev to explain why he tried to keep the CPSU functioning until the very end; Gorbachev reviews all the alternatives and claims that breaking the party up or starting a new party would have wrecked the state, since the right and left were so polarized at the time. His intention was to introduce the New Union Treaty, a constitution that would have left no room for the party bureaucrats. Only in this oblique way could he have established democracy and eased the old *nomenklatura* out of power. But they saw what was happening and tried to make a putsch instead. In response to one of Mlynář's rather DINOSAUR-like criticisms, Gorbachev says,

> I can agree with you when you argue that Soviet society was an extremely difficult and complex object for reform. In that you are correct. I was of the same opinion from the very beginning of the reforms, and that is the explanation for my choice in favor of evolutionary changes, my feeling that cavalry charges were unacceptable. The reason for the failure of the reforms is not that we took the path of democratic change. The reasons lay elsewhere, in the vindictiveness of the reactionary forces and the excessive revolutionism of the radicals.[35]

How much influence did each man have on the other's thinking? They do not discuss this question in the book, so we cannot answer it either. Since they were out of touch for so long, both of them had taken many political positions that could not have been directly influenced by the other. And when they recounted the changes forced upon them in those years, they debated the questions vigorously, with each standing his own ground and defending his views. Even then they were not trying to reach agreement but only to understand each other.

What they demonstrated is that they both remained committed to socialism—but a kind of socialism that is completely contrary to old Marxist-Leninist dogma. It is a socialism based on human values, one that honors diversity and is compatible with liberalism and democracy. Would each have reached this political philosophy without having known the other? I doubt it, but they do not say.

Another Termite Network: *Problems of Peace and Socialism*
This chapter has described, so far, the influence of two networks: the reformers in the Prague Spring and the Western European Eurocommunists, especially the Italians. As we have seen, the Czechs (especially the economists) actually did not cease to be influential as soon as they left the Party and became dissidents. However, their influence thereafter was indirect when it existed at all, for Soviet officials (except KGB agents) dared not communicate directly with a dissident.

Mlynář and his dissident Czechoslovak allies were absolutely isolated from a third important network that existed in the same city, Prague: certain Soviet intellectuals who were functionaries in the world communist movement. The remainder of this chapter will be concerned with this latter group of insiders. They were to become the key reformers in Gorbachev's government. Who were these remarkable people and how did they happen to be together in Prague? To explain, I must pick up the history of the international communist movement where I left off—with the "Comintern" and "Cominform."

The Third Communist International, or "Comintern," had been the main organized body of Communist Parties around the world until World War II. Stalin replaced it with a more limited organization, the "Cominform," which existed primarily to supervise the new Eastern European communist states and to coordinate the positions of all the Communist Parties.

The Cominform was abolished in 1958 and much of its work was taken over by a journal, *Problems of Peace and Socialism*,[36] which was housed in Prague in what had been a seminary until the Party expropriated it from the Catholic Church. For over thirty years, that journal would play a unique role in disseminating ideas through socialist countries and affording intellectuals a relatively safe space where they might discuss un-Soviet ideas. It was created and supported by the International Department of the CPSU—a group that was tolerant in comparison to the rest of the Party. It was the Soviet Union's most lively quasi-civil society—sponsored by the Party, but run by "half-dissidents."

The first editor-in-chief was Aleksei Rumyantsev, whose TERMITE tendencies were already known and who would become the leader of the progressive wing of the party. His efforts to build empirical social science would be blocked by the party's reactionary chief ideologist, Mikhail Suslov, who would dismiss him from all his posts in 1971.

Political scientist William Smirnov, who had worked closely with Gorbachev's aide, Georgi Shakhnazarov, told me what was expected of the staff of this unique journal. He said,

> They would be in constant communication with the different political parties and left movements all over the world. There was a strict selection because you must be ready to resist the temptation of Western ideas and revisionist ideas. But they can't send just a stupid apparatchik because you would be in dialogue with very skillful Western leftists. So there were two requirements: allegiance to the CPSU and the ability to write, to discuss, to negotiate. The journal was the primary ideological channel of influence of the CPSU with the leftist movements all over the world.[37]

One staff member of *Problems* was Gennady Gerasimov, who would later become the most famous press secretary during the Gorbachev period. TV viewers in the West watched him on the news every day or two. He described his Prague years with special enthusiasm in our phone interview. He said,

> It was our second university. In Prague we had free discussions that we had no opportunity to have in Moscow and we were in touch with the world. For instance, among other duties, I was in charge of buying books for the library and there was no limit. So I was subscribing to *Bookseller* of Britain and *Publishers Weekly* in the United States, a publication from France, the *New York Times Book Review*, and books on arms control and disarmament. Many friends of mine who were there changed their views on certain subjects. When they came back to Moscow, many of them went to the Central Committee—including me. I went to the department in charge of relations with the socialist countries, to-

gether with Shakhnazarov and Arbatov. Once Fyodor Burlatsky came to Prague and picked me up when he was hunting for additional people for the Central Committee, so I spent three years there.[38]

Besides Rumyantsev, Shakhnazarov, Gerasimov, and Ambartsumov, a few of the select group of Soviet staff members at *Problems* are listed in the endnotes. With few exceptions they were TERMITES would play important roles in Gorbachev's circle of reformers.[39] The journal employed a staff of some 400, including typists, accountants, and so on, of many nationalities. Any Communist Party could participate. The Chinese never joined. The French and Italians joined at first but withdrew later. The British, Canadians, and Americans joined and stayed on until the downfall of the journal when the Soviet Union collapsed. *Problems* was published in all Eastern European languages, plus French, Italian, English, Arabic, Spanish, Portuguese, and Kurdish.[40] However, not all articles appeared in all the different editions.

The masthead never identified the editorial board, or even the editor-in-chief. Some CPs existed underground and their members might suffer if their activities became known. Most articles were written by staff journalists, but some were submitted by correspondents from various Communist Parties, or even from non-Communists—especially after 1986, when editorial policy became more open, reflecting *glasnost.*

Staff members lived scattered across the various districts of Prague and were transported to and from work by special buses. The USSR paid the main expenses, and the editor-in-chief was always a Soviet; the secretary was always a Czechoslovakian. Some Czechs told me that they had feared to go near the *Problems* building because it was close to the headquarters of the secret police, with all their electronic surveillance equipment. But the Soviets recalled their stay in Prague as intellectually exhilarating.

One staff member was Vsevolod Rybakov, who had worked at *Problems* between 1971 and 1983, later joining the International Department of the Central Committee, CPSU. In 1991 he joined Gorbachev's secretariat. He told us,[41]

The magazine was considered to be a branch of the International Department of the Central Committee, though officially they were independent. . . . Yet 90 percent of the Soviet employees were concealed dissidents and sometimes even open ones, from the very beginning of the magazine. . . .

If you could attend the meetings of the Party members who were working in the magazine—such as Zagladin, Chernyayev, Karyakin—you'd be amazed. The record of those meetings could have been a reason for being arrested at that time and the best advertisement for these persons today.

Rybakov said that *Problems* had been designed as a clearinghouse for Communist theory from around the world, rather than a Soviet propaganda tool. This exposed its staffers to a broader range of opinions than would otherwise have been the case. As he pointed out, "because new employees were hired on the recommendation of existing *Problems* staff, it became almost an 'asylum for dissidents.'" He said,

Most materials from the Parties were written by non-professionals and often it was necessary to re-write them. Actually, that was the biggest part of our job. But the representative of a Party wouldn't accept it if I re-wrote it from the CPSU position. Often a Party asked us to write an article on a particular issue on behalf of their leader, so I was mainly writing articles for other people. . .

In the seventies a deep split was already evident in the Communist movement. The so-called Eurocommunists appeared. The U.S. or Canadian CPs stood on classical, orthodox positions. They supported everything that the Soviet Union was doing. The Eurocommunist-oriented Parties took a different view. For example, they said that both Western and Soviet missiles are bad; both sides are driving the arms race, sharpening the situation, and so on. Naturally, this was anathema to the Soviet side but anyway it influenced the struggle for peace.

When I was working in the magazine, our editor-in-chief was Konstantin Ivanovich Zarodov, a really remarkable person. At first glance he seemed to be a typical Party functionary—completely orthodox—but later, when he started to trust you, he turned out to be an absolutely different person, very free-thinking. Thanks to his support, it was sometimes possible to publish incredible things. For example, in 1979 Soviet troops invaded Afghanistan. The reaction of the Communist parties was not simple. Eurocommunist parties condemned it as aggression and started to say so in the materials they proposed to publish.

Another example: In 1980 in Berlin our magazine and the Socialist United Party of Germany organized a conference of the socialist camp and the national-liberation movements. These movements were pro-Communist but not really Communist. . . There was a speech by an old friend of mine, a Spanish leader who said that the war was aggression. I told him, "See what you can eliminate from [your speech]. Whatever you think it necessary to publish will be published, but please realize the level of harm it can bring to me."

So he crossed out some sharp passages that, if published, could bring us to jail. But such phrases as "aggression," and "invasion" were left in. After that I took it to Zarodov.

It certainly was unpleasant for him but he agreed. It was published and sold in Moscow. One can read that the representatives of prominent Communist Parties called our international assistance in Afghanistan "aggression."

As usual, we received a call from Moscow, and scandal. But Zarodov always said, "If you want to break relations with these parties and split the communist movement permanently, okay. Let the Politburo make the decision and we will put the blame on them. If not, we'll continue to publish material of this kind."

When in 1976 the French Communist Party eliminated the notion of the "dictatorship of the proletariat" from its statutes, they submitted an article to the magazine and explained why they refused to use the notion anymore.

It was an uneasy situation for us. Already almost thirty Communist Parties didn't have that notion in their regulations but this particular change happened on a wave of Eurocommunism and it filled the Central Committee with indignation, especially the Department of Propaganda. But anyway, it was published.

We asked Rybakov whether the ideas of the Prague Spring had been discussed and whether the staff of *Problems* had much contact with local Czechs, or especially with dissidents. There seems to have been little such contact. One of his friends, an Italian Eurocommunist, had contacts with Czech dissidents and wanted to organize a meeting between Rybakov and them, but, he said, "I was scared to do it. He understood that, though for him it wouldn't have any consequences (he might simply be forbidden to enter Czechoslovakia) for me it could be a disaster."

Besides, the Prague Spring ideas were not discussed as much at *Problems* as the ideas of the Eurocommunists. However, when the Eurocommunist Parties attempted to condemn the military intervention in Czechoslovakia, it was never published. There was a rule in the magazine against criticizing another Party without its permission and the Czech representative wouldn't allow it.

We asked Rybakov whether Western ideas were published in the magazine or sent to the Kremlin in the form of notes. He explained that such views were mainly reflected in the official published positions of the parties. However, there had been a separate department of the magazine that dealt with the struggle for peace. Rybakov himself had been working in the Asia and Africa Department, where the representatives of those countries used to say that it was not their task to fight for peace. They were struggling against starvation, disease, and colonialism. Peace was of interest only to the developed countries. Rybakov added,

> The President of the World Peace Council was an Indian, Romesh Chandra. He was a talented person but a demagogue at the same time. So the position of Eurocommunists certainly influenced the official peace movement, though ninety percent of the time it followed Soviet policy directions. As the Eurocommunist Parties changed their views further, they established relations with peaceniks. The Italian Communists were especially active in organizing discussions with them.

We asked him whether he had retained some loyalty to the socialist system later, while he was working in the International Department of the Central Committee. Two reformist approaches were possible: belief in a possibility of "socialism with a human face"—reforms from the top—or a total rejection of socialism. We asked which view was his own. He replied as a true TERMITE:

> In 1956, soon after I had read Khrushchev's report, I took the view that, "right or wrong, it's my country." I thought that one must make a choice: Either you refuse to collaborate or you work in the system—and in that case, regardless of your attitude to the system itself, you must honestly work for it. You must professionally do your job and maximize the true facts and arguments you provide to the Party leaders (which was my job), even if, according to the rules, you must dress a fact in propagandistic clothes.
>
> For example, in 1962 I defended my dissertation on "Imperialist Aid to the Developing Countries." At that time our official position was that this aid is complete robbery and only harms the developing countries. In my dissertation I used all the usual angry words against capitalism and then proved that this help really helps the developing countries to develop but at the same time it involves these countries in the capitalist system. So after pronouncing all the required abuse, it was possible to give the real facts and propose concepts. And after

1986 when the possibilities expanded, it became possible to write openly what we wanted to propose.

I believed that changes in the system were possible only by reforms "from the top." That idea was discussed secretly in IMEMO while I was working there: that it's necessary to try to change the system by "revolution from the top" to make it more human. We welcomed the Prague Spring until 1968. We believed that things were being done in a proper way, initiated from the top, that the odious features of the system were being eliminated and normal, human relations were being established.

Even later I didn't change my conviction that the Soviet people would never rebel. The system must be changed in the only possible way—from the top. Since our leaders were incapable of reform, it was necessary to propose changes in a way that wouldn't arouse their suspicion. For instance, during the Prague Spring Ota Šik, the Czech Minister of Economy, proposed changes no more radical than those that were being worked out at that time in Soviet Union for the economic reform of 1967–68. That means that here reforms were proposed in a way that didn't raise suspicions. Still, the reforms were stifled later anyway.

Our goal was to show that we want to improve the system, not explode it. . . . The leaders had similar views, though they didn't express them openly. Gorbachev held the same conviction that changes must be done from the top.

Rybakov's most rewarding task came in January 1986 when he worked on preparing the policy of disarming intermediate range nuclear-armed missiles. He recognized it as a utopian plan, but it "had the same influence on the social atmosphere as peaceniks' initiatives." He added,

It also overturned our international policy. We started to support the termination of civil wars in Africa where formerly we supported one side. Then we stopped quarreling with the dissidents in the international Communist movement. Gorbachev was meeting with the Italian Communist leaders and these conversations were better than with anybody else because there were common views between them.

The last remarkable initiative (because after that the fight inside the Party blew up) was Gorbachev's intervention at the UN General Assembly in December 1988. For the first time, the Soviet leader said that the way proposed by Communists and Social Democrats is not the only possible one, that the capitalist and socialist ways are parallel, and that they tend to converge and must establish a common civilization for all of humankind. This was a recognition of the theory of convergence, the position of Social Democrats. For a Soviet leader it was a huge step forward, a step that required lots of courage because the Politburo was split and only part of it supported Gorbachev.

This new position was prepared mainly by Rybakov and a group of consultants under the guidance of Gorbachev's assistant, Chernyaev. The approach toward the Social Democrats was initiated by the International Department. The consultants all understood where the limits were, but kept trying to enlarge them in every new document. "We were Gorbachev's allies," he said. "He is a naturally gifted person."

When the group of consultants went abroad they could not express their own personal opinions. For example, Rybakov said,

> In August '88 I was in Paris as an official representative and at a meeting I was pressed to answer a question about Soviet intervention in Czechoslovakia. First I said that, as an official representative here, I can criticize my leaders but not the leaders of Czechoslovakia. But they pressed me anyway to state my position. Finally I said that, as my private position, I remember clearly when I heard the news on the radio about the invasion of our troops in Czechoslovakia. For me it's still one of the darkest days in my life, a tragedy not only for Czechoslovakia but also for our country.
>
> At that time if the Czech leaders had learned that the official representative of CPSU expressed such an opinion I would have had trouble—not from the Soviet side but because of the Czechs. They would complain.

* * *

Most Russian academics today call their post-Khrushchev period of Soviet governance "authoritarian" rather than "totalitarian" to indicate how much better it was than the Stalinist system. Gorbachev, however, continued using the harsh term. Totalitarianism is hideous, anti-human. Decency requires every human being to prevent its occurrence anywhere, for it is a trap that cannot easily be disarmed.

Dictators are only a tiny fraction of the population, but they can control everyone else unless some powerful groups—especially the police and military—defect and disobey orders. But in a totalitarian system, communication is so constrained that it is hard to organize any such opposition. It's even dangerous to try to locate other potential resisters. A dictator can rule only by keeping most people ignorant of significant facts and afraid to compare their own theories and opinions.

As we have seen, there were a few shelters where Soviet intellectuals could communicate enough to develop alternative ideas. Only a few university students, such as Gorbachev and Mlynář, formed enough trust to speak frankly with each other. Their experience differed from that of foreign cadres (even loyal, pro-Soviet cadres) at the Institute of Social Sciences, who were isolated, not for their own sake, but to keep them from contaminating the opinion of ordinary Moscow citizens. In a dictatorship, foreigners are dangerous.

Yet there were locales of contact with foreigners—especially for Party officials who were sent abroad. Groups formed right inside the Central Committee. There were opportunities to learn true facts and pass them on, even to build trust, most notably in a certain former seminary in Prague. We can call these groups civil society.

And yet, they only partly count as such. Civil society confers several advantages on its members. It gives them know-how—as these TERMITE groupings actually did. But it also enables them to organize and promote their ideas publicly, possibly with enough strength to challenge the rulers and effect alternative political solutions. This the "TERMITE civil society" never accomplished. The allies of Gorbachev and Mlynář knew they could go to jail for expressing ideas openly. They never became BARKING DOGS, and as cautious, careful, astute people they saw no opportunity for a "revolution from below" in Russia. Popular uprisings in Poland and Hungary had been crushed, as was the Prague Spring. They could only wait for their moment to come, wait for a "revolution from the top" to bring "socialism with a human face." It would be Gorbachev who gave them that opportunity.

But in the end, the society would be too polarized for evolutionary progress. Gorbachev would have to zigzag between powerful Party DINOSAURS and the impatient BARKING DOGS with their new, radically democratic, allies. For this seeming ambivalence he would lose the trust of the TERMITES. And by abandoning him, the TERMITES would prevent him from giving them the kind of governance that they all wanted: democratic socialism.

Notes

1. The strongest evidence of his intentions can be seen in the transcripts of his prolonged discussion with his closest friend from university days. See Mikhail Gorbachev and Zdeněk Mlynář, *Conversations with Gorbachev: On Perestroika, The Prague Spring, and the Crossroads of Socialism*, trans. George Shriver. (New York: Columbia University Press, 2002).

2. Len Karpinsky, "The Autobiography of a 'Half-Dissident,'" in *Voices of Glasnost: Interviews with Gorbachev's Reformers*, ed. Stephen F. Cohen and Katrina vanden Heuvel (New York: Norton, 1989), 299–300.

3. Victor Sumsky, in discussion with the author, 1992, Moscow. Sumsky had been a staff member of the Soviet Embassy in Indonesia.

4. See Oleg Kalugin, *The First Directorate: My 32 Years in Intelligence and Espionage Against the West* with Fen Montaigne (New York: St. Martin's, 1994).

5. John Bacher, "Eurocommunism: Showing a Human Face to Both Blocs," *Peace Magazine* 2, no. 7 (February–March 1987): 27–32.

6. Andrzej Korbonski, "Poland," in *Communism in Eastern Europe* 2nd ed., ed. Teresa Rakowska-Harmstone (Bloomington: Indiana University Press, 1984), 51–54.

7. Bennett Kovrig, "Hungary," in *Communism in Eastern Europe*, 94–96.

8. Santiago Carrillo, *Eurocommunism and the State*, trans. Nan Green and A. M. Elliott (Westport, CT: Lawrence Hill, 1978).

9. H. Gordon Skilling, *Communism National and International: Eastern Europe After Stalin* (Toronto: University of Toronto Press, 1984), 12.

10. Bacher, 27.

11. This is the opinion expressed by the economist Rudolf Zukal, in discussion with the author, summer 1994, Prague. Zukal says he was one of the generation of intellectuals who had been raised to replace the ones liquidated in 1948. However, for participating in the 1968 reforms, he was made into a bulldozer driver for 19 years. Nevertheless, he managed to work one day a week as an independent economist. At one point he showed the authorities that their statistical yearbook was full of lies. They assumed that he must have received this information from outside agents and arrested him as a spy. Because he was able to show them how he had figured it out independently, he was released. Ironically, after the Velvet Revolution, the "lustration" law that was introduced labeled him as an informer to the Communist government because he had told them about the false statistics and for this he was punished yet again.

12. Vanek Silhan, in discussion with the author, summer 1994, Prague. Silhan was an economist and a leader in the Czechoslovak Central Committee who stood in for Dubček during his absence. See Alexander Dubček, *Hope Dies Last: The Autobiography of Alexander Dubček*, ed. and trans. Jiři Hochman (New York: Kodansha International, 1993), 217. Silhan continued as a dissident in the "normalization" period after the invasion of 1968. He had lived in Leningrad in 1955–56, and a number of fearless Russian intellectuals continued to speak freely with him during the normalization period.

13. The Action Program can be seen in the appendix to Dubček's *Hope Dies Last*. Hochman finished the book after Dubček's death. Václav Slavik, a friend of Dubček's who had been a member of his Politburo in 1968, complained of the book's numerous errors during his interview in Prague, spring of 1994. Dubček had died in a car accident without reading several of the last chapters.

14. Ulc, 123.

15. Rudolf Zukal, in discussion with the author, 1993, Prague.

16. Zukal, discussion.

17. Čestmír Císař, in discussion with the author, 1993, Prague.

18. Dubček, 157.

19. Dubček, 209–14.

20. Eva Hoffman tells the story of Goldstücker and his family in her book, *Exit into History: A Journey Through the New Eastern Europe* (New York: Penguin, 1993), 129–38.

21. Eduard Goldstücker, in discussion with the author, September 1993, Prague.

22. Pelikan had been general secretary of the International Union of Students. In 1968 he was director of Czechoslovak television, and after the invasion he worked in Rome.

23. Jaroslav Šabata, in discussion with the author, 1993, Prague. Šabata had been ideology secretary of the CPCS during the Prague Spring and continued to be a leading dissident in Slovakia until the Velvet Revolution of 1989.

24. Dusko Doder and Louise Branson, *Heretic in the Kremlin* (New York: Penguin, 1991), 20.

25. Fyodor Burlatsky, in discussion with the author, 1994, Moscow.

26. Archie Brown attributes this comment to a report by Olga Kuchkina, See Brown's introduction to Mikhail Gorbachev and Zdeněk Mlynář, *Conversations with Gorbachev*.

27. Fyodor Burlatsky, discussion.

28. Zhores Medvedev, *Gorbachev* (New York: W.W. Norton, 1987), 37.

29. Medvedev, 37.

30. Goldstücker, discussion.

31. Dubček, 258.

32. Gorbachev and Mlynář, 41.

33. Jaroslav Šabata interview, Prague, September 1993.

34. Gorbachev and Mlynář, 128–29.

35. Gorbachev and Mlynář, 79.

36. The English version of this journal was titled *The World Marxist Review*.

37. William Smirnov, in discussion with the author, summer 1993, Institute of State and Law, Moscow.

38. Gennady Gerasimov, telephone discussion with the author, 1994.

39. The former staff members of *Problems* include: Georgi Arbatov (Academician, Member of the Central Committee, Head of the USA. and Canada Institute and close adviser to Andropov, Brezhnev, and Gorbachev); Anatolii S. Chernyaev (who would become Gorbachev's aide); Ivan T. Frolov (later an editor of *Kommunist* and also of

Pravda, Frolov became a leading specialist in environmental issues); Timur Gaidar (a reformist economist whose father was a famous writer of children's stories and whose son, Yegor, would become the architect of "shock therapy" under Yeltsin); Richard Kosolapov (later Editor of *Kommunist* and one of the few people on this list who could not be called a reformist); Yuri Karyakin (a prominent writer, social commentator); Otto R. Latsis (reformist historian who wrote a book about Bukharin. He was repressed, then elected to the Central Committee of the CPSU); Merab Mamardashvili (a former classmate and friend of Gorbachev's at Moscow State University, who would become an eminent philosopher); Konstantin I. Milkulski (who would become an academician); Marina Pavlova-Silvanskaya (a journalist with important contacts to Eastern European dissidents, especially Polish Catholics); Vadim Pechenev (later Chernenko's assistant); Vsevelod B. Rybakov (a consultant in the International Department of the Central Committee, who then worked for President Gorbachev); Aleksandr S. Tsipko (who was later to work at International Department of the Central Committee, and as Deputy Director of Bogomolov's institute); Alexander I. Volkov (who would later work at Gorbachev Foundation); Yegor V. Yakovlev (a journalist who would become head of *Moscow News*, then head of Russian television after the 1991 putsch attempt); and Vadim Zagladin (specialist on East-West relations who became first deputy head, International Department of the Central Committee, part-time adviser to President Gorbachev).

40. Mr. and Mrs. Zaki Khairi, in discussion with the author, 1993, Prague.

41. My research assistant, Julia Kalinina, fully participated in and occasionally conducted this and several other interviews in Moscow.

Chapter 5: Three Freelance Diplomats

The Cold War started before World War II had even ended. Although the Soviet Union bore the heaviest burden in the alliance against Germany, its status as an ally was always limited. Stalin learned that an atomic bomb was being developed secretly and even was told (mainly by a Manhattan Project scientist named Klaus Fuchs) how to do likewise.

The Americans had begun work on a bomb because they thought Hitler was developing one. When that proved untrue, they kept going anyway. The head of the project, General Groves, told one of his scientists, Joseph Rotblat, that the bomb soon would be needed in the forthcoming war against the Soviet Union.

Horrified, Rotblat quit his job at Los Alamos and devoted the rest of his long life to the abolition of nuclear weapons. Although he was the only researcher to quit on moral grounds, many of the other scientists were also shocked by the outcome of their work when Japan was bombed. They formed the Federation of American Scientists (FAS) to counter the nuclear threat.

When the first atomic bombs were dropped on Hiroshima and Nagasaki in August 1945, Stalin already had known for three years that such weapons were probably being developed and had launched a similar Soviet project under the direction of Lavrenti Beria, the head of the secret police. The scientific director was Igor Kurchatov. By August 29, 1949, the first Soviet atomic bomb was tested. It was followed on August 13, 1953, by a hydrogen bomb whose designer was the physicist Andrei Sakharov—later the leading dissident.

The nuclear arms race was on. Whatever cooperation had existed between East and West during World War II ceased throughout this Cold War. Einstein warned, "The splitting of the atom has changed everything save our modes of thinking, and thus we drift toward unparalleled catastrophe."

In such a situation of enmity, how could mutual trust be restored? Stalin permitted almost no civil society contacts across the new "Iron Curtain," though person-to-person contacts are the most common precondition for the establishment of trust. Soviet citizens were not allowed to go abroad, and there were hardly any transnational non-governmental organizations.

For a decade or more, the main East-West contacts that could take place were with individual Western travelers who visited the Soviet Union on business or, rarely, as private tourists. Nevertheless, a few such persons, whom I call "freelance diplomats," did attempt to build trust with the Soviet officials whom they met. Gradually some of them would be able to create genuine civil society organizations to bring together Soviets and Westerners, but at first virtually the only trust-building efforts were the solo campaigns of individual visitors.

I want to describe in this chapter the "freelance diplomacy" of three such Western travelers who all sought independently to improve relations between East and West, to promote human rights, and to end the arms race. They are Norman Cousins, Jeremy Stone, and Ernst van Eeghen.

Norman Cousins

Among every peacenik's pantheon of saints is a man whose main source of fame was something quite different—his demonstration of the healing power of laughter. This was Norman Cousins, a writer and, for thirty years, the editor-in-chief of an influential magazine, *The Saturday Review*. On the day that Hiroshima was obliterated. Cousins wrote a long article expressing his sense of guilt over the terrible use of this weapon. The article was reprinted widely and an expanded version was published in several languages as a book. For the rest of his life Cousins worked tirelessly to curb nuclear weapons and to build a system of world governance in which nations would become states within a global federation. As we'll see in the next chapter, he founded the Dartmouth Conferences, one of the most influential transnational civil society organizations.

In 1979 Cousins published a book, *The Anatomy of an Illness*, which recounted his own experience with a painful, ordinarily fatal illness, ankylosing spondylitis. He reported having experimented on himself with Vitamin C and laughter, stimulated by watching countless humorous movies—a regimen that actually cured him. He went on to teach in the UCLA medical school, where there is now a department named after him. His discoveries led to the development of a branch of medicine called psychoneuroimmunology, which deals with the impact of emotions on health. He is best known for this work, but here I want to describe his personal diplomatic missions to the Soviet Union.

The closest the world ever came to nuclear war was probably the Cuban missile crisis of October 1962. Fidel Castro and Premier Nikita Khrushchev had agreed to install nuclear-armed missiles in Cuba, and the Soviets were preparing to do so when American surveillance systems spotted their activities. President John F. Kennedy and his advisers resolved to impose a quarantine on the island and even to use nuclear weapons unless Khrushchev backed down.

In the end, Khrushchev did relent, on the implicit understanding that the United States would not invade Cuba and would forgo developing military installations in Turkey, which the Soviets regarded as equally threatening. Years later, the participants in this drama from both sides came together to review the crisis and found that they had been even closer to launching nuclear war than they had realized at the time. As Soviet General Anatoly Gribkov said, "Nuclear catastrophe was hanging by a thread . . . and we weren't counting days or hours, but minutes."

In the months following the crisis, both Kennedy and Khrushchev, still shocked by the experience, decided it was necessary to reverse the nuclear arms race. But how could they break the impasse between themselves? Kennedy was impressed by a method called Graduated and Reciprocated Initiatives in Tension Reduction (GRIT), proposed by the American psychologist Charles Osgood.[1] Instead of trying to negotiate an agreement for each side to make equivalent concessions at the same time, GRIT would allow either side to take the initiative by voluntarily making a significant but affordable peace gesture, then wait for the other side to reciprocate with a similar concession. Step-by-step, the two sides could take turns demonstrating their willingness to move toward peace, each side in its turn reciprocating to the other. Kennedy undertook exactly that approach, announcing that the United States would stop testing nuclear weapons in the atmosphere so long as no other country tested. In response, Khrushchev ended the production of Soviet strategic bombers, established a hotline between the Kremlin and the White House, and signed a treaty limiting nuclear testing: the Partial Test Ban Treaty of 1963.

It was while all these dramatic events were going on that Norman Cousins was astonished to find himself serving as an intermediary between President Kennedy, Pope John XXIII, and Chairman Khrushchev. He later described those momentous meetings in a book aptly titled *The Improbable Triumvirate*.[2]

In this situation Cousins, our first "freelance diplomat," did not offer his services but was asked to serve. He was acquainted with a representative of the Vatican who realized that Cousins had already met Chairman Khrushchev to create a civil society organization. (I will describe it, the Dartmouth Conferences, in the next chapter.) Sensing that Cousins might be an ideal emissary to perform new back-channel negotiations, the priest asked him to go meet with Khrushchev secretly to discuss religious affairs in the Soviet Union.

Cousins, who had a deep interest in religion, agreed to perform this shuttle diplomacy between the pope and the general secretary. However, before setting off on the trip, he visited the White House to ask whether President Kennedy wanted him to convey any message as well. Kennedy asked him to make it clear how much he wanted to overcome the Cold War and the recent Cuban missile crisis. Thus Cousins set off on his travels with two momentous but unrelated diplomatic missions to carry out.

On December 1, 1962, he left for the Vatican to find out what concerns were uppermost there. Besides asking that Christian Soviet citizens be granted improved opportunities for religious practice, Rome also wanted to secure the release of an archbishop of the Ukrainian church who remained in prison for having collaborated with the Nazis.

Next Cousins went to Moscow and spent three hours with Khrushchev, mainly discussing the recent missile crisis. After a time, Cousins proposed the release of the archbishop, but Khrushchev began heatedly describing the actions of the Ukrainian Church during the Nazi occupation. Cousins did not disagree, but claimed that the archbishop should be released from prison on humanitarian grounds, since he was old. Khrushchev saw the point but objected that the bishop would tell the world about the bad conditions of Soviet prisons. Cousins promised that this would not happen. He would talk to the pope and make sure of it. Khrushchev wavered. Then Cousins conveyed Kennedy's message.

Since the missile crisis, Khrushchev was under a lot of pressure from hard-liners who thought he had succumbed to Kennedy's pressure. Indeed, his vulnerability on this account would play a part in his subsequent ouster. Khrushchev believed that the Americans wanted mutual coexistence, but he needed to reach a substantial breakthrough, such as an agreement over a test ban treaty, to prove to his hard-liners that he was not overly trusting. Accordingly, he asked Cousins to tell Kennedy that he was genuinely ready for such a treaty, and that it should be possible to surmount the main obstacle to that goal: disagreement over the type of inspection necessary for each side to be sure that the other was not cheating. He also ordered some Christmas cards for Pope John and President Kennedy, and asked Cousins to deliver them.[3]

Returning to Rome, Cousins went directly with the Christmas greetings to the pope, who was pleased by the turn of events. The archbishop was released from prison, but Cousins's promise was not kept. Newspapers in several countries published stories about the bishop's account of abusive Soviet prison life.

Worse yet, the test ban negotiations in Geneva soon reached an impasse over the question of inspections. Khrushchev, having heard through several back channels that the Americans would be satisfied with three inspections per year, used all his powers of persuasion to get the hard-line members of the Politburo to go along with the plan, though they interpreted his attitude as appeasement. Then he found out that the Americans actually insisted on eight inspections. He felt betrayed, since the misunderstanding was being interpreted in the Soviet Union as proof that the United States was not negotiating honestly.

Again in April 1963 Cousins was sent by the Vatican to ask for the release of a bishop, this time a Czech archbishop, and by Kennedy to find out what had gone wrong with the Geneva negotiations. After a flight to Sochi, Cousins visited Khrushchev in his country house, where they spent most of the day together, strolling, playing badminton, drinking vodka, eating lunch.[4] Yet it was a difficult day. Cousins apologized for the Ukrainian bishop's news leak but pressed on, now requesting the release of the Czech bishop. Khrushchev, who knew nothing of this priest's case, agreed to look into the matter and would, indeed, authorize his release after some weeks. Alice Bobroshova recalls the visit, for as usual she was present to interpret. She said,

> Khrushchev felt he had been deceived, since he had got the impression that the Americans would be satisfied with three inspections. Cousins said, "Let's not talk about how it happened. Let's start again."
>
> Khrushchev said, "No, I don't want to discuss it with you. How would I look to my Council of Ministers? I believe what I was told by them. I can't go back to them again."
>
> Cousins didn't show it in his book—you will not get an impression of how awful he felt. It finished late at night and he said, "I can't leave tomorrow. I must talk with him again." But Khrushchev said no.[5]

When Cousins reported back to Kennedy on April 22, 1963, the President understood Khrushchev's predicament, commenting that he himself was also under similar pressure. The lack of progress in reaching agreements between the two countries strengthens the hard-liners in both so that the DINOSAURS in the Soviet Union and the United States each use the actions of the other to justify their own position. Cousins explained that it was up to Kennedy to break the impasse—and quickly, for a Chinese delegation would visit Moscow within a couple of months and, if no progress had been made on the treaty, Khrushchev would probably have to admit that his coexistence policy was a failure.

Kennedy admitted that this was true, and six weeks later, he delivered a historic commencement speech at American University. That was the occasion when he announced new steps to end the Cold War, promising not to test nuclear weapons in the atmosphere so long as other states did not resume such testing. Then he sent Ambassador Averell Harriman on a mission to Moscow; two weeks later, the Partial Test Ban Treaty was initialed.[6]

At first, it seemed that this treaty could not be ratified by the senate, since public opinion was clearly opposed to it. However, Norman Cousins debated the "father of the Hydrogen bomb," Dr. Edward Teller, on television several times. Public opinion shifted, and by September, the treaty was ratified by a vote of 80 to 19. Cousins, the discreet citizen diplomat, had served his country well, and in so doing may have also preserved humankind.

* * *

At the time, it had seemed that the tide had turned, that the Partial Test Ban Treaty was only the first step among many. It banned nuclear test detonations in the atmosphere, in outer space, and underwater, but allowed testing to continue underground. Most people expected that it would be followed soon by a Comprehensive Test Ban Treaty, but that did not happen. Kennedy was assassinated and public opinion became focused on other matters, including the Vietnam War. The next big advances toward nuclear disarmament would not take place for more than twenty years and would be led by Mikhail Gorbachev.

Yet challenges arose throughout the interim. As everyone could foresee, a full-scale nuclear war would probably be fought with weapons propelled on missiles, and the motivation was growing for weaponeers to devise not only the missiles for offensive attacks but also a defensive system that could knock down the opponent's incoming missiles—a scheme that foreshadowed Ronald Reagan's favorite "Star Wars" system.

The nuclear arsenal kept growing. When I became an anti-nuclear weapons activist in the early 1980s there existed some 50,000 nuclear bombs and the number would increase to a maximum of 70,000. Though nothing was stopping the infernal production line that multiplied these devices, several treaties were negotiated (not all of which were ever ratified) to limit their testing, deployment, and the creation of missiles and anti-missile systems that would deliver them in a war. Several "nuclear weapon free zones" were established where no such weapons could enter. In 1972 and again in 1979 Strategic Arms Limitations Treaties (SALT) were adopted by the two superpowers.

In 1968 there was the Nuclear Non-Proliferation Treaty (NPT), an especially important agreement between the non-nuclear weapon states and the nuclear weapon states whereby those non-nuclear states would not acquire such weapons if they received access to peaceful nuclear technology, and if the five states having weapons would disarm them and move toward general and complete disarmament. Thus, although there was no significant nuclear disarmament until the INF Treaty of 1987 and the START Treaties of 1991 and 1993, there had at least been some modest success in limiting the deployment of weapons.

The most controversial negotiations between the nuclear states involved the banning of anti-ballistic missile defense systems. Already in the 1960s, long before Reagan proposed his Strategic Defense Initiative (SDI or "Star Wars") there was a serious public debate in the West about this subject. Pugwashites, in particular, focused on the issue, as we shall see in the next chapter. And so did a young Harvard mathematician named Jeremy Stone. In 1972 the ABM Treaty did indeed become a reality (probably in part because of his freelance diplomacy) though later the United States would abrogate it for the sake of building an extensive system of missile defenses.

Jeremy Stone

In 1963 Jeremy Stone, the elder son of the journalist I. F. Stone, was a young researcher with nuclear weapons on his mind. He wrote a paper called "Should the Soviet Union Build an Anti-Ballistic Missile System?" His answer was no. In 1964, he presented it to a group of influential Russians and Americans in Cambridge, Massachusetts. The Americans liked his paper, but the Russians did not, so Stone began visiting the Soviet Union on his own to promote his ideas. He and his wife B. J. financed their own travels as tourists, and B. J. learned Russian for the purpose. Between 1966 and 1970 they made five trips—lecturing, lobbying, and presenting Stone's arguments for a treaty banning ABM systems.

Stone, who was then younger than most Pugwash members, felt somewhat rejected by the group, but decided to forge ahead independently. By traveling privately, he managed to form relationships with certain top-level Soviet scientists—notably the Pugwash regulars Mikhail Millionshchikov and Vasily Emelyanov. "They were the transmission belt," he said, "and it wasn't a question of when they changed their tune. It was a question of when they were permitted to express the views that, I think, scientists all along understood."[7]

Initially Stone focused largely on human rights issues; he began speaking up on behalf of Andrei Sakharov in 1973. By then he was president of the Federation of American Scientists (FAS), and was prodding Western scientists to defend Soviet dissidents.[8] After meeting Sakharov in 1976, he encouraged Western scientists to refuse to attend Soviet meetings until dissidents were provided their human rights. However, by 1983 the FAS saw the overriding importance of discussing nuclear issues with Russian scientists, so Stone called off the boycott, but seized every opportunity to speak on behalf of Sakharov.

Stone invented a simplified arms control strategy. He suggested that, once the SALT II treaty was ratified, new complex agreements need not be negotiated to decide upon further cuts. Additional reductions could just be a matter of shrinking each ceiling by a certain percentage annually. Heads of state could negotiate the next steps of disarmament themselves, just by deciding whether to reduce limits set in a treaty like SALT II by perhaps 2 or 7 percent a year. President Carter secretly tried his idea during a summit in Vienna, said Stone.

However, during the early 1980s, arms control was impeded by a new problem: President Reagan's fervent commitment to the Strategic Defense Initiative, which most Soviets feared. By any conventional reading of the ABM treaty, SDI would have been a violation. Still, Reagan refused to trade away his program, even for remarkable Soviet offers, thus stalling negotiations to reduce the numbers of both intermediate-range and strategic (long-range) missiles.

In 1985, addressing forty scientists in Moscow, Stone proposed a way of breaking the impasse. He combined it with his older idea of percentage reductions: "You people are saying that if we go ahead with Star Wars, there can be no disarmament. I agree, but you should turn it around. You should see that if both sides go ahead with disarmament, there can be no Star Wars. Disarmament in and of itself might be the answer to Star Wars. With offensive reductions under way, there would be no political support for Star Wars [in the United States]. . . . Only one number needs to be negotiated—the percentage for annual reduction of SALT II limits."[9]

Stone called his idea a "bear hug." He proposed that the Soviets announce, "Okay, we won't complain about Star Wars. We'll go right ahead with disarmament, but we'll do it on a year-by-year basis, under a continuing agreement. If you go beyond talk and actually violate the ABM treaty in any way, then, boys, we'll stop the agreement."

After Sakharov regained his freedom in 1986 and became influential in nuclear politics, he adopted a version of the bear hug. He argued that SDI was technically unfeasible anyway, and that there was little risk involved. Unlike Stone, however, he proposed that disarmament be halted only if Star Wars were actually deployed. His model, called the "Sakharov finesse," was widely credited for making possible the Strategic Arms Reduction Treaties (START) of 1991 and 1993. In fact, however, it was Stone's version that the Soviets adopted.

Gorbachev and Reagan reached agreement on START I, but only after the world had passed through an even more perilous phase of nuclear confrontation in the 1980s. Both nuclear blocs, NATO and the Warsaw Treaty Organization (WTO), fearing and mistrusting each other, planned to install new missiles in Europe in preparation for an ultimate nuclear holocaust. Millions of activists poured onto the streets around the world, calling for a halt to the madness. Gorbachev and Reagan did begin to move toward disarmament, but after them, the mutual threat of nuclear war continued.

* * *

Still, Jeremy Stone persevered with his personal, freelance negotiations. He offered two more proposals during the Yeltsin and Putin years, both of which came close to succeeding.[10] Partly for the sake of countering potential nuclear capability in North Korea, the United States continued pursuing the development of anti-missile defense systems, which would require them to abrogate Stone's main achievement—the ABM Treaty of 1972. This prospect alarmed the Russians, since a U.S. missile defense system would give them a decisive edge if they chose to launch a first-strike against the Russian arsenal. But Stone offered Yeltsin's newly independent Russia this original solution: the notion that disarmament itself might be the best way of preventing a disarming U.S. attack.

Stone gave this solution a strange but catchy title, "Truncate the Sword and the Shield Becomes Harmless." In 1999 he went to Moscow again and visited Prime Minister Sergei Stepashin. Although, as always personally committed to the ABM Treaty, Stone could foresee its limited future. He had been informed, however, that if the U.S. had no more than 1,000 nuclear warheads, they would not be able to launch a first strike anyway, even if they had a functioning defensive system, for a first strike would require at least 1,000 weapons. Hence, he reasoned, the best approach for Russia would be to reach a treaty limiting itself and the U.S. alike to no more than 1,000 warheads. In exchange for that agreement, they would allow the U.S. to develop a small missile shield, which would not eliminate enough of the Russian missiles to let the shield fulfill its protective purpose against Russia. (It might nevertheless be adequate to defend against a fledgling nuclear state such as North Korea.)

Stepashin liked the idea. He was going to Washington to see President Clinton soon, with whom he promised to broach the subject in the Oval Office. And so he did, but without success. He later explained to Stone that Clinton's response was, "Gore is running for President and he doesn't want any trouble."

Of course, it was George W. Bush, not Gore, who became President, and he was not interested in disarmament. So Stone tried to think of yet another way to preserve his treasured ABM Treaty. After discussing his idea with White House staffers (who sounded negative) he went back to Moscow to try again there.

Stone pitched his new proposal, called "Mothball the ABM" to the chief Russian negotiator, Georgi Mamedov, and then to Yuri Ossipyian, an arms control committee chairman, on September 11, 2001, only hours before the terrorist attack. The basic idea was that Moscow would agree to permit testing of the ABM technology for the next few years if Washington would agree not to withdraw from the ABM Treaty during President George W. Bush's first term. The ABM treaty would still be an official agreement, but would be interpreted so loosely that the U.S. could proceed quite far without abrogating it.

Stone visited everyone influential whom he could reach. All signs looked favorable in Moscow. But the U.S. was mobilizing for war. To Stone's amazement, Secretary of State Condoleezza Rice had reversed her initial rejection and was now favorable to his Mothball plan. President Putin went to visit President Bush at his Texas ranch, but they reached no agreement. It seems that the U.S. side insisted, not merely on the freedom to develop a small ABM system, but any testing that it wanted. Indeed, on December 12, Bush announced his intention to withdraw from the ABM Treaty on six months' notice.

This was one of the issues that spoiled the U.S./Russian relationship, creating what some Russians call, not without justification, "the new Cold War."

Ernst Van Eeghen

When Gorbachev came to power in 1985 some NATO countries were still unde-
cided whether to deploy cruise missiles on their soil as a counter to the continuing Soviet deployment of SS-20 missiles. The Dutch opposition to NATO's missiles was led by the IKV, a coalition of religious organizations coordinated by
Mient Jan Faber, a lanky mathematician-turned-activist, who told me,

> In the Netherlands the peace movement managed to block the deployment of
> cruise missiles. The government had decided to do nothing for a certain period.
> The deadline was the first of November, 1985. If the Soviet Union at that time
> had deployed more than 378 SS-20s, then Holland would deploy NATO's
> forty-eight cruise missiles in the Netherlands. That limit, 378, was chosen be-
> cause it was the number that the Soviets had at that time and the Dutch gov-
> ernment wanted them to stop.

Ernst Van Eeghen was the wealthy head of a trading company owned by his
family for over 300 years. Like most other Dutch churchmen, he felt obliged to
do his utmost to block the nuclear arms race. Unlike most others, however, he
had some influence in the Kremlin, and he decided to try to use it. Having
served as an officer in World War II, he was vice-president of the Dutch war
veterans' association and knew many veterans and military people in other
countries, including the Soviet Union. He had also engaged in numerous major
business deals over the years, through which he had formed friendships in both
the USSR and the United States. On the American side, he was a friend of
Senator Sam Nunn, the head of the Senate Armed Services Committee, and
General David Jones, who had chaired the Joint Chiefs of Staff.[11]

As a devout Christian, Van Eeghen was invited to presidential prayer breakfasts in Washington, a practice that he liked so much that he introduced it to the
Netherlands. In Moscow his friendships deepened, and some of his prominent
friends disclosed the sense that their spiritual needs were unfulfilled by Communism. Van Eeghen prayed with them. Privately, they became Christians.
Among these secret converts was a high-ranking KGB officer.

Mr. Van Eeghen would not tell me about these matters. Informants who
knew him well told me that he never takes credit or puts himself out in front.
They alluded, however, to facts that he never mentioned: that with his friends
occupying decision-making posts in both the Pentagon and the Soviet military
establishment, he was an excellent person to serve as intermediary between
them, and that he did so on matters relating to cruise missiles. As well, Van
Eeghen organized dialogues on a variety of issues, including arms control, between experts in the West and in the Soviet Union.[12]

In 1985, then, Van Eeghen had friends in high places in Moscow—people
with direct access to the Politburo—and he visited them, asking how the new
general secretary might be persuaded to stop deploying missiles. Gorbachev was
still in a period of transition and had not yet indicated his interest in disarmament. According to Mient Jan Faber,

Van Eeghen went there and talked to Arbatov and other people and said, "You have to do something. Please tell Gorbachev and the others that they really have to respect this limit of 378 missiles." He talked to me and I informed some people in the Dutch government that he was doing this kind of thing. I had the feeling that it was not completely hopeless; there was a possibility that he would manage it, because of the kind of man he was. Nobody in the Dutch government believed that. So at the end of October, he went again to Moscow. This was one week before the first of November, the deadline. He was put into a hotel room and Arbatov and other people told him to stay there: "We are now negotiating. It's going quite well with the Gorbachev people and we might succeed." He told me this later.[13] He stayed in the hotel for days. They said, "Don't leave your room. It's still going on. We will do our best. Wait, wait, wait."

So after three days they came back to him and said, "It's okay: 378. No more."

Van Eeghen came back to Holland and rang me. He said, "It's arranged." I couldn't believe it, but he was definite. I went to Amsterdam immediately and we had lunch together. We were happy. And then there came a phone call from Moscow saying that it was not okay. Some people from Gromyko's office in the Foreign Ministry had said, "This is unacceptable."

It failed but I think he almost managed it. Anyway, the Dutch decided on November 1 that we had to deploy. But actually, we never deployed because things were changing so rapidly in the Soviet Union. They were confused. This was a sign that they were in transition that they were even willing to deal with a tradesman. The Netherlands was this intermediary.[14]

I discussed this story of "freelance diplomacy" with Mr. Ruud Lubbers, who had been the prime minister of the Netherlands while the events were going on. He added some details:

Those days I was prime minister. There was a big demonstration in The Hague just before the Cabinet had to come to a conclusion.

As a matter of pure coincidence I received that Friday evening before it a visit of Prime Minister Rajiv Gandhi [of India] and his wife Sonia. They paid me a visit on their trip back from Washington to New Delhi and used that opportunity. As a matter of fact, I had known his mother, Indira Gandhi, very well and that was the reason for their visit.

However, during our conversation Rajiv Gandhi received a telephone call from the Kremlin, urging him to make another stopover in Moscow. While they were very tired, the decision was taken to stay over in The Hague and they flew Saturday morning to Moscow. I used that opportunity to talk over with him the SS-20 problem and asked him to talk it over with Mikhail Gorbachev. He did so and Monday morning he called me from Delhi with the results.

No, Mikhail Gorbachev had no room to reduce the numbers at that very moment, but he invited me if I would take a positive decision on deployment in the Netherlands to arrange that the actual deployment would be somewhat later because he, Gorbachev, saw good possibilities to agree on zero-zero with Washington within one year.

And so it happened. There was a positive decision from the Dutch, but it never came to actual deployment.[15]

If Mr. Van Eeghen failed to limit the Soviets' deployment of SS-20s, he was more successful in the area of human rights. He established the De Burght Conferences, a series of events named after the location of the first meeting, a Dutch resort on the sea. The conferences had a peculiar origin, according to Landrum Bolling, the co-chairman of the group. He explained to me,

> Some Ukrainian Baptists who had settled in Chicago approached their congressmen, asking them to intervene with the Soviets to secure the release of an underground minister, a man named Khailo. He had refused to register with the authorities and his activities therefore were illegal. He had been in prison and mental hospitals for about fifteen years. The congressmen took a petition to Moscow but never got to see any authority. Then they heard of the pious Dutchman so they appealed to Van Eeghen and he agreed to try to help.
>
> He went to Moscow and looked up a friend, a high KGB officer, who said, "I'll see what I can do."
>
> Soon Khailo was released and Van Eeghen went to visit him in his Ukrainian village. He was an impressive person, determined to emigrate to America with his whole family of twenty-nine people.

Van Eeghen and his friend Bolling worked out the arrangements and the family did emigrate. In the course of these negotiations Van Eeghen dealt with Soviet officials in the ministries of justice and foreign affairs who said they would like to be rid of the whole embarrassing problem of religious persecution. But they said,

> We're not going to do it in a way that would cause the Americans to have a propaganda circus against us. We would like to have an international conference on human rights in which we could discuss these things with many countries. Can you arrange some such conference to which we could be invited? Then we could begin to work toward releasing all of these people.

That prompted Mr. Van Eeghen to organize the De Burght conference. He asked Bolling to organize the American delegation. Bolling said,

> I decided to start with Jimmy Carter, whom I know well, because that had been one of his strong interests when he was president. So Mr. Van Eeghen and I flew down to Plains, Georgia, and talked it over with him and Rosalynn. Carter said, "It's a great idea, but I shouldn't be involved in it because I'm too high-profile, but Rosalynn can take part in it." She was willing and I said, "Okay, Rosalynn, you're going to be co-chair of this with a Soviet."
>
> Professor Burlatsky, who was editor of *Literaturnaya Gazeta,* was chairman of the Soviet delegation and Van Eeghen got Madame Giscard d'Estaing to come along. She and Rosalynn were friends. We had an interesting group of parliamentarians and former cabinet ministers from Sweden, Holland, and Italy. On the American side there were three sitting congressmen, two former congressmen, a court of appeals judge, Father Hesburgh, president of Notre Dame University. The Soviet delegation included a Metropolitan from the Orthodox Church, the minister of justice in the Russian Republic, some academics, and

journalists. We also had representatives from Poland, Czechoslovakia, Hungary, and Poland.

In the middle there was a crisis. Without notice, a Protestant pastor from Switzerland came up with a list of about 200 names of people said to be in prison. This upset the Russians and Eastern Europeans. A Czech representative there blew up. But Burlatsky was extremely skillful. He said, "We are surprised at this way of presenting these names and we're not prepared to respond to this. We don't know who these people are, but I assure you that when I get back to Moscow, I will take this up with the proper authorities and we will see what can be done."

Later in 1988 President Carter hosted another meeting in Georgia, followed six months later by a meeting in Moscow. Eventually all 500 known religious persecuted persons were released. Bolling told me in 1994 that the De Burght Conferences were still continuing,

> We got involved in urging them to pass a law on religious freedom. The Supreme Soviet passed a progressive law before it went out of business, but that law has been under attack. . . . There is a strong row going on in the Duma about a [proposed] law that would entrench the Orthodox Church. The Russians are put off by the American evangelists who are swarming in there. Mr. Van Eeghen has just been in Chicago discussing what to do to prevail on the Soviet authorities to pass a more even-handed law.[16]

Ernst Van Eeghen's effectiveness depended, of course, on the existence in the Soviet Union of persons who were as concerned about human rights as he. His most prominent counterpart was Fyodor Burlatsky, a lawyer by training whose name we have already encountered as one of the group of TERMITES who connected with *Problems of Peace and Socialism* in Prague. Burlatsky had served as speechwriter to Khrushchev, Andropov, and Gorbachev.[17] I became well acquainted with Burlatsky and in one of our numerous conversations he gave me additional insights about the reforms that he had led:

> The first problem which Rosalynn Carter explained to us was the problem of the Baptist religious groups who were in prison. After the first conference I had a talk with Mr. Gorbachev, gave him a list of more than 400 prisoners, and asked him to release all of them. In the beginning he refused to do this and told me each case should be investigated separately, but then I argued and he decided to release everybody. He gave this instruction to Mr. Lukyanov, who, as a secretary of Central Committee, managed many services: KGB, and Ministry of Internal Affairs. Everybody was released at that time. It was the first step.
>
> I was elected to the Congress and to Supreme Soviet and I became the president of its sub-committee. I managed this commission, which prepared three drafts of laws: freedom of press and mass media, freedom of religion, and freedom of movement and migration. They were very big commissions which included not just the deputies, but representatives from the Ministry of Defense, the Ministry of Foreign Affairs, the Ministry of Domestic Affairs, from the KGB—all the ministries interested in this topic.

My Western partners helped me as consultants. I sent two drafts of laws to Mrs. Rosalynn Carter and to Mr. Van Eeghen, who was secretary for the International East-West Conference of Human Rights. They gave me many remarks, especially about the draft on freedom of religion and conscience, and the second draft on freedom of movement and migration. I prepared this draft with another commission from our parliament, a commission on law.

Then we had a session of Supreme Soviet—a very big story. Especially this freedom of movement part, because Gorbachev was against it. He worried about a brain drain. Bureaucrats [estimated our loss at] about eight million—the best, our specialists. He told me that Americans now are not interested in this law because they are afraid about Russian immigration.

I had two meetings with the Secretary of State, James Baker. The first was in Washington during a prayer breakfast. I like those prayer breakfasts because it's some sort of community, of national feeling. I asked Mr. Baker to help us influence Gorbachev directly with the freedom of movement issue. And the second time I met him, when he came to Moscow, I understood during our discussion that Mr. Bush had had a talk with Mr. Gorbachev on James Baker's advice. After this, Gorbachev changed his mind and decided okay. But he told me, "Please, let's compromise." We discussed this in the spring of 1991. I said okay and then the last draft of the law was adopted. Every human rights law we prepared had a very big struggle.

* * *

We have reviewed the bold peace activism of three freelance diplomats. They are not typical of Western peaceniks, of course, but were able to be effective precisely because of their connections with Soviet TERMITES who did not lack power. It is stretching a point to call Nikita Khrushchev a "TERMITE," or, as such people sometimes called themselves, a "half-dissident," but he was vastly more flexible and fair than his predecessors or immediate successors as general secretary.

As we shall see in the next chapter, Cousins developed excellent connections with numerous other genuine Soviet TERMITES, such as Georgi Arbatov. Real trust developed through contacts in the transnational civil society organization that he founded.

For his part, Jeremy Stone acquired good, trusting relationships with several eminent Soviet Termites who were also active in Pugwash—Millionshchikov and Emelyanov—as well as with the preeminent BARKING DOG, Sakharov. Van Eeghen almost succeeded in turning the tide of the nuclear arms race because of his connection to the remarkable TERMITE Arbatov. He did achieve a remarkable change in democratizing Soviet society through his connection with yet another TERMITE, Fyodor Burlatsky.

These high-level Soviet TERMITES did not necessarily find it easy to carry out democratic or peace-oriented reforms. There were risks involved, though perhaps not such serious ones as the BARKING DOGS incurred. I asked Fyodor Burlatsky more about the challenges confronting leading TERMITES such as himself. He explained that he had been "pushed" from his jobs three times:

First was 1967 when I published an article against the dictatorship. I was a political observer with the newspaper *Pravda* and they pushed me from this position. The second was in the Institute of Sociology. Mr. Rumyantsev and I created it together. He was president, I was vice-president. We worked together
from 1969 till 1972. Then they pushed all of us, about 140 sociologists. The
third time was in 1975 when I started to create political science in our country.
I published an article in 1965 and created a political science sector inside the
Institute of State and Law. They pushed me from this position too and abolished the sector. It was the Brezhnev epoch.[18]

I asked Burlatsky how he had decided to work on the human rights commission in 1988, and how much support he had enjoyed. He replied,

I was a lawyer and all my publications, even during Khrushchev's time, were
about democracy and the process of democratization, especially about human
rights, juries, courts, and such questions. That's why I had this in mind. I published many books and articles in Aesop's style. I published a biography of
Mao Tse Tung and everybody understood at that time that it's not just about
Mao Tse Tung but Stalin too. I published a book about Machiavelli, and everybody understood that it's just not about the prince in Italy, but about the cult of
personality of Russia. Not just I, but many of us did it this way. That's why I
was prepared and I just used the chance.

The decision came when I asked Mr. Gorbachev indirectly (Mr.
Shakhnazarov helped me), and Gorbachev said it was okay if we created this
commission. That was important because before this time I was like a Party
dissident. People could not support me officially but [they could] after we created this commission. That's why the initiative came from me.

Of course, there was a big influence from the Helsinki Commission. The
very important first conference was in Moscow in 1988 when people came
from different countries—the Helsinki Watch Commission, the American Congress, and Amnesty International. Reagan, Bush, Margaret Thatcher—all of
them—emphasized that human rights problems are very important for Soviet-
European relations.

* * *

How much influence did prominent Western individuals have in Soviet policies?
The instances I have cited here may be almost unique or may reflect a fairly
common phenomenon. We can never say with certainty. Anyway, it is probably
impossible to measure influence or power directly, since often it is wielded in an
implicit, invisible way. For example, there is *potential* power, which has the
strange property of being self-fulfilling. People often avoid clashing with others
who may not appear overtly intimidating at all, if they are believed *capable* of
wielding power. Hence power may never have been demonstrated overtly in any
contest, but if it is attributed to a person or group, if may have extreme effects.[19]
Manifest conflicts and the open use of power to dominate others are only the
visible tip of an iceberg.

Influence actually works in many other ways—some of them so subtle that
people do not even realize that they *have been* affected. Influence is expressed

even in the way that questions are formulated, or in the way they are ignored. Unfortunately, there is rarely any empirical way to gauge this kind of influence.

Norman Cousins succeeded in negotiating the release of some Czech bishops, but failed to persuade Khrushchev to accept a higher number of on-site inspections that would make a comprehensive test ban treaty possible.

Ernst van Eeghen tried to block the deployment of the last SS-20 missiles, which would have prevented the Netherlands from accepting cruise missiles. He came close, but not close enough. He had more success, however, in negotiating the release of a religious figure and creating the institutions by which Soviet human rights became protected by effective laws. For that achievement, he wins a very good score.

But scorekeeping is meaningless, for we cannot know what *might* have happened if what *did* happen had *not* happened. Van Eeghen, Stone, Cousins, and numerous others were able to get close enough to the centers of Soviet power to "make their pitch." When a good idea is added to a discourse, we should normally assume that this is beneficial. However, one person alone is rarely influential in any single issue.

The peace workers we have considered made a difference because they had counterparts in the Soviet Union—people such as Fyodor Burlatsky, Georgi Arbatov, and the pious Christian KGB general whom I shall not name here. Our friends in high places had good ideas and were convincing when they promoted them. But no one owns ideas. When they are working their effects, they are just "in the air." Ideas, taking the shape of words, are propelled through the air, whether by sound waves or by satellites in space. We can launch them and give them a vigorous push. After that, God only knows where all they will go. And when they have done their job, only God may know from whence they came.

Notes

1. Charles E. Osgood, *An Alternative to War or Surrender* (Urbana: University of Illinois Press, 1962). Amitai Etzioni suggested the same approach at about that time.

2. Norman Cousins, *The Improbable Triumvirate: John F. Kennedy, Pope John, Nikita Khrushchev.* (New York: Norton, 1972).

3. His interpreter, Alice Bobroshova, told me that in his book, Cousins makes the Christmas card business seem offhand. It was not. She recalls sitting with him in the Hotel Metropol, anxiously waiting for those cards to be delivered, since his plane would be leaving soon and he thought they were so important that he would not go without them.

4. Gale Warner and Michael Shuman, *Citizen Diplomats: Pathfinders in Soviet-American Relations—And How You Can Join Them* (New York: Continuum, 1987), 243.

4. He served as a roving trade ambassador under President Kennedy with great effect. Cousins, 175.

5. Alice Bobroshova, in discussion with the author, 1994, Moscow.

6. Warner and Shuman, 177–78.

7. Jeremy Stone, in discussion with the author, April 1995.

8. For a discussion of his views about human rights, see Jeremy J. Stone, *Every Man Should Try: Adventures of a Public-interest Activist* (New York: Public Affairs, 1999).

9. Strobe Talbott, *The Master of the Game* (New York: Vintage, 1988), 261.

10. Stone describes his efforts on his NGO's web site, catalytic-diplomacy.org (accessed April 20, 2010).

11. Landrum Bolling, in telephone discussion with the author, spring 1994.

12. Mient Jan Faber's interview is the source of much of this information. Faber was not accepted by the Soviets as a participant in such dialogues, however, because of his close connection to dissidents. Hylke Tromp, a Dutch peace researcher and a board member of IKV, helped in organizing these dialogues.

13. Arbatov alludes to the Netherlands' decision in his memoirs, saying "I tried in vain to persuade Georgi Kornienko and Akhromeyev—this was already in Gorbachev's time—to slow down, if only a little, the number of SS-20s being deployed, bearing in mind that the Netherlands was committed to forbid the deployment of American cruise missiles on its territory if the number of our SS-20s did not go above a certain ceiling." Georgi Arbatov, *The System* (New York: Times Books, 1992), 206–07.

14. Mient Jan Faber, in discussion with the author, 1993, Ankara. I also heard a slightly different version of the same story from a leading Belgian peace activist, Robert De Gendt, who had been in Moscow trying to negotiate a similar deal for Belgium. The outcome of course was the same.

15. Ruud Lubbers, e-mail message to the author, February 4, 2010.

16. Landrum Bolling, in telephone discussion with the author, May 1994.

17. Burlatsky would again lose his position in 1991 as editor of *Literaturnaya Gazeta* after the August coup attempt for allegedly not having protested against the plotters in print. Bolling, who knows him well, looked into the evidence and insists that his behavior was faultless in this matter. According to Bolling's Moscow informants, Burlatsky, who was away on vacation at the time, instructed his subordinates by phone to publish a protest against the coup. Instead, they published a pro-coup editorial, for which he was unjustly blamed.

18. Interview with Fyodor Burlatsky, April 1996, Toronto.

19. Robert Dahl, *Who Governs? Democracy and Power in an American City* (New Haven: Yale University Press, 1961).

Chapter 6: A Civil Society: Elite Bears and Doves

People often call Russia a "bear" but Russians don't seem to mind. They were more like teddy bears during the 1980s when they met us "pigeons"—the Western peace activists. (Russian-speakers do not distinguish between a pigeon and a dove; both are called "golub.") Friendship and a cordial civil society grew up between Teddy Bears and Doves.

These friendships were between Soviet and Western elites, not average citizens. Ordinary Western peace activists had no contact with Soviet officials, high or low, and certainly did not expect to influence their decisions. But that is what the civil society of elite bears and doves actually accomplished.

Peace Movements, East and West

I'll begin not with these elite peaceniks but with the huge mass movements on both sides. Even in Warsaw Pact countries, some demonstrations were enormous. For example, I was one of thousands of Westerners invited to a peace event in Prague in 1983, the "World Assembly for Peace and Life, Against Nuclear War," which filled all the posh hotels. We guests received lavish gifts, banquets, pieces of children's art, and excursions to bathe at the spa in Karlovy Vary. Throngs of Czechs lined Prague's streets, waving identical paper flags (no homemade banners). There was a scuffle near the platform as the female cosmonaut Valentina Tereshkova spoke. Some protesters had tried to hoist a sign calling attention to the plight of repressed dissidents (including, I later learned, Václav Havel, who would become the country's beloved president after the Velvet Revolution). But these protesters were quickly arrested and hustled away.

Our Czech and Slovak hosts were desperately afraid of nuclear weapons—no less so than my Canadian and American friends—and they longed to reunite the two halves of Europe. One young reporter interviewed me. When I mentioned democracy he agreed with me but admitted he couldn't publish my remarks unless he could figure out how to "propagandize" them.

Western mass movements were different, though also animated by strong feelings. For example, in 1982 I was one of a million people who paraded through Manhattan to rally in Central Park. Some "Hibakusha" women—victims of the atomic blasts in Hiroshima or Nagasaki—were standing at a curb. I stopped there and apologized to one of them, recalling with shame my joy, at age fourteen, on hearing about the bombing of her city. We hugged, weeping.

The placards in Western demonstrations were homemade. Instead of receiving gifts we paid our own way and often slept on the floor of another activist's apartment. Western speeches differed from those in the Eastern rallies. Speakers on both sides criticized the United States and NATO's nuclear arms, but only those addressing Western rallies also criticized the WTO bloc for their nukes.

In the U.S. there were large organizations such as SANE and the Freeze Campaign. In Britain the Campaign for Nuclear Disarmament (CND), revived public concern, led by Bruce Kent. In Western Europe national organizations sprang up, such as the Dutch inter-church group (IKV) and the international European Nuclear Disarmament (END), which held a conference each summer.

END was led by the eminent English historian E. P. Thompson; a British political scientist, Mary Kaldor; and the Dutch leader of IKV, Mient Jan Faber. END sought not only to stop the nuclear arms race but also to liberate millions of Europeans from communist regimes To put Europe back together again, its agenda promoted freedom and democracy.

In 1990 Kaldor, Faber, and a Serbian woman, Sonja Licht, formed the Helsinki Citizens Assembly (HCA), which also sought to stimulate changes from below. HCA urged the establishment of civil society in Eastern Europe.

The mass-based Western anti-nuclear movements expected to have no influence on the military and political leaders in Moscow, and END and HCA were especially remote from the centers of East bloc power; they cultivated contacts with dissidents instead of government officials. That is, they aligned with the Eastern European equivalents of BARKING DOGS instead of TERMITES. Therefore END and HCA leaders were not invited to peace conferences in Moscow until *perestroika* was well advanced. Later they would enjoy considerable influence because of their friendship with Eastern European dissidents who came to power after the peaceful revolutions of 1989. In Russia, genuine BARKING DOGS never came to power, so END and HCA never took root there.

The Cold War was ended by two dissimilar kinds of influences. In the West, intellectual peaceniks barely influenced any of the governments participating in NATO. It was mass-based, popular movements of voters in the streets who finally had some impact on these governments. But in the East, where there was no authentic grassroots peace movement of significant size until the late 1980s, the rulers paid surprisingly close attention to the suggestions of democratic-minded intellectuals—indigenous TERMITES—who in turn were keenly attuned to the ideas of Western political scientists and peace researchers. The Soviets were more elitist than Western politicians. Theirs was a "revolution from above."

At that time, Western activists believed that they had no influence at all, for they certainly were not invited to the White House or 10 Downing Street for discussions with the leaders. However, David Cortright published a book arguing that the grassroots movement had won, if we compare the positions taken by Ronald Reagan at the start and end of his presidency, as the Cold War ended.[1]

There is a widespread belief in America that it was Reagan, not Gorbachev, who took the initiative to end the nuclear arms race. That is patently false. Reagan came to office in 1981 pledging to achieve "technological and military superiority" over the Soviet Union. Superiority—not mere parity! This remained an objective for his advisers, who, had they wanted to, even during the Brezhnev years, could have reached an arms control agreement with the Soviet Union that was as good as the INF Treaty of 1987.

Two factors arose that forced Reagan to change. First, his nuclear policies brought thousands of protesters into the streets. Films were shown on TV and town meetings were held that changed public opinion away from his militaristic views. And second, Reagan became involved in the famous "Iran/Contra" scandal in 1986. Senior members of his administration were trying to help Iran obtain arms, in violation of an embargo, in exchange for the release of hostages and the funding of Nicaraguan Contra fighters. Some members of his cabinet were charged and convicted. This scandal ruined Reagan's popularity, and in an effort to repair it, he began to adopt the disarmament policies that the voters wanted. Cortright, among others, attributes the U.S. willingness to end the Cold War to these two developments. If, as he suggests, the American peace movement pushed the government to change, it was an indirect victory, not one in which peace activists were ever invited to meet political leaders face-to-face.[2]

Moscow's policies, on the other hand, were influenced by prestigious Western "doves" and elite "bear" friends in transnational civil society organizations that I'll explore here. (Forgive my mixing of all these animal metaphors.)

Let's consider the impact of two elite transnational civil society organizations: the International Physicians for the Prevention of Nuclear War and the Dartmouth Conferences. The former was open to all physicians and other health-care professionals, but its influence mainly came from intense lobbying by its highly influential leaders. The latter was a small exclusive club.

As the experienced negotiator Landrum Bolling described his Soviet counterparts in the elite Dartmouth Conferences, "They obviously want to be in touch with U.S. 'ruling circles.' The more our delegation seems to be plugged into our national establishment, the better the Soviets like it."[3] The Soviets wanted to meet with former high government officials, leaders of industry, and academics with ties to government. They were particularly fascinated by David Rockefeller, who regularly participated in the meetings.[4]

The Dartmouth Conferences
You met Normal Cousins in the preceding chapter, which recounted the effectiveness of elite, highly motivated individual peace activists. But Cousins was also remarkably effective in organizing and leading *groups*. As early as 1960 he launched a particularly influential organization, the Dartmouth Conferences.

Cousins was a peacenik *par excellence*. He had been one of the founders of the United World Federalists, had participated in founding SANE, and had enlisted the most honored Christian humanitarian of his day, Dr. Albert Schweitzer, in calling for a halt to the risky nuclear tests.

As the editor of *Saturday Review*, Cousins had published editorials during the 1940s promoting world government. In response, Dwight Eisenhower had written letters of support, and they had become friends. In 1958, President Eisenhower asked Cousins to set up a small group of private citizens in both the Soviet Union and the United States for "people-to-people" discussions. Cousins was already planning to go to the USSR in 1959 for a series of lectures, so he proposed the idea to the Soviet Peace Committee. His original plan was to organize grassroots meetings between citizens, but the Soviets regarded contacts with ordinary citizens as out of the question. They did not rule out meetings of elites, though nobody expected any to be approved.

I interviewed Cousins's interpreter Alice Bobroshova in 1994. She was a researcher at the Institute of USA and Canada with thirty-four years experience in the Dartmouth Conferences. She described with affection Norman Cousins, her old friend who had died in 1990: "He stimulated me. When I was with him I felt so interesting!. . . Norman Cousins was the greatest experience of my life."

Bobroshova recalled that during the first meeting with officials, when he proposed the conference, Cousins mentioned the good changes he had observed in the Soviet Union. He also said that he couldn't keep silent about things that he considered completely wrong, such as their involvement in Hungary. He was delighted when they approved the proposed conferences. Bobroshova said,

> But then the U2 spy plane happened. Khrushchev had to go to Paris. Everything fell through and we thought that all our efforts were in vain. There were articles in *Pravda* against it. There were always factions in the Central Committee. I think that Khrushchev himself [saved the plan].[5]
>
> The head of the Soviet delegation was Alexander Korneitchuk, a Ukrainian playwright who was at one time President of Ukraine. Some people didn't like him. He was very open—maybe not very sincere, but he could be a nice guy. Though they were like two poles in their differences (Norman was so critical of communism!) Korneitchuk and Cousins complemented each other. I think the success of the first conference was because they were so good with each other. It was a kind of chemistry. Korneitchuk didn't speak a single word of English and Norman didn't speak a word of Russian, but they got along.
>
> The American group included Walt Rostow, Philip Mosely, and Agnes de Mille. We had one of our cinema producers and a general secretary of the Baptist church here, and they had their counterparts. It took place at Dartmouth College in 1960. The conferences were closed; no press people were there until the end. The idea was that it should be away from cities. People lived together for a week, then a few days before and after. They would play tennis, go for walks together. The first time, there were two simultaneous interpreters. Later we had all the proper equipment and there were four interpreters from each side from the United Nations. At the first conference very few Russians knew English, but later we tried to get people who did. Language was never a problem.
>
> It was difficult for the Soviet group. This was a whole new idea of how to talk to each other. It was not supposed to be a confrontation or a defense of the policies of your own government, but to learn to understand each other and find a way out of these old confrontations. The agenda addressed the most vital problems of the time: disarmament, nuclear weapons, the development of trade, and later on, ecological problems. The same problems were discussed all over

the world, but in the 1970s these conferences were important. These people were experts in their field. They could influence their government.

These topics were [covered] in official negotiations but there you can't retreat. Everybody feels that they are representing their government. As in a war, your country is depending on you not to back up a step.

But this was different. At any new conference, the majority were always the old people who knew the ways. We would involve some new people but explain to them first not to be defensive. You had to learn to yield in some ways.

The Dartmouth meetings were bilateral: limited to Americans and Soviets. Unlike the Soviet participants, the Americans did not represent their government (they freely criticized it) but none of them held radical views. This conservatism was not off-putting to the Soviets. In fact, Alice Bobroshova admitted that she preferred this group to the supposedly more congenial western leftists. She said,

I often had to work with "our friends," the American Communists. They didn't have hard ground under them. But when the Dartmouth Conferences started, those people were sure of themselves. They understood that the other side was not an enemy; the other side had its own ideals.

But with the Communist visitors here—well, we tried to show them the best, but you can't hide everything, so I had to defend everything. Our favorite year to refer to was 1913, so I would say that in 1913, 90 percent had been illiterate and now only one percent are illiterate. In 1913, there were *this* many of something, and now there are *this* many. Of course, there *had* been such changes. But the costs! Millions of lives![6]

George Sherry, the chief interpreter for the conferences but whose main job was as assistant-secretary-general at the United Nations, described Dartmouth:

Of course, there is constant talk. There are discussions at meals and sitting around—trying to push forward this Dartmouth process, which is designed to facilitate understanding, but in a very realistic and serious way. None of the silly peacenik stuff! And I would say that it has had an enormous impact on the Russians.[7]

If "peacenik stuff" seemed silly to some American participants, it did not seem so to the founder, Norman Cousins, or to Georgi Arbatov, who ran the Soviet half of Dartmouth during most of its life. Both men promoted views that many within their respective governments regarded as radical nuclear pacifism.

I wondered how far the Soviet participants could go in expressing disagreement with their government's position. According to Alice Bobroshova,

They could never say, "My government is wrong." Sometimes they would say, in small ways, "Maybe our government could do things a little bit differently," but they couldn't give up the idea that it was "my country, right or wrong." The Americans could criticize their government quite freely.

The meetings were always bilateral, though some problems were global. Some new organizations arose from a Dartmouth Conference, such as the American-Soviet Trade and Economic Council. Donald Kendall of Pepsi was involved in that, and some people from the U.S. Chamber of Commerce.

Some arms control ideas began there. There were generals from both sides, such as David Jones, Chairman of the Joint Chiefs of Staff. Also, Brent Scowcroft, Graham Allison, and Zbigniew Brzezinski.

Unlike academic conferences, the participants did not present papers. Statements were limited to about ten minutes on each side to get a conversation going on a particular subject and, after that, nobody spoke longer than four or five minutes. The ground rules called for dialogue, no speeches.[8]

In the spring of 1961 the Soviets hosted the Americans in the Crimea. Cousins said he had observed there some changes in the Soviets' views of war. Marxists had always held that war was inevitable between the socialist and capitalist countries, but the nature of nuclear war was such that the Soviets were beginning to regard coexistence as necessary and possible.[9]

While the third conference was being prepared, a new crisis erupted between the superpowers over the stationing of American troops in Berlin. Informally, both countries had been observing a moratorium on nuclear testing. In August, 1961, the Soviets responded to the Berlin crisis by announcing that they were forced to resumed testing. Cousins and Korneitchuk appealed to each other by cable, but without success. Korneitchuk defended his country's resumption of testing and reproached Cousins for stating in the *Saturday Review* that people everywhere should protest those tests. In his reply Cousins pointed out that if it had been the U.S. that had announced plans to resume tests unilaterally, he would have done everything possible to persuade them not to do so. "Our hope is that advocates of peace inside the Soviet Union are prepared to do the same."[10]

But they were not. Relations between the two countries continued to deteriorate, with the U.S. then resuming its own nuclear tests. In view of this bleak climate, the third Dartmouth Conference was delayed until October 21–27, 1962.

* * *

The delegates arrived at a preparatory school in Andover, Massachusetts just at the outset of the Cuban missile crisis. President Kennedy's television announcement of a naval blockade of Soviet military shipments to Cuba made it apparent that nuclear war was imminent. The worried Soviet delegates discussed the situation among themselves and both delegations called their own governments. Officials told them that it might be useful for private citizens to work on the question too, so the Soviets decided against leaving for home. All week the issue was debated. The Soviet delegation was headed by a scientist, Yevgeny Fedorov, who argued that the Soviet missiles in Cuba were needed to keep Americans from invading the island. The conference participants established a communication channel between Moscow and Washington, mediated by Pope John XXIII, through whom several useful messages were passed.[11]

Even as their political differences sharpened, the American and Soviet delegates became more positive toward each other personally. Their impact on decisions was marginal, but they stayed together unceasingly, trying to solve a life-and-death problem for all humankind. On the last day, Cousins invited them to his home for dinner, where they learned that the crisis had passed; Kennedy and Khrushchev had reached an agreement.[12] They cheered and toasted each other, recognizing that they had formed a partnership for work that was far from over.

It was during the next few months that Cousins carried on the "freelance diplomacy" between Kennedy, Khrushchev, and the pope, as described in the previous chapter. These were part of the negotiations that resulted in the Partial Test Ban Treaty—the first real breakthrough in stopping the nuclear arms race.

Making the most of this, Kennedy began planning to offer the Soviets nuclear non-proliferation terms, a staged disarmament program, a strengthening of the United Nations, and security agreements for Berlin and Southeast Asia.

These accomplishments were not to be fulfilled, however. Kennedy was assassinated, Khrushchev was ousted, and Pope John XXIII died. When the fourth Dartmouth Conference met in June 1964, the relations between the superpowers had again begun to deteriorate and soon thereafter the American side was actively waging war in South Vietnam, while the Soviets were supplying weapons to the North Vietnamese. Between 1964 and 1968, no Dartmouth meetings were held. Cousins kept trying to organize one, but Korneitchuk refused to do so until the Americans stopped bombing North Vietnam.[13]

In 1969 the conferences started again in Rye, New York, with some changes. Whereas formerly the Ford Foundation had sponsored the meetings financially, from that point onward, it was the Kettering Foundation that paid the bills and handled the administration for the U.S. side. In the Soviet Union, the organizing was transferred to Georgi Arbatov's Institute for USA and Canada; Arbatov led the delegations, which included people from IMEMO and other research institutes.[14] Agendas became more oriented toward specific issues, including trade and economic relations, science, and environment, plus regional tensions in such places as the Middle East. In 1975 a Dartmouth task force proposed a solution to the Arab-Israeli conflict that was incorporated in a joint agreement announced two years later by the governments of the two nations. This agreement did not please the American Jewish community, however, so the U.S. government dropped it. By 1979, the Soviet participants in Dartmouth XII objected that they were being kept out of the Middle East negotiations.[15]

Harold Saunders, who had been assistant secretary of state for the Near East and South Asia, became co-chair of Dartmouth's task force on regional conflict in 1981, and the Afghanistan War was added to that task force's agenda in 1986. The Soviet co-chair was Yevgeny Primakov. Afghanistan was perhaps the topic about which Dartmouth made the largest impact in changing participants' interpretations. As Harold Saunders told me,

> When I first joined, the Soviets were still absolutely inconvincible when Americans said that the Soviet invasion of Afghanistan had put the final nail in the coffin of the SALT II exercise. The Soviets said, look, Afghanistan is a

faraway place. It has nothing to do with U.S.-Soviet arms control or the arms race. Jimmy Carter wanted to renege on the SALT II treaty and he just used Afghanistan as an excuse.

The American response was: You don't understand how the American body politic works. There is no way that an American government could ratify through the Senate of the United States a treaty vitally affecting the interests of the United States when the American people had seen the Soviet invasion of Afghanistan as a major breach—perhaps *the* major breach—of international law since the Cold War, since '48 or '49, except for Hungary and Czechoslovakia. Therefore, Americans are saying, we just don't trust those people. We don't want anything to do with them. [The effort from this side] was try to get the Soviets to see that the U.S.-Soviet relationship had to take account of American citizens' perceptions of Soviet actions, and the mistrust or trust that would build up. Ultimately, Gorbachev was smart enough to see that and in a December 1988 speech to the United Nations, he addressed it directly. But, in '81, the Soviets were inconvincible.

The same people, Vitaly Zhurkin for one of them, who took that line in '81 were acknowledging by '83 or '84 the linkage of issues. They didn't like the word "linkage" because Kissinger had used it, but they began to change their minds about the way U.S. policy-making toward the Soviet Union worked. . . [16]

Dartmouth input on the Afghanistan War was well-received. In his memoirs, Georgi Arbatov recounts having returned from a Dartmouth meeting in 1980 with Yuri Zhukov and going to see Brezhnev. They told him that "our intervention in Afghanistan was ruining détente and helping the American extreme right in the forthcoming elections. We persuaded him to make a symbolic gesture by recalling ten percent of our contingent from Afghanistan."[17]

The regional conflicts task force had an Afghan specialist who spent time in the analytical office of the Soviet Foreign Ministry and the Oriental Studies Institute. One Saturday morning, Saunders recalls, he and his task force went to see Yuli Vorontsov, the second level person in the Foreign Ministry, who was shortly to become Soviet Ambassador to Afghanistan. For two hours Vorontsov questioned them about that country, for the next day, U.S. Secretary of State George Shultz was coming to Moscow to talk about Afghanistan. Vorontsov sought their opinion about what might happen in Afghanistan if the Soviet troops pulled out. The task force argued that the Najibullah government did not have wide support.

One shouldn't assume that, because the Western participants regarded the Dartmouth meetings as fruitful, their Soviet partners would necessarily think so too. To check whether this was so, I asked the impression of several people from the Soviet side. Georgi Arbatov had already made his opinion clear in his memoirs, noting that the meetings "seriously helped my institute, and me personally, to become familiar with various American points of view on extremely important questions of foreign, military, and economic policy." I also asked Vladimir Petrovsky, formerly deputy foreign minister, who was, when I first interviewed him, under-secretary-general of the United Nations, with responsibility for disarmament affairs. He told me,

I participated in Dartmouth nearly from the very beginning. The Dartmouth meetings, for me, were of particular importance because they helped me to understand the political thinking in the West in all its aspects, from right to left. It was one of the most educational meetings. I have very good feelings about it. I was participating even as a young diplomat. I participated in the first meeting with the famous Ukrainian writer, Korneitchuk. . . All these groups—Pugwash, Dartmouth—brought fresh air.

This view was echoed by Harold Saunders, who told me,

If you look at the people who wrote the articles and speeches between 1985 and 1988 or so that became called the "New Political Thinking" in Moscow, you'll find that virtually every one of those authors on the Russian side had been part of Dartmouth or one or two of the other parallel dialogues—the UN Association or Graham Allison's group at Harvard. I remember one time Arbatov was asked what the most important product of Dartmouth had been and his answer was, "The people whose minds have changed." I think when Vitaly Zhurkin and Primakov and others wrote their articles, you can't say that they adopted one particular idea at one particular moment—but their way of thinking had changed.

International Physicians for the Prevention of Nuclear War

Everyone—even the head of a government—needs a doctor. Those who doctor people in high places may be influential. Two such physicians were Yevgeny Chazov, whose patients included Brezhnev, Andropov, Chernenko, and Gorbachev, and Bernard Lown, whose patients since about 1980 have included Georgi Arbatov. Together these two men created an international organization that contributed significantly to ending the Cold War: International Physicians for the Prevention of Nuclear War (IPPNW). In 1985 the organization received the Nobel Peace Prize. In 1994, Bernard Lown told me how this all came about:

The IPPNW emerged largely because of a sense of desperation in my personal life. I had founded Physicians for Social Responsibility in 1961 and had been the first president for about nine years, but by 1978 it was clear that we had failed. We had made no impact on public opinion; in fact, the arms race had intensified under Carter. Everywhere we were stalemated by five words: "You can't trust the Russians." I heard that phrase a thousand times over. So the idea came up of working with the Soviet physicians and establishing a model of cooperation and trust-building. It was fortunate that I was able to reach out to Yevgeny Chazov, the physician to Brezhnev.

   Chazov was initially very opposed to getting involved in this. We had been good friends for twenty years, having worked together in cardiology. The medical profession has links that transcend boundaries in a way that made intimacy and trust like very few other professions. When I came to Chazov, he supported the formation of a global movement but was opposed to his own personal involvement—for legitimate reasons. He felt that we would be tilting at windmills and undermining our own professional careers. The movement would become politicized and we would be destroyed. This kind of black pre-

diction is typically Russian! We argued for many hours and finally he agreed to
work with me. It was March of 1980.

From the moment Chazov got involved, he began to speak out. He was
one of the first to go on Soviet television late in 1981 to talk about the nuclear
issue. This was courageous because, although the Soviets were spouting all the
time about how they are for peace, they never encouraged any discussion of
nuclear disarmament. A number of them told me that this was because they
were afraid of undermining support for the military. But by speaking out,
Chazov began to crack this intractable apparatus.

In 1982, I think it was, Chazov decided to speak to the Central Committee
on this issue. First he had to submit his speech to Suslov, the head of ideology.
They said it was no good and sort of rewrote it. Chazov got upset, and because
Brezhnev was out of town, reached Chernenko, who encouraged him to give
his original talk. Suslov was perhaps the second-most powerful man in the Soviet Union, but Chazov ignored him and gave his talk. Afterward there was silence, and then Brezhnev ambled over to the podium and said, "Those are the
most sensible words we have heard in a long time." Chazov then got a standing
ovation.

During those years we began to shape public opinion in America. By
1983, there was deep thinking in the American establishment about it. The reason I know this is that we had requested a message from Reagan [to the IPPNW
conventions] in 1981 and '82 and he had refused, but in 1983 he sent us a message. It made one categorical statement: "Nuclear war cannot be won and must
never be fought."

We blazoned that statement in neon and complimented the White House.
There had been people like [George Herbert Walker] Bush acting like, well, we
can absorb 40 million casualties. They did not just have a change of heart; they
had to placate a large, restive public. This became a clarion call a year later in
the elections when Reagan used it all over the place: "Nuclear war cannot be
won and must never be fought."

The third Congress of IPPNW was in Amsterdam in 1983. Lown invited
Yevgeny Velikhov, who later became the science advisor to Gorbachev. Lown
was urging him to organize a "think tank" on nuclear issues, for he could see
that the Soviets had no idea how to get out of the impasse. They were reacting to
British and American position papers instead of thinking it out independently.
Lown told me,

They'd take a paper that we gave last year and sort of put the Soviet imprimatur
on it. At the third congress, I introduced Velikhov to [Princeton physicist]
Frank von Hippel and told them to get to work on it together, which they did.
They made a major contribution.

It seemed to me that if we depend on arms controllers, we are doomed. So
in 1983 in Amsterdam, I proposed in a sentence, without elaborating, a new
policy—Unilateral Reciprocating Initiatives—as a substitute to arms control.
That will loom large as time moves on.

I was testing this idea in '83, going back and forth to Moscow all the time.
I made about thirty-five trips in ten years. It did not have a warm reception
there. They said, "Okay, suppose we take an initiative. The Americans do not
respond. Where do we go from there?" My answer was: *more initiatives.*

"But say we've disarmed completely. Then what happens?"

I said, "The public will step in at some point." They didn't buy that.

In 1984 I prepared two talks for our Congress. One dealt with trusting the Soviets in our intertwined destinies. The other dealt with unilateral initiatives. Chazov got frantic. He did not want me to give the unilateral initiatives speech because any speech given by me was regarded as a joint statement and he knew damn well that any statement by him had to be approved by the Politburo. It would imply that this is Soviet policy.

The talks were for two sessions: a private session for the organization and a public plenary in a bigger hall with [Greek Prime Minister] Papandreou, the Mexican Nobel laureate, Garcia Robles, the Finnish prime minister, and a lot of politicians. Chazov did not want me to give it there. He said, "Give it to the IPPNW people instead."

After the Congress, I urged our executive director to circulate the speech and Chazov objected. I went to Moscow to argue with him that we must address this issue and that the first step in the unilateral initiative must be a cessation of nuclear tests. That is the first visible step. This was late '83. He said, "I'm sick and tired of listening to you talk like this because they are never going to agree to it." I said, "Well, thank you for agreeing with me personally, anyway. Whom should I meet in the Soviet Union?"

He introduced me to a lot of arms control guys and Central Committee members, but he refused to come along. I talked with them, including Dobrynin. Most of the scientists absolutely supported me: Goldansky, Velikhov, Sagdeev, the people in the USA/Canada Institute. I got a cold reception from only one guy: Alexander Bessmertnykh, who was then deputy foreign minister. He was articulate and sophisticated. He said, Suppose we do as you say. We stop the nuclear tests. It makes a headline and then nothing else appears in the press. After six, eight, or nine months, America makes no response. Then we begin to test again. They will say: The Russians broke their pledge. They are liars. So what is the value of your policy?'

I was naïve. I argued that it could not happen because there will be a lot of talk about the Russian initiative. He laughed and said that I did not realize that the capitalists had complete control of the media. They could turn it off and on at will. He turned out to be right. But he did listen, and there were key people with him.

Gorbachev came to power in March of 1985. I went to Moscow in April and again talked to a number of people. Then the next month, in early May, they gave me a banquet. I was surprised. There were people from the Central Committee, people from here and from there. No speeches, but a lot of toasts. Several people took me aside and told me, "You have been successful. On July 29, Gorbachev is going to give a speech to announce that on August 6, we will stop nuclear testing."

They expected me to say "Wonderful!" but instead I felt very uneasy. I realized that there was no movement strong enough to compel reciprocation by the other side. It was just not there. So I said, "Can the announcement be delayed?" But they couldn't understand what was bugging me. A Hamlet who didn't know his own mind.

In any case, the policy of reciprocating initiatives became the hallmark of Gorbachevism and helped break the whole impasse. If you look thereafter, one initiative after another—the moving of 500,000 troops and tanks—was a part of that policy that we had urged. But nobody identified it with IPPNW or my own urging.[18]

* * *

Did Lown's notion of unilateral initiatives catch on? I asked Vladimir Petrovsky whether or not there had been a specific discussion of the notion of unilateral initiatives in Russia and he said yes. Indeed, Gorbachev acknowledged it himself and I would later discover that the Soviet apparatus had been collecting everything that had been written in English about unilateral initiatives (which peace researchers called "GRIT"). And when Lown retired as co-president of IPPNW in 1993, he was given a banquet and a book of testimonials. The message from Gorbachev stated that without him the INF treaty might never have been realized. Lown told me that IPPNW had an impact in another area as well:

> In June of 1982 we taped a discussion that was broadcast on Soviet television on Saturday at 7:00 PM; they estimate that between 100 and 150 million people watched. They rebroadcast it a week later. It was the most outspoken discussion ever. Six American doctors and six Russians talked for one hour on prime time. We tried to have it shown in the United States, but failed. One of our doctors took it to New York but NBC, ABC, and CBS wouldn't even look at it. This happens all the time with the *New York Times* and the *Washington Post*.
>
> Anyhow, that broadcast had enormous impact because, among other things, it says that the Soviet Union could not be protected by the military. It discussed the cost of the military, which had never been discussed before. Moreover, it discussed civil defense, which was a big bugaboo in America. Morning, noon, and night you heard that the Soviet civil defense was going to defeat us! After that broadcast, try to find me an article in America about Soviet civil defense. It put an end to it. We said that civil defense is a deception, it cannot work. People will be incinerated and asphyxiated in shelters. Civil defense's only meaning is pre-emptive strike, for how else would you know to get your people into shelters unless you intended to strike first?
>
> One columnist at the *New York Mirror* wrote that the American doctors have saved the United States $3 billion by putting an end to the civil defense hoax.
>
> Another interesting impact is that we contributed to the liberation of East Germany. The East Germans could not organize. They could go to church because the Protestant churches were not proscribed, so many dissidents moved into the church. But another movement that was not proscribed was IPPNW. If you look at the Forum, the group that played a critical role in getting rid of the East German government, you will find that of the thirty key members, I think twelve were IPPNW activists. But their agenda was social democratic and they were swept over by Kohl and disappeared.[19]

I was curious about Chazov. At first he had been anxious about Lown's promotion of unilateral initiatives. How had he come to change his attitude? Lown said that it happened during the winter of 1984–85 when the two of them had traveled around the U.S. holding big meetings to promote nuclear abolition—and saying that the first step must be the cessation of nuclear testing [by a unilateral moratorium]. Lown said,

We put enormous pressure on Chazov to agree to that position. He resisted because they wanted parity. They had an inferiority complex because they were backward in technology and could not keep up with the United States. There was a lot of pretension. Arbatov tells me that they once put up wooden missiles with metal in them so that satellites could see them and think they had thousands of missiles when they had very few.

So in the winter of 1984–85, Chazov and I argued night and day in Chicago. Then in Los Angeles we were sitting in Mayor Bradley's office. We were going to get the keys to the city in a press conference. I told Chazov that we were going to announce that our policies were unilateral initiatives and cessation of nuclear testing. I said we must come out and call on the Americans to do that, and also call on the Soviets. I gave him the document. He was hemming and hawing. Our deputy executive director, Norman Stein, was there. He was very clever and had prepared three different versions of the same thing. Chazov was standing there with Tulinov, who was not a doctor but a representative of the Central Committee to ensure that the party line is maintained. A lovely guy, but an apparatchik. Chazov showed him the document and he said, "No way!"

So I said to Chazov, "Don't listen to him. What do you, yourself, think is wrong with it?"

He said, "I don't like this line." So I said, "Okay. Norman?"

Norman was a genius. He had anticipated which line he wouldn't like and he gave him the second version. Chazov was shocked. How could we have corrected it already? So he looks at Tulinov and Tulinov makes a sour face.

I said, "What don't you like in this?" He said, "I don't like this." I said, "Norman, do you have another version?"

Norman comes through with the third version. Now the correspondents are starting to come in. Chazov was in a state of exasperation and Tulinov was cringing and angry but he did not dare indicate that he was in control because there were too many people around. At this point, Chazov said, "Ah, to hell with it!" And he signs. So we announce it at the press conference and it goes out over the wires.

In the Soviet Union there is an interregnum. Chernenko is dying. In fact, two days later Chazov would be called back early, leave me in Cleveland, and race back to Moscow. So in the Soviet Union they hear Chazov making this announcement of the new policies: The Soviet Union is going to engage in unilateral initiatives, of which testing cessation will be the first policy. Now they know damn well that Chazov wouldn't say anything unless it was approved by the Politburo and Chernenko. But Chernenko is dying, so who knows? Chazov was in effect saying, "I am determining Soviet foreign policy right now," although he wasn't. He was tense and uneasy. I knew him very well. We were like brothers. I knew why Tulinov almost had a stroke on the spot. Chazov was uneasy about sacrificing his career but he had a lot of courage.

Chernenko died within a month. But in the meantime nothing happened. He was too sick. And in March, the moment Gorbachev steps in, one of his first actions is on this issue. By May I knew about it so they must have made the decision in at least April.

BARKING DOGS generally blamed Chazov for not being courageous in defense of Sakharov. He had signed a letter condemning Sakharov. I asked Lown about that issue and he replied,

> I personally don't feel like making a saint of the father of the H-bomb—neither Sakharov nor Dr. Teller, who regarded each other as buddies. And the effectiveness of IPPNW is largely because we put ourselves in Soviet shoes: If I were a Soviet, what would I be able to do? We ask them to do likewise.
>
> So let me ask you this. If a Harvard professor of theoretical physics, very influential, came out appealing to the Soviets to strengthen their SS-18s to be able to strike at the evil empire of Washington, which is the source of imperialism and misery the world around, what would happen to him? Would there be an outcry? Would a number of other professors write letters saying that what he is doing is outrageous? Well, that is exactly what Sakharov did in 1973. He came out in support of American missiles. To Russians, that was the act of the greatest traitor. Chazov and another twenty guys wrote a letter of protest against him.
>
> I think Sakharov did many courageous things. He disavowed nuclear weapons. But he wanted the nuclear industry to continue. He and Yelena Bonner were playing their own game. He was not for the abolition of nuclear weapons and he was not a saint to me.

It is difficult to appraise this allegation about Sakharov's position by referring only to his own memoirs. He certainly did get into difficulty in 1973 and was excoriated by many more than twenty letter-writers—some of them people who had been in trouble themselves for their critical statements. However, Sakharov pins the trouble on an interview that was published in Sweden. It is critical of the Soviet system with perfect accuracy, but it says nothing about Western nuclear weapons. However, ten years later, in an open letter to Sidney Drell regarding the U.S. freeze movement, Sakharov does make the points for which Lown criticizes him. It was after writing that letter that he was exiled to Gorky. Of course, there may be other relevant documents that Sakharov does not mention in his memoirs that would call for a different verdict about his conduct as of 1973.

* * *

Lown had worried about being able to mobilize sufficient power to ensure reciprocity from the West to Gorbachev's unilateral testing moratorium. His misgivings were well-founded, since the United States in fact did not match the moratorium. Lown described his own campaigning on both sides of the Atlantic during the Soviet moratorium. In 1987 he was still trying to prevent the Soviets from ending the moratorium. Philip Schrag recalls,

> In February, Lown attended the Forum for a Nuclear Free World and the Survival of Mankind, an international "peace forum" that Gorbachev had convened in Moscow. There, he pleaded with Anatoly Dobrynin, former Ambassador to the United States, not to resume testing. Dobrynin scoffed, and he teased Lown. "I have a suggestion. I'll arrange for you to argue your case be-

fore the Politburo. One member will appreciate it, but he is the only one on the Politburo who supports you."

"Who's that?" Lown asked.

"Gorbachev," Dobrynin said. "As for the rest of them, you have to understand that the Central Committee has received 30,000 letters from Soviet citizens opposing our unilateral halt in testing."

Lown did not speak to the Politburo, but he did address the thousands of peace activists at the Forum. When he returned to the rostrum, Gorbachev reached into Lown's breast pocket, took out the speech that he had just given, and wrote on it, in Russian, "I agree with every word of your speech." Nevertheless, the Soviets soon resumed testing.[20]

Lown did not mention all of his contributions toward ending the Cold War. I discovered one important influence of his from Matthew Evangelista. In 1983 a huge phased-array radar had been built near Krasnoyarsk in Siberia in violation of the Anti-Ballistic Missile Treaty, which permitted such radars only on the periphery of the country. All objections raised by the Americans were ignored and the radar station's workings were kept secret. Bernard Lown, in a conversation with the top Soviet scientist Yevgeny Velikhov, described the U.S. military buildup and Russian secrecy as "two sides of the same coin," and eventually Velikhov came to agree. He convinced Gorbachev to let Americans come and photograph the place. Those who did so still concluded that the radar was basically a military project, designed for early warning in case of a missile attack. A year later, the Soviet Foreign Minister Eduard Shevardnadze insisted on admitting the truth and dismantling the radar before it became operational.[21]

* * *

Much of Lown's power came from his prestige as leader of a civil society organization representing dedicated physicians. And of course Norman Cousins's personal influence was also enhanced by his position as founder of the Dartmouth Conferences. Yet such meetings have declined since the end of the Cold War. It is time to create new, regular, sustained conversations about serious issues—not just among the elite bears and doves, but even among ordinary citizens who otherwise cannot meet each other in person.

Notes

1. David Cortright, *Peace Works: The Citizen's Role in Ending the Cold War* (Boulder: Westview, 1993), 240–46.

2. Cortright, 240–46.

3. Landrum R. Bolling, "The Dartmouth Conference: Subjective Reflections," in *Private Diplomacy with the Soviet Union*, ed. David D. Newsom (Lanham, MD: University Press of America, 1987), 41.

4. Philip D. Stewart, "Informal Diplomacy: The Dartmouth Conference," in *Private Diplomacy with the Soviet Union*, 18–19.

5. Alice Bobroshova, in discussion with the author, 1994, Moscow.

6. Bobroshova discussion.

7. George Sherry, in telephone discussion with the author, April 1992.

8. Harold Saunders, in telephone discussion with the author, 1993.

9. The first official Soviet statement that war was not to be considered inevitable came in a textbook edited by Georgi Arbatov, Fyodor Burlatsky, and others under the direction of Otto Kuusinen, *Fundamentals of Marxism-Leninism Manual*, trans. and ed. Clemens Dutt (Moscow: Progess Publishers, 1964), which had already appeared in Russian in 1959.

10. These events are recounted in Gale Warner and Michael Shuman, *Citizen Diplomats: Pathfinders in Soviet-American Relations—And How You Can Join Them* (New York: Continuum, 1987), 171–73.

11. Philip D. Stewart, "Informal Diplomacy: The Dartmouth Conference," in Newsom, 10.

12. Warner and Shuman, 157–59.

13. Warner and Shuman, 179.

14. When he was asked to create the Institute for USA/Canada studies in 1967, Georgi Arbatov had never visited America. See his *The System* (New York: Times Books, 1992), 297. He soon made up for lost time.

15. Warner and Shuman, 180–81.

16. Saunders gave an example of how the Dartmouth meetings changed American perceptions as well. This was a meeting in Austin, Texas, at a time when Americans still thought Gorbachev was trying to fool them with his reformist policies. He would change into a tiger at any time, they believed. Arbatov brought along a cast of stars and convinced the Americans that the new general secretary was authentic.

17. Arbatov, *The System*, 200. Arbatov points out that Andropov heard about their appeal to Brezhnev and scolded him. Andropov was still hoping for a quick victory.

18. Bernard Lown, in telephone discussion with the author, spring 1994.

19. Lown discussion.

20. Philip G. Schrag, *Global Action: Nuclear Test Ban Diplomacy at the End of the Cold War* (Boulder: Westview Press, 1992), 56.

21. Matthew Evangelista, *Unarmed Forces: The Transnational Movement to End the Cold War* (Ithaca, NY: Cornell University Press, 1999), 325–27. According to Tom Cochran (interview, April 1995) it was largely Velikhov's pressure that resulted in the decision not to complete building the radar installation.

Chapter 7: Scientists and Weaponeers

Scientists, including some weapons scientists, probably deserve the most recognition for influencing their political leaders to end the nuclear arms race. This chapter is about their accomplishments.

The network of scientists is a key component of transnational civil society. Top researchers and theorists must maintain contact with their peers abroad. This fact enabled several key scientists of both blocs, especially during the 1980s, to cooperate with wonderful and historic effect.

Pugwash and the ABM Treaty

In the United States and Britain, scientists' dissent against the nuclear arms race came early and openly. *The Bulletin of the Atomic Scientists* and the Federation of Atomic Scientists (later, the Federation of American Scientists, or FAS) were founded in the fall of 1945 by Manhattan Project scientists who wanted to ensure that nuclear weapons would never again be used in war. The Atomic Scientists Association in Britain was founded a few months later with the same goal.

In contrast, Soviet scientists worked in a police state where dissent was dangerous and sometimes life-threatening. It was not until after Stalin's death in 1953 that it became thinkable for TERMITE scientists to meet with Western scientists to discuss, unofficially, a wide range of arms control concerns. The foundation for cooperation between Soviet and Western scientists was built, brick by brick, by the Pugwash Conferences on Science and World Affairs.

The Pugwash movement got under way in July 1957. In attendance were three scientists from the Soviet Union; three from Japan; two each from Canada and Britain; one from Australia, Austria, China, France, and Poland; and six scientists and one law professor from the United States.

That meeting was inspired by a 1954 "manifesto" drafted by British philosopher Bertrand Russell and signed by a host of prominent scientists, including Albert Einstein. The manifesto urged humankind to abolish war, and it enjoined the world's scientists to "assemble in conference to appraise the perils that have arisen as a result of the development of weapons of mass destruction."[1]

The annual Pugwash Conferences cover a wide array of topics on science and world affairs, with several symposia and workshops every year, mostly relating to nuclear weaponry. There have been fifty-nine major Pugwash meetings since 1957, as well as many smaller meetings.

Although never a large movement—it recruits by invitation only—Pugwash played pivotal but behind-the-scenes roles in influencing the political leaders of the superpowers. All participants were invited as individuals, not as representatives of their government or any institution. However, the Soviet delegates had to be approved by the top level of the Party and were monitored while they were abroad. Long-time Pugwashites sometimes recall the mischievous role of Vladimir Pavlichenko and I. A. Sokolov, who watched over the Soviet Pugwash delegations for years.

Sokolov, in particular, made little effort to disguise his authority over the sometime official head of the delegation, Academician M. A. Martov, greatly to the embarrassment of participants from other countries and—one supposes—Martov himself. Sometimes Western participants who spoke excellent Russian would catch Pavlichenko changing or adding something while translating a paper. Eugene Rabinowitch, the Russian-born editor of the *Bulletin*, and Joseph Rotblat, the Polish-born British physicist and founder of the Pugwash movement, would challenge him openly at times, saying: "This is not part of the paper."

Although some Soviet scientists were clearly intimidated, suggests Rotblat,

> there were other scientists who didn't care a hoot about people like Pavlichenko and Sokolov. [Lev] Artsimovich was a brilliant scientist. He didn't care! He would even speak up openly, a bit like [Andrei] Sakharov. He was the first person to invent the big machines that produce fusion. And Peter Kapitza was another person who would speak up. Igor Tamm, another giant physicist. They spoke their mind.

* * *

Of the early Soviet participants in Pugwash, two made especially important contributions in moderating their nation's engagement in the nuclear arms race: Academicians M. D. Millionshchikov and Lev A. Artsimovitch.[2] Both were eminent nuclear physicists: Millionshchikov was vice president of the Soviet Academy of Sciences, and Artsimovich was in charge of Soviet fusion research.

Early on, Pugwash began looking into the matter of antiballistic missile (ABM) defenses, already among the most contentious weapons issues in the 1960s. Both superpowers had been working toward the development of ABM systems since the mid-1950s. The early versions consisted of missiles that were supposed to intercept incoming ballistic missiles. These were crude precursors of the Star Wars scheme, which thirty years later would include not only missiles but also x-rays and lasers for intercepting incoming nuclear weapons. In 1964 the Soviets deployed a primitive system around Moscow. Meanwhile, the United States was attempting to upgrade its Nike surface-to-air guided anti-bomber missile so that it, too, could destroy incoming missiles.

Even then, there were strong arguments against engaging in a race for defensive weapons. In chapter 3 you met Peter Kapitza, who published an article supporting Bertrand Russell's appeal not to develop defenses against nuclear weapons.[3] Kapitza's reasoning had no effect on his government's policy but most Western arms control experts were also wary of defensive systems. In bald terms, according to the prevailing arms control view, nuclear stability—deterrence itself—depended on the fact that the United States and the Soviet Union were both held hostage by nuclear weapons. Defense Secretary Robert S. McNamara called their joint predicament "assured destruction." (ABM proponents added the word "mutual," giving the twentieth century one of its most descriptive acronyms, "MAD.")

In the United States, pressure for an ABM system had become irresistible by the mid-1960s. The Pentagon wanted it; a majority of Congress wanted it; and the American people seemed to want it. Congress appropriated money for a new post-Nike system, "Sentinel," which was supposed to provide coverage to most of the continental United States. However, this ambitious project could not be fulfilled.

McNamara, along with most arms control experts, was against building anything but a limited system, nominally to protect the country from accidental Soviet launches or an attack from China. President Johnson sat on the fence, dubious about a full-blown ABM system, but mindful of the political pressure to build one. Even the best system would be porous and easily overwhelmed by more and better offensive weapons, argued McNamara. ABM defenses would accelerate the arms race and perhaps create East-West instability, which could lead to a nuclear first strike.

In contrast, Soviet Premier Alexei Kosygin was wholly in favor of defensive systems. The topic was a hot button at the June 1967 summit in Glassboro, New Jersey. At one point, Johnson ordered McNamara to explain to Kosygin why the Soviet ABM system was pointless. McNamara told the premier that no matter how strong Soviet defenses were, the United States would build the weapons necessary to overcome them. "The blood rushed to his [Kosygin's] face," writes McNamara, "he pounded the table, and he said, 'Defense is moral; offense is immoral.' That was essentially the end of the discussion."[4]

The official Soviet war-and-peace position of the day had few gray areas. The Soviet Union said it favored general and complete disarmament. If that could not be attained, then defenses against nuclear weapons would seem to be a benefit, not a disadvantage. The United States dismissed the Russian position, announcing that it would retain nuclear stability by developing multiple independently targetable reentry vehicles (MIRVs) for its intercontinental missiles. In other words, a single intercontinental ballistic missile might carry a number of different smaller nuclear rockets, which could break apart while in flight and hit different targets. No defensive system could stand up to such an onslaught.

Some first-rank Soviet scientists soon saw the dangers posed by ABM systems.[5] By about 1964, Artsimovich and Millionshchikov, who were well positioned to influence their government, were quietly adopting the anti-ABM view propounded by most U.S. arms controllers. Further developments in the scientists' position could be seen in a December 1967 meeting of the Soviet-American Defense Study Group, whose members all were Pugwashites, including Millionshchikov.

According to Raymond Garthoff, then a senior fellow at the Brookings Institution in Washington, D.C., "Several senior Soviet officials have privately identified this meeting as having made a significant contribution toward shifting Soviet policy away from support for ABM and toward acceptance of the stabilizing function of mutual deterrence."[6] Rotblat confirmed this view:

> At that time, the Soviet Union was officially in favor of developing anti-ballistic missiles. They looked at it almost as a moral issue. They said, "We want to defend our people."[7] The Americans at the time were against having such a defense system. We knew that the offensive weapons are much cheaper than the defensive weapons. You can always saturate the defenses, either with offensive weapons or with decoys. . . . Somehow we had to explain this to our Soviet colleagues.
>
> The leader of the Soviet delegation was Mikhail Millionshchikov, who was a physicist and a very powerful figure in the Soviet Union; he was also the speaker of the Parliament, the Soviet. The speaker in the Soviet was not like the speaker in the House of Commons. He had even more power, though the Soviet met only once a year.
>
> At a meeting in India, he put forward arguments why the Soviet Union should develop these defenses. There was a good paper from Jack Ruina [a professor at MIT] that provided the counter-argument and we argued about this. We did not think that we convinced him. He just listened and explained why his views were right.
>
> Then we met the following year and we took up this discussion again. It was clear to us that he had presented his views to the government and the generals back there and they again came out asking for more details: In what way would such a development affect the future arms race? It was clear to us that he wanted to be armed with such arguments that he could present back on the other side.

Rotblat said that Millionshchikov generally took the Soviet position in the Pugwash meetings, but upon returning to Moscow argued the Western view. By the time of the Pugwash Conference in Sochi, on the Black Sea, in October 1969, which was attended by twenty-one Soviet scientists, Millionshchikov definitely said he opposed ABM systems. The topic was debated, and the final statement of the conference included the following regarding the deployment of ADMs and MIRVs:

> Deployment of either of these weapons systems . . . will not only increase the waste of resources and the danger of accidental or unauthorized launching of nuclear-armed missiles but will also increase the probability of nuclear war, since one or the other major nuclear powers might conclude that there are advantages to be gained by striking first rather than accepting the risk of a first blow by its adversary.[8]

A month after the Pugwash meeting in Sochi, the Strategic Arms Limitation Talks began in Helsinki. One outcome was the ABM Treaty of 1972, which (until President Ronald Reagan revived the goal of missile defense in 1983 with his Strategic Defense Initiative) successfully prevented a destabilizing race for defenses against ballistic missiles.

Why did the Soviet government abandon its simplistic position that "defense is moral; offense is immoral"? No doubt there were many factors, including cost and the growing conviction, nourished over the years by Soviet participants in Pugwash, that made-in-America MIRVs could defeat any defensive system. But U.S. political scientist Matthew Evangelista offers a distinctive speculation: that Ludmila Gvishiani, a historian who was at the Pugwash conference in Sochi, may have been able to explain to Kosygin what McNamara had failed to convey at Glassboro. After all, she was his daughter.[9]

Millionshchikov later gave substantial credit to the Pugwash process. He noted that he had privately come around to the anti-ABM position in 1964 during a Pugwash meeting at which the participants "had learned much from each other," and that he had "passed the lesson on to his government."[10] Artsimovich had also come to the same position, recognizing the connection between offensive and defensive weapons, and he openly stated his concerns about ABMs in 1967 at the Pugwash conference in Sweden.[11]

Georgi Arbatov, head of the Soviet Union's Institute of USA and Canada Studies and another Pugwash participant, published an article critical of ABMs in the newspaper *Izvestia* in 1969. Evangelista also believes that the Soviet government was influenced by Academician Vladimir Kirillin, a deputy to Kosygin, who attended a Pugwash meeting in 1963 and later kept up with further discussion of the ABM issue with Artsimovich, Sakharov, Millionshchikov, and other Soviet scientists.[12]

"Very often in Pugwash," noted Joseph Rotblat in an interview with me, "we seem to talk and that's the end of it. We often have to wait years before we can see any real effect of our debate, but this time we could see how it happened."

Finally, as you'll recall from chapter 5, in addition to the Pugwash meetings, another "freelance diplomat," Jeremy Stone, also independently contributed to the crucial ABM debate.

* * *

Both Millionshchikov and Artsimovich died in 1973. They and their cohort were succeeded by able scientists who would eventually pick up the East-West dialogue and carry it forward. Especially notable would be Yevgeny Velikhov and Roald Sagdeev, both of whose careers were advanced by Artsimovich. Nevertheless, their main contributions to ending the nuclear arms race would have to wait until Mikhail Gorbachev came to power in 1985.

In the 1960s, Artsimovich had already singled out physicist Velikhov for promotion. Although Velikhov's initial specialization was in developing computer technology, he became director of the Soviet fusion program in 1977.

Gorbachev, who was then national Party secretary for agriculture, wanted to learn how computers might be used in farming. Velikhov introduced him to the world of computers, and from then on, he would be a key science adviser to Gorbachev. In fact, Velikhov ultimately had more contacts with Westerners during the 1980s than any other Soviet figure except Arbatov of the USA-Canada Institute.

Roald Sagdeev was also a protégé of Artsimovich. Having spent a lengthy period in Academic City in Novosibirsk conducting research on fusion power, Sagdeev returned to Moscow in the early 1970s. By 1973, he was director of the Space Research Institute of the Soviet Academy of Sciences.[13]

The Brezhnev era lasted seventeen years, and during that time little was accomplished in arms control or disarmament, although the failure was not just the fault of the Soviets. Apart from Pugwash, there were few meetings between Soviet officials and their counterparts abroad. It was the time of Watergate, the aftermath of Vietnam, and Cold War competition for influence in Africa, Asia, and Central America. Détente came and went, and the East-West arms race lurched onward with MAD momentum.

But then came President Reagan's Strategic Defense Initiative speech in March 1983, a proposal to develop the technical means to destroy ICBMs in flight. The speech alarmed the Western arms control community as well as peace activists. Reagan's "Star Wars" proposal seemed certain to revitalize the nuclear arms race.

Key Soviet scientists were dismayed, too. Frank von Hippel, a Princeton physicist and then chairman of the FAS, recalls that shortly after the speech, a group from the Soviet Academy of Sciences sent an open letter to the American scientific community. The gist of the letter, in von Hippel's words: "You people convinced us that it would be counter-productive to have an anti-missile race. There were talks going on through Pugwash about these matters in the late 1960s. Have you changed your mind?"[14]

One of the scientists behind the letter was Yevgeny Velikhov, who was already well known to U.S. scientists working on magnetic fusion. In response to the Star Wars speech, he founded the Committee of Soviet Scientists for Peace and Against the Nuclear Threat, commonly known as CSS. It was made up of high-level Soviet Academy scientists, and it had been responsible for the open letter to American scientists. The FAS responded positively to the letter, and Velikhov invited them to send a delegation to Moscow to meet with the CSS. The FAS accepted, beginning a long and useful collaboration between the Washington-based FAS and the Moscow-based CSS. Von Hippel, for instance, estimated that he had been to Russia more than thirty times between 1983 and 1995, when I interviewed him.

The CSS, said von Hippel, played a key role in persuading Gorbachev, who took the reins of power in March 1985, that the Soviet Union should not engage in a Star Wars race. SDI was unworkable, said the CSS scientists, and could be easily overcome with more cost-effective counter-measures. Sagdeev's expertise as a space scientist was particularly crucial in the Soviet debate about Star Wars, said von Hippel.

Eastern and Western Lobbying for Sakharov
The achievements of leading Soviet scientists such as Vitaly Goldansky, Yevgeny Velikhov, and Roald Sagdeev owe much to the assistance of their sci-

entific counterparts on the Western side. After Reagan's "Star Wars" speech of March 1983, Sagdeev's expertise as a space scientist became pivotal in the Soviet debate about how to respond to the Strategic Defense Initiative. He later succeeded Velikhov as chair of CSS and continued the constructive collaboration that Velikhov had begun with von Hippel. For example, he and von Hippel edited a book together.[15]

The chemist Vitaly Goldansky had already been one of the leading Soviet Pugwashites even before the eighties. In our interview he mentioned an event that illustrates how Eastern scientists were supported in their political activities by their Western counterparts. It had happened during a large gathering of scientists who had been invited to Moscow to discuss disarmament issues.

As Goldansky recounted the story, "I was the chairman of one of the sessions in July 1986. It was one day before the end of the meeting. Eric Fawcett [a Canadian physicist] took the floor and suggested that we immediately invite Sakharov to come here from Gorky [where he was under house arrest]. I told him that this is an interesting idea that deserves attention. 'Unfortunately,' I said, 'it is too late to do anything. We end tomorrow, but it should be taken into account and we should think about this possibility.' And in December, Sakharov was here. It was a useful step along the way."

But Fawcett's suggestion came after a long effort had been made by Soviet scientists—interventions about which Sakharov was unaware. Goldansky said,

Starting from '85 or even earlier, Velikhov had asked Sagdeev and me to prepare a letter to Gorbachev, giving the arguments in favor of Sakharov's immediate return to Moscow. Sagdeev and I made many drafts of such a letter.[16] We gave them to Velikhov, and Velikhov passed them through [Arkady] Volsky and [Alexander] Yakovlev and then finally to Gorbachev. Then they kept asking us to make another draft, taking this or that into account. I remember that Sagdeev and I, over the course of a year or more, wrote five or six drafts of this letter, trying to convince our leaders.

It was not so easy because it was a special way of writing. You couldn't describe anything openly. It should be a kind of Aesopian language. You try to develop arguments in the language familiar to them. Otherwise, if you just wrote something in another language, they would treat it as an anti-Soviet letter and it would not work. It was quite difficult to explain that Sakharov should be brought here and, at the same time, explain that this will be favorable to the Soviet Union, our country, and that it will not be treated as the result of pressure from outside. . . .

The purpose of our letter was to help Gorbachev. We knew that he was willing to do it. He needed some help in preparing a letter in language that could be understood and accepted by his colleagues in the Politburo.[17]

Seismometers in Semipalatinsk

Since the early years of the nuclear era, a primary goal of the international arms control movement had been to see a comprehensive nuclear test ban treaty (CTBT) enter into force, as a means of slowing down and perhaps even ending the nuclear arms race. Twice the Soviet Union proposed a moratorium on nuclear testing—once, in 1958 under Nikita Khrushchev, which President Dwight

Eisenhower accepted, and again in August 1985 under Gorbachev, which President Reagan rejected.[18]

Velikhov was a major figure in responding to the 1986 Chernobyl disaster, and his experience at Chernobyl was directly related to his opinion about nuclear tests, as he explained to Western researchers in 1989:

> Before the Chernobyl explosion, many important specialists and political figures believed that a nuclear reactor could not explode. Now they know the truth. That is why it is wrong to believe that there cannot be accidents involving nuclear weapons. And there will be an accident if we don't start eliminating them very soon. Gorbachev agrees. He doesn't believe in the infallibility of nuclear weapons, and Chernobyl strengthened his feelings about them. After Chernobyl, he extended the Soviet moratorium on nuclear testing, and he thought you would have enough sense to follow this example. But you didn't.[19]

In September 1985, von Hippel and Velikhov met at a workshop in Copenhagen that commemorated Niels Bohr's efforts to prevent a nuclear arms race. Velikhov was distressed that the Reagan administration had reacted so negatively to the moratorium. At one point, says von Hippel, Velikhov said the Soviet government might be willing to let a Western group observe the moratorium within the Soviet Union to show that there was really no testing going on.

This was the first suggestion that the Soviet Union might accept seismic monitoring stations on Soviet soil. A generation earlier, the CTB idea had foundered even though Khrushchev and Eisenhower (and then Kennedy) had wanted one. U.S. weaponeers had argued that the Soviets might be able to conduct "decoupled" underground tests. Decoupling means conducting the explosion in a big air-filled cavity. If the cavity is large enough, the seismic signal would be reduced to that of an explosion about seventy times smaller. Early claims were that this would be feasible for explosions with yields up to 300 kilotons but today it is thought that it would only be practical to build a cavity large enough to decouple an explosion with a yield of up to 5 kilotons.

If it were possible, as initially believed, to successfully disguise large nuclear explosions by decoupling, the only remedy for this deception would be onsite inspections, backed with a worldwide system of seismic monitors. Khrushchev had rejected all but a sharply limited number of inspections, saying that they would be little more than "spying" expeditions. But in the mid-1980s, with a truculent U.S. administration accelerating the nuclear arms race and a man who favored "new thinking" in the Kremlin, it was the time to raise the issue again.

Several Western organizations began developing the seismic monitoring idea at almost the same time, and they explored it together. Parliamentarians for Global Action (PGA) in particular used the opening to test out some new ideas regarding verification techniques. It had already begun work to design a verification system adequate to monitor a permanent CTB Treaty.

PGA is an innovative voluntary association of parliamentarians from all around the world who want to promote their shared approaches. During the mid-1980s, it launched two constructive new initiatives, the better-known being the

Six Nations Peace Initiative (sometimes called the "Five Continent Peace Initiative" or the "Delhi Six").[20] The leaders of six nations (Sweden, India, Mexico, Tanzania, Greece, and Argentina) issued a joint statement in May 1984 calling on the five nuclear powers "to stop testing, production, and deployment of weapons of mass destruction and to undertake substantial reductions in nuclear forces." The Six Nations Initiative especially addressed verification issues, for which they engaged an organization called VERTIC to conduct a technical study. It differed from the opinion of the Conference on Disarmament's advisory group, which had said that verification could be done with fewer than 100 monitoring stations. PGA proposed 300-plus, and the CTBT that was adopted by the UN General Assembly will ultimately involve 337 such stations.[21]

In December 1985, before the six-month moratorium was to expire, Gorbachev announced the first of two extensions. A PGA delegation, with von Hippel as its science adviser, flew to Moscow in April 1986 to try to get Gorbachev to extend the moratorium again. They met with Foreign Minister Eduard Shevardnadze and Velikhov. Von Hippel, who wasn't sure much had been accomplished, suggested that the PGA talk further with Velikhov before returning to America.

The meeting with Velikhov turned into a brainstorming session. Velikhov wanted to move even faster and involve scientists in verification, even if there was no bilateral moratorium. Before the Westerners left Moscow, the PGA and the Soviet Academy of Sciences had agreed to organize a joint workshop on verification in May.

When they got home, von Hippel and Aaron Tovish, executive director of the PGA, asked Tom Cochran and Adrian De Wind of the National Resources Defense Council (NRDC), a Washington-based organization that does legal and technical work on environmental, energy, and disarmament issues, to take part in the up-coming workshop. They also invited Jack Evernden, a seismological monitoring specialist with the U.S. Geological Survey, to go along. A seismologist from Sweden, Ola Dahlman, was also part of the team. Dahlman, Evernden, and the NRDC had done impressive recent work with the Six Nations Peace Initiative on monitoring, in anticipation of a possible comprehensive test ban.

The Soviet and Western scientists met only two weeks after Chernobyl, and Velikhov had to shuttle back and forth between Moscow and the stricken area, leaving the Soviet and Western scientists to work out details. The PGA's Tovish had supposed that they were discussing a long-range monitoring plan, a scheme that would be ready when, and if, the Reagan administration agreed to make the moratorium bilateral. Despite Velikhov's earlier enthusiasm for monitoring without a bilateral moratorium, no one really expected the Soviet government to accept seismic stations on Soviet soil while the Americans continued to test.

However, to everyone's amazement, Velikhov persuaded Gorbachev to accept the idea of monitoring in the absence of a bilateral agreement. In fact, Velikhov asked the group to work out a plan for Gorbachev's unilateral initiative then and there. The Westerners extended their stay while Velikhov returned to Chernobyl. When he came back, the group quickly drafted an agreement and the seismologists started drawing designs on the blackboard for seismic stations that would be grouped around the Soviet test site at Semipalatinsk as well as the American test site in Nevada.

The monitoring system that the PGA had proposed would have required the United States to join the test moratorium, which wasn't in the cards. But the NRDC was able to make an immediate commitment to the project, bilateral or no. Therefore, the agreement that emerged from the meeting was not between the two governments but between the Soviet Academy and NRDC.

Back in Washington, there had been a months-long effort by the Reagan administration to portray the moratorium as just another Soviet propaganda ploy. The Reaganites made it clear that they wanted no part of a CTB. Nuclear testing was necessary for the nation's security, went the argument—the weapons labs had to test to refine weapons scheduled for deployment; to improve safety and reliability; and to develop a "third generation" of weapons, including the nuclear-pumped X-ray laser, a possible keystone for Star Wars. Lies were deliberately spread alleging that the Soviets had accelerated nuclear testing before calling the moratorium. But now with Gorbachev's response to the PGA's original initiative, and with the NRDC's seismic monitoring, it was obvious that something new was afoot. Colonel Ed Nawrocki, an assistant to then Assistant Secretary of Defense Richard Perle, later put it this way:

> The NRD's goals were totally the opposite of our own. They went into this project to prove that a comprehensive test ban treaty is verifiable. [And we'd made verification the main public objection to a comprehensive test ban because] verification is such a "show-stopper," as Perle is fond of saying. So the government didn't go much beyond verification as a reason why we shouldn't have a CTB. And the NRDC was out to undermine the verification argument against a CTB.[22]

Led by NRDC's Cochran, an American team of seismologists was in Kazakhstan by summer, collecting data that would be useful in designing systems to verify a low-threshold underground test ban treaty. The U.S. government reciprocated by allowing the group to set up monitoring stations around the U.S. test site in Nevada. The reciprocity was only symbolic, for there were already university seismic stations in the area, but it was an important symbol anyway.

In the Soviet Union, American scientists worked with scientists and technicians from the Institute of Earth Physics to set up ten stations. The political impact of the project may have been even more important than the technical information generated. It suggested that the Soviet government was willing for the first time to accept intrusive monitoring.[23] Aaron Tovish, the PGA's executive director, told me in 1993:

> [Rep.] Tom Downey has on his office wall, framed, the first seismograph of an earthquake coming from the station near Semipalatinsk. And [Rep.] Ed Markey got up on the floor of Congress and said, "Look at this. I have evidence here of the change in the Soviet Union. This is information gathered by American scientists in a militarily sensitive area." It had quite an impact. There were streams of delegations going over to look at the seismic stations.

In 1996, the United Nations General Assembly adopted a comprehensive test ban treaty—several years after the events that we have been describing—though the U.S. Senate did not ratify it. Nevertheless, the terms of the unratified treaty have been observed: The Soviet Union last tested a weapon underground in 1990 and the U.S. in 1991.[24] Thus the aforementioned international scientific efforts were major contributions to the cessation of nuclear testing. As Frank von Hippel recalled in our 1995 interview,

> We had a workshop on it in Moscow in the spring of 1990 with weapons scientists from all four labs and also Ray Kidder, a key scientist from Livermore, who supported the test ban and made important rebuttals to arguments that the scientists made. Out of that we produced a report for making a technical argument with Congress. . . . Ray and I were invited by Velikhov to testify in front of a Committee of the Supreme Soviet on the test ban.

Nongovernmental organizations such as the PGA and NRDC had opened the door by proving conclusively that the Soviet Union was ready to cooperate on verification issues.

Disarmers and Nuclear Detectives

The ABM issue and the test ban verification issues were the most conspicuous areas in which scientists were able to make vital contributions to reversing the arms race, but there were also many other topics toward which their technical expertise counted. In the 1980s most of these had to do with various other aspects of verification. For example, could warheads be detected from a distance? Could the dismantling of warheads also be monitored? How advanced were the Soviets in their radar installations for monitoring ballistic missiles or objects in space? Were they developing ground-based lasers that might be used to destroy satellites or even re-entry vehicles? American scientists proposed, and often carried out, activities that helped to answer such questions, and which may have given the Soviets the answers they needed as well.

Not all the scientists' proposals could be carried out. For example, during the Reagan years PGA was interested in promoting a proposal by the American "spacewoman" Carol Rozin for mutual inspections of space launches. Nicholas Dunlop, who then led PGA, explained the reasoning behind this suggestion: "If international inspectors were observing every space launch, [U.S. Defense Secretary] Weinberger couldn't say any more that the Russians are putting up space weapons. He would then have to admit that he's doing it, not because the Russians are doing it, but because he wants to do it."[25]

Dunlop and his team went around Washington discussing the idea with congressional representatives. They saw Senator Al Gore, who was a leading proponent of the MX missile and hence not as popular with the peace movement as with environmentalists. Gore dismissed the idea on the grounds that Bell Telephone would certainly not let international inspectors look at all the hi-tech equipment they send up in their rockets. On the other hand, Dunlop remarked,

When we went to see the Soviet deputy foreign minister, Vladimir Petrovsky, he said, "This is a very interesting idea." Within two weeks, the Soviet Ambassador at the disarmament talks in Geneva had formally proposed this as Soviet policy—international inspection of space launches. Petrovsky got the idea right away. We also had lunch on that trip with Arbatov and Primakov and their respective deputies, and they got it too. Petrovsky actually came to see us in our office in New York—the only person of that rank who ever came to visit me in my office. There weren't any parliamentarians there, just Aaron [Tovish] and me. He said, "I wanted to see where all these good ideas come from."[26]

The space launch inspection idea foundered in Washington, but Frank von Hippel and the Soviet scientists, especially CSS, continued their friendly and vitally important cooperation. The two sides, while observing the rules of military secrecy, shared whatever they were allowed to tell and engaged in mutual detective work to find out the rest, all for the sake of their common goal: nuclear disarmament. Von Hippel explained in our interview,

In January 1986[27] Gorbachev had given a speech saying we should go to zero [i.e. totally eliminate all nuclear weapons]. The question was how deep we could go. Even the most radical arms controllers said, "Let's not talk about zero. Let's talk about deep cuts." Sakharov had just been released from Gorky. He didn't give Velikhov much credit because Velikhov had not seemed responsive to his appeals while he was in Gorky. The following year, there was a conference in Moscow on the anniversary of Gorbachev's bold speech.

Velikhov had organized a five-ring circus. He had the writers' meeting, the artists' meeting, the businessmen's meeting, doctors' meeting, political scientists' meeting going on in parallel. He and I organized the scientists' meeting, which turned out to be the most important. I selected the Western scientists.

We had sessions on deep cuts and a session on space-based weapons systems. John Pike was most important in that. Out of it came a debate between Andrei Kokoshin [who would later serve as Yeltsin's deputy defense minister] and Sakharov. At that time the Soviet government was saying that they could not negotiate cuts in offensive weapons unless we re-committed ourselves to the ABM treaty. Jeremy Stone on the Western side and Sakharov on the Soviet side were saying, "Look, the Star Wars program is so ridiculous. Just go ahead and decouple. Don't let this crazy Star Wars program hold hostage our opportunity for making deep cuts." Sakharov said that in that session and then later on he and Kokoshin had a debate, with Kokoshin defending the linkage. Later on they did deal.

Another important topic was non-offensive defense, which some West Europeans were promoting there: Anders Boserup, Robert Neild, Albrecht von Mueller. Kokoshin was interested in this. Some time later he showed me things along those lines that he had put into Gorbachev's speech. The non-offensive defense guys and I were invited back to talk further about security in Europe.

The crowning event of the conference was that we went to the Kremlin and met with Gorbachev. One person represented each of these meetings. I spoke for the scientists. . . .

While we were in Moscow, we signed an agreement between FAS and CSS to do a joint research program. Velikhov was turning the group over to Sagdeev at that time. Sagdeev and I organized the research for a book we wrote together that focused on nuclear warhead arms control. When the INF treaty came up for ratification, Jesse Helms asked, "What about the warheads? We're talking about destroying the launchers, but what about the warheads? Aren't those the things that hurt people?"

The administration said, yes, yes, but we can't verify the elimination of warheads because there is all this science that we don't want to reveal to the Russians. So we had a press conference and [nuclear weapons expert] Ted Taylor explained it all.

At that time, I was agitating for a cutoff on the production of highly enriched uranium on both sides. I was trying to sell that over there and after some years, I finally did. With two other people, I had written an article about it in *Scientific American* (September 1985).[28] There was a big struggle about whether they would include that in the Russian edition of *Scientific American*. It took two years before the censors allowed them to print it. I think Velikhov had to go to pretty high levels to get it approved.

Why, I asked, had the Soviets been so sensitive about this issue? Von Hippel replied,

Maybe because I had estimated how much plutonium the Russians had produced from the Krypton 85 in the atmosphere that was released when the plutonium was reprocessed. It has a ten-and-a-half-year half-life and it accumulates. So on the global level, if you subtract out the sources that you know, the residual is the Soviet plutonium production. So Velikhov was amused that I had penetrated one of their deepest secrets.

We kept pushing it and finally in 1989, they got Gorbachev to agree to it. . . . Anyhow, in the July 1989 meeting, one of the people from the foreign ministry came in with the Russian edition of that *Scientific American*, all underlined. It had been used heavily in briefing Gorbachev.

On one trip while I was agitating for a cutoff of highly enriched uranium Velikhov took us to their first plutonium production site—their equivalent of Hanford—in the Urals near Chelyabinsk. Westerners had never been inside this place. People gathered around a U.S. congressman who had come along with us. They said, "We always dreamed of this." We went inside. They were shutting down the plutonium reactors. We discovered the reservoir into which they put high-level radioactive waste. I just couldn't believe it when they said 120 million curies. I made them repeat it about six times.

I asked von Hippel, "Was this Lake Karachay, the place where, if you stand on the edge for an hour you get a lethal dose?"

"That's right," he replied, laughing. "They asked us whether we wanted to go there!"

Von Hippel and the FAS did a major study of warhead detection. There was a public controversy about that at the time. He explained that in 1987 Gorbachev stated that it was possible to detect warheads on cruise missiles from a distance.

This claim actually came from a guy who had an idea that the neutrons coming out of the warheads would make argon in the atmosphere radioactive and then you could detect that radioactive argon downwind. Velikhov picked up that idea and told it to Gorbachev. The context was that the Russians wanted to include sea-launched cruise missiles in the START negotiations and the Americans were resisting this because they said you couldn't verify it. That was the context in which Gorbachev made that incorrect statement.[29]

In his memoirs Sagdeev described his exasperation when Gorbachev made this announcement. He was also shocked that Velikhov could have believed it himself and, without checking with his colleagues, promoted it at the top levels, including to Gorbachev. Sagdeev knew it was an extremely dubious scientific claim, yet Gorbachev had introduced it as if an important breakthrough by Soviet scientists had ended all problems involved in verifying submarine-launched-cruise missiles. "These exaggerations and overstatements could eventually harm the credibility of our position at the negotiating table," Sagdeev wrote.[30]

Von Hippel and an American named Steve Fetter became interested in the false claim Gorbachev had made. From a distance of tens of meters you *could* detect gamma radiation—but then you could shield it too, so the verification problem remained unsolved. Von Hippel said,

Tom Cochran picked up this idea and said, "Boy, this sounds like an opportunity for another NRDC demonstration." I was ambivalent because it might be misleading; you *could* conceal these things. But there was something else behind this crazy idea, which we learned later on. Anyway, Velikhov loves demonstrations, so he and Cochran organized a group, built around Fetter and his calculations. In July 1989 Velikhov asked Gorbachev, who said, "Okay, we'll provide a warhead if you can measure the radiation from it."

Tom organized a group that included a couple of journalists and three congressmen. We went on a Soviet cruiser off Yalta and the NRDC group measured the gamma rays coming out of the launch tube for this sea-launched cruise missile.[31] Then the Russians showed us how *they* detected warheads. They set up a neutron detector in a helicopter that flew by and detected the warhead from up to seventy meters away.

Later I talked to the guy who designed this detector. He said it had been in use for over ten years and the Soviet navy had actually flown over U.S. ships with it. I asked, "How did the U.S. ships let you get that close?" He showed me pictures of the U.S. sailors waving.[32]

Sometimes the American Star Wars people claimed that the Soviets were making a lot of progress with some kind of SDI program of their own. I asked von Hippel whether he had looked into that. He replied,

They were referring to a mysterious ground-based laser facility in Kazakhstan that supposedly had the potential to damage U.S. satellites. This was Sary Shagan, their test site for ABM technology, where they had a powerful laser that they could shoot things down with. So John Pike agitated with Velikhov, and Congressman George Brown got into this. We'd like to visit this place.

There was a big building in the desert with a beam director on it. We went inside to look at the lasers and later I showed the pictures we took. Somebody from Livermore said, "Toys!" There were some desktop ruby lasers and an industrial size twenty kilowatt CO_2 laser, and that was it—sort of 1950s electronics. They were having trouble even tracking airplanes and had never managed to track a satellite, whereas out in White Sands, we had a 2,000 kilowatt thing. Tom Cochran and I had an article in the *New York Times* about the killer laser that wasn't.[33]

* * *

Relations between Soviet and Western scientists were more mutual than were the relationships between, say, political scholars, among whom "New Thinking" innovations tended to flow mainly from West to East. Aware that American scientists were influencing Gorbachev, Soviet scientists sometimes tried to exert a reciprocal influence on U.S. policy-makers. For example, several Soviet researchers became real experts on the plans for "Star Wars." Velikhov, Roald Sagdeev, and Andrei Kokoshin of the USA/Canada Institute wrote a book on the subject that was published in 1988 in both Russian and English. They showed how easy and inexpensive it would be to neutralize American space-based defenses. The book had little or no impact on American politicians but it upset numerous Soviet citizens. Unaccustomed to reading public discussions about their country's military plans, they demanded that the scientists be prosecuted for revealing how the Soviet Union would counteract the Reagan's Strategic Defense Initiative. Gorbachev ignored their grumbling.[34]

For his part, Velikhov had been visiting the United States and had become acquainted with the impact of private foundations such as Carnegie and MacArthur, which sponsored research projects. He decided to create a transnational outfit to carry on such activities and in 1988, with grants from a number of American foundations and the Soviet Peace Fund, he launched a new civil society foundation with a clunky name: the International Foundation for the Survival and Development of Humanity. It would have offices in Moscow, Washington DC, and Sweden. Velikhov recruited to its board of directors Frank von Hippel, Sakharov, David McTaggart of Greenpeace, and especially Jerome Wiesner, who had been President Kennedy's science adviser. It is still pursuing a transnational agenda: international security, environmental protection, Third World development, and human rights.

Nevertheless, the great period of international collaboration among scientists lasted only as long as Gorbachev led the Soviet Union. During the Yeltsin years the CSS's leaders would turn to other pursuits. Sagdeev would marry Susan Eisenhower, the granddaughter of President Eisenhower, become a professor at the University of Maryland, and co-author a book with von Hippel.

And my interview of Yevgeny Velikhov in 1997 would take place at the Kurchatov Institute in Moscow, which he headed. As in the case of most other former TERMITES, he would then be estranged from Gorbachev. Instead of telling me about his scientific work, he would describe with enthusiasm his new project—to establish "Junior Achievement" clubs for adolescents, training them after school to run small businesses and become capitalist entrepreneurs.

Listening to Sagdeev and Velikhov reminded me of an important truth: Idealism can be expressed in infinitely varied, sometimes astonishing, ways.

Notes

Part of this chapter was covered in a previously published article by the author: "'Political' Scientists," *The Bulletin of the Atomic Scientists* 31, no. 1 (July-August 1995): 62-68.

1. For a history of Pugwash, see Joseph Rotblat, *Scientists in the Quest for Peace: A History of the Pugwash Conferences* (Cambridge, MA: MIT Press, 1972).

2. They were not necessarily the most frequent attenders. During the first decade, of the fifty Soviets who attended Pugwash conferences, twelve attended five times or more. They were: Academician Artsimovich (5); Academician A. A. Blagonravov (7); Academician M. M. Dubinin (10); Professor V. S. Emelyanov (6); Academician V. M. Khvostov (10); Professor A. M. Kuzin (6); Academician M. D. Millionshchikov (5); V. P. Pavlichenko (15); Professor M. I. Rubinstein (7); Professor N. A. Talensky (11); Academician A. V. Topchiev (5), and Academician A. P. Vinogradov (8). See Joseph Rotblat, *Pugwash—the First Ten Years: History of the Conferences of Science and World Affairs.* London: Heinemann, 1967), 219–20.

3. Peter Kapitza, "The Paramount Task," *New Times* 39 (September 1956): 10–11.

4. Robert S. McNamara, *Blundering into Disaster: Surviving the First Century of the Nuclear Age* (New York: Pantheon, 1986), 57.

5. Another early opponent of ABM systems was not a scientist but a well-informed Soviet journalist, Gennady Gerasimov, who would later become famous as Foreign Ministry spokesman under Gorbachev. See his article, "The First-Strike Theory," *International Affairs* (Moscow), no. 3 (1965): 39–45. He elaborated the same points in a subsequent book opposing Star Wars, *Keep Space Weapon-Free* (Moscow: Novosti, 1984). However, in an interview Gerasimov told me that he did not have much influence with Gorbachev on this topic at first. Though Gerasimov was present at Reykjavik and gave his reasons for discounting SDI as impractical, Marshal Akhromeyev offered a more conventional view that won out on that occasion. Later, almost everyone came to accept Gerasimov's arguments.

6. Raymond Garthoff, "BMD and East West Relations," *Ballistic Missile Defense*, ed. Ashton B. Carter and David N. Schwartz (Washington, DC: Brookings Institution, 1984), 298 as discussed by Matthew Evangelista in "Soviet Scientists as Arms Control Advisers: The Case of ABM," IV World Congress for Soviet and East European Studies, July 1990. See also Evangelista's thorough account of this issue in his book *Unarmed Forces: The Transnational Movement to End the Cold War* (Ithaca: Cornell University Press, 1999). His work is especially convincing regarding the influence of these Soviet scientists on ABM policies.

7. Joseph Rotblat, *Scientists in the Quest for Peace* (Cambridge, Mass. and London: MIT Press, 1972), 337–38.

8. Rotblat, 337 38.

9. Evangelista, "Soviet Scientists," 30.

10. Rudolf Peierls, *Bird of Passage: Recollections of a Physicist* (Princeton, NJ.: Princeton University Press, 1985), 286, cited in Evangelista, "Soviet Scientists," 24.

11. Bernard Feld, "Artsimovich and the Pugwash Movement," in *Reminiscences about Academician Lev Artsimovich*, ed. B. B. Kadumtsov et al. (Moscow: Nauka, 1986), 84; and Evangelista, "Soviet Scientists," 16.

12. Evangelista, "Soviet Scientists," 30.

13. Roald Z. Sagdeev, *The Making of a Soviet Scientist: My Adventures in Nuclear Fusion and Space From Stalin to Star Wars.* (New York: Wiley, 1994).

14. Frank von Hippel in discussion with the author, April 1995, Princeton, NJ.

15. Frank von Hippel and Roald Z. Sagdeev, eds., *Reversing the Arms Race: How to Achieve and Verify Deep Reductions in the Nuclear Arsenals* (New York: Gordon and Breach, 1990).

16. Sagdeev reports this letter-writing activity in his memoirs, *The Making of a Soviet Scientist*, 252–53.

17. Vitaly Goldansky, in discussion with the author, April 1993, Moscow.

18. On the Soviet moratorium and Western influences on its extensions, see Matthew Evangelista, *Unarmed Forces: The Transnational Movement to End the Cold War* (Ithaca: Cornell University Press, 1999), 264–88.

19. Yevgeny Velikhov, "Chernobyl Remains on Our Mind: Interview with Yevgeny Velikhov," in *Voices of Glasnost*, ed. Stephen F. Cohen and Katrina vanden Heuvel, (New York: Norton, 1989), 161–62.

20. Evangelista, 274.

21. The other key PGA initiative at that time was the plan to convene a conference of the existing Partial Test Ban Treaty members to amend it and convert it into a Comprehensive Test Ban Treaty. There was a provision in the PTBT whereby signatory states could require the United States to convene an Amendment Conference. The initial supporters of this Amendment Conference idea were Mexico, Tanzania, Venezuela, Peru, Indonesia, and Sri Lanka. The PGA undertook to round up supporters and PGA's leader, Aaron Tovish, and David Koplow of the Georgetown Law School put the results of the VERTIC study into an annex to the amendment.

The Amendment Conference did take place in 1991 and 1992, but ended (as expected) in a stalemate. The organizers actually had not expected the U.S. to accept a CTBT at that time, but had simply intended to show which states were creating obstacles against it. In the end, the initiative aroused public concern around the world about nuclear weapons, which helped prompt the UN General Assembly to adopt a CTBT in 1996. Unfortunately, as of mid-2010, it has not entered into force, mainly because the United States has not ratified it. President Obama has indicated his support for it. For a comprehensive history of the Amendment Conference project, see Philip G. Schrag, *Global Action: Nuclear Test Ban Diplomacy at the End of the Cold War* (Boulder: Westview, 1992).

22. Philip F. Schrag, *Listening for the Bomb: A Study in Nuclear Arms Control Verification Policy* (Boulder: Westview, 1989), 84.

23. From interviews with Thomas Cochran, Nicholas Dunlap, Christopher Paine, Aaron Tovish, and Frank von Hippel.

24. Not all other countries immediately suspended testing, however; India and Pakistan continued until 1998 and North Korea tested a bomb in 2009.

25. Nicholas Dunlop, in discussion with the author, April 1992, Bratislava.

26. Dunlop discussion. Vladimr Petrovsky later became under-secretary-general of the UN and head of its Geneva office, which deals with disarmament affairs.

27. There had been many earlier statements to much the same effect. In 1986 Gorbachev had met with Reagan at Reykjavik, almost reaching an agreement to eliminate all their nuclear weapons.

28. A version of this paper appears as "Fissile Weapons Materials," with David H. Albright and Barbara G. Levi in a collection published by the American Institute of Physics, *Frank von Hippel: Citizen Scientist* (New York: Simon and Schuster, 1991), 105–16.

29. Von Hippel discussion.

30. Sagdeev, 302–04.

31. See Thomas B. Cochran, "Black Sea Experiment Only a Start," *Bulletin of the Atomic Scientists* 45, no. 9 (November 1989): 13–16.

32. Von Hippel discussion 1995.

33. Von Hippel discussion 1995.

34. Frank von Hippel, "Non-governmental Arms Control Research: The New Soviet Connection," in Frank von Hippel, *Citizen Scientist* (New York: Simon and Schuster, 1991), 89.

Chapter 8: In the Hands of Experts

I can't help smiling at some of the business cards I've been given in Slavic countries. Where a Westerner's card might identify her as "Jane Smith, Researcher," lots of Russians identify themselves as, say, "Sergei Ivanov, Expert." That always takes me aback, much as you might react if my card identified me as "Metta Spencer, Plenty Smart." If Ivanov makes more than a decent ratio of mistakes in a given year, shouldn't his card be changed to "Sergei Ivanov, Inexpert"? This does not happen. Perhaps their experts really are.

At least it is evident that Gorbachev's foreign policy and military experts really were.

But who are these "experts," and what do they do?

They are not bureaucrats or politicians, for they do not have administrative responsibility for running government or industry. They are not regular university professors. They are intellectuals, who offer suggestions to real policymakers. They are usually regular staff members of a research institute or government agency. And they are indeed smart. They deserve much of the credit for ending the Cold War.

Gorbachev was no military man. He did not claim to know much about military matters. He supported democratization and liberalization (the suddenly fashionable "New Political Thinking") that emphasized interdependence, mutual security, and a willingness to live with the West in an undefended space: "our common European home."

Ideas of cooperation and common security are antithetical to conventional military assumptions. When Gorbachev came to power, over a quarter of the Soviet GNP was devoted to the military. He sought information and advice from civilians. Indeed his military policies were as strongly influenced by "experts" as by generals and admirals.

Those civilian experts maintained an ongoing dialogue with Westerners who were critics of militarism. In the fields of international relations and military doctrine, Gorbachev's policies were strongly influenced by a transnational community of experts among whom foreign peace researchers were especially prominent.

New Political Thinking

The security policies that were discussed and adopted during those years include the doctrines of *common security, reasonable sufficiency, non-offensive defense,* and *unilateral initiatives.*

As a general approach to international relations, the Gorbachev innovations involved shifting toward a principle of *common security* or "mutual security" as opposed to the practice of seeking to establish one side's security by intimidating or threatening all potential enemies.

Common security policies assume that enemies become more dangerous when they feel threatened. In pursuing one's own security, therefore, this policy advocates enhancing the security of the other side as well, since neither side can gain true security at the expense of the other. One example of this principle is the negotiation of *confidence and security-building measures* (CSBMs), such as, say, telling your suspicious neighbors in advance when you will hold military exercises and perhaps even inviting them to come and watch. This will allay any alarm they may feel on seeing your troops assembling.

Reasonable sufficiency is a principle that became official Soviet policy during Gorbachev's period. Unlike the principle of "parity," which insists that both adversaries should be armed to an equal degree, the Soviets came to recognize that in weaponry, "enough is enough." They need not acquire more or better weapons just to stay equal to their adversary, for it is pointless to be able to kill each enemy fifty times over. Once is enough. This insight saves money while also observing the principle of common security.

Consistent with the notion of common security is the military doctrine of *non-offensive defense.* This principle advocates aiming to be armed more strongly defensively than offensively. All potential enemies should be able to recognize that your side is well-prepared for self-defense on your home territory, but completely unable to attack them. This fact should reassure them (unless, of course, they do intend to attack your side).

Unilateral initiatives have already been mentioned as a policy promoted by Dr. Bernard Lown. Many Soviet arms reductions and agreements were undertaken as unilateral initiatives, rather than through agreements established by negotiation. Previously, arms limitations had been established mainly by treaties, but negotiating a treaty was tiresome, for each party insisted on keeping as strong as the other, though their forces contained different mixes of components. Negotiators, then, had to balance apples against oranges—or submarines against aircraft carriers. A unilateral initiative is a different approach. One side simply disarms a certain affordable amount of weaponry and invites the other side to reciprocate in some appropriate way without dickering over the terms.

Gorbachev's team soon began to take bold unilateral initiatives. After fifteen years the negotiations over conventional forces in Europe (MBFR) had failed to reach an agreement between the Warsaw Pact and NATO for mutual withdrawal of troops. Gorbachev simply announced that he was withdrawing 500,000 soldiers and 5,000 tanks. The impasse was broken and the Conventional Forces in Europe Treaty soon followed.

The Intermediate-range Nuclear Forces (INF) Treaty is a second example. At first Gorbachev refused to agree to a treaty calling for both sides to remove its medium-range nuclear missiles from Europe. The Americans insisted on a "zero-option"—the removal of all such missiles, both Soviet and American, from Europe. Since the Soviet weapon deployments were already ahead of the NATO deployments, this would require the Soviets to give up something real in exchange for keeping out the Americans' still-hypothetical missiles. The American offer was designed precisely because it was sure to be rejected, allowing the West to claim the high road. Suddenly, however, Gorbachev dropped his objections to the zero option and agreed to sign the INF Treaty, demonstrating one of his many surprising unilateral initiatives. Always, Gorbachev's unilateral initiatives were based on the principle of common security, for they were intended as confidence-building measures—ways of enhancing security on the other side.

This chapter will show the significant role of Soviet experts and their Western counterparts in developing the aforementioned concepts. But first I'll show the extensive teamwork of the liberal Eastern and Western experts who promoted these ideas. Some of these experts were already TERMITES, but many of them were perfectly normal Communist SHEEP—not yet very critical of their society. Still, good ideas were diffusing across borders, and almost entirely in their direction. Here are some examples.

* * *

Nikolai K. surprised me when he came from Moscow to a conference in Toronto and stayed with me a few days. I took him for a drive around the city and casually asked what he had studied in graduate school in international relations. I was so startled by his answer that I whipped out a tape recorder and asked him to start over. It seems that the Soviets had been studying Western theorists longer than I knew. He said,

> The main ideas of the Confidence and Security Building Measures (CSBMs) as a mechanism for dampening tensions between states and establishing mutual influence in the military and the political sphere had been worked out in the early 1960s. Indeed, some parts of these mechanisms were already worked out in the 1950s and were suggested in the international negotiations on the military and political future of postwar Europe. These were mostly developed by German and English specialists and strategists. Analytical researches were made, for example, in Ebenhausen, one of the main strategic institutions in Western Germany on Lake Starnberg, near Munich. Very big books were written on this topic between 1963 and 1965.
>
> Some people in the Soviet Union argue that it was just speculation and that it became politically realistic only after "New Political Thinking" was declared under Gorbachev. But from my point of view this is not true—not only because such measures were already to [be seen] in the Helsinki Final Act, but also because a very developed political concept of security and confidence building was laid out as an official policy by Chancellor Schmidt in 1978 at the UN Conference on Disarmament. That really changed the field. However, the idea of CSBMs was applied at first only to the military sphere. And then at the end of the 1970s, it was displayed in political steps in Europe. CSBMs became

one of the major instruments of the relations between countries. It has yet to be applied also in the sphere of economy and other spheres so that they will be comprehensive instruments of the foreign policy.[1]

Nikolai said that the neutral countries of Europe—the countries of Northern Europe and the Federal Republic of Germany—were the first to take interest in what were, at that time, called "security building measures." Such countries as the United States and the USSR were not interested in such confidence building measures. The West Germans—especially the Social Democrats—were leaders in developing a notion called "Security for All."

Egon Bahr's group within the Social Democratic Party worked out this concept, but the most active countries in this sphere were Sweden, then Austria, partially Switzerland and Finland. What we now call "common security," in which all the parties respect the interests of all their counterparts, was established at the end of the 1970s on a political level, but as a theoretical idea it was established much earlier. Nikolai said,

> Soviet researchers became familiar with these ideas five or six years after they had been launched in Western Europe, especially under the CSCE process. When we speak about the interdependent world, you know that this idea is one of the basic principles of the so-called "New Political Thinking." The first official publication on this question was I think made in September of 1982 in an article by Mr. Genscher in an American journal and was called "Western Policy Towards the Interdependent world."
>
> Our political science is one step behind the ideas developed in the Western countries, especially in Western Europe. Political science in the Soviet Union was of course mostly ideological and tightly controlled. Some researchers tried to bring the ideas of Western political science to the Soviet Union and they found a way,"

Nikolai chuckled. "They published books of 'criticism'—for example, criticisms of Western foreign policy theorists. The main part of the book was just summaries of the books that had been published in the other countries. That was the whole point of publishing these 'critiques'! But some also tried to develop original theories and original political science for the Soviet Union—not just to repeat what was said abroad. One such person was Mr. Shakhnazarov, one of the advisers to Gorbachev. He did something special. It was real science and original."[2]

* * *

A few months later I had a chance to interview a prominent expert at his office in Moscow—Sergei Karaganov—about the same subject: the influence of Western political theory on Soviet experts. Karaganov was a civilian specialist on military affairs based in the Institute of European Studies, a renovated old building near the Kremlin that had once housed a department of Moscow State University before it moved up to the Sparrow Hills around 1950. Karaganov had been especially influential in promoting the doctrine of "reasonable sufficiency."

In our interview he confirmed and amplified Nikolai K's account of the Western origins of "New Political Thinking." Karaganov said,

> I started to study military and political matters sometime around 1979 or '80 and I had the feeling that something was wrong [about over-armament]. However, in my case, the crucial influence was the debate over the INF. I defended the Soviet position with less and less enthusiasm. By that time I started to study the Western policies seriously, and also the history of Russian defense policy. I started to change my mind. The INF debate was extremely crucial. Larger policy-making circles here and in Europe became involved in the security debate for the first time, and the Russian elite was exposed to the *official* Western argumentation—which was extremely weak—but also, for the first time, to *liberal* Western argumentation. Massive contacts started to be forged between the Soviet elites and liberal social democrats. The main source of this thinking is German social democracy: Egon Bahr, Karsten Voigt and others. They were all over the place here. . . .
>
> A [somewhat weaker] intellectual influence was the globalist and interdependence policies of the 1970s—such [political theorists] as Joseph Nye and Robert Keohane.[3] I remember reading them some years ago. They had an influence on certain groups of Western-oriented Soviet elites, especially scholarly debates on these matters and also the re-evaluation of our own policy. Mostly they were liberals. Conservative thinking never had any influence here.
>
> Also, immense amounts of information were for the first time brought to the surface. We never had information until the INF debate, when we got some.

I was still surprised by such statements. I interrupted him and asked, "Really? You were a professional military analyst and you didn't have critical parts of the information you needed?"

Karaganov smiled at my naïveté. "Absolutely," he replied.

> We still don't have all the information we need now. But at that time, the only information we got was from American sources. Even the military didn't know their own secrets because they were so closely [guarded]. Most of the military were unable to analyze [structures within the defense establishment]. Many of the arguments were wrong but most of the information was correct. If you developed a certain proficiency you could see where the truth lay and where there were certain exaggerations. So you were able to have your own opinion.

His role had been to explain the policies of the West and provide sophisticated argumentation for the Russian position. "We were apologists. But still the institute's directors and deputy directors were scholars and they conducted studies on their own. And some of us in our circle were trying to push the boundaries."[4]

* * *

The experts kept referring to the Palme Commission and the German Social Democrats as major influences, especially in developing the notion of "common security," so in 1994 I phoned Egon Bahr, the most eminent of these Germans, to ask about his own influence during the 1980s. He told me,

I was a member of the Palme Commission. [The Swedish prime minister] Olof Palme, who was a long-time friend of mine, asked me at the end of 1980 to start thinking about the rules of security in the nuclear age. So I did. And I came to an astonishing result. Based on mutual assured destruction, its quite obvious that neither side in a major nuclear exchange can win a war.

So if this is true, then the result is that the potential enemy becomes the partner of your own security and the other way around. In other words, despite the fact of the East-West conflict, both sides can live together or can die together. If this is true, we live in a period de facto of common security.

I was surprised at this result because it was against the experience of history. In history, when you fought, you had to beat the enemy. To become secure, you had to win a war. So I wrote this down, left it on my table for two months, and read it again. I could not find a mistake, and I asked Karl Friedrich von Weiszacker, one of Germany's most brilliant brains. He's a philosopher, a physician, and the brother of the president. He couldn't find a mistake so I gave it to Olof.

At a Palme Commission meeting there was a long debate and at the end, the concept was accepted unanimously. Georgi Arbatov was the Soviet commissioner. David Owen was the British commissioner, and Cyrus Vance was the American representative. Arbatov mentioned Mikhail Gorbachev as a promising new political leader, and eventually Bahr met Gorbachev. He told me,

I met him in a long conversation in, I suppose, April 1985, just a few weeks after he became number one. To my surprise, he developed the idea of common security. He wanted to teach me, to explain it, as if it were his personal idea! I didn't react, but told him after ten or fifteen minutes, "I agree completely!" . . . Later I met Arbatov and asked him to explain how Gorbachev came to these ideas. Arbatov said, "No miracle at all. As I told you some years ago, I have personal relations with this man and whenever I came back from the Palme Commission, I explained to him our discussions and our ideas. He accepted these ideas so that he got the impression that they are his ideas. I didn't want to argue with him!"[5]

* * *

Andrei Melville is the political scientist who was mentioned earlier in connection with the Soviet Peace Committee, where he worked briefly as Secretary—before discovering how hard it would be to introduce *perestroika*. Melville also acknowledged that the "New Political Thinking" of the Gorbachev era was largely imported, but he argued that this could not have happened had it not been supported from the top. In fact, the top leaders themselves were especially open to foreign ideas. Melville told an anecdote that illustrates how the influence worked. He said,

One can hardly call Seweryn Bialer a "New Political Thinker" in the strict sense of the word, but I am fond of his writings and he is one of the authorities in political science in the West. Some of his ideas were connected with what later emerged as "New Political Thinking." A brilliant lecture that he delivered

at Columbia University in '84 or '85 about the nuclear revolution was published in a booklet. There he explored many of the ideas of this sort—that the
world after the nuclear revolution has changed, politics has changed, etc.—
ideas that were developed later in the context of the New Political Thinking. . . . I was following his writings and I saw that Robert Jervis originated
many ideas that Bialer absorbed.

So Bialer comes to the Soviet Union just after publication of this brilliant
lecture. I remember escorting him to Shakhnazarov's office, who was the usual
contact for him in the Central Committee. I have no idea what they discussed,
but I watched what was published. And in three months or so, Shakhnazarov
publishes an absolutely amazing article, "The Logic of the New Thinking," first
in the magazine *XXth Century and Peace* and then in an expanded form, in the
Problems of Philosophy Journal. Many basic notions from the Bialer lecture
you can find in Shakhnazarov's article. That was an exciting experience because I could see the channels of ideas.[6]

* * *

Peter Gladkov, an expert on Soviet-American relations, shed light on the ways
in which new—especially foreign—ideas made their way through the Soviet
system. He was head of the department of multilateral negotiations at Georgi
Arbatov's USA/Canada Institute. This interview took place in October 1991,
while Gorbachev was still President of the Soviet Union. Gladkov said,

The influence is mostly indirect. The ideas are rolled through numerous Western magazines and books. There you try to see them in the light of our reality
and then use them as bricks for constructing your own concept of the problem.
Then you expound them in so-called "closed" publications for the government,
the Ministry of Foreign Affairs—or you can try to publish it in the open press.
So the most important influence is the creating of an environment of scientific
discussion. Through this environment, Western ideas influence our thinking
and, later on, the process of decision-making. "New Political Thinking" is an
example. All its main ingredients were taken from Western ideas. Jimmy Carter's speeches stated lots of ideas that were repeated by Gorbachev.

In *Moscow News* I published an article in about 1990 on Soviet-American
relations regarding changes in Europe. I was the first to state that sooner or
later the USSR will find a way to cooperate with NATO. At that time the future
disintegration of the Soviet Union was not evident, and it was still a question
what would happen with Germany. I proposed a three-step plan: 1. GDR and
West Germany leave the Warsaw Treaty and NATO; 2. Something else, I don't
remember what; and 3. WTO and NATO end their existence and the Soviet
Union finds a form of association with former NATO countries. That, I said,
will be the way to create European security. I can't say that it's my own idea.
I'd read and heard about it but I can't recall the source. But this idea was "in
the air." It is often impossible to say who was the first to state this or that idea.
Though I expounded the same ideas in all kinds of notes and reports, I don't
know what the reaction was.

Here's another story. My September (1991) article in *Moscow News* says
that UN peacekeeping forces can be used in Karabakh for separating Azeris and
Armenians. That idea was stated by Shevardnadze; he mentioned it when he
was in the U.S. But before his mission, we had prepared notes on the possible

use of UN peacekeeping forces in our internal conflicts. He read the notes and remembered the idea. When he got an opportunity he set it forth. I know that my article was cited because a person who had been present told me that Chairman Kryuchkov had criticized this article, claiming I was trying to attract external forces to decide our internal conflicts. Again, where did we get the idea? I don't know who said it first. It was mentioned in the Western press. . . .

Western publications and communication with Western peace activists and scientists played a decisive role. In our country it used to be impossible to [learn anything new] from the discussions because everybody was dancing to the same tune. It was like scorched earth here. Communication with Western people was like a breath of fresh air. People such as Robert Legvold from Columbia University, Seweryn Bialer, Joseph Nye. Their work on Soviet foreign policy gave a very important insight and it was useful to compare their views with ours and sometimes correct ourselves. Senator Sam Nunn was also useful.[7]

* * *

The American peace researcher Dietrich Fischer contributed this story about his friend Johan Galtung to *Peace Magazine* in November, 1992. I had heard the same story from Galtung himself but I like Dietrich's dramatic way of telling it.

Act I
When Johan Galtung, who is widely regarded as the father of peace research, founded the International Peace Research Institute in Oslo in 1959, he and his colleagues sent copies of their working papers to a number of institutes around the world, including the Institute for World Economy and International Relations (IMEMO) in Moscow. They received acknowledgments from many quarters, but never heard from IMEMO. It was as if the papers disappeared in a black hole, leaving no trace. Despite this lack of feedback, the members of the Oslo team persistently kept sending their papers on alternative approaches to peace and security to IMEMO throughout the 1960s and 1970s.

Act II
In 1979, Johan Galtung attended an international conference at IMEMO. During a break, the librarian approached him and asked, "Are you Professor Galtung? I would like to show you something." She took him to the basement in the library, opened a locked room, opened a locked cabinet inside the room, and showed him a pile of papers. Here was the entire collection of papers that he and his friends had been sending over the years. Surprisingly, the papers were worn out from having passed through many hands, edges bent and torn, with portions underlined and numerous notes in the margins.

Act III
Last year, Vladimir Petrovsky, then the Soviet deputy foreign minister [later the under-secretary-general of the United Nations for disarmament affairs], came to Oslo to see Johan Galtung, gave him a big hug and said, "I really wanted to tell you how grateful we were for all your papers that you kept sending us. During the Brezhnev era, I was part of a group of young scholars at IMEMO who met frequently to discuss new ideas, and we studied your books and papers intensively, among others. We knew that our system needed reform, and that the time for change was coming. You provided us with valuable new concepts and concrete ideas of how to proceed.[8]

* * *

Sergei Blagovolin was the man who had told me about being locked in his office at IMEMO and guarded by Yevgeny Primakov while writing a report for Gorbachev. However, beginning in 1985, civilian analysts began to receive some valid figures from their own military sources—though such information was transmitted unofficially. Blagovolin also told me,

> For many years, we had prepared an analysis for the Soviet General Staff, estimating American military-industrial capabilities. The General Staff, and some civilian persons who were in close relations with them, tried to convince our political leaders that the real size of the American military-industrial capability was much higher than it really was. For example, our assessment of forcible military tank production was 80 thousand tanks a year! In reality, the highest American tank production was 1,200.
>
> "When we received some real information," he said, "not only about Soviet tank production but also about the size of American production, we were completely shocked because only two plants—in Lima, Ohio, and Detroit, Michigan—produced tanks in the United States. All our official sources claimed that they had at least twenty-two plants. . . . To me, this was the first strong evidence that something was completely wrong. We were shocked because we found that we all were simply liars! It was terrible because all those figures were in the "red books"—special books published annually for the Politburo and our top military officers. . . . Absolute miscalculation, on a huge scale! It was not 10 or 20 percent or even 50 percent, but much more serious.[9]

Blagovolin then expected that the results of his studies would lead to sharp cuts in military spending and force sizes. This happened, but only to a limited extent. He says the military budget was cut by only about 25 percent during the Gorbachev years. When I interviewed him, he was still hoping to see military reforms in Russia. The armed forces would be reduced to a small fraction of their recent size, while improving their efficiency and professionalism.

If these stories are convincing proof that Westerners did influence Soviet politics and military doctrine, we can turn to a more important question: What new policies did Western experts promote? I'll discuss two military policies, (a) *reasonable sufficiency* and (b) *non-offensive defense*; a diplomatic procedure, (c) *unilateral initiatives* instead of conventional negotiating practices; and a new doctrine of international relations—(d) *non-intervention* in the affairs of other sovereign states. Taken together, these four principles are all elements of *common security*, as introduced above.

Reasonable Sufficiency

In the Cold War, the Soviet public believed that the West had vastly greater military strength in all spheres than the East, and that its leaders presumably had the worst conceivable intentions. NATO intended war; it was not a question of *whether* this would happen, but only a question of when. Then other experts began to publicize the fact that the supposed crisis had been exaggerated. It became possible to question the whole doctrine of weapons parity and to argue that what was needed was *sufficiency*, not balance.

Some of the leading proponents of this novel idea were civilian TER-MITES—experts on military affairs and Soviet-American relations at Arbatov's institute. Sergei Karaganov, whom you have already met, co-authored some influential papers with a young scholar named Andrei Kortunov in the early eighties. In 1994 I interviewed Kortunov about those early papers. We met at the USA/Canada Institute, where he was head of the foreign policy department. He recalled what it had been like to publish an article that challenged generally accepted Soviet ideas. Kortunov said,

> The first piece on reasonable sufficiency was basically a reassessment of the Western threat to the Soviet Union.[10] It was one of the ground breakers on this question because it appeared in 1987 or 1988 in *Kommunist* magazine, the official theoretical magazine of the Communist Party. That is why it was interpreted as a semi-official statement that had to be taken into account, including by the military. But my initial idea to write something like that came from my experience as a lecturer in the early '80s.
>
> Our institute had educational programs in different parts of the former Soviet Union. We toured the country and gave lectures about the current international situation. This experience gave me some sociological data about what people are interested in, what they believe, what they do not believe. And I was repeatedly asked, "Do we really need to fear the West? Is the West still planning war against Soviet Union? If yes, what are the reasons and rationale behind such plans? If no, what are we to do for our own national security?"
>
> People were scared. In 1983 there was propaganda and a rather tense situation with the Soviet-American relations. But at the same time, the fear that had been present in the '50s and '60s had largely eroded by the '80s and people started to question the military budget. Do we really need aircraft carriers? Do we need to keep close to a million troops in Central Europe? Do we need to keep Germany separated? Of course, you should also take into account that the Reagan administration distorted the picture in those years, making crazy statements about how nuclear war could be fought and won. But nevertheless, my knowledge of the United States suggested that there were no real threats of war against the Soviet Union—especially surprise war. The Western policy was mostly one of containment. . . . So I wanted to write an article where I could throw those ideas onto the table. My first try was a Liberal weekly, *Oganyok*. It was '86, the very beginning of the Gorbachev period, and they failed to publish it because they were scared. It took me another two years and two co-authors to put this paper through. Ultimately, we got published in *Kommunist*[11] but we had to balance this recognition of the new situation with the idea that what the West was trying to do was just to exhaust the Soviet Union economically—that the main purpose of the arms race was to bleed the Soviets white as a purposeful strategy and that it would be stupid for us to go into this blind. We had to balance our ideas with a more conservative assessment of the Western strategy.

After the INF treaty was negotiated, a basic shift took place in assessing the validity of Soviet doctrines. For many years, the Soviet position had rejected the zero option, arguing that it would ruin parity; it would have grave political and military implications.

"But then all of a sudden," says Kortunov, snapping his fingers, "Gorbachev signs the treaty—and nothing happens! There was something fishy about this. . . ."

> Our article compared the situation of the mid '80s with the situation just before the Second World War. We still had many generals then for whom the real danger was something like the German offensive back in 1941, so we just tried to compare the situation of 1941 with 1985. Obviously the situation had shifted immensely in the favor of the Soviet Union. We could not justify a defense posture that was supposed to confront a possible offensive from the West of the 1941 type.

While he had been going around the Soviet Union giving lectures, Kortunov had made the same point in public—though in 1985, the exact wording was important. He had picked some slogans out of Gorbachev's statements that could be interpreted in very different ways.

> We said we were just trying to develop his ideas. It's like Christianity. If you want to give a new reading of the Bible, you pretend to be more consistent in your interpretations than those who did it before you. And we just tried to find something in Gorbachev's statements—or for that matter in Brezhnev's statements, because the idea of reasonable sufficiency appeared before Gorbachev. In his notorious Tula speech somewhere in the very early '80s, Brezhnev mentioned something like that. Basically, what you had to do is just to find something to justify your reflections on this or that issue. Of course, it would be perfect to find a quote. You could put in a footnote, saying, "As Comrade Brezhnev stated back in 1975, we can avoid a nuclear war with imperialists." And then you could develop this idea into something useful. You could just say, if you can avoid war with the imperialists, this means that imperialism is not as militant as it used to be. If it is not as militant as it used to be, probably they do not have committed war plans. And if they don't have committed war plans, that means we can limit our defense expenditures. If we can limit our defense expenditures, probably we can change the role of the military—and so forth. And of course if you could quote from Lenin, it was even better, especially after Gorbachev came to power.

"He was playing the same game quoting Lenin," I ventured.

"Yes," agreed Kortunov."Probably he was sincere. We were not. We realized that it was the rule of the game, and I studied Lenin carefully. I remembered a number of good quotes that could be interpreted as showing that Lenin had foreseen reasonable sufficiency. Everybody understood the rules of the game, especially people who read *Kommunist*."

Still, to get such an article approved was quite a breakthrough in those days. If the editor-in-chief didn't want to take responsibility himself, he could solicit opinions from prestigious persons serving on the editorial board. In Kortunov's and Karaganov's case, the blessing came from having Vitaly Zhurkin as one of the co-authors. Zhurkin held a prominent position—Deputy Director of the USA/Canada Institute—and was known for his cautious views. The article had a lot of influence simply because it was published in *Kommunist*.[12] If something was published in that journal, people in higher education, in the military, in political committees were expected to read and accept it. However, since the authors were civilians, some of the generals were irritated. But as Kortunov recalled,

> I think that there was only one, General Gromov, who made a speech saying, "There are some notorious comrades who even claim that there is no longer a threat to the Soviet Union. They are wrong!" Later I wrote another article about minimum deterrence that was pretty provocative. I wrote it together with another deputy director of our institute, who was a KGB general.[13] Basically, the case that I made was that we might disarm unilaterally, leaving just 500 warheads in Europe. I think that was published in 1989. Of course, the military went after us because that was *too* blunt.

While Kortunov and his colleagues were promoting the military doctrine of "reasonable sufficiency," a number of Westerners had been promoting a doctrine called "non-provocative defense," the notion that a country should limit its weapons to ones that can only be used to defend its own territory. But in the early 1980s it had been hard to engage the military in any discussion of either of these topics.

> Their regular answer was, "You civilians don't understand anything. You have no information and no data. There's no point in talking to you because you are amateurs. We are professionals." Since they wouldn't discuss anything with us, we couldn't get any information from them and it was a vicious circle. However, we consider *our* military to be our friends and colleagues. The USA/Canada Institute did not tolerate conservative military. Here we had intelligent military people who spoke foreign languages and participated in international conferences. They were not typical. We didn't have many contacts with the General Staff.

Kortunov had worked in Washington at the Soviet embassy, where he had become interested in the U.S. peace movement. In the early 1980s he and a small group of friends translated and published a series of books in Russia by Americans—liberal articles on nuclear and security issues. These were not the numbered white books but ones meant for the general public. These included articles about the anti-war movement in the United States, which influenced Soviet public opinion. He thinks these were even more important than his papers on reasonable sufficiency and military policy. "Also," Kortunov added, "such bodies as the Palme Commission, of which Arbatov was a member, were able to publish their findings in Russian. It had an impact on experts, diplomats, students—especially on scholars, because many of them [otherwise] couldn't even get access to original materials published in the States."[14]

Non-Offensive Defense

Non-offensive defense also goes by several different titles: non-provocative defense and defensive defense. Whatever terminology we use, it refers to a military strategy that was developed independently by various groups and individual writers. The group that was most influential in promoting the idea to the Soviets comprised several members of the Pugwash movement: a Dane, Anders Boserup; an Englishman, Robert Neild; and a German, Albrecht von Müller.

Still, the most readable portrayal of the general logic of non-offensive defense can be found in a popular book by a Swiss-American peace researcher, Dietrich Fischer, *Preventing War in the Nuclear Age*.[15] Along with Michael Johansen, a young Dane who was visiting Toronto at the time, I interviewed both Fischer and Boserup and published the conversations in *Peace Magazine* in August, 1985.

Fischer became familiar with this type of military defense in his native Switzerland, a neutral country that has avoided war for centuries. The Swiss Army has no way of projecting power to fight beyond its own borders, but has credible ways of defending the society against aggression. Swiss families have bunkers in their homes, and the men keep their rifles ready. During World War II, the Swiss deterred an invasion by Hitler by threatening to blow up their own Alpine tunnels and make it impossible for his army to march through. Some of these principles could be applied more widely, according to Fischer. He told us,

> Offense is not really defense but is aggression. Weapons with long range, such as intercontinental nuclear missiles, are offensive. Weapons with short range, like a land mine that cannot be moved around, or a bunker, or a fixed obstacle to a tank, are defensive because they are non-mobile or mobile within only a short range. Also, if a weapon's destructiveness is very localized (like an anti-tank weapon that can destroy one tank) it's defensive. On the other hand, an incendiary weapon that can destroy a large area or especially a nuclear, biological, or chemical weapon that can wipe out entire populations, is offensive.
>
> A defensive weapon favors the side that responds to an attack, while an offensive weapon favors the side that initiates the attack. For example, if two aircraft carriers approach each other, whichever fires first—let's say a nuclear cruise missile—at the other one can destroy it before it can fire back. When such an offensive weapon is involved, whoever hesitates and allows the other side to strike first takes a serious risk. But with defensive weapons, the one who initiates combat is at a disadvantage. An example might be two sides facing each other in bunkers or fortresses. Whichever side first ventures out into the open field to storm the other is far more vulnerable than the one who waits inside and only fights off an aggressor.

I said, "So a purely defensive system improves the security of a country that acquires it, without threatening the security of anyone else."

> Exactly. A purely offensive weapon, on the other hand, reduces the security of potential adversaries without contributing anything to the country's own defense. Most military systems are of an intermediate type. They improve our own security while reducing the security of others.[16]

In April 1985, when Gorbachev first came to office, one of the first things he did was to declare a unilateral moratorium on the stationing of the medium-range Soviet missiles SS-20s in Europe. At about that time, Fischer sent a copy of his book to Gorbachev and another to Reagan. He received a card from the White House, but no mention of his book. Three weeks later he got a call from the Soviet Embassy in Washington, saying that Gorbachev had particularly asked that he be thanked for his book. A while later there was a twelve-page review of his book by Georgi Shakhnazarov, one of Gorbachev's closest advisers, in the *Journal of Foreign Literature* in the USSR. When I obtained a partial list of the famous series of numbered white books, Fischer's book was included on it. Any book published in that series would automatically have exceptional influence on the decision-makers. Probably Gorbachev read it himself, though the evidence is circumstantial. For example, Fischer referred in his book to Herbert York's argument to the effect that a test ban moratorium will improve stability. Gorbachev quoted the same argument in his own book, *Perestroika*.[17] Gorbachev also used the metaphor that the nations are like a group of mountaineers, who can aid each other or pull each other down. This is the same metaphor that Fischer had used in his book.

Johansen's and my *Peace Magazine* article also included an interview with Anders Boserup, who then was on the sociology faculty in Copenhagen. We were fortunate to interview him when we did, for he died soon afterward. He was a gaunt chain-smoker who seemed stressed and somber. But, compared to conventional military strategists, his views were refreshing. He told us,

> Non-provocative defense is not the same as nonviolent defense. It's an actual kind of military defense, but without any offensive capability. So it cannot be perceived as threatening by an opponent. Under present circumstances, where people are scared about the defense problem, you will not get acceptance of anything less.

We asked: "People feel they have a right to have defense?"

> Yes. They may be right or wrong, but the political realities are that we'll get nowhere unless we have something to propose that people can recognize as a genuine defense but which has advantages compared to what they have now.
>   Non-offensive defense has two advantages. First, it improves crisis stability. We want a kind of defense that does not encourage quick escalation or panic if something is about to go wrong. Then we and the potential enemy can sit back, take it easy, wait, and assume that things will settle by themselves. That's one thing to achieve.
>   The other objective is to create such a situation that we can start disarmament. It helps if I have strong defenses and therefore don't feel the need to match whatever the other side does, but if I also have weak offensive capability, he does not have to be very nervous whenever I do something. That enlarges our margin of safety, which allows us to negotiate a disarmament that needs not even be very well balanced to be acceptable. So these two objectives are really the advantages—crisis stability and making disarmament possible.

We asked: "What kind of weapons improve 'crisis stability'"? Boserup said,

Weapons that are invulnerable. They can't be destroyed in a quick attack by the other side. Also, they have to be non-threatening to the other side. It's easy to give examples of the kind of weapons that we would *not* want. Cruise and Pershing missiles stationed on European soil are good examples. They are frightfully threatening to the other side and also vulnerable to quick attack. Before the war starts, while they are still in their bases, one big bomb might destroy all of them. So there is an enormous incentive to be the first to strike. That is what I call crisis instability.

Now for crisis stability we'd use a non-offensive, widely disseminated, in-depth defense, based on infantry that is concealed and can go into hiding.

"When you say 'widely disseminated,'" Michael asked, "do you mean scattered around in the territory?" Boserup replied,

More or less evenly distributed. This means, for example, that you cannot destroy big contingents of forces by bombardment. You'd have to destroy the whole country before you'd have destroyed those forces. So there's no quick crisis move that can improve your situation.

I said, "I've heard that given as a reason why nuclear weapons were not used in Vietnam. The soldiers were scattered around the jungle, so it wouldn't have done any good. You'd have had to destroy everything." Boserup nodded.

I think that's true, yes. The only target for these weapons was Hanoi, and it was not a military target. That is very much on one's mind in relation to Europe too. It's important to have forces that do not provide the other side with any useful military targets for nuclear weapons. For non-offensive defense, you scatter people as much as possible, to reduce vulnerability and make it easier to hide.

On the other hand, that leaves you with the problem of gaining sufficient fire-power to stop an invading enemy if he concentrates his forces.

"So if you play it one way," I said, "you distribute your forces across the countryside, but that makes it harder to fight the adversary if they come in a concentrated assault. What's the answer to that?" Boserup replied,

The answer is to try to use some modern weapon types that are now in the pipeline: long-range or intermediate-range missiles, for example, with warheads that can find and home in on heavy armor, on aircraft, or whatever. You scatter over the whole country both your infantry and also missiles of a range of 100 kilometers or so. Since they have this range, you can concentrate on firing into that point instead of bringing all your troops in. Therefore, you remain invulnerable. You do not concentrate your own forces, but only your fire. Such technical solutions are becoming possible now, but they've not always been possible. You need very high precision—fire over a range of 100 km that is almost as accurate as fire within line of sight.

"But I guess you wouldn't want really long-range weapons because it would look like you could shoot them into their territory," I said. Boserup replied,

Yes, that is true. But also, whether you pose a threat depends on what other forces you have. As long as the only thing you can do is to shoot 100 km into enemy territory and destroy some military installations there, that does not really pose a threat of invasion. It's only a threat of invasion if you also have armored forces that can move under enemy fire and can come in behind. So if your combination is missiles of 100 km, plus unarmored infantry, then you do not pose a threat at all, because you cannot move into enemy territory with infantry. You'd be too vulnerable nowadays.

We asked, "What countries are relying on that system now?" Boserup said,

None yet. But it is coming. Technology is imposing it. Modern weapons have so many defenses built into them that they are inordinately expensive. We stand at a historical turning point. The cost and the possibility of decentralized technology will establish defensive systems that will facilitate disarmament. If we see clearly, we may get out of the arms race. On the other hand, if we just sort of bungle into it, we may decentralize and build up these new weapons without getting the benefit from it. Technology now allows us to move toward disarmament, but it also allows us to create something highly de-stabilizing, such as the AirLand Battle, the Deep-Strike concept, and so on.

I said: "The psychology of the defensive strategist that you're describing doesn't sound like the militarists I know. The ones in Washington seem keen to keep the Russians vulnerable." Boserup said,

You're absolutely right. The United States believes it is engaged in a global confrontation with the Soviet Union and that it must manage to prevail in the end. But plenty of people in Europe do not think that way. Our feeling is that we'll have to live with this big neighbor of ours. We can hope but we cannot force it to change. Weapons are for use only to preserve peace. In Europe that fact sank in forty years ago.

"Did you say that there is no country that's using defensive defense now?"

Right, but several countries have elements of it. Yugoslavia is a good example. And of course, the guerrilla strategy that you saw in Asia—Mao's China and Vietnam—had certain similarities. It was also a kind of hide and seek game in which the attacker really cannot find any worthwhile targets. But on the other hand, it lacks the high technology.

Michael and I objected: "But these are all conventional wars. In a day when nuclear warfare is possible, isn't it almost irrelevant to pay much attention to conventional military situations?" Boserup replied,

No, I think this enormous focus on deterrence gets us away from the real problems, which are the instabilities in the nuclear . . . and conventional forces all around the world. They could blow up, escalate. It won't come from a sudden strike by the Soviets through some "window of vulnerability"—a strike at the missile silos. The danger is that the Russians will be very scared and try to achieve the same thing that the Americans have. That produces an arms race, which can be unstable. You can have accidental war in that situation.[18]

With hindsight, re-reading these two interviews two decades later reveals negative aspects of non-offensive defense systems that one couldn't see in our 1985 discussion. For one thing, experience with land mines shows that, although they are immobile and would be classified as "non-provocative," they are virtually as dangerous to one side as to the other; it is the local population that has to go on living among land mines for generations after the fighting stops. Since de-mining is costly and dangerous, only rarely are mines a good defensive weapon.

Moreover, the example of Yugoslavia illustrates another serious shortcoming of non-offensive defense. As Boserup mentioned, the Yugoslav Army was comparatively non-offensive in its structure and could have fought off many a would-be invader. With its short range weapons and disseminated forces, the Yugoslavs could not have invaded a foreign country. However, that very hardware was excellent for fighting an internal war, as the world has since found out. For all the numerous advantages of non-offensive defense, therefore, one should also recognize its limitations, for it does not inhibit all types of warfare.

Nevertheless, in the context of the Cold War that existed in 1985, non-offensive defense offered an alternative to the dangerous game of nuclear deterrence. The Americans never took it seriously as a option, for they remain convinced that their stature as a superpower brings a right or even a duty to intervene around the world. To do that, a military force must be capable of projecting power vast distances, which implies immense offensive capability.

The Soviets, on the other hand, became quite interested in the ideas proposed by Boserup and his small Pugwash group. The door was opened to Moscow's inner decision-makers by the Soviet ambassador to Denmark, Lev Mendelevich, who became acquainted with Boserup in Copenhagen. Jørgen Dragsdahl, a Danish journalist covering military affairs, told me about him:

> In the 1960s and 1970s, Lev Mendelevich had held a lot of significant positions. He was involved in changing Soviet policy toward the EEC—showing them that they simply had to relate to the EEC. Also, he negotiated on, I think it was the Indian Ocean Arms Limitation Treaty, where his counterpart was Paul Warnke. But then he was sent as a representative to Denmark. He's absolutely the key in what happened next. First of all, Denmark is so insignificant that if one of the top people in the Soviet Foreign Ministry is sent there, it can only be called retirement—or even political exile. What he did in Denmark, however, showed that the old man was not finished. Over some objections at the embassy, he ordered them to collect all available material on non-offensive defense. He analyzed it and kept sending things back. It was very significant for developing a policy on that issue.

Mendelevich was recalled from Denmark in 1986 and put in charge of long term planning for the ministry and as a member of the Council of Ministers. So he came to one of the most significant positions late in life. As a person, he was extremely respected. He died in 1990.[19]

Besides Mendelevich, Anders Boserup benefited from another important relationship. Since childhood, he had known Robert Neild, a Cambridge University professor who had been the first director of the Stockholm International Peace Research Institute (SIPRI). When Boserup worked at SIPRI, he convinced Neild of his ideas and the two started work on a book. In our phone interview, Neild described the period when the Soviets had begun taking an interest in their notions of non-provocative defense. He said,

> In my SIPRI days I believed that disarmament will come about through negotiation. The chief contribution one could make at SIPRI then was to provide a better flow of information about what was going on in the arms race. I had the idea of starting the yearbook because there was incredibly little information available. What was released was what governments chose to release. One hoped that by making politicians and diplomats better informed one might contribute to the debate.
>
> Later I came to doubt whether negotiations were a way of stopping an arms race because they implied that you could get balance in arms.[20] They operated on the criterion that balance was necessary. So long as you do that, you are in an almost hopeless game. You can't tell what balance is because weapons are unmeasurable. You always think the other side has got more and you are always negotiating to avoid inferiority.
>
> It was in disillusionment with the pursuit of balance that I teamed up with Anders Boserup. He got me interested in the ideas on defensive defense. A German, Horst Afheldt, was in it too. Anders and I started to write a book about it, the pure theory of strategy.[21] We wanted to show logically why, to go defensive was the way to get out of an arms race—because balance ceases to matter.
>
> At Pugwash we met another German, Albrecht von Müller, who became excited about the same idea. Our main contact with the Russians came in February of '87 at the big "nuclear forum" in Moscow. There were seven extraordinary gatherings. One for scientists, another for international relations experts, writers, everything. I went ahead early with Anders . . . to see Georgi Arbatov.
>
> We said to him, "Look, Gorbachev wants to get out of the arms race. The way to do it is to change your strategy and go defensive."
>
> Arbatov said, "We're listening." He suggested that Anders and I come back to Moscow soon as a small group with one or two other people. They agreed to pay all our local costs. So Anders, Albrecht von Müller, Frank von Hippel, a Dutchman, Egbert Boeker, Andreas von Bulow, and I went to Moscow in May. On the Soviet side, they called it defensive defense. They included Alexander Konovalov, Andrei Kokoshin, and Oleg Bykov, who was deputy director of IMEMO. Konovalov did a lot of work on this.
>
> We spent a number of days with meetings. Arbatov himself didn't deal with it so much. The chap who did was Andrei Kokoshin, who became the Russian deputy minister of defense [after the USSR came apart].
>
> While we were there, we went to see a lovely old man at the Soviet foreign office, Lev Mendelevich, who had been ambassador in Denmark. Anders had sold him these ideas and they had become good friends. I've got his card here: director of evaluations and planning at the Ministry of Foreign Affairs.

And then there was a Pugwash meeting in August '88 at Dagomys on the Black Sea.... [22] After Pugwash, I was in Moscow again. Reasonable sufficiency had already been proclaimed as Soviet policy. We said, what does it mean? That you should have enough to defend yourself or what? And they hedged a little, though they were pretty open. I said, "Look, I think I understand this. You've obviously had to strike a compromise in an argument with your military and you've struck on some ambiguous word, which one always does in politics."

One of them said, "Ah, Mr. Neild. You understand the world very well." They had been having a fight with their military over it.

I reminded him that an important piece had been written a little earlier by Zhurkin, Karaganov and Kortunov on reasonable sufficiency.[23] That language had already been promoted. Neild replied,

While there I went to see Mendelevich again with several of his young men. We had free conversations about how to advance in the Gorbachev era. It was wonderful. A propos the meaning of reasonable sufficiency, I said, "You really need to define this and sort it out because the West doesn't understand it. I see you've got a compromise, but what can be done about it?"

Mendelevich then suggested that our small group write to Gorbachev and ask what it meant. We were to let him and Arbatov know when we were writing. It was clear what he meant. I have worked in government. In other words, we should send a letter saying, this isn't good enough, isn't clear. Do you mean defensive defense or does it mean offensive? What the hell is it? Plainly, he was saying, you send Gorbachev a letter. Let Arbatov and me know when you send it, and we will draft an answer ... saying it means only defensive sufficiency, with which we can give another kick to the military, if we can get it on your initiative. They were using us to give ideas with which to fight an internal battle. And on this occasion, one was providing ammunition for this battle. So we went in for a curious exercise that, in the end, changed shape a bit.

Albrecht von Müller got involved and turned it into, not just a letter asking that question, but rather laying out a scheme as to what would be the right level of forces. We sent it. [Text in footnote.][24] And we got back Gorbachev's reply:

16 November 1987
Dear Messrs von Mueller, von Hippel, Boserup and Neild,
I was interested in your letter, in which you laid out some ideas on the complex and very poignant problem of how most effectively to lower the level of military confrontation in Europe from the Atlantic to the Urals, in order to limit the possibility of a new war on the European continent.

You approach this in conceptual and practical terms which might well provide the basis of a solution to the problem.

In practical terms, as I understand it, the question concerns the realization of measures to limit and restructure the armed forces and conventional weapons with which the two sides confront each other in Europe, in such a way as to keep on both sides a basic capability for non-offensive defense.

This is very close to our understanding of the problem. The Soviet Union abides by the principle of reasonable sufficiency of armed forces and armaments. This reflects the strictly defensive orientation of the military doctrine of our country and our allies in the Warsaw Pact. The path towards the realization of reasonable sufficiency we see in governments not having more military strength and armaments than is necessary for their reliable defense, and also in their armed forces being structured in such a way that they will provide all that is needed for the repulsion of any possible aggression but could not be used for offensive purposes.

We are actively engaged in preparing for negotiations in the near future on the limitation of armed forces and conventional weapons in Europe. As you know, at the moment a mandate is being agreed for such negotiations at the CSCE in Vienna.

In this preparatory work, we are basing ourselves on the known proposals of the Warsaw Pact concerning real and radical reductions, and the elimination of asymmetry and imbalance by reducing accordingly the arms of the power that is in the lead, by removing from a zone between the Warsaw Pact and NATO the most dangerous offensive weapons, and by reducing to a minimum agreed level the concentration in this zone of armed forces and armaments. In the course of this work we will pay attention to the concrete ideas laid out in the memorandum attached to your letter.

I want to underline again that we attach great significance to the active participation of learned people in seeking solutions to what are the most pressing military-political and international problems. We are all doing one thing directly connected with the central problem of the contemporary world—the problem of how to ensure the survival of mankind.
With respect,
Mikhail Gorbachev

The Western experts, Boserup, Neild, von Hippel and von Müller, had reason to feel satisfied with such a reply. Their basic principle was affirmed in Gorbachev's most significant clause, "armed forces being structured in such a way that they will provide all that is needed for the repulsion of any possible aggression but could not be used for offensive purposes." The principle of reasonable sufficiency, originally bold enough simply for having suggested cuts in military forces, had been rendered even bolder by Gorbachev's new definition: The official Soviet policy now specified not merely cuts but a restructured composition of forces to reduce offensive capabilities in particular.

Meeting with Gorbachev a few months later, Frank von Hippel proposed (as Soviet scientists had asked him to do) a defensive-defense formula as the Soviet negotiating proposal for the upcoming new negotiations on conventional forces in Europe (CFE): Both sides should cut their offensive conventional arms to 50 percent of whichever of the two sides is lower in each category. This did become the Soviet proposal. However, the Reagan and Bush administrations rejected this proposal and demanded that essentially all cuts be made on Soviet side. They got away with it.[25] The CFE treaty was asymmetrical; about 10 percent of U.S. forces were covered, but 80 percent of Soviet forces. To be fair, other Westerners visiting Moscow had advocated this asymmetrical agreement, saying that it would be a constructive unilateral initiative from the Soviet side.[26]

It is evident that the main notion of non-offensive defense came from the West. However, there were not only Soviets who understood the merits of this doctrine, but a few who had thought of it independently. I know of two different retired colonels who wrote separate papers arguing along the same lines. One of these persons declined to be identified here, presumably from modesty, since the Soviet Union was in its last months when we talked and there would have been no punishment for his inventiveness.

However, there had previously been ample reason for caution, as the other retired colonel had found out. He can now be named—Viktor Girshfeld—but he was better known in the West as "Colonel X." In 1983 and '84 three articles were published about him. Girshfeld proposed unilaterally halving Soviet conventional forces, plus re-structuring them along the lines of defensive-defense. The British peace researcher Mary Kaldor met him in Moscow. She told me,

> He had been a colonel under Khrushchev. . . . He was at IMEMO. He came up with the notion of sufficient defense for the Soviet Union. Stephen Shenfield discovered him, interviewed him, and publicized this in the West. When we went to Moscow in '86, as an END delegation, we went to see Colonel X. He didn't call it "reasonable sufficiency," but "sufficient defense." And he had very radical, well worked out ideas about an alternative defense policy for Russia, which were his own ideas but very influenced by ideas of defensive defense in the West. He was sort of a semi-dissident, one of those guys who came into the open during the Khrushchev period. Big beard, elderly guy, who felt that because of his dissident views he had suffered. He was sacked. But then his ideas were taken up in the USA/Canada Institute and IMEMO.[27]

Unilateral Initiatives

One innovation coming from Western peace researchers is the use of reciprocal unilateral initiatives rather than conventional negotiations, which over-emphasize parity. Bernard Lown kept promoting that idea, as we have seen, and he was not alone. There have been several previous successful uses of this procedure, one in particular being exceptionally memorable. It had happened at the end of an earlier phase of the Cold War, yet the story had apparently been forgotten.

American psychologist Charles Osgood published a book in 1962 entitled, *An Alternative to War or Surrender*,[28] which proposed abandoning the effort to stabilize deterrence as the only hope for humankind. He believed it possible to reduce tensions between states, and he called his method "Graduated Reciprocation in Tension Reduction," or GRIT. The source of interstate tension was a breakdown in trust, leading to a situation of fear, even where the states still had some common interests. Osgood's solution was to apply the golden rule, with certain safeguards for self-protection, to allow the parties to restore trust and mutual understanding. For this, deterrence was not a satisfactory solution, but it could not be given up easily when there were grounds for mistrust. Therefore, a minimal deterrence would be temporarily necessary, but everything should be done to change the basic situation.[29]

The solution that Osgood proposed was a series of incremental unilateral initiatives, each constituting a conciliatory gesture. They should be varied in nature, announced ahead of time without bargaining, but continued only in response to comparable moves from the other side.

It was the year of the Cuban missile crisis, and Osgood was president of the American Psychological Association. He took this occasion to go on a lecture tour, promoting his idea of GRIT. In the White House, President Kennedy, still shaken from the serious showdown with the Russians, was looking for an alternative way to peace. Told about GRIT, he ordered an aide to work with Osgood. The result was seen in his famous American University speech of June 10, 1963, which followed Osgood's formula exactly in proposing new measures for peace. In fact, Osgood had been involved in drafting that speech.

Kennedy spoke of the danger of nuclear war in a conciliatory tone toward the Soviet people, saying, "No nation in the history of battle has suffered more than the Soviet people suffered during the Second World War." Since the poor relationship between them and the Americans was man-made, a solution could also be made by man. He urged a re-assessment of American Cold War attitudes and declared a unilateral moratorium on U.S. nuclear tests in the atmosphere.

Khrushchev responded immediately. *Pravda* and *Izvestia* printed the Kennedy speech and the Soviets stopped jamming radio broadcasts, letting the Voice of America send this speech in Russian to the Soviet populace. Next the Soviets took a conciliatory step by allowing a team of UN observers to go to Yemen. Khrushchev announced on June 19 that production of Soviet bombers had ceased. The U.S. responded by allowing the Hungarian delegation to be seated in the United Nations. Thereupon the Soviets accepted the newly proposed hotline and announced their own moratorium on atmospheric nuclear testing.

Within a few weeks the Partial Test Ban Treaty of 1963 was signed—not as a result of negotiation but as another step in the GRIT process. In October, President Kennedy approved the first wheat sales to the Soviets. Who knows where this series of reciprocating initiatives might have led if he had not been assassinated two days later?

President Gorbachev consciously attempted to revive this GRIT process. High Soviet spokespersons sometimes use the term GRIT in their speeches. Ironically, the term is no longer used in America, except by peace studies specialists. Even Americans who urge "reciprocating unilateral initiatives" generally do not know the origin of the term or recognize the acronym GRIT.

The eminent peace scholar Johan Galtung praised Osgood in our interview:

> To my mind, he was by far the best peace researcher on the North American continent. Peace research is not simply a question of bright, intellectual models or concepts with no concrete suggestions. So, by presenting the image of asymmetric disarmament—you cut down 10 percent, and then you wait for the other party to follow suit—he proposed something between balanced disarmament (which never came about because nobody could ever agree what is balanced) and the stupid position of the unilateralists in the peace movement who said, "Let's abolish all nuclear weapons right now, unilaterally." Stupid, because the world doesn't move in jumps of that type. The Osgood approach was put forward by many of us, by myself for instance. It meant enormously much

in giving Gorbachev the basic tool of the INF. The basic tool of the INF was essentially to say, if you don't agree with this, I am going to do it anyhow.

And then, when the Western side said, "This is a bluff," Gorbachev said, "Okay, I'll cut even more," until the point came that the Western side discovered that it had turned the whole public opinion against itself. So the cooperation there between peace research, a statesman in the Soviet Union, and world public opinion was a triangle of supreme significance.[30]

I said, "I remember noticing something remarkable at an END convention in France. Sergei Plekhanov, then deputy director of the USA/Canada Institute in Moscow, used the word GRIT in a dialogue with Mient Jan Faber. I thought, there are very few people in Western political science who would know the word GRIT. This guy has been reading something!" Galtung replied,

That only shows the irrelevance, in general, of Western political scientists. They are only interested in what governments do. They are so superficial, such bad intellectuals! I mean—to write about politics as though social movements didn't exist, women didn't exist, children in the Intifada didn't exist, nonviolence didn't exist! They're just blind people.

I laughed and said, "Anyway, hearing a Soviet talk about GRIT made me aware that peace research was having an impact there." Galtung said,

Oh, there's no doubt about it. . . . The Soviets didn't want superiority, they wanted parity. But parity would be much better if it could be at a low level. And I think they saw GRIT as a practical method by means of which they could [bring the arms race] down to a lower level. . . . What were the intellectual ideas that were available to the Gorbachev inner circuit? One was GRIT.

Pieces of the puzzle were falling into place. Vladimir Petrovsky was in the Gorbachev inner circuit. He had been deputy foreign minister in the early Gorbachev years, and it was he who had hugged Galtung and thanked him for all those papers he had sent to IMEMO, which would have included Galtung's endorsement of Osgood and GRIT. I reviewed my interview of Petrovsky, who had later become the under-secretary-general for disarmament affairs in Geneva. Indeed, I had asked him whether there had been a conscious decision to use unilateral initiatives instead of ordinary negotiation procedures. He had replied,

There was a discussion because certain people advocated some kinds of negotiations. But there was an understanding at that time that the situation was really so bad, especially in the military and political field, that it was necessary to take drastic measures, for something might happen—not intentionally, but still, something could happen. We have a famous writer, Chekhov, who said that the hunter's gun that is on the wall always has a chance to fire unexpectedly. We had a long debate and we thought that this is unilateral in the sense that we took the initiative, but we also believed that this strategy of unilateral decisions was a policy of good example. In other words, you take a step, and you believe that the other side will match it. And we believed at that time that this would happen, that there would be opportunity to go deeper. And there

were times when the United States responded in the process. . . . This idea of
the unilateral move as a kind of good example was advocated by the foreign
minister. I always considered it in my writings. You had the precedent for it in
the relations with the United States. . . . The idea was in the air.[31]

I had other evidence that the Soviets were using unilateral initiatives as a
conscious policy. Lindsay Mattison was the executive director of the International Center for Development Policy in Washington. He had worked with some
people around President Gorbachev and had been a go-between to try to end the
war in Afghanistan. At that time, a high-level KGB agent named Aksilenko was
assigned to assist (and presumably also monitor) him. Mattison told me,

> I started getting requests four or five years ago [i.e. in about 1987] from the
> Central Committee through Aksilenko for anything on the subject of unilateral
> arms control initiatives. They were collecting everything on the subject.
>   Now one of the things that became clear to me in the Afghan conflict was
> that Shevardnadze and the gang at the Foreign Ministry and the Central Com-
> mittee of Gorbachev had designed a policy. If it was good for the Soviet Union,
> they decided just to do it. They announced that they were going to get out of
> Afghanistan and the U.S. government started running around saying, "Let's ne-
> gotiate," because they wanted [to keep it] bogged down. It took me about two
> to three years to put the pieces together.
>   Clearly they had adopted a policy approach. . . inside the Foreign Minis-
> try, and God knows what they had inside the Central Committee, but as I look
> back at those original requests from Aksilenko for everything on unilateral
> [initiatives], it indicated to me that a set of very high-up people inside the sys-
> tem had decided. And this was how they played Eastern Europe and the mis-
> siles and Western Europeans. You know how they pulled the damn troops out.

"Yes," I said. "Don't talk about it, just do it. Interesting." Mattison replied,

> They totally took the initiative away from the West. And that I'm sure was all
> the master framework in which Shakhnazarov, Petrovsky, Shevardnadze, and
> the gang were operating.

"The stuff you were asked to collect, do you think it was sent to them?" I
asked,

> I know it was. Aksilenko wasn't [collecting it for a hobby.] No, he was their
> agent. The KGB worked for the Party. . . . If you go through Shevardnadze's
> stuff [in the archive], I am just sure it's there. We were concentrating on for-
> eign policy regional conflicts. It was true of the Angolan negotiations. It was
> true of the Ethiopian stuff, it was true of the relations with Vietnam. They were
> a little more paranoid in how they dealt with China, but . . . they did not want to
> get locked in with negotiations.
>   Call up John Tirman at the Winston Foundation. I took him to Mos-
> cow. . . . He was writing a book on unilateral initiatives and Aksilenko went
> bananas and demanded that I get a copy of that book. Even though it was still a
> manuscript, I got it from him and I took it. A lot of stuff they just announced:

they were cutting their troops by so much and their weapons by so much. If you go over that period, the characteristic of almost everything was unilateralism. Nobody has ever written about that or ever noticed it, as far as I'm concerned, but I noticed it when the State Department started jerking around with Afghanistan and they just kept moving. They were not interested in spending years in Geneva.[32]

I took Mattison's advice and talked to John Tirman. I happened to meet him in a noisy cafeteria in Ankara, where the Helsinki Citizens Assembly was convening. Tirman was the executive director of an organization that provides funding for various peace movement publications and activities. He said:

I wrote a book called *Sovereign Acts: American Unilateralism and Global Security,* which was published in 1989 by Harper-Row-Ballinger.

I should have written instead a book with the title, "How to respond to Gorbachev," and set it in contemporary events, as people understand them. And then I would have needed to deal more with the Soviets themselves. But I didn't study the Soviet side much. My approach was to demonstrate the utility of unilateral measures and also to demonstrate the historical precedents for them. . . . in arms reduction.

For example, I had a chapter on the Comprehensive Nuclear Test Ban and I discussed how Congress could recapture its constitutional prerogative to involve itself in foreign policy and the steps that it has already taken on certain other kinds of bans like anti-satellite weapons testing. So that was the premise of the book, and I had a chapter or two on nuclear policy and nuclear weapons doctrine. That is, not every single thing has to be negotiated because there are many constraints on negotiation as a route towards arms control, and there are numerous other measures one could take to stabilize the relationship and reduce the cost of the arsenal. I argued that the United States should be taking the leading initiative towards arms control and that the Russians would probably follow suit. Unilateral measures could circumvent many of the problems that the legalistic part of the bilateral relationship had fallen into.

Negotiations are very easy to subvert. For example, if you are completely dedicated to negotiation, then you constantly have to answer charges about Soviet misbehavior, Soviet duplicity. You have to deal with loopholes, treaty writing, the legalistic aspect of treaties, the tendency to compromise, the ability of the Joint Chiefs of Staff to bargain with the President—a long litany of criticisms. Among military people, I think that there is a conviction that negotiations can enhance a military position and that negotiations are inherently part of the strategic environment, to which they have to pay attention. Of course, there never was a better negotiator than the Joint Chiefs of Staff. They would negotiate with the President on anything. So they were very adept at it and they could sink any negotiation just by going to Congress and saying it was dangerous.

I said: "Well I wouldn't say that you had a roaring success on the American scene. It sounds as if you had more success on the other side." Tirman replied:

I don't know if I had any success. I don't think that there's any question that the Soviets took many of the ideas of Western peace researchers and incorporated them into their actual negotiating positions and military doctrine, not just when Gorbachev was talking at the rhetorical level, but what they actually put on the table. This was certainly true in the case of the CFE Treaty —The Conventional Forces in Europe. The proposal that they put on the table there was a defensive defense doctrine. That did not come from Soviet military thinking. That came from the West.

And the acceptance of zero-zero option was a recognition by the Soviet Union that the West really was not a particular threat to them. And that, I think, is something that was conveyed from years and years of contact through the Dartmouth Conferences and Pugwash meetings, much more significantly than the peace movement per se of the 1970s and 80s. The Gorbachev generation, having been more exposed to the West, and having been part of these meetings for so many years, had sort of accepted this. And Gorbachev's overall direction was influenced by Westerners in some more specific ways—by peaceniks.

The Soviets were avid consumers of Western literature of all kinds. I remember one incident. The first time I was in Moscow, someone mentioned to me that I should meet Sergei Kapitza, who wrote a book on Star Wars.

"He had footnoted a book that I had done. Not on Star Wars, but an earlier book that I had done on the militarization of high technology. That book had a small loyal readership among people who had an interest in that topic, but it certainly had not received a great deal of notice anywhere. I was amazed at the attentiveness to something like that. That just said to me that these people are reading everything that they could get their hands on from the West.

A coterie of people formed, I think, who saw these as good ideas, a way to get out of the arms race. They were basically the sons and daughters of Prague Spring, and they believed in liberalization. As far as I know, this was an unintentional effect of peace research, which was always aimed at the Western governments more than the East. Maybe the Europeans were taking Moscow into account more than we do here but those ideas took hold there first and then reverberated back to the West. That fact is really astonishing.

"It is," I said. "And it's so counter-intuitive that I don't even know many peace movement activists who realize that it's true. The reason I find this research so interesting is that nobody seems to know it."

"Right, exactly," said Tirman.

Non-Intervention

Reasonable sufficiency—for what? Non-offensive defense—against whom? Unilateral confidence-building initiatives—toward whom? All these policies fit together as the coherent foreign policy of a nation that does not plan any wars outside its own borders. If attacked, it will defend its territory, but otherwise not.

What a refreshingly novel idea!

The Soviet Union was, until the last hour of its existence, a "superpower." It is widely imagined that superpowers (and even "great powers" that fall a little short of "super") have an invisible "sphere of interest" within which they may rightfully intervene at will. For example, the U.S. usually presumes that the "Monroe Doctrine," legitimately entitles it to invade any Central American country, whereas no great power from other quarters of the globe may do the same. Nor, indeed, is the U.S. limited to its claimed sphere; it has bases around the planet and a record within living memory of direct engagements in such places as Lebanon, Iraq, Somalia, and Vietnam. These military adventures are described as "responsibilities" but it was understood for forty years that such American "responsibilities" ended where the acknowledged Soviet sphere of interest began. There were some ambiguous areas—in Africa and the Middle East, especially—but there was clarity about East Central Europe. If anyone still harbored illusions after Yalta, no one did so after the Hungarian uprising of 1956. No Western power was going to intervene militarily in Eastern Europe. The people of those states—and indeed the whole periphery of the USSR, including Afghanistan—would have to accommodate their big socialist neighbor.

Until Gorbachev came to power. His new concept, "common security," was not just rhetoric. His genial foreign policy spokesman, Gennady Gerasimov, who had become a nightly star on American newscasts, announced the "Sinatra doctrine"—that all neighboring countries could do it *their* way. He was announcing a unilateral Soviet policy of military non-intervention in the affairs of sovereign states. What are the origins of this unusual doctrine?

Gerasimov was a spokesman for Gorbachev[33] and therefore was not responsible for the policy that he was enunciating, but in fact he was already an expert on several important aspects of military doctrine, including the prospect of space weaponry. He was especially familiar with the theory of non-intervention.

Since 1978 or '79 Gerasimov had known Randall Forsberg, a leader in the American peace movement and director of an institute for military policy analysis. Forsberg was famous for another innovation, the nuclear freeze, which became the main peace campaign in the United States. However, over a decade or more, she devoted even more energy to promoting the non-intervention regime as a policy. She was director of the Institute for Defense and Disarmament Studies in Cambridge, Massachusetts. Soviet military experts and conservative Americans alike took her seriously. (For example, she was one of the five people who briefed President George H. W. Bush on arms control matters before the Malta summit.) Still, instead of claiming any special influence, she said, "I have no way of knowing the extent to which these meetings may or may not have played a role." But Gennady Gerasimov told me,

> She traveled to Russia many times and she was influential because this lady sometimes knew the details of the military things better than some of the military people. She impressed everybody with her knowledge of details—not only that she was the author of the nuclear freeze movement.[34]

In 1981 Forsberg visited the Soviet Union twice, giving talks on the nuclear freeze and on the idea of conventional nonintervention and nuclear disarmament to gatherings of senior experts at IMEMO and other institutes. Sometimes she would be the only speaker at a dinner.

In the early '80s she convinced a state department official, Arthur Macy Cox, that a nonintervention regime had to be the foundation of building confidence. "The benefits are high, the costs are low," the two of them agreed, "and it would benefit both countries equally. It would be much more feasible bilaterally than unilaterally, just like the freeze, though it would make sense unilaterally."

Cox set up a working group to discuss the idea under the sponsorship of Brown University's Foreign Institute. The members met over a period of years and produced a final report before Gorbachev announced that the Soviet Union was going to withdraw from Afghanistan and not use force to maintain their presence in Eastern Europe. Cox was one of the people who, like Frank von Hippel, traveled back and forth between the U.S. and Moscow all the time, conferring directly with Shevardnadze and his ministry.[35]

In 1988 Forsberg organized a joint seminar on arms reductions in Moscow. Her group of Americans included Stanley Resor, Jonathan Dean, and Ted Warner, of RAND, Frank von Hippel, Arthur Macy Cox and Bill Green, plus staff members from the institute that she headed in Brookline, Massachusetts. This was the first conference that IMEMO had ever co-sponsored with an American organization, and the topic for two days was the upcoming Conventional Forces in Europe (CFE) negotiations. She and Oleg Bykov, deputy director of IMEMO, co-chaired the event. The group also met with two former U.S. ambassadors, two generals who were advising Gorbachev, and with Lev Mendelevich, the old ambassador who had returned from Copenhagen to the Foreign Ministry.

Three months later, Gorbachev made his remarkable speech at the United Nations, announcing unilateral cuts of half a million troops from Europe, a unilateral withdrawal from Afghanistan, and changes in Eastern Europe. It was the turning point in Soviet policy. Forsberg had lunch with Gerasimov and discussed those issues.

The next July, she was back in Moscow teaching a summer school at the institute that trains the foreign diplomats, which had never had any foreigners on its campus before. That summer she also visited IMEMO, the USA/Canada Institute, and Gerasimov.

When Gorbachev announced his principle of non-intervention in Eastern Europe, he also announced confidence-building troop reductions in the same area, as well as in the western part of the Soviet Union. Forsberg told me,

> He did not expect the initiatives in Eastern Europe to lead to a complete Soviet withdrawal, because he did not see that they would be pressed to do that. But he did enunciate the principle that *if they were*, they would. And then the Eastern Europeans turned right around and said, "Thank you very much, you can leave."
>
> I think that the initiative to reduce troops in Eastern Europe was made primarily, not in the spirit of the non-intervention regime, but to get going a process of conventional arms reductions, which would save money and improve relations. And I think that [Jonathan] Dean, who in many . . . meetings had pressed Soviet officials to take initiatives, I think it is likely that he had an instrumental impact on those initiatives.[36]

Let the Dissidents In!

Mention Randy Forsberg's name, and some Soviet generals seem to pull themselves up taller, barely suppressing an inclination to salute. Mention Mary Kaldor's name and you do not see the same reaction. At the end of the Cold War, both women were at the top of the prestige scale, but unlike the self-possessed

Forsberg, Kaldor is a born dissident. She and officials recognize each other instantly as natural enemies. Her hosts could hardly have known how to prepare when she followed Forsberg the next year in Moscow, teaching a summer course at the Party's school for diplomats. Yet she was the perfect choice for the job, since she was certain to insist upon the next step that should logically follow after the Soviets had announced their commitment to nonintervention. It was time to open up and let the Eastern European dissidents in, as proper members of European society, indeed as guests to Soviet-sponsored events.

Mary Kaldor, then a peace researcher at the University of Sussex, had visited Eastern Europe frequently during the previous few years as a key figure in the END movement. She had family ties in Budapest with relatives of her father, the eminent expatriate economist Nicholas Kaldor. And some members of the spin-off body from END, the East/West Dialogue group, had reached the point of trying to contact Russians.

In particular, the Czechoslovak dissident Jaroslav Sabata had been released from jail and had been a leader in writing the "Prague Appeal," which he hoped would gain some attention in Moscow. Sabata and others, including the Obrada Movement in Czechoslovakia, believed the time was ripe to contact Soviets who had been sympathetic to the Prague Spring. Sabata was not allowed to leave his country, but in that period he was meeting with the END leader Mient Jan Faber three or four times a year. Hearing of Kaldor's conference in Moscow, he sent a Slovakian woman friend, Dana Ferenčáková, to read a statement there. When Ferenčáková arrived, Mary Kaldor already had her hands full, waging a struggle for her other dissident friends. I interviewed Kaldor and Mient Jan Faber simultaneously, for he had been present too. Mary said,

> This was held at "MGIMO" [the Moscow State Institute of International Relations], which had been a very closed institute known as the KGB school. Our summer school with them in Moscow was held in the summer of 1989. Jim Skelly, the other organizer, and I insisted that we should be free to invite whom we liked. And so I invited opposition figures. From Hungary I invited Konrad, Haraszti, and István Rév. From Czechoslovakia, I invited Jaroslav Šabata and from Poland I invited Bronislaw Geremek. And the Russians made a terrible fuss, as you can imagine. "This is impossible! It's enough that we opened our doors to foreigners, let alone these people." He said, "We'll only do it if our allies agree."
>
> So I called up the foreign ministries in Hungary, Poland, and Czechoslovakia. The Hungarian Foreign Ministry was great. They sent someone to MGIMO, saying as far as they were concerned, I could invite whomever I liked. At the last minute, Geremek couldn't come and suggested Adam Michnik instead. And they said no to Michnik. But he was already on his way to Moscow. And of course at that time Poles didn't have to have visas. So he simply came.

Mient Jan Faber said,

> When I arrived in Moscow, Mary was already at the airport, and some guys with a big black car were waiting to bring us immediately to some kind of din-

ner party. But Michnik arrived at the same time, and they refused to take him in the car because he was this awful dissident from Poland. So we refused to go with them. Instead, we went with Michnik to a press conference somewhere.

It was '89, so Bush was in power in America. Michnik was by then a Member of Parliament and the head editor of a major newspaper. On that very day, Bush was in Warsaw and Michnik had been invited for a dinner with him. He went there and said, "I can only stay for a while because I have to go to Moscow," so he left early. But then, when he came to Moscow, they refused to let him in!

[We laugh.] Mary Kaldor continued the story:

I said, "Look here, he's already informed the Western press. You're going to look very stupid when it's all over the Western press that you refused to allow a Polish Member of Parliament to speak." But they refused so I took a taxi to go meet him. One of them said, "I will not let that man ride in an institute car."

He arrived. He was so funny. He was in jeans, as always, but he said, "Kuron put on a suit to meet Bush! It was really an amazing occasion. There was Jaruzelski, there was Bush, and then there was a bunch of us criminals." [We laugh.]

I negotiated that, but it was a terrible strain because the Americans couldn't really understand why I was making such a fuss about it. Just when I had negotiated this thing about Michnik, this woman [Dana Ferenčáková] turns up with Jaroslav's paper. They wouldn't let her into the seminar room.

I said, "I can't do any more," so Mient Jan and Michnik staged a little demonstration and said, "We won't go inside the seminar room unless she's allowed in." And so she was allowed in to listen, but not to read it. The next day we arranged that the paper would be presented at Bogomolov's institute. So we all went there to discuss it.

I asked, "Were Soviets there listening?" Kaldor replied,

Of course. They were very official. There was Dubinin, who has been appointed, I think, number three in the talks in Geneva on Yugoslavia. And Gavriil Popov. And when I met them again six months later they behaved as though they had forgotten, after the events of '89. "We were the avant-garde,' they said."

The important [breakthrough] I would say, was not so much the particular documents as the symbolism of having those people there, in forcing the others to listen to them and recognize that we and the Americans and everybody else thought it was important that they should be there. So in that sense I think it had an influence. What influence Jaroslav's paper had, I don't know.[37]

* * *

I have considered five crucial innovations in foreign policy and military doctrine that were adopted during the Gorbachev years: (a) non-offensive defense; (b) reasonable sufficiency; (c) the use of unilateral initiatives instead of negotiation; (d) a commitment to non-intervention in the decisions of other states; and (e) the admission of dissidents into the discourse between officials and foreign peace researchers.

Considered as a package, these are a remarkable departure from any policy that had previously been in either the East or the West. How could such a remarkable U-turn in Soviet policies have come about? I have argued that it happened largely as a result of the contact between TERMITE experts and foreign peace researchers. But there was more to it than that.

Let's recall that Soviet foreign policy became discredited in the early 1980s. Indeed, Gorbachev's rise to power was based largely on his critique of that policy. The decision to deploy SS-20 nuclear missiles in Eastern Europe had produced a crisis for Soviet ideologists, stimulating a peace movement in Western and even Eastern Europe to protest against the deployment of—not just American missiles—but Soviet missiles! "A plague on both their houses."

Within the Soviet political structure, that caused a major upheaval. The ideologues were astounded to find that "peace-loving forces" were blaming them for escalating the arms race. Their critics included all the Communist sympathizer organizations on which the Soviets had traditionally relied in the West. According to official Soviet ideology, this could not happen. The Soviets, by definition, were the peace-loving forces against Western imperial forces.[38]

Gorbachev proposed a simple explanation: We made a mistake. We don't need these missiles. They're provocative. They're contributing to the escalation of East-West tensions, they're strengthening anti-Soviet feeling. The whole thing has backfired. It has brought the Western governments even more under the orbit of the U.S. government. It's forced a demonstration of NATO's solidarity at the very moment when we had been weakening NATO politically.

Gorbachev and the TERMITES around him, the experts whom we have met in this chapter, called the SS-20 a big mistake. Adding that to the fiasco in Afghanistan, they could show that the Soviet government's approach to foreign policy was mistaken and that they needed a more conciliatory approach.

Thus began a remarkable interest in new ideas, an eagerness to listen to all kinds of people, even including peaceniks from abroad. What I was seeing in Georgi Arbatov and Vladimir Petrovsky, and what others saw in Lev Mendelevich, Georgi Shakhnazarov, and Yevgeny Velikhov was a team of experts who were on a mission—a quest for new ideas.

They listened well.

They listened to Anders Boserup, Robert Neild, Dietrich Fischer, and Johan Galtung, who promoted non-offensive defense. Colonel Viktor Girshfeld, Sergei Karaganov, and Andrei Kortunov listened and invented "reasonable sufficiency." Kortunov and Sergei Blagovolin listened to American reports about the stockpiles and productions of weapons and concluded that the Soviets were amassing far more than they needed for "balance," when even "balance" was an excessive objective. (Anyone could understand that "sufficient" means enough, and that parity, as an objective, may therefore lead to excess.)

Gorbachev's experts also listened to Westerners such as Charles Osgood, Bernard Lown, and John Tirman, who proposed that they give up dickering over "bargaining chips" at the negotiating table and adopt a policy of "unilateral initiatives." The term "GRIT" seems to have become a household word for these people. Not only did they use it with an easy familiarity in their discussions with

Western peaceniks, but they sent the KGB out to find everything written on the subject, even in manuscript form before it appeared in print.

They listened to Randall Forsberg when she spoke sensibly about the merits of a non-intervention regime, a promise not to dominate the affairs of the states that had previously been satellites. This commitment, expressed jokingly as the Soviets' new "Sinatra Doctrine," actually was the momentous change that allowed Central European countries to move toward democracy.

The hardest part was to listen to Mary Kaldor when she demanded that they let dissidents speak. She won that breakthrough only because the leaders in the Soviet Union were serious about overcoming totalitarianism and the Cold War.

Yet that breakthrough was only grudging and partial. At that point, the TERMITES could tolerate almost anything more easily than accepting BARKING DOGS, whether they were from Poland, Hungary, Czechoslovakia, or the Soviet Union itself. As we shall see, the Soviet dissidents would never take their place as leaders in the post-Communist state, as did the dissidents from other Eastern European countries, such as Geremek, Michnik, Havel, and Dienstbier.

Yet my interviews established in this chapter that "experts" in the Soviet Union, like the Soviet scientists, were seeking ideas from their Western counterparts. They were on a quest and international civil society welcomed their participation in solving the most serious global problems of the day.

Notes

1. I wish I could properly acknowledge Nikolai K. for these valuable comments but I don't know his location and cannot ask permission to quote him. This interview was in Toronto, September 1992.

2. Nikolai K. discussion.

3. Although Karaganov does not refer specifically to any book, a likely one of that period would be *Transnational Relations and World Politics*, edited by Robert O. Keohane and Joseph S. Nye, Jr. (Cambridge, MA: Harvard University Press, 1972).

4. Sergei Karaganov, in discussion with the author, May 1992, Institute of Europe, Moscow.

5. Egon Bahr, in telephone discussion with the author, April 1994.

6. Andrei Melville, in discussion with the author, spring 1991, Moscow.

7. Peter Gladkov, in discussion with the author, October 1991, Moscow.

8. Dietrich Fischer, "The Black Hole," *Peace Magazine* 8, no. 6 (November–December 1992): 18.

9. Sergei Blagovolin, in discussion with the author, 1993, Moscow.

10. Vitaly Zhurkin, Sergei Karaganov and Andrei Kortunov, *Reasonable Sufficiency and New Political Thinking* (Moscow: Nauka, 1989). See also Georgi Arbatov, "How Much Defense is Enough?" *International Affairs* no. 4 (Autumn 1989), and P. Baev, Sergei Karaganov, et al., *Tactical Nuclear Weapons in Europe* (Moscow: APN, 1990).

11. Vitaly Zhurkin, Sergei Karaganov, Andrei Kortunov, "Old and New Challenges to Security," *Kommunist* no. 1 (January 1988): 42–50.

12. *Kommunist* was later published under the title, *Svobodnaia mysl'* (Moscow: 1991).

13. Informants from the USA/Canada Institute believe that this must be the KGB general with whom, as described earlier, Van Eeghen prayed, and who helped engineer the release of the Ukrainian Baptist pastor. As he was dead, I could not interview him.

14. Interview with Andrei Kortunov, Moscow, March 1994.

15. Dietrich Fischer, *Preventing War in the Nuclear Age* (Totowa, NJ: Rowman and Allanheld, 1984).
16. Michael B. Johansen and Metta Spencer, "Nonprovocative Defense," *Peace Magazine* 1, no. 5 (August 1985): 20–22.
17. Mikhail Gorbachev, *Perestroika* trans. Georges Peronansky and Tatjana Varsavsky (London: Collins, 1987). However, the *New York Times* had quoted almost the same argument, so Gorbachev may have read it there instead.
18. Johansen and Spencer, 16–20.
19. Jørgen Dragsdahl interview, Moscow, August 1991. Also see Jørgen Dragsdahl, "How Peace Research Has Reshaped the European Arms Dialogue," in *Peace Research in Europe, Annual Review of Peace Activism, 1989*, ed. John Tirman (Washington, DC: Winston Foundation for World Peace, 1989), 39–45.
20. Robert R. Neild, *An Essay on Strategy as it Affects the Achievement of Peace in a Nuclear Setting* (Basingstoke: Macmillan, 1990).
21. Boserup died before the book was complete and Neild published it himself.
22. One such influence came from Bulgaria. Dietrich Fischer reports that Professor Nansen Behar, Secretary of the Union of Scientific Workers, organized a conference on "European Security and Non-Offensive Defense" in Varna, Bulgaria, in October 1987. This was the first event of its kind in Eastern Europe. There were twenty participants from the East and twenty from the West, including retired British Brigadier General Michael Harbottle. Behar later spent a year in New York at the Institute for East-West Security Studies.
23. Zhurkin, Karaganov, and Kortunov.
24. The text of their letter was published in the journal of the Federation of American Scientists, *FAS Public Interest Report* 41, no. 2 (February 1988). It follows:
10 October 1987:
Dear General Secretary Gorbachev:
We are a group of scientists from Western countries who have been working on the problems of easing both the nuclear and nonnuclear military confrontations in Europe. We have noted the statements, made by you (most recently in *Pravda*) and by the Warsaw Treaty Organization (from Budapest and Berlin) that the doctrine of WTO and NATO forces should be defensive and that a stable balance should be achieved by reductions in offensive forces rather than by build-ups.
We are very much interested in these statements. We have reached similar conclusions. We would like to share them with you and ask you to respond with an elaboration of your ideas.
Current fears of war in Europe are due primarily to the offense-capable structure of the military forces on both sides. These structures give forces the capability for surprise attack and conquest. They feed the fears which are used to justify very high levels of military spending and a continued technological arms race after more than 40 years of peace in Europe. These same fears are also used to justify reliance on nuclear weapons as a deterrent to nonnuclear aggression.
Reductions of the current forces without changes in their composition would preserve their offensive structure and the associated fears of aggression and therefore would perpetuate the justification for relying on nuclear weapons in Europe. We believe that there should be reductions in non-nuclear forces designed so as to simultaneously cut drastically their offensive capabilities and preserve the defensive capabilities on each side. That would implement the doctrine of defensiveness and lead to a stable condition that we would term "mutual defensive sufficiency." At that point, we believe that the popular willingness to maintain large armed forces and to sustain the risks of the nuclear confrontation would rapidly erode.
We would suggest the following approach: from the Atlantic to the Urals, reduce the numbers of strike aircraft, tanks, armed helicopters, and long-range artillery on each

side to equal levels well below the current levels of the lower side; and ban ballistic missiles in Europe with ranges greater than approximately 50 km.

Although the reductions required to reach equality will be unequal, the security of both sides will be increased. Reducing long-range strike capabilities would reduce incentives for preemptive strikes in time of crisis. Reducing numbers of tanks and artillery available for massed attacks relative to decentralized defensive forces would reduce the capability for capturing foreign territory. And, with the fear of conventional aggression reduced, "battlefield" nuclear weapons could be withdrawn from Europe and destroyed, thereby reducing the danger of nuclear war. Then the technological resources of both East and West could be freed to concentrate on the social, economic, and environmental improvement of Europe and the rest of the world.

We would also urge that, as part of the new extension of *glasnost* to the military area, the Soviet government publish its own numbers for Soviet weapons systems in different categories. Otherwise, independent analysts will continue to have only NATO estimates—which are often biased upwards by worst-case assumptions.

We would be interested in your reactions to these thoughts and in your own ideas for implementing your proposals for reducing the continuing senseless and dangerous military confrontation in Europe.

Sincerely,

Anders Boserup, Robert Neild, Frank von Hippel, and Albrecht von Mueller

25. Dietrich Fischer, memorandum, 1991.

26. Randall Forsberg, in discussion with the author, 1992. Forsberg was part of a group visiting IMEMO. She favored cuts of weapons based in the U.S. but maintained in opposition to the Soviet Union. The other members of the U.S. visiting team promoted disproportions of the kind that actually would be adopted in the CFE Treaty.

27. Mary Kaldor, in discussion with the author, December 1993, Ankara. See also Stephen Shenfield, "The USSR: Viktor Girshfeld and the Concept of 'Sufficient Defense,'" *ADIU Report* 6, no. 1 (January–February 1984): 10.

28. Charles Egerton Osgood. *An Alternative to War or Surrender* (Urbana: University of Illinois Press, 1962).

29. I am borrowing heavily here from a fine account of these events outlined by John Sigler in a lecture to Science for Peace in Toronto in 1991. See also Amitai Etzioni, "The Kennedy Experiment," in *Western Political Quarterly* 20, no. 2 (June 1967): 361–80. See also Etzioni's article in *Psychology Today* (December 1969): 43–45 and 62–63.

30. Johan Galtung, in discussion with the author, December 1993, Ankara.

31. Under-Secretary-General Vladimir Petrovsky, in discussion with the author, United Nations, New York.

32. Lindsay Mattison, in telephone discussion with the author, 1992.

33. Actually he was spokesman for the Soviet Foreign Ministry, but Gorbachev often borrowed Gerasimov's services. Eventually he appointed a staff of his own

34. Gennady Gerasimov, in telephone discussion with the author, spring 1994.

35. Randall Forsberg, in telephone discussion with the author, 1992. I was unable to interview Cox, who died in 1993. Forsberg died in 2007.

36. Forsberg discussion 1992.

37. Mary Kaldor and Mient Jan Faber interview, December 1993.

38. I am indebted to Christopher Paine for this analysis.

Chapter 9: Do Peace and Democracy Work?

I adore Mikhail Gorbachev. Almost all other peace activists feel the same way. He did everything we could have asked of him when it came to promoting peace and democracy in the Soviet Union and around the world. I can hardly think of another ruler in history whose actions and values were equally commendable. Under his leadership the ailing Soviet system was peacefully dismantled, the Cold War came to an end, Eastern Europe became free, and the arms race was reversed, for Soviet leaders could see that their country needed peace and democracy to deal with its systemic crisis. What a record of success!

But most Russians disagree. Indeed, public opinion there holds Gorbachev in low esteem bordering on contempt and considers most of his actions wrong-headed. For example, here is part of an e-mail from a Russian friend:

> Gorbachev himself doesn't understand now what he did. Was it positive or negative for his country? The consequences of his openness were unfavorable for Russians. That is evident even to him. Western countries used Gorbachev as a naïve child. He weakened Russia's military strength and the West immediately took advantage of the opportunity. Now we face an expanded NATO, an American military base in Poland, and color revolutions in the countries that we considered to be our zone of influence.
>
> That's very unpleasant. Whom shall we blame for that? Certainly him: Gorbachev. Not long ago the Duma passed a law to create foundations of presidents' heritage. Every president will have his heritage foundation: Yeltsin, Putin, and Medvedev. But not Gorbachev. No. The Duma said he wasn't a president of Russia. He was president of the Soviet Union. That's the official explanation, but the real reason is that they think it will be better for Russians to forget his heritage. Imagine his feelings about the role he played!

In this chapter I'll appraise his landmark decisions as objectively as possible, taking account of his own personal orientation and the key TERMITES on his team—his foreign minister, his advisers, his economists, and the top KGB and military leaders who advised him and administered his policies.

Gorbachev was committed to peace and democracy—not only as a goal but as a means. He tried to make the Soviet Union accountable to the citizens and he tried never to resort to police or military action to enforce his political actions. If

171

we want to know whether peace and democracy work, his experience is an excellent test case.

Of course we know the objective outcome: The Soviet Union was dismantled. Did Gorbachev's reliance on peace and democracy determine the breakdown of the Union? To anticipate my conclusion, I will say here only that three factors caused that outcome: the *weak economy*; the *demands for secession* by nationalist leaders of various republics; and the desire of *Party elites to retain their monopoly of power* rather than become a democracy. We'll ask whether his peaceful and democratic approach was the source of these conditions.

Besides the Russians who retrospectively consider Gorbachev's goals disastrous for the country, there are others who originally shared his goals but believe now that he executed them badly.

And many severe problems did arise, such as an economic crisis, the loss of superpower status, separatist riots and insurrections, and eventually the break-up of the country. When blame is assigned for such events, it must be pinned on the leader, though when discussing calamities that could not reasonably have been foreseen, no one actually deserves blame. Hence in deciding how much credit and blame to assign to Gorbachev and his team, we must consider not only whether their intentions were sound and fulfilled, but also whether the obstacles that arose were foreseeable.

First, let's acknowledge that we cannot be sure what his intentions were at any particular time or how much he knew. He would certainly never have become general secretary of the CPSU if he had been completely frank and straightforward throughout his life. As a master TERMITE, Gorbachev knew when not to show his true intentions—not only before he came to power, but indeed throughout his tenure in office, since there were powerful opponents around him at all times. You can call him tricky if you don't respect such political maneuvering, but I call him politically savvy. In any case, when analyzing his policies we must admit that they were not always what they seemed to be, and we cannot know all the intentions that lay behind them. Even honorable politicians are complex.

In appraising Gorbachev's performance, we are not just playing a scholarly sport. We need to judge the astuteness of this man so as to learn from his mistakes and failures. And there were abundant failures; many results of his actions were exactly what he tried to prevent. But, just as he studied Khrushchev's failings carefully, so too other leaders and activists will study how to create peace and democracy. A critical appraisal may yield helpful warnings about possible pitfalls to avoid. If history offers any advice, Gorbachev's experience is the most useful case study of all.

We can identify six clear goals of Gorbachev's, which I will review sequentially. They are:

- to protect human rights and maximize human freedom;
- to promote peace and disarmament;
- to improve the quality of life of the Soviet population;
- to increase democracy and political accountability;

- to relinquish Soviet control of the Warsaw Pact countries to their own governments and citizens;
- to prevent civil war and strife, holding the Soviet Union together.
-

How well did he and his policy-makers succeed in upholding those values?

Goal: To Protect Human Rights and Freedom

To increase freedom and protect human rights were Gorbachev's primary objectives all along. Both of his grandfathers had been incarcerated during Stalin's time, and as a young man he had committed his life to keeping totalitarianism from ever arising again.[1] As a democratic socialist he believed that no regime can be truly socialist unless also democratic. In *Conversations with Gorbachev*, the transcript of long discussions with his closest friend, Zdeněk Mlynář, the two men show that even during their university days they had been democratic socialists and that they had remained so.[2]

Freeing oppressed people would seem to be a winning strategy. Peace activists generally assume that if you treat others well, they will reciprocate. Presumably Gorbachev believed so when it came to freeing prisoners of conscience. For example, he freed Sakharov from house arrest and invited him to return to his activism. Sakharov did so. But soon he became Gorbachev's opponent in the new, democratic parliament[3] and, after his death, his widow continued her fierce opposition to Gorbachev. They and Gorbachev's other rival, Boris Yeltsin, were the leaders of the leftist movement—a political wing that identified themselves as the "democrats" and claimed to be vastly more democratic than Gorbachev himself, whom they criticized bitterly. With respect to these people I write the word "democrats" in quotation marks, since not everyone who claims to be democratic really is so. Especially Yeltsin's allies.

As we shall see, the polarization between this group of radical "democrats" and the hard-line DINOSAURS would widen so much that Gorbachev would worry about the prospect of civil war. In order to placate the DINOSAURS, he would temporarily adopt some of their anti-reformist policies. In reaction, many of his own team would join the radical "democrats" and bring about his downfall. The center would not hold; his TERMITES would abandon him.

Surely he did not anticipate such results. Rather than embracing the BARKING DOGS as allies, he gave them a way to attract a wide following of impatient intellectuals who would become his strongest enemies.

A similar shock awaited Gorbachev when he authorized Fyodor Burlatsky to work for human rights and religious freedom. As described in chapter 5, it was Burlatsky who joined the pious Dutchman Ernst Van Eeghen in holding an international conference on religious freedom. In 1988 Burlatsky created the Human Rights Commission, which he co-chaired with Rosalynn Carter. They held two conferences, first in the Netherlands and then in Moscow, inviting members of the American Helsinki Group and some dissidents who had been in the Gulag—notably Sergei Kovalev—as well as Ludmilla Alexeyeva, a co-founder of the Moscow Helsinki Group who had emigrated to America.

Probably Gorbachev expected the human rights BARKING DOGS to be grati-
fied by his freeing of the prisoners of religion and by the human rights legislation that Burlatsky prepared and steered through the Supreme Soviet. They were
not, for they disliked the fact that the initiative was government-led. Their logic
was impeccable, whether or not it was wise in that situation. If you want to form
an independent civil society, as surely the dissidents did, it must not be a crea-
ture of the regime. As we will see later, the independence of civil society is still
in jeopardy in post-Putin Russia.

However, I must also recognize Burlatsky's understandable disappointment
that these former dissidents had not participated in the Russian commission but
in the American one. He had invited them to join his group but they preferred to
continue to represent the American Helsinki group. He said,

> Timofeev and Kovalev and some other [dissidents] created their own groups—
> Memorial and some others—and didn't want any contact with us. They ex-
> plained that we are an official group and they are real unofficial groups. And
> really it was that way because I became a member of parliament and had big
> official influence with the government, which gave me a very good possibility
> to work for human rights.[4]

I never understood the BARKING DOGS' antipathy toward TERMITES—especially toward the very man who had liberated them. Once I asked Academician
Vitaly Goldansky, "Suppose I am in jail. Somebody unlocks the door and lets
me out and I don't say thank you. That is incomprehensible. What had he done,
while unlocking the door, that made it impossible for people to thank him?"
Goldansky replied,

> First they need to know why he opened the door. They didn't understand
> sometimes. I told you that we had prepared many drafts of this letter [asking for
> Sakharov's release] because it would help Gorbachev. We knew that he would
> be willing to do that. He needed some help in preparing a letter in language that
> could be understood and accepted by his colleagues in the Politburo. But Sak-
> harov was maximalist. And there were also other dissidents who were maxi-
> malists. And while being certainly thankful for their own release, they immedi-
> ately demanded other steps.[5]

That explanation still seemed insufficient to me. Would these "maximalists"
have preferred for Gorbachev to lose his position because the DINOSAURS were
still so strong? Evidently so. That seemed irrational to me.

Eventually I came to ask a different question. Suppose dissidents actually
had not *wanted* to be released from prison. After the Velvet Revolution, the
Czech dissident Václav Havel was freed and immediately became president of
Czechoslovakia. I read a conversation between him and a former Polish dissident, Adam Michnik, who had become editor of a Warsaw newspaper. Speaking
of the average citizen in post-totalitarian society, Havel said,

> It is these people who really despise the old totalitarian regime. But at the same
> time they had spent their entire lives under that regime and became accustomed

to it. They became accustomed to the fact that above them a large, strong state was developing which was able to know everything, which supposedly looked after all their needs, and which was responsible for everything. The citizens became accustomed to such relationship with the state and to its habits. And these are habits which are difficult to get rid of. . . .

[P]eople want to find a guilty party. They are in a state of shock caused by freedom, by the absence of guarantees, by disillusionment with the hierarchy. This is a state which I have many times compared to that of a person who's just been released from jail. When you are in prison, you are happy for the moment. When you are let free, and when it happens so suddenly, you become totally helpless; you don't know what to do. You may even have a desire to return back to prison, because you know what awaits you there. But you don't know what to expect of this newly acquired freedom. The same thing is happening with this society. It does not know what to do with this freedom. Hence, this search for an enemy who could be blamed for all the misfortunes.[6]

Havel's interpretation fits comments that I heard from former dissidents in Russia, though of course they never quite stated that they preferred prison life to the challenging stresses of freedom.

Besides, there is also another possible explanation that is unique to the Soviet Union—the dreadful experiences of the former prisoners of Stalin's Gulag whom Khrushchev freed.[7] After his "secret speech" denouncing the crimes of Stalin, Khrushchev released some four million prisoners, many of whom had spent most of their adult lives in the Gulag. They were a scruffy looking bunch, conspicuous for their tattoos and crude prison slang. Most people could not believe that Stalin had made a mistake and incarcerated millions of innocent people. Therefore they resented and feared the release of these "criminals" into respectable Soviet society.

Knowing this history, one might expect the dissidents whom Gorbachev released also to feel wary about their new freedom. But it was different this time. Soviet citizens had been listening to the BBC, Voice of America, and Radio Liberty; they knew a lot about dissidents and admired them. Shortly after these extreme BARKING DOGS were released, many people idolized them and joined them as radical "democrats" in opposition to the man who remained the leader of the reviled CPSU.

Thus my question remains unanswered. I still cannot quite fathom how these formerly persecuted people could fail to support their liberator and his advisers and ministers. In any case, the truth is that Gorbachev's commitment to freedom and human rights did not receive the respect and allegiance that he may have expected. The results were only partly successful.

Goal: Peace and Disarmament
To promote peace and disarmament was the second of Gorbachev's goals. As he told his friend Zdeněk Mlynář,

From the very beginning of *perestroika* I proceeded on the basis that change must be carried out democratically through reforms and most importantly, without bloodshed. My own experience, which I accumulated while holding the highest post in our government, showed unambiguously that the use of force as a method of long-term resolution of fundamental problems is unacceptable.[8]

But Gorbachev took office during the worst phase of the Cold War. Two military alliances, NATO and the WTO, had been attempting to harm each other almost continuously since the end of World War II. Although direct fighting had been narrowly averted, there were "proxy wars" in which each camp supported opposite sides of wars in other countries, such as Angola, Korea, Vietnam, the Middle East, and, since December 1979, Afghanistan. Both sides had been undergoing massive military build-ups. The Soviet military was consuming, by some estimates, up to 25 percent of the country's gross national product and had achieved approximate overall parity with the Americans.[9]

After the Soviets had deployed intermediate-range ballistic missiles targeting Western Europe, NATO had responded during Jimmy Carter's administration by planning the deployment of Pershing and cruise missiles in Europe that could strike Moscow within about ten minutes of flight. The danger was mounting when Gorbachev took office, intending to reverse this ominous trend.

But he faced a determined opponent in the White House—Ronald Reagan, who was building up U.S. weaponry while refusing arms control measures. Reagan announced a new Strategic Defense Initiative (SDI), popularly dubbed "Star Wars," to intercept incoming nuclear missiles and denied that the Anti-Ballistic Missile Treaty of 1972 applied to it, since his system would involve a new technology.

Gorbachev and his foreign minister, Eduard Shevardnadze, were cultivating good relationships with their counterparts in the United States and, especially, in Britain. Margaret Thatcher had quickly taken a liking to Gorbachev and persuaded the initially skeptical Reagan to trust him too.

Reagan had already made an offer to the Soviets—one that they *could*, and almost certainly would, refuse: the "Zero Option." In 1981 he had offered not to proceed with the deployment of his planned intermediate-range Pershings and cruise missiles in Europe if the Soviets would remove their existing missiles targeted on Europe. Since this involved trading real missiles for mostly drawing-board missiles, he knew that there would be no takers.

But to everyone's astonishment, Gorbachev accepted the offer. The Zero Option became the basis for the Intermediate-Range Nuclear Forces (INF) Treaty, which was signed in December 1987.

The INF Treaty was, however, only a consolation prize. The previous year Gorbachev, Reagan, and their advisers and ministers had met for a summit in Reykjavik, Iceland. The Americans had not expected anything dramatic to happen there, but Gorbachev had arrived with big plans. He proposed the complete elimination of all nuclear weapons. Reagan was tempted to agree, but he would not give up his beloved SDI plan. It was SDI that killed the deal. Nevertheless, the INF Treaty was completed within a year. It called for the elimination of nuclear and conventional ground-launched ballistic and cruise missiles with intermediate ranges (300–3,400 miles). By its deadline, June 1, 1991, 846 such weapons had been destroyed by the U.S. and 1,846 by the Soviet Union.

A month before the August 1991 coup attempt against Gorbachev, another important treaty was signed in Moscow—the START Treaty. Finalized by Reagan's successor, George H. W. Bush, it covered long-range nuclear weapons and eventually resulted in the removal of about 80 percent of all strategic weapons then existing.

Moreover, Bush Sr. began eliminating short-range nuclear weapons that were scattered around the world on ships and artillery. Gorbachev matched him and even raised the ante, withdrawing about 12,000 Soviet short-range weapons in comparison to the American withdrawal of 4,000. Indeed, all such weapons had been removed from Soviet republics before they gained independence.

As the Cold War wound down, progress began to occur in conventional weapons too. For years negotiations had been stalled between NATO and WTO over conventional arms control from the Atlantic to the Urals. In December 1988 Gorbachev announced at the United Nations the withdrawal of 50,000 troops from Eastern Europe and the de-mobilization of 500,000 Soviet troops—another of his audacious unilateral initiatives.

In late 1989, the whole situation changed in Europe. The Berlin wall came down and nonviolent revolutions swept the WTO countries, resulting in the overturning of all their Communist regimes. The Soviet Union concluded even faster troop withdrawals from those countries. Its leader was now speaking in peaceable tones about "our common European home" and "common security."

America's Gulf War presented a new quandary for Gorbachev. He had firmly rejected all pressures for the Soviet Union to intervene militarily abroad, but he was also cultivating good relations with George H. W. Bush, who fully intended to punish Saddam Hussein for his attack on Kuwait. Gorbachev consulted his ministers, whose opinions were divided. Foreign Minister Eduard Shevardnadze was firmly on the American side, and Gorbachev finally accepted his arguments, though he also sent Yevgeny Primakov off to Baghdad to see if he could bend Saddam Hussein enough to prevent the impending war. Primakov had long experience in the Middle East and did return with a proposal that was not taken seriously enough to prevent the invasion. Still, Shevardnadze was irked by Gorbachev's ambivalence about supporting the American war.[10]

By then the Cold War was tepid. Proxy wars were over. Even the Soviets' brutal war in Afghanistan had ended, though it had lasted far longer than Gorbachev had hoped.

* * *

Soviet participation in the Afghan war had started at the end of 1979, when Brezhnev sent troops as a gesture of fraternal solidarity toward the communist government in Kabul, which seemed to be losing a civil war. Then, of course, matters went from bad to worse. The modernizing communists, the People's Democratic Party of Afghanistan (PDPA), and their Soviet allies attempted to reform Afghan society by such means as improving the status of women and changing other local Muslim traditions. Offended by these alien interventions, various local warlords took up the struggle, which became a proxy war for the United States and the Soviet Union. However, other states—notably Saudi Arabia, the UK, Egypt, China, Iran, and Pakistan—also got involved, supporting the Muslim insurgents, the Mujahideen, while India supported the Soviets and the communist Afghan government.

The Soviet invasion cannot have been a complete surprise to the Americans, who had been secretly funding the Mujahideen for six months, funneling the money through the CIA and Pakistani intelligence service.[11] As President Carter's adviser Zbigniew Brzezinski later admitted, CIA aid to the Mujahideen did not begin after the Soviet army invaded Afghanistan, but well in advance.

> We didn't push the Russians to intervene, but we knowingly increased the probability that they would. . . . That secret operation was an excellent idea. It had the effect of drawing the Soviets into the Afghan trap. . . . The day that the Soviets officially crossed the border, I wrote to President Carter: We now have the opportunity of giving to the Soviet Union its Vietnam War.[12]

That war was to last nine years. It stopped being regarded as the Soviets' international duty in 1986, when Gorbachev openly called it "a running sore." Behind the scenes, he was trying to find a responsible way of withdrawing, though the last Soviet troops would not actually be removed until early 1989.

One of Gorbachev's secret interventions during that interval has not been widely told, for it drew upon the transnational civil society connections of Georgi Shakhnazarov, one of his closest advisers from 1988 onward.

Shakhazarov had long been based in Prague, working at the *World Marxist Review* (*Problems of Peace and Socialism*) and developing a broad perspective. Then he worked in the International Department of the CPSU, specializing in relations with communist countries. He created a political science association in the Soviet Academy of Sciences and advocated democracy and a liberal international approach. He wanted a world order that would transcend national identities and borders. In his new political science association, he came into contact with an American, Lindsay Mattison, who does international development work from an organization in Washington, D.C. They liked each other. In 1992 I phoned Mattison, a plainspoken man who recounted his remarkable adventures as a back-channel diplomat during the Soviet-Afghan War.

> The Political Science Association, though small in staff (it was really a kind of secret club, a network headed by Shakhnazarov) enabled me to break the standard exchange relationships with those institutes. Normally the director controls it and sends his friends because traveling abroad is a privilege. This way we were able to reach in and select people to create conversations that were much more intelligent. . . . I had my own KGB guy, a fellow named Valentin Aksilenko, who was quite famous, actually, in some circles. . . .
>
> In any case, Shakhnazarov was given a bunch of jobs by Gorbachev. Job number one was Afghanistan, because it was a communist country. So Shakhnazarov said to me: "Go find me the Mujahideen and let's negotiate."
>
> And so I went around. They asked me to organize a delegation to Afghanistan. I got Bill Sullivan, the former ambassador and a bunch of people. We took the first American group and flew in over the rockets, throwing flares out of the airplane, went to Kabul, and met with [then-President] Najibullah and all the

fun people in Afghanistan. Primakov led the Russian delegation. We took a *Post* reporter with us. Afterwards, Shakhnazarov basically told us they were getting out. That was a year before everybody else knew.

Then Shakhnazarov asked me to set up negotiations with the Mujahideen. There is in AID a training program for Mujahideen, [which made] contacts. We took six of the seven groups, rented a chateau outside Paris, and brought in Aksilenko, who by then was an important member of the Soviet Political Science Association, and [William] Smirnov, who was Shakhnazarov's aide, and did negotiations with the Mujahideen.

[Vladimir] Petrovsky, who is now under-secretary-general of the UN, is one of the Political Science Association people. He did things like pull the foreign ministry off us. They didn't particularly like an independent negotiation coming out of the Central Committee. You know, they were professional diplomats. They were having trouble with the negotiations but they issued visas, little things like that. They allowed expenditure of hard currency by the embassy in Paris to keep people alive. You don't make independent moves in the Soviet system, and Shakhnazarov was using his network. Shakh is in that crowd that Burlatsky put together years ago which became Andropov's brains trust.

We set up a set of secret negotiations and we did it again in Bad Godesberg in Germany. We sent somebody to Peshawar to meet secretly with the Mujahideen leaders, Rumani and the rest of them. The Salang Road is in a mountain pass that Rumani controlled. We cut a deal that got him to open the road and let the Russian troops out. The liberals around Gorbachev were afraid that the road would be cut and the conservatives would yell that we have to go back into the country to rescue the troops and the whole thing would start over again.

I had a lot of meetings with Shakhnazarov. Primakov was peripherally involved, off and on. There was a brawl between the two of them in the Central Committee. Primakov likes a lot of credit for things. He took the public position of the Russian government, which was that they wouldn't deal with the Mujahideen without the PDPA or Najibullah crowd present. But these were secret negotiations that I was doing. We were dealing directly with the Mujahideen. In the official talks they never got anywhere because they constantly had to argue on behalf of the PDPA. Shakhnazarov was pleased that we didn't leak it or publicize it because it would have embarrassed them and might have caused Najibullah's government to collapse.

We'd do things like, the Muj would tell us they have to say so and so and apologize for this and do that. We'd write stuff and Gorbachev would speak over Radio Moscow, and the Muj would say, Well, I guess we're dealing with the right guy here. (laughs.)

We were getting no help from the State Department because Zalmay Khalilzad, who ran the firm, is an Afghan who didn't want peace. He was the person in the State Department in charge of Afghan policy. The Reagan people put a Pakistani at the National Security Council and an Afghan at the State Department in charge of the policy. I don't know whether you know that Zia [Prime Minister Muhammed Zia-ul-Haq] and Pakistan backed [Gulbuddin] Hekmatyar and tried to make it a religious fight because they didn't want the ethnic brawl with the Baluchis to spread into Pakistan. So they didn't want peace in Afghanistan; they wanted a religious war.

And further, they were getting enormously rich on the arms trade, narcotics, and huge U.S. funding of the Mujahideen through the CIA. That was all in the hands of the military intelligence, ISI, in Pakistan and to this day they still control the nuclear program. The CIA was not giving stuff directly to the Mujahideen; it was giving it through the Pakistan Intelligence. So U.S. policy was, they just wanted to deal with the Soviets and talk. They wanted to set up more talks and so on, but the Soviets said they just wanted to get out. So it's fair to say the U.S. government didn't lift a hand to help the Soviets resolve it. But I went over and briefed them a lot.

Because we were not officials and because, wearing one hat, Shakhnazarov and Aksilenko and all the gang could be the Soviet Political Science Association, if we got caught in France or Germany doing these talks, it would just be "citizen diplomacy" and a group of amateurs rather than anything official, so it wouldn't embarrass them. . .

After Afghanistan, the next thing for Shakhnazarov to do was preside over the devolution of Eastern Europe. If you see pictures of Gorbachev traveling, or at meetings of the Warsaw Pact, you always see Shakhnazarov at his side. And Shakh is very proud of having got through that without killing everybody.[13]

I asked Mattison what sort of Westerners Shakhnazarov had been close to. He said he had not known Westerners until late in his career, but had become acquainted with Saul Mendlovitz, a law professor at Rutgers who, with Richard Falk, had developed something called the "World Order Models Project" (WOMP). Mendlovitz had accompanied Mattison to Moscow for the last conference before the Soviet Union ended. Mattison said,

I was with Shakhnazarov and Yakovlev and the others [when they took] down the flag in the Kremlin and got out of there. I took the guy from the Supreme Court, Scalia, and Governor Ashcroft of Missouri and a whole gang of about fifty Americans over there and did the final conference on the Union Treaty.

Mattison also told me more about the Institute of Social Sciences (described in chapter 4). This had been the training facility for elite foreign communists, but as *perestroika* gathered strength, it had to be shut down. He said,

It belonged to the International Department of the Central Committee. Shakhnazarov basically gave that to me a year ago, saying: "Think of something to do with it." So I was setting up a center for constitutional democracy and I brought in congressional delegations. I was setting up a relationship between the Supreme Soviet and the U.S. Congress.

But times change. When the Soviet Union came apart, Gorbachev was left with no presidency to occupy. He established two foundations instead: Green Cross International, which is based in Geneva and addresses environmental and peace issues, and the Gorbachev Foundation, which was initially housed in the swanky buildings that Mattison had expected to use for his center. I interviewed several members of the Gorbachev Foundation there, including Shakhnazarov. Later Gorbachev would feel cramped in that space, which was controlled by his vindictive and triumphant rival, Boris Yeltsin. With financial support from the founder of CNN, Ted Turner, the Gorbachev Foundation built an elegant new edifice elsewhere, which it now occupies.

* * *

Did peace work? As we have seen, Gorbachev and his ministers and advisers tried hard to avoid imposing their policies with violence—and in this they generally succeeded. If for no other reason, the remarkable progress they made toward nuclear disarmament assures their status in history. As one Soviet colonel said to me, "We should put up a solid gold statue of Gorbachev."

But not everyone shared that opinion. Indeed, public opinion generally turned against Gorbachev, concluding that he had given away the country's most priceless assets. But I had opportunities later to question members of his team of peacemakers about their regrets. For example, my research assistant Julia Kalinina interviewed Eduard Shevardnadze for me in 1995. She asked him about

> all these *perestroika* agreements—the elimination of missiles, the withdrawal of Soviet troops, and the unification of Germany. For the same deeds that the West thanked you, you are severely criticized here. And now a kind of revision is going on about what you had done. Was it really necessary to conclude these treaties? Are the politicians right nowadays—that they ought to follow a "power" line in politics, and not agree so rapidly to all the demands of the West?

Shevardnadze replied,

> You know, at that time the threat of a new world war really existed. I could feel it in my skin. And nuclear war and nuclear weapons—that's not an ordinary war. Today people don't remember much about it but at that time everybody was yelling. "We are going to a nuclear catastrophe; we'll all die!"
>
> On the unification of Germany. . . . Now people judge the situation differently but at that time a huge group of our armed forces was located there in the middle of Europe. And in the background—mass demonstrations for unification of Germany that could easily turn into serious collisions. There was a real threat of World War III. Now time has passed and things look different. That happens.

Julia asked, "As for *perestroika* and the breakdown of the Soviet Union, do you wish you could re-do it somehow?" I like Shevardnadze's reply:

> Concerning *perestroika* in this country, I think we could have chosen another way. The formation of new states—sooner or later that would have happened anyway. But we could have moved toward confederation, except that, as a result of the coup, everything collapsed. And I don't know if it's worth regretting that now.[14]

Goal: Improve Quality of Life for Soviet People
Improving the quality of life of the Soviet population was a third goal of Gorbachev's. There were two main factors involved: first, low income levels and, second, the poor health of the population, mainly caused by high rates of alcoholism. Both were enormous challenges, beyond his control.

He began by addressing alcoholism, the main factor explaining the shocking mortality levels among Soviet males, whose life expectancy at birth in 1985 was only 63.3 years, compared to 72.9 for females[15] and 73.1 for Canadian males that year.[16] Only two months after his elevation he raised the price of liquor and curtailed its availability. This did reduce the sale of alcohol, thereby improving the purchasing power of the citizens, but it also cut government revenue by about 100 billion rubles. In any case, the production and sale of alcohol soon resumed, though largely as a black market commodity. And, after a brief upward blip in life expectancy, males continued to decline in health.

By all accounts, the anti-alcoholism campaign failed and would not be tried again until 2010 when, for the same reason, President Medvedev would again impose a higher price on alcoholic beverages.

The low standard of living of the Soviet population mainly reflected the general economic condition, which was plunging when Gorbachev took office. This need not be regarded as an inevitable effect of socialism for, except in wartime, the Soviet economy had shown high rates of growth—higher, indeed, than in capitalist countries. In part this could be explained by the fact that growth is greatest when a country is industrializing, and industrialization already had taken place in the U.S. before intensifying in the Soviet Union.[17]

Another major factor was the price of oil. Russia is the world's second-largest oil-producing country. The oil crisis of 1973 created hardship for the rest of the world but benefited the Soviet economy. New oil and gas fields were opened just when prices were rocketing upward, but the Brezhnev government wasted the new money that poured in from exports. Instead of finding new solutions to the increasing food shortages, or upgrading the backward construction industry, the regime spent lavishly to import grain and even meat and butter, enabling the population to live beyond their realistic means.[18] During the 1970s and early 1980s, the Soviet Union received over $170 billion from oil exports, but no one seemed to know where most of that money went.[19] In fact, this new oil money served to disguise the actual deterioration in the Soviet productive economy, which was declining seriously from about 1975.

Only after taking office did Gorbachev discover the magnitude of the economic crisis facing the country. Although he had been regarded almost as the "heir apparent" to the leadership, he and the other Politburo members had received reports about the economy that were heavily censored and "cooked."

Moreover, Gorbachev himself was not much of an economist. As a democratic socialist his economic notions were changing rapidly to resemble those of the social democratic parties of Western Europe. In the meantime, he had to depend on Soviet economists who were themselves confused. The progressive ones were secretly leaping from doctrinaire communism into doctrinaire neoliberal capitalism influenced by Milton Friedman's monetarist theories.[20] Unlike his team of international advisers, who had developed wider perspectives at *Problems of Peace and Socialism* in Prague, his domestic advisers were not up to the tasks before them. As Gennady Gerasimov explained to me, Gorbachev "relied on people in other departments of the Central Committee. And the people in the domestic departments were just awful. . . .So he had no good team."[21] The country was already running a budgetary deficit and the world price of oil was falling dramatically.

At one point the world oil price would sink as low as $7 per barrel. Allegedly this decline was engineered by Cold Warriors on the Western side. The Reagan administration may have encouraged Saudi Arabia to lower the price of oil to such an extent that the Soviet Union could not make a profit and would have to deplete their hard currency reserves.[22] The infliction of such painful conditions on the Soviet Union was a normal, if deplorable, Cold War maneuver in those days, which Gorbachev could not have countered.

He had quickly started cutting military expenditures but was spending heavily importing machine tools. Probably his primary emphasis instead should have been on improving agriculture, for the country could not feed itself and could hardly afford imported grain. In one speech Gorbachev contemplated increasing the size of collective farmers' private garden plots, which was actually the only effective sector of the agricultural system.[23] Had that been done, he might have solved the food problem, but that is not certain because the agricultural infrastructure for harvesting, storing, and transporting food was inadequate. He might also have profitably studied the agricultural changes that had been taking place in China since 1982, but his advisers showed no interest in them.

By 1987 Gorbachev realized that the emphasis on machine tools was a mistake and he launched an economic reform, introducing a limited market system by permitting small private cooperative businesses to operate. However, he made no move toward private ownership of large-scale productive property or the replacement of planning by free markets.[24] Consumer goods were scarce and by 1988 the food stores were almost empty. The SHEEP were losing patience.

Oddly, however, this did not mean that they were actually deprived. Indeed, the quantity of consumer goods was increasing but the money incomes of families rose even faster. There was a widening gap between the availability of consumer goods and the money demand for them. Since prices were controlled, this led to a breakdown in the distribution system. With more money in their pockets, people were actually consuming more while complaining about the shortages.[25] Every household kept a stash of hoarded goods, although the grocery stores were almost bare.

Opinions were becoming polarized about the economy, with the radical so-called "democrats" demanding more moves toward a capitalist system, and the DINOSAUR elites resisting ever more strongly. Gorbachev did move toward a market economy, but hesitantly and tardily. His slow responses were irritating everyone and turning public opinion against him.

But Gorbachev was acknowledging that more should be done, and in 1990 he established a team of sixty economists and lawyers under Deputy Prime Minister Abalkin to develop a new economic plan. They recommended a gradual freeing of most prices, denationalizing small companies and turning large ones into joint-stock corporations. Instead of promising jobs to all workers, they would provide unemployment benefits. Still, some sectors of the economy would remain state-owned and price-controlled.[26]

This plan seemed too radical for Gorbachev, who consulted other advisers. Soon several groups were developing different plans. The one that came closest to being implemented was the so-called "500-day plan" of Stanislav Shatalin and Grigory Yavlinsky. Their team had been authorized by both Boris Yeltsin, who had become president of the Russian republic, and Gorbachev. It was a plan for transitioning to capitalism. With foreign investors encouraged, at least 70 percent of all industrial firms would be turned into joint-stock corporations.

But Gorbachev was losing popularity and worrying about objections from DINOSAUR Communists, who would not tolerate such a drastic change. Instead, he tried to tinker with the 500-day plan, combining it with a less radical plan by Prime Minister Ryzhkov. Jack Matlock, the American ambassador, considered his new mish-mash "a proposal to combine opposites. To their respective authors, the plans were totally incompatible and could not be combined."[27]

Now Gorbachev was desperate, for the political center that he occupied was being torn in opposite directions. He could find no solution acceptable to both the polarized right and left wings,

It was in this situation in 1991 that he went to the G7 meeting in London, hoping that his new Western friends would recognize his predicament and offer financial assistance to tide his country over this difficult transition.

They did not. His ally Margaret Thatcher was no longer in power and could not help him. His past peacemaking concessions to the United States evidently had no "cash value" now. He had accomplished many important reforms successfully, but his goal of improving the quality of life for the population could not be counted among them. He returned to Moscow to deal with the other crises that were destroying his authority in the country. But soon the DINOSAURS would attempt a coup against him. The end was nigh.

Goal: Democratization

Democratization was a third goal of Gorbachev's. He had sworn to combat Stalinism, which of course required not only the cultivation of peace and human rights but also a form of governance accountable to the people. In doing so, he would be sawing off the limb on which he sat, giving away the source of his own power and potentially limiting his capacity to fulfill his goals for the country. Surely he knew this, and yet he never hesitated.

He chose as his closest advisers—Alexander Yakovlev, Eduard Shevardnadze, and Georgi Shakhnazarov—men who lacked authoritarian tendencies. I will describe some events that illustrate their democratic personal traits.

Alexander Yakovlev had been an exchange student at Columbia University in 1958 and, back at home, had worked his way up the ladder, becoming head of the CPSU's department of ideology—until he published an article blasting Soviet anti-Semitism. He was punished for his audacity by being sent to Canada, where he was ambassador for ten years. (I wish Gorbachev had used that undemocratic way of disposing of his enemies. He should have made Boris Yeltsin ambassador to Bolivia.)

Anyway, in Toronto I heard stories about Yakovlev's friendship with our prime minister, Pierre Trudeau, who supposedly named one of his sons after him. I also heard a story from some of my friends who went to Ottawa to picket the Russian embassy. (In those days we made a point of criticizing not only NATO's nuclear missiles but also those of Russia.) It was a bitterly cold night and the peaceniks were parading around in the snow with placards, chanting slogans. The front door opened and Ambassador Yakovlev appeared. He beckoned them indoors, gave them something warm to drink, and spent the evening chatting with them all by the fire. They were impressed. Our own political leaders never showed such democratic ways!

* * *

I heard an equally endearing story about Shevardnadze from Margarita Papandreou, an American-born woman who had been first lady of Greece. Margarita is a feminist who used to organize other women as peace lobbyists. They were a transnational civil society group, both Eastern and Western. Somehow Margarita and her women got a chance to sit down with the foreign ministers of the Warsaw Pact countries. Eduard Shevardnadze was chairing the meeting and they talked at length about military doctrine. Then, she told me,

> we said we had found training booklets that were used for training soldiers in the Soviet Union. They were based on more of an aggressive, rather than a defensive, military posture. And we said, since you claim this is a defense system and has no aggressive intent, why are your soldiers being trained for aggressive action? The response at that time was that that was not really so, but there was kind of a thoughtful response on their side.
>
> At the end of the meeting, Shevardnadze congratulated us on the kind of knowledge we had about issues, and I must say, we were not being flattered. Not by any of the ministers. They listened to us seriously.
>
> He said, "We would find it very interesting at some point if a group of your representatives would sit in, totally, at one of our meetings and listen to what we discuss and what we are concerned about. And then at the end of the meeting we would like to have a kind of critique from your group of women."
>
> Our mouths just fell open. Now, we did not get to that stage because after a certain time things were changing. But we asked if we could send to each minister our list of questions and get their response later. They agreed to that.
>
> Later we went to Moscow again. When we saw Shevardnadze he handed us the answers to our questions. He said that they had discussed them thoroughly and that a number of the issues that we had brought up they had started taking care of. They were moving ahead to make some of those changes. One thing he pointed out was that, as far as military training was concerned, they were in the process of writing a new military manual for their soldiers.
>
> It wasn't just the manual because other things also had to be changed. They were making sure that their military establishment was defensive and it was not meant to take any kind of aggressive action.

* * *

My story about Shakhnazarov comes from Saul Mendlovitz, the Rutgers University Law professor who had directed the World Order Models Project (WOMP) that Mattison described above. Mendlovitz told me a little about the project, which was based on the premise that the way to get world peace is through world law.[28] It involved building networks of people around the world who were interested in the same topics—another instance of what I'm calling here "transnational civil society." What they wanted to do was blur the national boundaries, mainly by creating sort of a "cultural globalization" that would transcend nation-states with these world-wide networks of personal connections. (If this book is preaching any sermon, it is precisely promoting that very idea.)

WOMP itself comprised a network of scholars living in various countries. In the U.S., the leaders were Mendlovitz and a Princeton professor of international law, Richard Falk, who co-authored a number of books about world order. The main members in Russia were a sociologist named Eduard Arab-Ogly and Gennady Gerasimov (whom Mendlovitz calls "Gene"), who would become spokesman for the Foreign Minister and Gorbachev. Mendlovitz called the former *Problems of Peace and Socialism* staffers

> a not-so-invisible conspiracy group. And they knew each other, were promoting each other. They became the Gorbachev men. I didn't know that Gene was part of that, but it turned out he was. . . . They saw this particular group [WOMP] as an important group for them to be part of because it gave them a window, not just to the U.S., but to the world. . . .We did keep in front of them the notion of global polities—that it's something to take seriously. . . . So they came to ten or twelve workshops and [discovered] that there were people in the rest of the world who were interested in producing a system in which neither the Soviet Union nor the United States was dominant. And that it was worth thinking about humanity as a whole, though we were going through wars of national liberation.

WOMP was not the only source of such ideas. Already Georgi Shakhnazarov, another TERMITE veteran of the Prague-based *Problems of Peace and Socialism*, had been writing futurist books that envisioned how a preferable "world order" would look and making exactly the same points. Mendlovitz said,

> Five years ago Georgi came to me in the United States, knocked on my door, introduced himself to me and said, "I know about you people, the World Order Models people. I would like to talk to you about it." I said, I think you should meet Dick Falk. So we had him speak at Princeton. And we dreamed up a project called "Global Civilization: Challenges to Sovereignty, Democracy and Security." The result was four years of work and three conferences, the first one at IMEMO on sovereignty, the second one at Yokohama on democracy, and the third one at Notre Dame on security. Shakh and his assistant, William Smirnov, were engines in making sure that that project went. Shakhnazarov was writing letters for funding. Went to the Rockefeller Foundation, tried to get people at the UN aboard. Thinks that it's one of the most important projects that ever happened! He came to see us, I didn't go see him. They spent four years with

us. And I was back there last July at the Gorbachev Foundation for the meeting
on global civilization.

Shakhnazarov had also invited me to that conference but I had to leave the
day before it began. In fact, Shakhnazarov had also lent me the only copy of his
memoirs that had been translated into English. I read it one weekend and returned it to him, offering to find an American publisher for him if he'd scan it
and send it to me. He never did so, but he did tell me about his interest in democracy. For example, he said that Gorbachev

> became secretary for agriculture while I was deputy chief of the International
> Department, dealing with our relations with the governments and radical parties
> in Czechoslovakia and Poland. He came there as chief of the delegation. Sev-
> eral times I assisted him. Once he said, "I have read your book on the New
> World Order." That was the first time I had met anybody from the Central
> Committee who had read anything besides Marx and Lenin. [We laugh] He
> said that he approved—that it was a very interesting book.[29]

One could infer that his thinking on world order, global governance, and
international law had influenced Gorbachev. In 1988, just after Gorbachev had
withdrawn six tank divisions from Czechoslovakia and Hungary, I was interviewing a friend for *Peace Magazine*, George Ignatieff, who had served as Canada's ambassador to the UN and also to NATO. We were exultant about Gorbachev's recent speech at the United Nations. Ignatieff said,

> Announcing this reduction, Gorbachev is saying that the Cold War is over. He
> says that the use (or the threat of use) of force no longer can be an instrument
> of foreign policy. What he's saying is revolutionary and it's what the UN
> Charter says. We in Canada should especially welcome this assertion of what
> we worked so hard after World War II to put into international law. Interna-
> tional disputes were to be settled by mediation and through the Security Coun-
> cil, and we'd set up peacekeeping forces. Under Stalin, we just couldn't get the
> Soviets to implement this principle of the Charter. . . . But in his speech at the
> United Nations, Gorbachev emphasized that he is now willing to deal through
> the UN with all regional disputes and that he invites the UN not only to help the
> withdrawal in Afghanistan, but to use UN peacekeeping forces there when the
> troops are withdrawn.
>   And in the same speech, he announced Soviet plans for conversion to civil
> from defense industries. He said that it's desirable for all states, beginning with
> the major military powers, to submit conversion plans to the UN.[30]

This sounded like WOMP to me, and also like Shakhnazarov's memoirs. So
I was not surprised in 1999 when Gorbachev published his book, *On My Country and the World*.[31] Every word of it might have been written by a WOMPer.

Goal: Increasing Democracy
Gorbachev's democratization plans involved three different kinds of change:
* *glasnost*: openness, transparency, freedom of expression;

- re-structuring the government, making it pluralistic and accountable to the citizenry rather than under the control of the party; and
- "switching on support from below" by encouraging civil society
and political participation.

* * *

Glasnost was introduced soon after Gorbachev took office. It became permissi-
ble to argue against government policy or particular leaders, both publicly and
even in the press. Censorship was relaxed, and even official Leninist ideology
could be questioned. People could gain access to libraries full of shocking secrets. Films could be produced that would have been forbidden before.

The government had to allow certain grim truths to come out that exposed
its past wrongdoing—such as the hidden fact that the Baltic republics had not
joined the Soviet Union freely, but had been divided between Hitler and Stalin
in a secret 1939 pact whereby Stalin tried to avoid going to war. The truth about
the Katyn massacre also was finally acknowledged: that the secret police had
murdered about 22,000 Polish prisoners of war in a forest in 1940 by order of
Stalin. These disclosures gave impetus to the growing demands of nationalists in
the Baltics to secede from the Soviet Union.

The trouble is, if you allow people to choose their own paths, they may not
choose what you prefer or even what is good for them. Democracy is desirable
because it inherently fosters human flourishing better than authoritarian rule,
and because it is a way of resolving disputes peaceably, but not because it yields
the best political decisions. There is no system that will always do that. As
Churchill said, democracy is the worst form of government except all the others.

In his memoirs Gorbachev recalls that the media's sensational new revela-
tions had influenced government deliberations during that early *glasnost* period.

> More and more often, before the start of Politburo and secretariat meetings
> there were discussions of the harshest criticisms from the press, radio, and tele-
> vision. Regardless of the agenda, such conversations continued at the meetings
> themselves, sometimes pushing aside important questions that needed an im-
> mediate decision.[32]

* * *

Perestroika was the re-structuring of institutions, especially the state itself. Gorbachev introduced an elected congress and an upper house resembling a senate
and became the country's president, rather than just leader of the party. He did
not, however, give up his post as general secretary yet because he worried that
the Party would choose a hard-liner as his successor and stop the reforms.[33]

Democratization required that the Soviet constitution be revised in several
ways, especially to eliminate the Communist Party's guaranteed monopoly of
power. Moreover, the relationship among the various branches of government
might need to change; the question was whether there should be a division of
power among them, as with the Americans' "checks and balances" or whether
instead the Party, the judiciary, the legislature, and the administrative bodies
should remain connected. Finally, there were new questions about the degree of

autonomy, if not independence, to be granted to the various republics.

The Soviet constitution thus included two especially problematic clauses. First, there was Article VI, which specified that the CPSU should play the "leading role" in government. It certainly did. For each government office there was a parallel CPSU office overseeing it, which could intervene in its decision-making. Gorbachev intended to separate the CPSU from the government, allowing it to function as only one of several parties, primarily to nominate candidates for elections. But this move was certain to cause conflict. Second, there was Article 72 of the Constitution, which guaranteed the republics' right to secede. In 1991 this would prove to be a fatal clause.

The most famous public fight concerned whether to abolish Article VI, the guarantee of the Party's "leading role." In the new Congress of People's Deputies (which had been created in 1988, but which met only twice a year, mainly to elect a smaller standing legislature, the Supreme Soviet) tempers flared between the DINOSAURS and a new, radical group of "democrats," the Inter-Regional Deputies, who identified with Sakharov and the BARKING DOGS and were suspicious of Gorbachev's reforms "from above." (It is not that there actually *were* many former dissidents among these Deputies, but that many of them evidently wished they *had been* dissidents while it was still a bold thing to be.)

Gorbachev fully intended to undo the Party's monopoly of power—but not in the way the Inter-Regional Deputies demanded. It seemed to him premature and unnecessarily confrontational to repeal Article VI just then, for the Inter-Regional Deputies were a minority in the Congress and to give in to their demands would have infuriated the reactionary CPSU deputies. First he needed to persuade the Central Committee of the Party to accept the change.

He had actually been preparing other ways of easing the DINOSAURS out of power. For one thing, he was setting a time-bomb—the new "Union Treaty," which would simply have no role for them. The Party elites would find themselves out of jobs. However, as the time approached for that treaty to be signed, they recognized its implications and attempted a coup against him. Unfortunately, in the meantime the radical "democrats" would be accusing him of being reactionary for hesitating to repeal Article VI. That accusation further diminished his dwindling popularity as the country's democratic pioneer.

He did persuade the Central Committee to repeal Article VI in March 1990, having been too careful to introduce such a change "before the time was ripe." By 1990 it was already "overripe" for a society that had watched other Communist regimes being toppled throughout Eastern Europe the year before.[34] He never intended to ban the CPSU altogether, as Yeltsin tried to do, but only to remove its monopoly of power. Some of his advisers wanted him to split the party in two, thereby instituting a multi-party system, but perhaps he considered that move too confrontational. Besides, it would have left the DINOSAURS in charge of both new parties, where they could perhaps stop *perestroika*.

Earlier, and even more important than repealing Article VI, were Gorbachev's plans to create a division of power among the country's governing bodies, especially by making the top executive into a president elected by the citizens, rather than a general secretary whose source of power was the CPSU.

His plans for this had been taking shape since he came to power, if not before, though few people knew about it. In a BBC program in 1991 Alexander Yakovlev, Ivan Frolov, and Georgi Shakhnazarov stated that he had realized as early as the autumn of 1986 that democratization would require the end of the one-party system, and that he had been planning steps toward a multi-party democracy, though the timing and details were influenced by outside events. They said that each step encountered opposition within the Politburo, so that he had to adopt certain tactics that made it appear that he was only improvising.[35] The inner circle of political advisers had intended in 1988 to put the idea to the Nineteenth Party Conference in the summer. As Shakhnazarov explained,

> Anyone who at that time had said openly that we were progressing towards canceling the leading role of the Party and introducing a multi-party system, and that the Party might lose power, would have been swept aside.[36]

I interviewed one of Shakhnazarov's aides, Yegor Kuznetsov, who told me that, when packing up and moving Shakhnazarov's office, he had found a stenographic notebook containing the minutes of Gorbachev's inner circle's early meetings to plan the creation of a division of powers. It had not been catalogued for the archive so Shakhnazarov casually gave it to him as a worthless item. In fact, Kuznetsov wrote his Ph.D. dissertation in political science on the basis of this notebook and his interviews of Mr. Shakhnazarov. I sent my research assistant, Ignat Kalinin, to the Institute of State and Law to read Kuznetsov's thesis and take notes for me. No public records exist of the debates about the plans for re-structuring the Soviet state, either the conversations of Gorbachev's small inner circle of advisers who had developed it[37] or the closed meeting of deputies where the constitutional re-structuring proposal was first debated openly.

Shakhnazarov and Vadim Medvedev had sent a note to Gorbachev in the very beginning of 1985 advocating a presidency. Thus, according to Kuznetsov's account, the inner circle had existed from the earliest days of Gorbachev's time in power. They all agreed on only two topics: their abhorrence of Stalinism and the need for reform. Everything else was debated, especially at the end of 1989. Ivan Frolov and Alexander Yakovlev wrote the political and philosophical parts. Georgi Shakhnazarov and Anatoly Lukyanov did the sections on law and structure. Vadim Medvedev worked on the economics, and Anatoly Chernyaev was responsible for the section on foreign relations.

Their intent was not to weaken the Party but to make Gorbachev less dependent on it. This was a middle-term strategy—to undermine the DINOSAURS and the "radical democrats," who alike threatened Gorbachev's reforms

The crucial debate had to do with the separation of powers. According to Gorbachev's preferred constitution, there would be a system of checks and balances dividing authority between the branches of the state. The president would not be able to dismiss parliament (i.e. the Supreme Soviet and/or the Congress of People's Deputies), while for its part, the Supreme Soviet would be able to reject anyone the president might appoint. Otherwise, the Supreme Soviet would be strictly a legislative branch and the president, with his cabinet, would be strictly the executive branch. (The judiciary would still not be an independent branch, but would be overseen by a committee of the Supreme Soviet.)

At bottom, the main debate was about which should be more powerful—the Supreme Soviet or the president. One aspect had to do with how the president should be elected. Except for the first election, which would be by an extraordinary session of the Congress of People's Deputies, Gorbachev wanted the president to be elected directly by a popular vote of the people. This would assure his independent authority. Others believed that the president should be chosen by the Congress of People's Deputies.

Since Gorbachev lost his office before being able to create his preferred new system, no one can say which approach would have been better. As we talked together, Kuznetsov speculated as to whether the Soviet people are able to "handle" a division of powers. He noted that checks and balances had been adopted by the American founding fathers to *protect* democracy, whereas in Russia and the other post-Soviet states the separation of powers just resulted in civil war. The new Russian Constitution resembled Gorbachev's preferred model. If the Supreme Soviet and the president disagreed, they would have to work their differences out in conferences. But in 1993, when the Russian Duma (legislature) rejected some of Yeltsin's appointments, he was outraged and tried to dissolve them, contrary to the Constitution. Since they refused to dissolve, he ordered tanks to shell them, then enacted a new constitution by decree, giving himself and all subsequent presidents all the powers that he wanted. No longer can the parliament refuse anyone the president chooses to appoint.[38]

Moreover, as Kuznetsov pointed out, the republics that became independent with the Soviet collapse all adopted constitutions embodying a separation of powers, as Gorbachev recommended. Several of them also have experienced civil wars. The Soviet system apparently did not teach politicians to resolve their issues by negotiation, compromise, or patient consultation. Democracy has not taken root as Gorbachev hoped it would. With a hollow laugh, Kuznetsov said, "Gorbachev's trouble was that he thought too highly of the Russian people."

* * *

"Switching on support from below" was, Gorbachev said, essential for democratization. He could give the people peace and democracy "from above," but they must learn to use these new rights and prevent any would-be Stalin from seizing control in the future. He sometimes quoted Solzhenitsyn, who had been imprisoned in the Gulag and who said that whenever anyone tried to gain dictatorial power, people should "make the ground burn under his feet" rather than accede to his demands. But there's a reason to call Soviet people SHEEP; they lacked the capacity for resisting a ruler's orders. They lacked independent associations—civil society—enabling them to act collectively to protect their rights.

Fortunately, civil society was beginning to develop. Thousands of new nongovernmental organizations formed during the late Gorbachev years, some of which were beginning to be active politically. In another chapter I will describe some of the peace groups, and there was a nascent environmental movement too.

Especially dramatic was the large new political movement—"Democratic Russia"—which was intensely anti-Communist, anti-Gorbachev, and pro-Yeltsin.

Gorbachev was confronted with mass nationalistic movements that threatened the stability and continuity of the union. His first concern was to persuade people in the Baltics to stay within the Soviet Union. Yet he did not seem perturbed by their demonstrations. I remember seeing TV news coverage of him, walking out in the crowd, trying to persuade the protesters in (I think) Lithuania.

He did have grounds for worry. There was much confusion about what democracy really was. Gorbachev understood that democracy required the intelligent construction of institutions. Many radical "democrats," however, seemed to define democratization as complete freedom. I heard a story (maybe true, maybe not) about a seaside town where there was a dangerous undertow. There had always been signs on the beach, warning people not to swim. When *perestroika* began, the mayor had the signs removed. Someone asked why and he explained, "Because we are a democracy now. We must stop telling people what to do."

Gorbachev worried about both extreme positions: the radical "democrats" who understood little about democracy, and the conservatives inside the Party or in the hinterland. As a leader he should not rush far ahead of the society, but now the intellectuals were impatient to adopt democracy and capitalism. The least popular political position now was Gorbachev's own careful, centrist approach. There was no longer any middle ground for him to occupy. In his memoirs he described radicals as people

> anxious to improve their social status and break into major politics, [and who] rushed headlong to expand the "bounds of what is permitted." Rejecting socialist values, these people, who only yesterday had been praising those same values in their dissertations, demanded a complete and immediate dismantling of the previous system.[39]

Soon many of his closest allies would join this group of radical "democrats" who were impressed by his impetuous rival, Boris Yeltsin—a man who claimed to be far more democratic than Gorbachev himself. Millions of people would believe Yeltsin's boasts, but live to regret it.

Goal: Relinquishing Control of Other Countries: From Brezhnev to Sinatra

Gorbachev's mentor, Yuri Andropov, had, as Soviet Ambassador to Hungary in 1956, been largely responsible for crushing the Hungarians who rebelled against a hated Communist government. Gorbachev had never criticized that military intervention, nor even the crushing of the Prague Spring, led by his best friend. But after taking office, he informed the leaders of the Warsaw Pact states that they could not expect his armed forces to keep them in power. They did not seem to believe him but the situation in Poland would prove that his was truly a different kind of Soviet government.

The Poles were the only Eastern European country that had a significant civil society. Poland had kept small farms instead of collectivizing them, as all other Communist countries did. It had a strong, free Roman Catholic Church, headed by a Polish pope who was by no means cordial toward communism. (I visited churches in Krakow and Warsaw in 1987 that held six masses per day and did not recognize the legitimacy of the Communist state's laws. One priest asked me to smuggle a large sum of money out of the country for one of his parishioners, which I agreed to do, though our plan failed.) And Poland had a trade union movement like no other: Solidarność (Solidarity) organized strikes with the support of the whole population.

Although many people expected the USSR to suppress Solidarność, that did not happen and by April 1989, the Polish government consented to negotiate with the union, which sent 100 representatives to "Roundtable Talks." Afterward, the now legalized Solidarność was allowed to participate in the elections. Its members won every contested seat in the Sejm and 99 of 100 senatorial seats. Poland's remarkable civil society organization had routed communism by sitting peaceably around a table with the government.

The other Eastern European countries lacked civil society organizations and had to use crowd demonstrations instead. Brave dissidents had gone to jail repeatedly, but none of them had developed plans for governing, for they surely did not expect to come to power. In fact, when I visited dissidents there, they all expected Gorbachev to fail.

For example, I interviewed Jiří Dienstbier in Prague shortly after Gorbachev came to power. He had been a journalist but because of his prominent role in the dissident organization Charter 77 he had spent three years in prison. He was then working as a stoker, since he was not permitted to hold any influential job. I asked what people in Prague thought about Gorbachev. He said,

> The majority of people simply don't believe that changes are possible. Even if Gorbachev understands well what is necessary for Russia and this part of the world, the opposition is terrible against such an understanding. It concerns the privileges of millions of apparatchiks. . . . .When I talk with Russians they are for Gorbachev, but they always say he will be lost. The bureaucracy will either destroy him or he will finally understand that he can't go further than the bureaucracy will accept.[40]

Dienstbier's predictions were not exactly fulfilled. For one thing, although Gorbachev was ousted, it was by "democrats," not by the Party bureaucrats, who tried to do so but failed. And for another thing, Dienstbier hardly foresaw that in 1989 he would become Czechoslovakia's first foreign minister after the "Velvet Revolution."

Unlike Poland, whose civil society had developed "social capital" and was able to negotiate, Czechoslovakia and the other Eastern European countries won their independence nonviolently by spontaneously crowding into the streets in the absence of any powerful civil society leadership.[41] And lacking Soviet military support, the Communist leaders simply walked away and let the people take over. Thus the overthrow of each regime was not caused solely by demands from below (though they were important) but also by the ruling Communist Party's abdication after Gorbachev refused to support it with military force.

Gorbachev was abandoning the "Brezhnev doctrine," which had been announced in 1968 to justify the Hungarian Revolution and the Prague Spring.

Brezhnev had stated: "When forces that are hostile to socialism try to turn the development of some socialist country towards capitalism, it becomes not only a problem of the country concerned, but a common problem and concern of all socialist countries."

In contrast, Gorbachev's policy was the "Sinatra doctrine." His spokesman, Gennady Gerasimov, explained it on an American TV show. "We now have the 'Frank Sinatra doctrine.' He has a song, 'I Did It My Way.' So every country decides on its own which road to take. . . Political structures must be decided by the people who live there."[42]

Ostensibly Gorbachev meant to shrug and let events run their course in Eastern Europe but in reality, from mid-1989 onward, he was putting pressure on all other Communist regimes, beginning with Poland, to begin reforms comparable to his own *perestroika*.[43] Mark Kramer, who has documented these pressures better than anyone else, writes:

> In each case, the Soviet Union helped to bring about sweeping political change while effectively depriving hard-line Communist leaders of the option of violent repression. The notable exception of Romania, with its bloody and chaotic revolution, merely proves the rule. Since the mid-1960s, Soviet influence had always been much weaker in Romania than in the other Warsaw Pact countries. If the Soviet Union had been able to maintain the same degree of influence in Romania that it enjoyed elsewhere in eastern Europe, the violent rebellion of December 1989 might not have been necessary.

How did the Soviet Union "effectively deprive" those leaders of the option of violent repression? Kramer gives a number of examples, to which I can add one here. In 1992 I interviewed Nikita M, who had been a Soviet official in East Germany when the demonstrations arose there that led to the opening of the Berlin wall. He said,

> One of the accusations against [the East German boss] Honecker that was pressed initially but now is waived was that he had given an order to use arms against demonstrators in Leipzig. Unfortunately, I was not present in Leipzig at that time but the witnesses said that some strange things occurred there. Many highways to Leipzig were blockaded by Soviet military vehicles that suddenly "broke down." And that meant that no other troops could be moved to Leipzig at that time. This story can be seen as a legend but there are witnesses to this. . . . . And I have a stale military secret for you. Any massive movement along East German highways was under control of the Soviet commanders. . . . The position of the Soviet forces prevented use of arms against demonstrators in East Germany. This hypothesis can be confirmed by the fact that the German government is quite tolerant to the presence of Soviet forces on German soil now.[44]

To verify this story I asked several well-informed persons, including Valentin Falin, the official who had represented the Soviet Union in East Germany. None of the experts I consulted believed the story. I want to believe it but in the absence of evidence, cannot. Falin insisted that there had been strict orders for the Soviet troops not to interfere with events in the country. However, he said, "the dynamics of events in these countries were certainly influenced by developments in the USSR, and you can hold Gorbachev responsible for this." Elsewhere, however, Falin has acknowledged a bit more deliberate Soviet influence:

> The CPSU Central Committee was aware of the unsavory processes underway in the [East European] countries and therefore—to the extent permitted by the principle of non-interference in internal affairs and respect of the right of peoples to choose—we tried to influence the situation.[45]

Falin acknowledged having opposed the re-unification of Germany, saying,

> I was of the opinion that, insofar as the unification process must embrace two independent sovereign states, each connected militarily, economically, and politically with different countries, they could not simply be unified mechanically by an on-paper agreement between the two states. In my view, and in the view of the experts whom I consulted, the unification agreement would have and should have very serious, far-reaching consequences for all concerned with the future, unified Germany, as well as for affairs within that country. In the way in which the unification took place, our concerns about security were disregarded. The former East Germany became a part of NATO and thus created the basis for the further spread of NATO in the East.[46]

This expansion of NATO was not an outcome the Gorbachev intended, so one must call his policies toward Germany at least partially a failure. Many Russians today resent the loss of what they call their "sphere of influence," as if major powers were somehow entitled to control certain other countries.

Goal: Preventing Strife and Civil War, Keeping the Soviet Union Intact

Some of my Russian and Ukrainian friends amaze me. They blame Gorbachev for breaking up the Soviet Union—yet I remember perfectly well that when it was first discussed they thought it was a great idea. I argued against it. One guy was even saying then that the USSR should break apart but that later it should re-combine. The others gave different reasons—mostly nationalistic ones—for favoring the breakup but then within months decided it had been a bad idea and that it was Gorbachev's fault. Putin calls it the worst catastrophe of the twentieth century, though he became president because Yeltsin gave him the job, and Yeltsin was obviously the real culprit, having broken up the country out of plain spite against Gorbachev.

Some blame the West, but there is no basis for that belief. The analysis of U.S. Ambassador Jack Matlock is more accurate. He wrote,

> If it had been in the power of the United States and Western Europe to create a democratic union of the Soviet republics, they would have been delighted to do so. But, of course, it was not in their power. So they could only watch with dismay as the empire fell apart and then scramble to establish ties with the bolting republics as best they could.[47]

Opinions also differ as to the mechanism by which Gorbachev supposedly destroyed the Union. Some people blame him for using state violence in Riga, Baku, Tbilisi, and Vilnius, where separatist groups were trying to seize power.[48] Such accusations were investigated by a commission in the Congress of People's Deputies of the USSR, which did not blame Gorbachev.[49]

In post-Soviet days, the opposite criticism is more common: that he did not use *enough* violence, as a ruler should do to maintain the integrity of a state that is threatened by separatists.[50] You can choose between these two arguments, but you cannot adhere to them both. Some Western sovietologists, including Jerry F. Hough, argue for the second view. He wrote,

> Gorbachev refused to use enough force to ensure obedience to Soviet laws and to suppress separatism. An enormous amount has been written about the handful of deaths Soviet security forces caused in Tbilisi, Baku, and Vilnius, as if these acts somehow destroyed *perestroika*. But continuing such limited applications of force would surely have preserved the Union. After all, the Soviet population was thoroughly cowed in 1988. . . . If any leader in any country indicates that he will not enforce laws or central authority, events will surely spin out of control.[51]

But most separatist actions were not crimes. They involved strictly nonviolent methods (especially in the Baltics), and were supported by transnational civil society. Although civil society groups had been weak in all socialist countries except Poland, they quickly began to flourish and multiply. In the Baltics, pro-independence groups organized a human chain of about two million persons in 1989 that stretched 370 miles across all three republics. Should Gorbachev have crushed them with tanks? Hardly! The Baltic people also organized a "singing revolution," wherein protesters met in public places for three years, singing nationalistic songs and hymns. On one occasion 300,000 Estonians were singing together. Should Gorbachev have set anti-riot troops against them with truncheons? I think not. Thus the peaceful methods of the Baltic protesters defeated the peaceful methods of Gorbachev—which seems preferable to the defeat of one army by another.

The ex-Warsaw Pact countries—people who had only recently been beneficiaries of the "Sinatra Doctrine"—now started urging Soviet groups of Latvians, Lithuanians, Moldovans, Estonians, and Ukrainians to claim sovereignty too and many came to express support as a new transnational civil society.

Nor were the new political leaders of Eastern Europe shy about helping out. Lech Wałęsa, for example, sent a public letter to Gorbachev in March 1990 urging him to extend the same "right to choose" to Lithuania that he had granted to Eastern Europe the previous year.[52] Adam Michnik addressed the congress of the Ukrainian independence movement Rukh, shouting "Long Live Ukraine!" and receiving thunderous ovations.

To them there was no difference between the rights of WTO countries to determine their own national destinies and the rights of would-be separatists in another country. As Stephen Kotkin notes, "Gorbachev's reward for having allowed the people of Poland to decide their own fate was Poles intervening to help decide the fate of the Baltics and Ukraine."[53]

Nobody expected democracy to be followed by such fervent claims for secession—but perhaps everyone should have foreseen it. The upsurge of nationalism was the logical result of a theoretical flaw that had been left unsettled since the end of World War I. Oddly, Woodrow Wilson and Vladimir Lenin held the same view on the question of nationalism—maybe the only time they ever agreed. Since then, both Communists and liberals have assumed (mistakenly, I think) that democracy entails national or ethnic "self-determination"—a right to a territorially-defined state for each nationality group. Because of Lenin's influence the Soviet constitution assured (theoretically, but not in practice) the right of nationalities to have their own republics and secede if they so chose. When Gorbachev started democratizing, the republics' leaders decided to take advantage of that right, thus destroying the Soviet state.

Separatism is usually unwise. Since populations sometimes intermarry or change their identities or place of residence, the aspiration to "national self-determination" in the sense of political sovereignty is unattainable, for there inevitably will be ethnic minorities in every country, however anyone re-draws the boundaries. States must be ethnically plural, like it or not.

However, when a country becomes democratic, it may contain a national community that is a minority within the state as a whole, yet a majority within a locality of that state. In that case, an incentive will arise for separatism. As a minority within the big polity, the national group must expect to frequently be out-voted, whereas if it can secede and become the majority within its own smaller polity, it will ordinarily win. Democracy doesn't mean much if you can't ever win elections. Hence the explanation for the rise of nationalism in early periods of democracy is the conventional system of geographically defined electoral constituencies. Some nationality groups know that their political issues and candidates will be defeated in fair, democratic elections, whereas if they could secede, they would constitute a majority and always win. This incentive arises from a flaw in almost all systems of democratic voting. Democracy is what people really need, not an ethnic homeland—but a democracy in which they have a chance to win sometimes.

An alternative, non-territorial approach would allocate an appropriate number of seats in parliament to various interest groups, occupations, or minorities so that gaining exclusive, sovereign control of a geographic area will not determine a citizen's prospect of satisfactory outcomes in elections.[54] Had the Soviet constitution provided for such non-territorial constituencies, nationalistic demands for separate republics would not have arisen. However, such an approach assumes that ethnic identities always are salient and permanent, which is untrue.

Separatist struggles are usually won or lost on the basis of violent protests or civil war. Thus in 1996, after the post-Communist wave of democratization, forty wars were being fought in thirty-four countries. In twenty-nine of those forty wars, the fighting was done by nationalistic groups.[55]

Most of the impetus for breaking up the USSR came from the political leaders of the republics, each of whom suddenly saw the possibility of becoming the head of a sovereign country. It is not clear that most ordinary Soviet citizens even in these republics wanted the Union dissolved. Only nine months before it was dismantled, a referendum was held on the question and 76.4 percent of the people voted to keep the Union intact.[56]

By no means was the dissolution of the Soviet Union a "revolution from below." The dynamics took place within the polarizing Party itself. The DINOSAURS stayed Communist and the radical "democrats" quit, leaving Gorbachev's careful, step-by-step approach without support. Gorbachev tried zigzagging, hoping to hold the two polarized extremes together by appealing to first one, then the other. That tactic failed; both sides turned against him even more decisively. There was a real prospect of civil war or, more likely, a putsch that would reverse all of his reforms.

The truly crucial time came in the winter of 1990–1991, when, for reasons that may never be fully explained, Gorbachev turned to the right. Appalling the reformists, he suddenly replaced his senior staff and ministers with several undistinguished opponents of *perestroika*—the very people who in August would attempt a coup against him. Many of his best TERMITE advisers and ministers abandoned him in disgust: Eduard Shevardnadze, Georgi Arbatov, and Yevgeny Velikhov, for example, though some of them reconciled later.

No one could comprehend what lay behind this change. He said it was a tactical maneuver and that he would revert to his true policies later on. But there were ominous rumors that his reversal was the result of duress. Was there an "invisible coup" before the August coup? I am uncertain, but here are clues.

Don Oberdorfer wrote a book titled *The Turn*, in which he noted that military officers (notably Generals Bronislav Omelichev and Aleksandr Peresypkin) started accompanying Gorbachev and Shevardnadze's negotiators to arms control negotiations with Americans. They were taking an active part in policymaking and were even exercising obvious influence over the civilian authorities. Oberdorfer recounted several events when one might reasonably conclude that the military people were running things.[57]

Lindsay Mattison speculated to me about the matter:

> by January, as far as I am concerned, Shakhnazarov and Gorbachev—they weren't exactly prisoners, but they sure as hell were being watched. This one guy would bully Shakhnazarov in my presence in a private meeting. . . . . He was nobody—just a toughie. And this clown is browbeating him and telling him what he has to tell me about upcoming activities and conferences and usurping the Institute for Social Sciences! You've got to be joking! . . . I think they gradually somehow squirmed out from under it and Gorbachev got more free.[58]

I asked Georgi Arbatov about that period and he expressed disgust. "He picked those people himself!" he exclaimed. He had given up on Gorbachev, after writing him a letter and speaking with him on the phone. He said that Gorbachev had assured him that his "turn to the right" was only a tactical maneuver, which he would reverse as soon as possible. Gorbachev had added, "You can't imagine what is going on inside the Party right now!" but Arbatov had not asked further questions, since they were on an unsecured telephone line.[59]

That sounded good enough to me. Gorbachev was saying that he had to do this, so I would have trusted him, but most progressive people around him did not. I thought back to the question I had asked Vitaly Goldansky about that period: Why had the "democrats" abandoned Gorbachev? Goldansky had replied that they had no grasp of tactics. He and I had been talking about the Inter-Regional Deputies, the "maximalist" members of the Congress who were led by Yeltsin and the eminent remaining BARKING DOG, Sakharov. Goldansky said,

> We had quarreled about that. For instance, in the last speech of Sakharov, the only name mentioned in his speech was mine and he disagreed [with me]. That was just a tactical disagreement. That was the meeting of the so-called Inter-Regional Group in our Supreme Soviet. Sakharov at that time suggested that we should announce a [general] strike and [declare] ourselves as opposition.
>
> I took the floor and said that I used to study history. And from history I remember that when Communists quarreled with Social Democrats instead of making a united front with them against Nazis, in fact that was useful for the Nazis. They helped the Nazis. Therefore, I said, I believe that what is suggested—this strike and the proclaiming of opposition—will be a gift to the rightist forces.Sakharov said, in the last words of his last speech (he died the same night), "And finally, what Goldansky has said—that this strike will be the gift to rightist forces, I disagree categorically." So that was a disagreement in tactics. Therefore, when you ask me whether I approved the behavior of these people who condemned Gorbachev, I disagreed with them. I think that leftist forces, from a practical point of view, made some mistakes. We had to keep much closer contacts to Gorbachev and try to understand each other better. Sakharov was a great thinker, a great scientist, a great humanist, but not always a great tactician or great politician. I think that sometimes his tactical steps were maybe wrong.[60]

Fyodor Burlatsky had also been at that meeting and his position had been the same as Goldansky's. He told me,

> Sakharov proposed that they must stop work at the same time all over the whole country, against Gorbachev and his policies. He said that Gorbachev doesn't fight for democracy. There was no concrete reason for it—just a general strike. This idea, as I understand it, came from his wife, Bonner. That was the topic of this meeting, and Goldansky and many others who were included in this group, criticized Sakharov.
>
> They gave me the floor with great respect because they believed that I would support them. And I said that, as I understand, you've started to create an opposition. But what kind of opposition—like in the West or in the East? In the West it's an open opposition, with a real program, with a shadow government like Great Britain, with concrete questions. ("We'll do this and that; we don't agree with this and that.") Or you'll create an Eastern style opposition to prepare a coup without any program. And I said that I don't understand what kind of program [you propose]. For example, I said that I see here in the presidium very different people—Yeltsin, a liberal former member of the Politburo, Sakharov, and a radical democrat, Popov [the mayor of Moscow]. But

you are sitting together and I don't understand what kind of political program brought you together. Can you explain what you fight for? Only for power? For some kind of program? What kind of program? If you'll explain the program maybe I will support you. And they became disappointed. Even Mr. Yeltsin. I saw hate in his face.

Sakharov died that night. It's a critical point in our struggle for democracy. I should write about this. The majority of the members of the Inter-Regional Group did not support Sakharov, but for different reasons than mine.[61]

Here we have two ex-TERMITES, Goldansky and Burlatsky, challenging two BARKING DOGS—an authentic one (Sakharov), and a recent convert to the radical anti-Communist cause (Yeltsin). But Goldansky and Burlatsky were not typical. Most TERMITES were switching over to Yeltsin in those days, and Sakharov's funeral would soon attract an immense following of them.

Finally, I asked Alexander Likhotal about that period when Gorbachev turned to the right. Likhotal was Gorbachev's deputy spokesman during the last months of his presidency and carried on as spokesman at the Gorbachev Foundation. Now, in 2010, he is president of Green Cross International in Geneva and remains one of Mr. Gorbachev's closest aides. I always used to visit him when I went to Moscow. It was in the Foundation, after the USSR had been dismantled, that I asked him why Gorbachev had lost the support of the progressives. Likhotal gave a fairly ordinary explanation, but that is not what interested me. I was surprised by something he said when I asked him to predict the fate of Yeltsin, who then occupied Gorbachev's old Kremlin office. Likhotal said,

I think that this government will be transformed with the input of new people into the government, representing the military industrial complex, and there will be a very dramatic but not visible change in the nature of the government.

"Not visible?" I probed, raising my eyebrows. But Likhotal only repeated,

Not visible. New people will come. The president will preside. It will seem to be the same government, but the government will be pursuing a different policy—totally different. And either Yeltsin, with this transformed government, will be obliged to impose martial law or something like that and become a dictator, or everything will be swept aside and national patriotic forces will put forward their leader, who will become a dictator. So, unfortunately, I am very pessimistic about the nearest future of this country.

I wondered whether this "invisible coup" was really describing Yeltsin's future or instead Gorbachev's past. It would have been tactless to ask, so I let the moment pass. As for Yeltsin, his rule would indeed become authoritarian, but without his being pushed.

Did Peace and Democracy Work?

There are two ways to judge the success or failure of a political leader. First, we may appraise his principles and whether his deeds are consistent with them. Or, second, we may appraise the observable consequences of his actions—whether they yield good or bad results in practical terms.

We must not rely solely on either of these approaches, but balance them. A person may be high-minded and ethical but feckless. Or a person may be effective but unprincipled and cruel. Both ideals and know-how are essential.

The first way of evaluating a ruler is far easier than the second. In Gorbachev's case, almost everyone gives him excellent marks. His decisions are obviously directed toward maximizing universal values and human flourishing: freedom, human rights, democracy, peace, and the highest quality of life of the Soviet population. He applied those principles with almost perfect consistency. This Gorbachev is a remarkably ethical man.

But how did his actions work out? That is a far more complex question. Are we asking whether Gorbachev himself is satisfied with his results? Or whether the average Russian is satisfied? Or whether you and I are satisfied? Or whether other particular interested groups are satisfied: Military officers? Zealous nationalists? Pensioners? The G7 leaders? What phase of the "outcome" should we judge—the immediate result, or the long-term result? And what if one satisfactory result then contributes to another different, but highly unsatisfactory, outcome? For example, allowing the East European countries to oust Communist regimes that they hated (a good result, we may agree) freed them to help the Baltic people demand their own independence (a bad result, if the goal is to keep the Soviet Union intact—which was, indeed Gorbachev's goal).

Or consider another example: disarmament. As a principle it is noble but its consequences are impossible to list. By preventing a war, it may save millions of lives. By reducing expenditures, it may improve the economy and divert funds to improve human well-being. It may make other nations feel more secure and trusting, hence more cooperative. Or conversely it may reduce the country's security by weakening its ability to suppress an insurrection or repel a foreign invasion. We cannot know all the consequences of disarming the Soviet nuclear arsenal, quitting the war in Afghanistan, and demobilizing 500,000 troops.

About some outcomes we can agree. Gorbachev did not improve the Soviet economy—at least in the short term. But he was transitioning to capitalism. Could anyone else have made a smoother transition? The Chinese did so, but they also suppressed democracy and violated human rights. Could Gorbachev have adopted their economic approach while also democratizing?

Although there could have been better or worse economic policies, even the best ones could not have fixed the crisis, which was largely caused by the drop in oil revenue.[62] Even in Russia, Bill Clinton's campaign manager's maxim explains which factor most influences a politician's popularity: "It's the economy, stupid!" (Yeltsin's presidency would be bumpy for the same economic reason as Gorbachev's. Not until Putin took office would the price of oil rebound, making the Russian economy apparently prosperous and boosting his approval ratings.)

Many Russians and even a few Western sovietologists argue that Gorbachev was weak, that he gave away Eastern Europe, sapped Soviet military power, and allowed the Soviet Union to disintegrate by refusing to use violence—which every competent ruler must be willing to use.

Clearly, peaceful, democratic methods do not always win in a power struggle. Sometimes harsh, repressive measures do restore public order, protect victims from harm, and enforce justice. That is why we need police and peacekeepers. But even excellent policing and peacekeeping do not elevate the quality of social life. Coercion sometimes seems unavoidable, but never desirable.

You may want a pithy answer to the question "Do peace and democracy work?" If we take Gorbachev as a test case (which is fair, since he was exemplary), our answer must be this: It all depends on what your goals are. If you want a country that spends its assets on weaponry and manages to intimidate people into submission, but where people experience the constant threat of warfare or even nuclear annihilation, then peace and democracy won't work. If you want a prosperous country that is growing economically, then peace and democracy will neither assure nor prevent that; economic policies matter more. If you want a country that is building a pluralistic parliamentary democracy, one that does not readily shed the blood of its own citizens or those of other countries, one that respects the freedom of neighboring countries, one where everyone may find out facts and debate issues freely, one that is respected, instead of feared, around the world, then peaceful, democratic methods do work.

What Gorbachev did was extraordinary. He showed how far a ruler can go in practical terms by relying on persuasion and mutuality instead of violence. He achieved much. Had the reformists stood by him, peace and democracy might even have triumphed. May other wise leaders learn from his example.

Notes

1. There is a story about Gorbachev for which I cannot find a written source. After learning of Stalin's crimes, he went to the spot in the Lenin (Sparrow) Hills where Alexander Herzen had once taken an oath to devote his life to combating absolutism, and there he too took an oath to devote his life to fighting totalitarianism. Zdeněk Mlynář wrote about this event somewhere and Fyodor Burlatsky told me that Mlynář had also told him about it in a conversation.

2. Mikhail Gorbachev and Zdeněk Mlynář, *Conversations with Gorbachev*, (New York: Columbia University Press, 2004).

3. I should note that in my interview with him, Georgi Shakhnazarov reminded me that Sakharov sometimes did endorse Gorbachev's policies.

4. Fyodor Burlatsky, in discussion with the author, October 1997.

5. Vitaly Goldansky, in discussion with the author, June 1992.

6. Václav Havel, "The Strange Epoch of Post-Communism: A Conversation with Václav Havel," by Adam Michnik in *Letters from Freedom: Post-Cold War Realities and Perspectives,* ed. Irena Grudzinska Gross (University of California Press, 1998).

7. Miriam Dobson, *Khrushchev's Cold Summer: Gulag Returnees, Crime, and the Fate of Reform After Stalin* (Ithaca: Cornell University Press, 2009).

8. *Conversations with Gorbachev*, 128.

9. Marshall Goldman speculates about the true percentage, mentioning 20 percent or even 25 percent. See his *What Went Wrong with Perestroika?* (New York: Norton, 1991), 84, 130.

10. Archie Brown, *The Gorbachev Factor* (Oxford: Oxford University Press, 1996), 218–19.

11. Robert Gates, *From the Shadows* (New York: Simon and Schuster, 1996), 118–144.

12. Zbigniew Brzezinski, interview by Vincent Jauvert, "The CIA's Intervention in Afghanistan," in *Le Nouvel Observateur*, January 15–21, 1998.

13. Lindsay Mattison, in telephone discussion with the author, 1992.

14. Eduard Shevardnadze, in discussion with Julia Kalinina on the author's behalf, September 1995, Moscow.

15. Michael Ryan, "Life Expectancy and Mortality Data from the Soviet Union," *British Medical Journal* 296 (May 28, 1988): 1513.

16. Human Resources and Skill Development Canada, "Indicators of Well-Being in Canada." www4.hrsdc.gc.ca/.3ndic.1t.4r@-eng.jsp?iid=3 (accessed April 27, 2010).

17. Fred Weir, *Russia's Path from Gorbachev to Putin: The Demise of the Soviet System and the New Russia* (Kindle edition, 2009) location 1007–11.

18. Georgi Arbatov, *The System: An Insider's Life in Soviet Politics* (New York: Times Books, 1992), 215.

19. Goldman, *What Went Wrong with Perestroika?*, 49.

20. Weir, Kindle location 1700–01.

21. Gennady Gerasimov, in discussion with the author, 1994.

22. Kenneth S. Deffeyes, *Beyond Oil: The View from Hubbert's Peak* (New York: Hill and Wang, 2005).

23. Goldman, *What Went Wrong with Perestroika?*, 79–80.

24. Weir, Kindle location 1441–45.

25. Weir, Kindle locations 1858–61 and 1937–42.

26. Weir, Kindle location 2086.

27. Jack Matlock, *Autopsy on an Empire* (New York: Random House, 1995), 414.

28. Interview with Saul Mendlovitz, New York City, 1993.

29. Interview with Georgi Shakhnazarov, Moscow, 1993.

30. George Ignatieff, interview by Metta Spencer, "On Gorbachev's Speech at the United Nations," *Peace Magazine* 5, no. 1 (February–March 1989): 15.

31. Mikhail Gorbachev, *On My Country and the World* (New York: Columbia University Press, 1999).

32. Mikhail Gorbachev, *Memoirs* (New York: Doubleday, 1995), 249.

33. Archie Brown, *The Gorbachev Factor*, 196.

34. Brown, 194.

35. Jerry F. Hough, *Democratization and Revolution in the USSR, 1985–91* (Washington, Brookings Institution, 1997), 150.

36. Shakhnazarov, as Hough quotes Angus Roxburgh, *The Second Russian Revolution: The Struggle for Power in the Kremlin* (New York: Pharos Books, 1992), 88–90.

37. The advisers working on the proposal were Alexander Yakovlev, Vadim Medvedev, Georgi Shakhnazarov, Anatoly Lukyanov, Ivan Frolov, and Anatoly Chernyaev on the first draft. The second draft involved Yevgeny Primakov, Valery Boldin, and Vitaly Ignatenko. Then Shakhnazarov, Frolov, and Chernyaev prepared the third draft and Gorbachev edited the decision in the end.

38. Yegor Kuznetsov, several interviews in Moscow and by phone in the U.S. He kindly gave me the unpublished transcript of an interview with Georgi Shakhnazarov and another paper of his: Egor Kuznetsov, "The Making of a President: A Glimpse of the History of the Top Executive Post in the USSR," *Demokratizatsiya* 2, no. 2 (Spring 1994): 222–227.

39. Gorbachev, *Memoirs*, 250.

40. Jiří Dienstbier, interview by Metta Spencer, "A Talk With a Samizdat Writer," *Peace Magazine* 2, no. 2 (April–May 1987): 16.

41. Stephen Kotkin, *Uncivil Society: 1989 and the Implosion of the Communist Establishment* (Kindle edition 2009) location 115–21.

42. Gennady Gerasimov, *Good Morning America* interview, October 25, 1989.

43. Mark Kramer, "The Collapse of East European Communism and the Repercussions within the Soviet Union (Part I)," *Journal of Cold War Studies* 5, no. 4 (Fall 2003): 178–256.

44. Nikita M. interview, Moscow, May 1993. I regret my inability to identify him properly, but I have not been able to contact him to obtain permission.

45. Quoted by Mark Kramer in "The Opening of the Berlin Wall: A Twenty-Year Retrospective," www.cceia.org/resources/ethics_online/0039.html (accessed April 27, 2010).

46. Valentin Mikhailovich Falin, in discussion with the author, February 1994.

47. Matlock, 672.

48. Gorbachev, *Memoirs*, offers his account of these events in Chapter 27.

49. Brown, 267.

50. Brown, 260.

51. Hough, 498.

52. Kramer, "The Collapse of East European Communism," 211.

53. Kotkin, *Uncivil Society,* Kindle location 2586.

54. Metta Spencer, "Politics beyond Turf: Grass-roots Democracy in the Helsinki Process," *Bulletin of Peace Proposals* 22, no. 4 (1991): 427–435.

55. Metta Spencer, "When States Divide," introduction to *Separatism: Democracy and Disintegration,* ed. Metta Spencer (Lanham, MD: Rowman and Littlefield, 1998).

56. Weir, *Russia's Path from Gorbachev to Putin,* Kindle location 314.

57. Don Oberdorfer, *The Turn: From the Cold War to a New Era* (New York: Simon and Schuster, 1991), 404–410.

58. Lindsay Mattison, in discussion with the author, July 1992, Washington.

59. Georgi Arbatov, in discussion with the author, 1994, Moscow.

60. Academician Vitaly Goldansky, in discussion with the author, 1992, Moscow.

61. Fyodor Burlatsky, in discussion with the author, October 1997, Toronto.

62. John Bacher, *Petrotyranny* (Toronto: Science for Peace and Dundurn Press, 2000), 188.

Chapter 10: The Soviet Peace Movement at the Time of the Coup

Moscow, August, 1991. Every morning there was a fresh red rose at the marble bust of Lenin, but that was the only old-fashioned sentiment one could detect at the European Nuclear Disarmament (END) convention. A thousand peaceniks had gathered here and, even as we met, a few of us heard, but discounted, rumors of baffling phone calls alluding to a possibly imminent coup. One day after our meeting ended, the DINOSAURS would attempt to oust President Gorbachev. Four months later, the Soviet Union would cease to exist. Yet between the 13th and 17th of August, the peace movement in the Soviet Union showed itself to the world as it could not possibly have done a year or two before.

I have previously described the only two Soviet peace organizations that existed in 1983: the Soviet Peace Committee and the Trustbuilders. But when *perestroika* began and civil society was encouraged, for a brief time the Soviet people enthusiastically began forming myriad unofficial associations, called *nyeformaly*—"informal organizations,"[1] which included lively peace groups. In this chapter I want to give a snapshot picture of that new, independent Soviet peace movement on the eve of the coup. But first I should draw the big picture, showing the changing political configuration of Soviet public opinion in 1991, by comparing it to the situation in 1982, which I described in the first chapter.

* * *

In the final years before Gorbachev's elevation, you will recall that the salient opinions fit nicely into a four-fold table defined by two variables: whether the state was accepted or opposed, and whether a person assumed that change would come from above or from below—that is, from the grassroots.

Only two different groups of people opposed the existing state—TERMITES, who believed that change must come from above, and BARKING DOGS (or dissidents) who believed that it would come from below. I called most other people "SHEEP" for, whether or not they supported the state fervently, at least they did not oppose it overtly. Virtually all SHEEP assumed that reforms could only be introduced from above—and the top leader did indeed prove to be the source of *perestroika*.

But by 1991 opinions had changed. I tried to make a new typology but it was useless; the categories and individuals were changing in four big ways:

First, there were then *two contending versions of the Soviet Union*: the old DINOSAUR-led CPSU state of the type that Brezhnev, Andropov, and Chernenko had ruled, and also the new Gorbachev-led democratizing state. The two versions differed markedly but according to both of them, the big changes were still expected to come from the top leadership.

Second, Gorbachev had made it *safe to disclose one's political beliefs* frankly; many people were doing so. For that reason it was inaccurate to call the TERMITES by that name anymore, since they functioned above-board rather than burrowing silently inside the Party. Indeed, many of them actually were in power; Gorbachev had appointed them as his advisers and new officials.

Third, *there seemed to be far more BARKING DOGS than before*. Because it was no longer dangerous to be a dissident, lots of people wanted to become one! Throngs of people began opposing both the old Soviet state and Gorbachev's regime. Admiring the authentic old BARKING DOGS, quite a few SHEEP joined forces with the few remaining dissidents under the banner of the late Sakharov. This new populist crowd of "would-be dissidents" included Boris Yeltsin (who had quit the Party) and two other important new groups: the various nationalists who were seeking to secede from the Union, and "Democratic Russia." The latter was a truly grassroots political movement that supported Yeltsin in criticizing *perestroika*, alleging that Gorbachev was actually only a DINOSAUR who wanted too little change and was advancing too slowly. But also, in 1990–1991, most of the TERMITES and virtually all of the other intellectuals were abandoning Gorbachev and joining forces with the new group: the remaining BARKING DOGS, now augmented in numbers and calling themselves "radical democrats."

Thus the previous TERMITES were divided into two camps, most of them now having joined Yeltsin and the radical "democrats," but some remaining loyal to Gorbachev. For example, as we have seen, Burlatsky and Goldansky retained their loyalty to Gorbachev, even when they deplored some of his decisions. Nevertheless, Gorbachev was rapidly losing his political base—his centrist TERMITES—and was increasingly vulnerable to the contradictory demands of DINOSAUR CPSU members on the right and "radical democrats" on the left. The defection of his TERMITES to Yeltsin would be Gorbachev's undoing.

Fourth, a major change during 1989–1991 was the emergence of a fledgling civil society. The SHEEP, by far the most numerous category in society, were confused by all these changes. About half of them leaned toward the DINOSAURS and half toward Gorbachev, with only a few of these ordinary citizens preferring the "radical democrats." Nevertheless, not many SHEEP became politically engaged; mostly they distrusted politicians or were indifferent to them.

However, they did become engaged in civil society for the first time. There were now thousands of new, active non-governmental organizations engaging in public affairs. If people were becoming democrats of some sort, they were not very politicized ones. In no sense could the burgeoning civil society groups be compared, say, to Solidarność in Poland, or to any confrontational dissident groups. They were still SHEEP by disposition. Whether they favored Gorbachev's state or the one led by his rival Yeltsin, they were not political partisans, nor, with certain exceptions, did their organizations protest against anything. Indeed, Gorbachev was ahead of them in promoting changes. But these non-political SHEEP were creating NGOs that, if sustained, would increase their "social capital," their capacity for working together with trust.

Many of these new civil society groups addressed peace and disarmament issues, but there were also environmentalists and even groups that called themselves "political parties," though most of them actually were only small discussion groups with no program and no aspiration to win an election. For example, one directory identified 130 such groups, the majority of which could claim only between three and 100 members. Some claimed as few as one member![2]

By 1991 there were hundreds of Soviet peace organizations. The END Convention showed that the independent peace movement had become pluralistic, democratic, and astonishingly free.

I had just returned to Moscow after a three-week tour of Russia and Ukraine, where I had visited peaceniks and environmentalists with a group of Americans and Soviets called "Promoting Enduring Peace." Our transnational civic group cruised down the Dnieper from Kiev to Odessa, stopping at cities along the way, and thence by plane to Leningrad (which would shortly resume its old name: St. Petersburg). That trip, preceded by weeks of interviewing in Moscow and followed by the stimulating END conference, gave me a panoramic view of the Soviet peace movement at a single dramatic turning point in history.

At the Peace Bazaar

END Conventions always were a marketplace of ideas. This time about half the participants were from the West; the rest were astonishing new Soviet activists.

To my amazement, the convention was organized jointly by both the Soviet Peace Committee (SCDP) and Civic Peace, a new coalition comprising many genuinely independent peace groups from across the whole Soviet Union. A year earlier, such cooperation would have been unthinkable, but the planning for this gathering had begun in 1990 soon after Andrei Melville had become the new secretary of the SCDP.

Melville was a political scientist, then in his thirties, who looked like a weight-lifter. He had a breezy, colloquial command of English that suited a democratic reformer. I had met him in Canada early in the eighties and we had immediately started talking about democracy—a topic that had not yet been common among Soviet ideologues. He was already one of the jet-set Russians who lecture in American universities. His new prominence in the SCDP seemed so promising that END's habitually skeptical officers agreed to cooperate with him. Unfortunately, the reforms that he attempted did not take root. By the time the convention opened, he had left his post and the SCDP had reverted to its top-heavy bureaucratic ways.

Many citizens were still contributing to the Soviet Peace Fund but, as the Soviet economic and nationalist crises intensified, 70 percent of the money that had formerly been spent on peace marches and conferences was now spent on the victims of Chernobyl and the refugees from nationalist conflicts, as well as on local environmental problems. The SCDP still occupied opulent offices, including a baroque mansion in Leningrad with gold panels, originally the home of a noble family. There were other grounds for concern about the organization's delayed democratization. For example, when any Western peace organization invited Soviet citizens to a conference, only SCDP officials were likely to come. Even in early 1991, invitations directed through the SCDP had continued to be "lost" if they were meant for independent activists. The END Conference was very open, but not other SCDP events.

* * *

The other co-sponsor of the convention, Civic Peace, was remarkable simply for existing, and doubly remarkable for attracting so many feisty peaceniks from the four corners of the vast country. This coalition had published a book on Soviet military policy and was working on a law to permit conscientious objection.

The coordinator was Tair Tairov, the fearless Uzbek from Tashkent who had been secretary of the World Peace Council in Helsinki until he uttered too many uncomplimentary observations in the Western press about his outfit. Getting fired only energized him. Tair enjoys verbal jousting and he never turned down a chance to appear on TV opposite a hard-liner or DINOSAUR bureaucrat, whom he taunted provocatively.

He had put together an interesting program, even while helping German relief workers during the winter, when food was scarce. They had generously sent supplies, which the Soviet army had distributed. Unfortunately, the food did not always end up where it should have gone, so the donors turned instead for distribution help to Tair's Civic Peace network of independent Soviet peace groups.

Over the years most members of my old friends, the Trustbuilders, had emigrated, but I had kept in touch with one member, Nikolai (Kolya) Khramov, who in 1991 was an organizer for the Transnational Radical Party. Now at END I found some young people who claimed to be Trustbuilders. One was Alexander Pronozin, who looked exactly like any young anarchist conscientious objector in the West—unkempt, unshaven, and overloaded with protest buttons—but who was about to become a stockbroker, idealistically volunteering his services to create a Russian stock exchange. The other Trust Group activists were Jana and Yury K,[3] a competent, ambitious couple of twenty-five, who had managed Civic Peace's office and now managed the logistics of the END convention.

I had already met the Ks one hot night in Pushkin Square, the famed meeting place of dissidents, now famed as the place to buy a Big Mac. (Forget your gastronomic prejudices. McDonald's and Pizza Hut have contributed greatly to democracy in Russia by providing convenient public meeting places.)

However, the queues at McDonald's that summer were long, so we sat on a park bench, swatting bugs. Yury and Jana said that the group had split over strategy. The most prominent member of one faction had deliberately misinformed the press, saying that the Trustbuilders had dissolved, though no one had ever decided to do so. Admittedly, it had not met for many months. (When *does* a group stop existing, anyhow?)

By then, however, there had been thousands of similar groups, so there was nothing special about this one except its honorable history. In post-Soviet days, no one in Moscow would seem to recall the Group for Trust at all.

Though in every specific feature they looked Western, Jana's and Yury's incongruities were as astonishing as those of the disheveled stockbroker. Unlike Pronozin or my young peacenik friends in Canada (who wore Doc Martens boots and nose-rings) this handsome Russian couple wore spiffy blazers and carried briefcases. They were faster with a business card than Clint Eastwood with a gun, and had registered themselves as a business firm. Yury was the president, Jana the vice president. After their biggest venture (the publication in Russian of a book on how to study for American SAT exams), a business partner had cheated them of their profits. They had appealed for help to the police, who had told them that, since no laws were in place yet to regulate contracts, the best thing to do would be to go to the "rackets" (organized crime) and pay to have their stolen money recovered.

Despite this setback, the Ks were lining up other deals, such as possibly building a styrofoam cup factory in Latvia. They had organized the other newly rich alumni of their university to help support the current cohort of impoverished students, for whom they expected to collect 3.5 million rubles. Also, they were playing with an idea to help their college cover its expenses by using its large fleet of cars to generate income.

The capitalistic Ks did not fit my image of veteran peaceniks, which they were. In secondary school, they had been fascinated by Radio Liberty's reports of the Trustbuilders. Crowds of non-conformist youths in those days had listened to the same radio bulletins and had gathered to drink and talk politics in the bushes on summer nights. A little earlier my friend Julia also had grown up in that adolescent subculture. Jana and Yury had become Trustbuilders in 1986 and had even lobbied officials in the Russian government about some peace issues. Indeed, one of these TERMITE officials had offered to support the Trust Group in every way possible.

* * *

The most common approach of the new Soviet peace groups was inter-personal, not political. I am skeptical about this method, for I believe that war is a social institution, held in place by forces that are far more powerful than personal attitudes and emotions. One small group was "Peace Through Family," which had come to the conference from Leningrad. At the student hostel where I stayed, I met a charming girl of fourteen who told me about them as we set off together in search of a *Herald Tribune* to satisfy my craving.

"Peace Through Family" was a network of families who had formed an intentional community and were teaching their children to deal constructively with conflicts. They would give a workshop the next day to demonstrate their method of working through conflicts by role playing. The girl said that the best discoveries of her young life had come from trading roles with adults. She and her mother regularly played each other in extemporaneous dramas about their real disputes. The approach was sweet, I thought, but not likely to end war.

More famous than Peace Through Family was "Golubka"—which means "Dove."[4] It too approached peacemaking on the interpersonal level. My interview with one of the key activists, Zhenya Andreeva, reminded me of the New Age encounter groups I had explored during the 1960s and '70s. Golubka held trainings in nonviolence, designed to help people confront each other honestly with their true feelings. Golubka's interpersonal adventure tours specialized in "citizen diplomacy"—putting Easterners and Westerners together and building friendships between them.

Every society can benefit to some extent from such practices, but Russian culture really needed it. Whatever fosters trust is beneficial, and Golubka was building up social capital by creating friendly transnational interactions.

For example, it was setting up e-mail links—still an unusual kind of international contact in 1991. Zhenya Alexeeva organized a roundtable at the convention for activists who had accounts, and instructed others who wanted to learn the technology.

Already, before the August coup attempt, Golubka had obtained copies of the famous 198 types of nonviolent sanctions listed in Gene Sharp's first book, *The Politics of Nonviolent Action.* This list includes such inventive activities as boycotts, skywriting slogans, protest disrobings, strikes, mock funerals, and sabotage. It was going to prove useful soon during the putsch.

Despite calling their activities "citizen diplomacy," groups such as Golubka did little political action. Instead, by bringing Eastern and Western citizens together in settings that are conducive to friendship, they hoped to overcome enmities. That cannot be harmful and may do much good. I think the main thing, though, is not the fun and friendship that such contacts bring about, but the actual global issues that are addressed by such transnational civic society organizations. And during that period these international networks tackled some real international problems together, building significant social capital.

* * *

Two peace groups at the END Convention were especially conspicuous: the Russian Peace Society and the Committee of Soldiers' Mothers. The former group was selling traditional lacquer boxes, icons, and pamphlets in English about Tolstoy's philosophy. They were also organizing tours to Tolstoy's ancestral estate, Yasnya Polanya.

I steered clear of the Russian Peace Society at the convention because of a prejudice of mine. The word "Russian" sometimes carried an anti-Semitic implication in those days by indicating what it is *not:* "not-Jewish." That was not the case with the Russian Peace Society, as I discovered when I became acquainted with its founder, Ruzanna Ilukhina, a pacifist historian of nonviolence in Russia.

A large, dark woman in her early sixties of Armenian and Jewish ancestry, Ilukhina invited me over for tea and later repaid my visit in Toronto. She lived in the famous "house on the embankment," the apartment complex built by Stalin for the top officials in his government. She had grown up there and inherited her suite from her stepfather. She recalls the purges of the 1930s—especially the noises in the stairwells at night when the secret police came to arrest, one after another, the men who lived there. Perhaps her opposition to all violence has its origins in those memories. She said,

> In '85 or '86 I began to read Tolstoy. In Russia we knew his novels but nobody knew his social and religious work. I became close to Quakers. I'm a very religious woman now because I'm old. Quakerism is not very Russian. When we organized the peace society in Russia, we took the model from the West and tried to put it in Russian soil. It was our fault. We should have made it more Russian.
>
> But Russian religious pacifists came to us: Doukhobors, Molocans, and Protestants. And now we try to revive the Tolstoyan movement as the basis of the Russian pacifist soul. It is difficult because our conception of Tolstoy is based on Lenin's book, which called Tolstoy a great novelist but bad social thinker. Now we try to understand who we are—to identify ourselves. We must write a book and we support a seminar about Russian nonviolent pacifists. If we have such a book, then we shall go on TV and publish a magazine. It must be Russian conception, not a Quaker conception. And it must have its Russian nonviolence heroes. Even before Peter the Great we had such a tradition.[5]

The sincerity of Ilukhina's pacifism would shine through a few days later, when the coup plotters put every Russian to the test.

* * *

"Mothers of Soldiers" were everywhere. In a hall outside the auditorium stood a number of tables, each one holding the black-bordered photograph of a young man. I made a *faux pas* by putting my handbag on one such table to rummage through it. A Mother came and reproached me for being disrespectful. In every workshop, usually before the scheduled speakers began, a dead boy's Mother would claim the floor and tell her son's story.

One of the women was particularly conspicuous. Her business suit and hairdo might have identified her as a professional woman, but as she sat there twitching before standing to speak, there was a fierceness about her that betrayed her silence. Her son had been shot dead by a warrant officer for refusing to peel potatoes. I heard her story in three different sessions. The chairperson always found it awkward to return to the agenda after listening to a Mother's tale.

My friend Sasha Kalinin knew the Mothers of Soldiers well. He had been promoting legislation that would permit conscientious objectors to enlist in some alternative service instead of being conscripted into the military. The Mothers of Soldiers supported his proposal wholeheartedly, but it was hard to work with them—especially those whose sons had died. In every street demonstration Sasha always tried to stand beside the most agitated Mothers to restrain them if they lost control and assaulted a military officer.

Most of the Mothers, however, were altogether peaceable. Sasha introduced me to the organization's founder and leader, Maria Kirbasova, who appeared delicate and feminine. Her Asian features and flowered silk dress reminded me of a Japanese lady from the days of kimonos, yet she must have been as sturdy as a rock. Once she and her Mothers had marched down to a recruiting station and demanded the unconditional release of some conscripts. The astonished army officer in charge had actually complied. (Four years later I would see news photos of a far older Maria Kirbasova, hobbling with arthritis, yet leading gangs of Mothers on peace marches to Chechnya. There they would embrace the Chechen women and order their own Russian sons to come home with them.)

Public opinion was on the side of the Mothers, Kirbasova had told me. Though the Soviet Union was not officially at war, 6,000 young men were dying every year in the army. Some of them committed suicide because of the miserable living conditions. Some of them were untrained in handling dangerous materials, and some were dying as a result of homicide. Ethnic violence was a major factor. Homicides against Slavic soldiers were disproportionate, which is why many republics were demanding that young men be required to serve only in their own national armies.

Many young men were also refusing to be inducted, not primarily because of ethical or religious objections, but political and practical ones. Youths from the Baltic republics, for example, refused to serve in "an army of occupation" riddled by violence, theft of military equipment, drug and alcohol abuse, and even homicide.

Grassroots resistance against militarism was everywhere. At one workshop of the conference, Kolya Khramov read out the percentages of draftees who had actually turned up for induction as ordered. Percentages ranged from 8 percent in Georgia and 16 percent in Armenia to 81 percent in Moldova. The pacifist groups were in tune with the times.

* * *

The two Soviet peace organizations that did most to stop the nuclear arms race were International Physicians for the Prevention of Nuclear War (IPPNW) and Nevada-Semipalatinsk. The latter group became increasingly important after it had become safe for ordinary citizens to participate openly in protest movements. It and the Mothers of Soldiers were exceptional; unlike most other peace groups at END, they resembled Western protest movements and cannot properly be described as SHEEP but as BARKING DOGS.

Kazakhstan and Nevada, where the Soviets and Americans tested their bombs, are both treeless deserts. In both places, citizens formed groups to protest against the underground explosions that were making people sick by exposing them to radiation vented from the test sites. The Soviet protesters named their movement "Nevada" to emphasize their spiritual kinship to their American counterparts.

Between 1949 and 1963, 179 atmospheric nuclear tests were conducted near Semipalatinsk, Kazakhstan. After the Partial Test Ban Treaty came into effect in 1963, all three signatory states, Britain, the United States, and the Soviet Union, held their tests underground. Until Gorbachev announced his moratorium in

1985, the Soviet carried out an average of eighteen tests per year. Public mention of health effects was taboo until *glasnost*.

In February 1989, after the radioactive gases were vented in the usual manner, the wind changed direction, alarming the military personnel on the site, who phoned Moscow for emergency instructions. The news of this accident reached Olzhas Suleimenov, President of the Kazakh Writers' Union and a deputy in the Supreme Soviet. Suleimenov was scheduled to give a campaign speech on live TV but, instead of delivering the expected address, he launched into describing nuclear testing, radiation leaks, and the related health effects. He ended by inviting all viewers to join him in a public meeting at the Writers' Union in the capital, Alma-Ata (now Almaty).

They came. Five thousand of them came. There they heard speeches by people who had such illnesses as cancer, known to be caused by radiation. Suleimenov said that the average lifespan in Kazakhstan had been reduced by four years over the past ten years, and that any further testing would be a catastrophe.

From that point on, Suleimenov was not kept from discussing the issue in public. Indeed, he was invited to join Gorbachev on a trip to Britain, where he held his own press conference. Kazakhs began writing him letters describing their children's cancers, noting that the hospital authorities would not indicate leukemia as the cause of a child's death, probably to disguise the epidemic caused by the testing.[6]

Nevada-Semipalatinsk's initial support came from citizens of Kazakhstan, many of whom were not protesting against the development of nuclear weapons, but only against testing them in their area. Those people were satisfied to have the tests moved to an island in the far north of Siberia, Novaya Zemlya. Others, however, were pleased when the international Greenpeace team went into the Arctic waters to try to prevent tests there too. Nevada-Semipatinsk also benefited from the support of IPPNW. The two organizations, acting together, put on seminars and other educational events that mobilized protests in the Kazakhstan area. Nevada-Semipalatinsk had become the most powerful disarmament group in the Soviet Union by the time of the END Convention and, accordingly, their sessions and workshops there attracted the largest numbers of participants.

* * *

Nationalism as a peace issue? Lenin insisted that nationalities are entitled to "self-determination," which means that they have a right to secede from any state, including the Soviet Union. This theory had been built into the Soviet constitution, but had not been critically analyzed by dissidents before *perestroika*, so it remained a belief of most "democrats" during the Gorbachev years. Rosa Luxemburg had warned Lenin that it would tear the Soviet Union apart, and she proved to be right.

The politics of the last Soviet period made strange bedfellows. Many of those attending the END Convention were not peace groups but nationalistic organizations advancing their separatist aspirations. To my mind they were the greatest threat to peace.

But there was another side to the matter. If nationalistic organizations wanted to be regarded as peace groups, they had to behave peaceably. This probably influenced their tactics for the better, although there were other obvious reasons for independence movements to limit themselves to nonviolent methods. A Lithuanian, for example, hardly needed to be told that it was impractical to launch a war against the Soviet Army.

Anyway, some of the independence movements sought recognition as peace organizations, though they were openly xenophobic, with chauvinistic objectives. Included in this list were the Estonian and Latvian Popular Fronts, plus the popular front in Lithuania that was known as Sajudis. In Ukraine, the nationalistic movement was Rukh.

Also some smaller groups were forming to demand independence for local minorities, as for example an organization seeking autonomy for the Gagauz, a small Turkish-speaking group in Moldavia, where there was a larger independence movement called the "Moldavian Popular Front." (Moldavia would gain independence sooner than anyone expected and change its name to Moldova.) Even before they dared hope for autonomy, most of the big popular fronts demanded that their men—and *only* their men—be allowed to do their military service in their home republic.[7] This would have reversed the integrationist practices of the Soviet Army, possibly reducing thereby the ethnic fights within the ranks, but at a high cost in terms of other integrative values. Because Soviet citizens could not travel during their vacations, the only way to see the other regions of their country was through military service.

The great majority of Soviet peaceniks accepted these secessionist movements and endorsed their objectives. It was considered progressive to celebrate ethnic diversity and, instead of seeing a danger in dividing up a society into mutually exclusive nationalities, most of them simply assumed that because the Soviet Union had been a totalitarian state, breaking it up was the way to bring freedom. Indeed, their immense admiration for Boris Yeltsin, even in those precoup days, derived from his willingness to break up the Soviet Union. His acceptance of nationalism, and not his other political views, was his supporters' usual reason for considering him more democratic than Gorbachev, who was trying to build liberal institutions in an integrated, multicultural society. Already, most of the rest of the world could anticipate the bloody battles that would result from these divisive movements, but Soviet "democrats" could not.

Thus on the day of the coup attempt, the nationalist movements were generally accepted as part of the Soviet peace movement. To some extent, this acceptance could be justified. Many of these groups maintained connections with the Green movement, which is basically anti-militarist. During the cruise on the Dnieper, I met many supporters of Rukh, including some Americans of Ukrainian origin. As with others born in diaspora populations, these Americans strongly favored independence for their grandparents' homeland. The talk that I heard among Rukh activists during my trip along the Dnieper did not seem to be framed in terms of nonviolence, but had an aggressive edge to it.

However, some of the Rukh people were genuinely nonviolent. For example, about a year before, Rukh had staged a hunger strike in the main square of

Kiev, forcing the Republic's prime minister to resign. They also extracted a promise: to phase out the remaining Chernobyl reactors—a pledge that would not be kept. At one point, a delegation of war veterans marched through Rukh's tent city to place flowers before the statue of Lenin. There was a possibility of confrontation, but the protesters kept total silence. Their leader spoke to the veterans and thanked them for their contributions to the defense of Ukrainian society, explaining that now it was Rukh's turn to do as much, but in a different way. The veterans, moved to tears, embraced the young protesters and gave them the flowers that had been meant for Lenin.[8]

The Lithuanian separatists had even stronger grounds for claiming to be part of the peace movement. Before launching their resistance movement, several people in the new, secessionist Lithuanian government had studied nonviolent forms of civilian resistance. The director general of national defense, Audrius Butkevicius, contacted Gene Sharp, the leading specialist on that topic, who had a manuscript in preparation. In April 1990 Sharp sent Butkevicius a copy of the booklet, which was translated into Lithuanian and circulated throughout the Lithuanian government and to some people in Latvia and Estonia. Butkevicius later told Sharp that the materials had been useful for planning the resistance movement, whose actions eventually created an excuse for the Soviet military attack on Vilnius on January 13, 1991.

Butkevicius would soon become minister of defense and invite Sharp to Vilnius to meet with parliamentarians and the security institutions. As a result, the Lithuanian government would adopt civilian-based defense as the primary security system for the newly independent state. Butkevicius would continue to work closely with Sharp in developing such nonviolent methods as a coherent approach to national defense.

* * *

Many of the so-called "political parties" should really be considered social movement organizations, for they did not field candidates for elections, and some of them even refused to vote. Two examples are the Transnational Radical Party and Democratic Union. They were related, with some leaders of both groups being recruited from the same network.

Democratic Union proclaimed nonviolence as a fundamental principle. However, its members were not all equally committed to this policy, and the party was divided from the very beginning. Most members also wished to prohibit their group from participating in elections, but failed to make this policy mandatory. The group's commitment to nonviolence seemed to vary unpredictably. A dozen of them proclaimed the people's right to "overthrow criminal power institutions by any method, including armed violence," and said that "Gorbachev deserves the fate of Ceauşescu." However, a majority of the other members steadfastly opposed violence[9] and the most prominent activist, Valeria Novodvorskaya, must have been of two minds on the subject. At least, that is the only way I can make sense of her pacifist-sounding replies to Alexander Kalinin's question about violence in a 1990 interview exactly a year before her inflammatory speech at the party's congress. Kalinin had asked her, "Do you know any problems that can't be solved without violence?" She replied,

> Not all problems can be solved, as a matter of fact. But if a problem can't be solved without violence, the more so it can't be solved violently. That's why Democratic Union rejects the death penalty in its program. When KGB inspectors during the interrogations asked us, "What will you do with us if you come to power?" we always responded: "We'll set a guard near your door to protect you from infuriated people." . . . The only possible punishment is to ostracize them.

The Transnational Radical Party has its main strength in Italy, where it has existed since the 1950s. Groups can also be found in Belgium, Hungary, Poland, Yugoslavia, and individual members are in many other countries. In Moscow, it was founded in 1986 and its early members included three former Trust Group activists—Evgenia Debrianskaya, Nikolai Khramov, and Alexander Pronozin (the stockbroker)—plus my friends Alexander Kalinin (then a deputy in the Moscow City Council) and Julia Kalinina.

The Radical Party's logo includes a drawing of Mohandas Gandhi and its platform includes the abolition of the death penalty, the legalization of conscientious objection to military service, and the release of animals from zoos. Less fittingly, the party would also like to legalize drugs and prostitution. During the convention the Radical Party put on a workshop on conscientious objection. Later Kalinin would serve on a commission for the Russian government developing a proposal for legislation, which would be adopted in an imperfect form in 1994.

* * *

The environmental movement burgeoned even more quickly than the peace movement. Early in the 1980s it managed to save the deep, pristine Lake Baikal from industrial pollution. Later, when nuclear disarmament seemed to be on the horizon, peace activists began attending to related environmental issues. Two organizations that illustrated this trend were Save Peace and Nature and, in Ukraine, Green World.

Vladislav Kornilov, the former secretary of SCDP who, during the coffee break so many years before, had privately urged me to keep talking about human rights, did not last long as a reformer in the Soviet Peace Committee. Upon being dismissed for their democratic ways, he and Tair Tairov attempted the same kind of substitute career: to found and lead a new, non-governmental organization. Kornilov's new organization, Save Peace and Nature (SPAN) initially seemed promising, However, funding would prove insufficient when the Soviet Union dissolved, and by 1993 SPAN would be out of business.

Green World, a longer-lasting environmental organization, existed only in Ukraine and had close ties to the Green Party and to Rukh, the nationalist group. It had at least half a million members all over Ukraine and was taking stands on controversial political issues. I interviewed its vice president, a mild-mannered engineer named Anatoly Panov, as we sailed down the Dnieper River. He said,

Right now we are working to close ecologically dangerous enterprises, such as nuclear power plants, old gas plants. We already closed the Danube-Dnieper Canal. We also were the initiators of the so-called "Chernobyl Trial." It's a public campaign in which we criticize our government for its poor handling of the situation after the disaster. . . . Also, we believe that Ukraine has at least five times as much military equipment and personnel as we need, so we'd like to see it cut.[10]

* * *

Memorial and Helsinki Citizens Assembly combined the approaches of several different levels, ranging from face-to-face dialogue, to peace rallies, to political campaigns. In the Soviet Union, the two groups overlapped.

Memorial was created by young Soviet citizens to keep alive the memory of those who suffered from Stalinism in the Gulag. The organization collected, catalogued, and filed thousands of documents which enabled some people to find out, for example, how their fathers had died.

If this had been all the members did, they would have accomplished much that is honorable, but they gradually expanded to take on even more tasks. Some of their members did research on the social psychology of totalitarianism. Others created systems for relieving the survivors who were suffering, in their old age, from poverty and the deterioration of the Soviet social welfare system. And some members formed teams to intervene in situations of ethnic conflict to prevent bloodshed. The organization still survives and is doing important human rights work in the post-Soviet era.

The Helsinki Citizens Assembly (HCA) was a network of Eastern and Western activists that held a big assembly every eighteen months somewhere in Eastern Europe. I was deeply involved in the organization for several years. The Russian delegation (mostly recruited from Memorial) was often organized by Marina Pavlova-Silvanskaya, a prematurely white-haired journalist who had worked for two decades in Prague at *Problems of Peace and Socialism*. When Marina couldn't come, there sometimes was no Russian delegation at all, though there would be participants from the (mainly separatist) republics, such as Dainis Ivans, a Latvian journalist who had been a major figure in the independence movement, and Natalie Belitser, a biochemist and fervent Ukrainian nationalist.

During the END Convention in Moscow, the officers of HCA—the Yugoslav leader Sonja Licht with her husband, sociologist Milan Nikolic, Mary Kaldor of England, and Mient Jan Faber of the Netherlands—gave a workshop on Yugoslavia. The Bosnian part of the drama had not yet begun, and HCA was organizing a peace caravan to travel around the country, urging people to put aside their secessionist ambitions and preserve peace. Milan drew a map on the blackboard and showed with swirling arrows how war might spread across the whole Balkan region, including Greece and Albania. Some people did sign up to go on the trip, which of course was fruitless.

HCA was more successful in the Transcaucasus region of the Soviet Union, where it kept a dialogue going among groups marked by ethnic rivalry. HCA maintained teams of volunteer mediators, such as Marten van Harten, a Dutchman who brought together representatives from the highest levels of the societies that are in conflict. More than once I witnessed the dialogue of twenty people around a table—such as a newspaper publisher from Baku, a Tbilisi psychologist, and two women parliamentarians, Anahit Bayandour from Armenia and Arzu Abdulayeva from Azerbaijan, who would later win the Olof Palme peace prize for sustaining their friendship in spite of the war and supporting other transnational civil society relationships as well.

But Then, a Coup

I had left Russia by train, still glowing with pleasure at the success of the END meeting and the prospects for a more peaceful Soviet Union. I had witnessed the beginning of a democratic movement from below, and I felt encouraged.

But just as we pulled into the station in Warsaw, someone said he'd heard on the radio that there was trouble in Moscow. Gorbachev was said to be "sick" and another group was taking over. I hurried to a hotel and, instead of interviewing Polish activists as I had planned, turned on CNN, and spent the day watching, along with (I guess) half the world's television owners. Then I caught my flight to Canada. On board, there was TV news from Moscow. Tair Tairov was being interviewed about the putsch. He sounded fatalistic.

Would civil society be able to mobilize opposition? Would the peace movement use nonviolence effectively? *Could the new grassroots Soviet peace movement face down an old-fashioned authoritarian regime?*

Notes

1. See Helsinki Watch, *Nyeformaly: Civil Society in the USSR* (New York: Helsinki Watch, 1990).
2. See Vladimir Pribylovskii, *Dictionary of Political Parties and Organizations in Russia*, ed. Dauphine Sloan and Sarah Helmstadter (Washington, D.C.: Center for Strategic and International Studies, 1992). For example, the single confirmed member of the "Right Conservative Movement" was its chairman, Nikolai Lanin, who described his party as nationalistic and "Right bourgeois"!
3. I wish I could name Jana and Yury, but I can no longer locate them to ask their permission.
4. Gale Warner, *The Invisible Threads: Independent Soviets Working for Global Awareness and Social Tranformation.* (Washington, DC: Seven Locks Press, 1991).
5. Ruzanna Ilukhina, in discussion with the author, 1991, Moscow.
6. Warner, 28–51.
7. Helsinki Watch, *Nyeformaly*, 91–92, 101–02.
8. Alex Kuzma, a U.S. Rukh supporter, in discussion with the author, August 1991.
9. Pribylovskii, 29–31.
10. Anatoly Panov in discussion with the author, August 1991, on a Dneiper river cruise ship.

Chapter 11: The End and the Beginning

The Soviet Union collapsed as the result of two *coups d'état*. The bare facts are well known, but the *meaning* of some facts may forever be disputed, though the debate hardly repays our attention. For example, some even say that Gorbachev was the author of the initial coup against himself—a notion that I do not bother to entertain.[1] (Maybe that's because I am Western. Russians often do think strategically, debating, for example, whether an act is what it seems to be or instead is a "provocation"—a move counter to one's own apparent interests for the sake of some ulterior motive. That's what comes of playing too much chess.)

The End of the Soviet Union

I'll recap the bare facts. Gorbachev was on vacation at Foros in the Crimea when the coup from the right occurred. He had been warned. The American ambassador, Jack Matlock, had received information from Mayor Popov of Moscow on June 20, 1991 that the KGB head, Vladimir Kryuchkov, and others were planning a putsch. He had told President Bush, who had instructed him to tell Yeltsin and warn Gorbachev, but Gorbachev had simply responded with a chuckle, "I have everything well in hand."[2]

He did not. He was negotiating the new Union Treaty with Yeltsin and the leaders of the republics, who had followed Yeltsin's example by declaring their sovereignty and trying to maximize their autonomy under the new treaty. The final controversy concerned the right of the Union to levy taxes. Yeltsin had wanted taxation to be the prerogative of the republics alone, but on July 29, a compromise agreement was reached and preparations began for the August signing ceremony,

Just then, Gorbachev met with Yeltsin and Nursultan Nazarbaev, the president of Kazakhstan, at Novo-Ogarevo, a state dacha outside Moscow. They discussed the possible appointment of Nazarbaev to a cabinet post, and Gorbachev revealed that he intended to replace two DINOSAURS, Defense Minister Dmitri Yazov and Kryuchkov, in the new government.

This disclosure was consequential, for Gorbachev later learned that their conversation had been taped by the conspirators themselves. He wrote, "When they heard that we intended to replace them, Kryuchkov and the others lost their heads. The claim that the plotters were driven by patriotic feelings alone is sheer demagoguery."[3]

Nevertheless, unaware of the impending coup, Gorbachev and several of his advisers had departed for their vacations in Foros, leaving a clear field for the putschists, who included the interior minister, Boris Pugo, the prime minister, Valentin Pavlov, the chairman of the Supreme Soviet, Anatoly Lukyanov, General Valentin I. Varennikov, and Vice President Gennady Yanayev, who would soon declare himself President.

On Sunday, August 18, as Gorbachev was preparing to return to Moscow for the treaty-signing ceremony, four men arrived unexpectedly at his dacha. He did not receive them but tried to phone Moscow, only to discover that all five phone lines were dead. Finally, the men barged in and gave him an ultimatum: he must sign the document issued by the new self-created "emergency committee." Gorbachev said that he would sign no such decree but would act legally, within the Soviet Constitution: "I told them that they were criminals who would be held accountable for their folly. That put an end to the conversation. As they were departing, I lost my cool and swore at them, Russian-style."[4]

When the men returned to Moscow and reported to the other conspirators, the main putschists were already beginning to wobble. Pavlov and Yanayev started drinking, while Lukyanov and Marshal Yazov regretfully started inventing fall-back positions. But it was too late to retreat. They had announced publicly that the president was sick, incapable of performing his duties. Crowds were milling around in every city, discussing the situation.

In Foros, Raisa Gorbacheva was keeping a diary that her husband would later publish in his memoirs. Everyone knew that their situation was grim. As Alexander Likhotal, Gorbachev's spokesman, told me later,

> I know pretty well the people who stayed there during those days in August. For instance, his bodyguards. He had around thirty personal bodyguards there and when he heard at the press conference that Yanayev invited the Russian deputies to go and to see for themselves that the president was incapable of carrying on his duties, he understood that in a couple of hours he would be incapacitated, just to show the visitors that he is incapable. At that time, he told his bodyguards to take their firearms and guard the perimeter of the building. His direct orders were not to permit anybody to come up more than thirty meters to these buildings. They were in this siege for several hours, and only two of the bodyguards did not obey this command and went away. They understood that in case of assault, all of them would be killed. I know this from the persons involved.[5]

The Gorbachev family was kept isolated in their dacha for seventy-three hours, though on Monday their television was working again. They also heard BBC news on a transistor radio, learning that Boris Yeltsin had called for resistance against the conspirators. In Moscow, exactly such a public mobilization was taking place, as I'll describe in another chapter. However, polls later showed that about 40 percent of the population sympathized with the coup, and the leaders of most republics were taking their time to think it over.[6]

On Wednesday the putschists again contacted Gorbachev. He met with four of them but refused to meet Kryuchkov and Yazov, who signed a statement admitting their guilt. He realized then that he was free, and told his family to prepare to fly back to Moscow.

But the stress had been too great. Gorbachev reported that as soon as his daughter Irina got into the car in Moscow, she had a nervous breakdown, and that his wife, Raisa, was "not well again for two years."[7]

Gorbachev asserted that he was now a different man, but he did not yet realize how different the country also was. Yeltsin was the great hero of the hour, having proved his courage by standing on a tank outside the parliament, urging the nation to defy the coup plotters. Public opinion of the party also had changed decisively during those three days. Crowds were gathering outside the Central Committee building, expressing outrage against the Party, but Gorbachev had not heard that almost the entire Party leadership in the country had betrayed him. At the press conference, he defended the CPSU and said he still hoped to reform it. As his interpreter Pavel Palazchenko, wrote about that event,

> I never allow my mind to be deflected when I interpret, but this time, even as I was speaking into the microphone, I thought, "This will cost him dearly." Indeed, the next day there was a lot of talk that Gorbachev had understood nothing, and the radical democrats, who had a justifiable feeling of triumph, could not forgive Gorbachev for trying to stay with the Party after all that had happened.[8]

On the afternoon of August 23, Palazchenko and Anatoly Chernyaev were watching a TV broadcast of Gorbachev's humiliating meeting with the Russian parliament. They were stunned to see the deputies insulting and jeering at him. "How can he continue as president after this?" Chernyaev said quietly.[9]

But he did—at least for a while. Indeed, on some fronts he was making progress. However, his closest advisers had to tell him the hard facts about the CPSU. Yakovlev, Bakatin, Primakov, Chernyaev, and Vadim Medvedev met him at his office and collectively told him that the hierarchy had betrayed him and that he must renounce them immediately or lose all credibility. He promptly declared himself no longer the general secretary and demanded that the Central Committee be disbanded.[10]

He still faced the matter of the Union Treaty, however. The Ukraine parliament declared independence, showing that they would probably not sign the treaty. Nevertheless, before Gorbachev met the Congress, he found compromises that all the republics except the Baltics would probably accept. In October, opinion polls were taken in major cities across the country. They showed that public opinion in favor of preserving the Union had not changed significantly during the last six months. Some 75 percent of those questioned favored keeping the Union.[11]

Other work progressed too. In late September, President Bush sent a proposal for a major disarmament agreement—a real breakthrough. And Grigory Yavlinsky had an economic plan that the republics seemed likely to sign.

Nevertheless, Boris Yeltsin was becoming more difficult every day. He made it clear that he was now the authoritative leader of the Soviet Union, and that Gorbachev could simply be disregarded. He announced his intention to release price controls from almost all products, triggering a round of panic buying in the shops.[12] Then on November 25, at a meeting of the State Council, Yeltsin refused to initial the draft Union Treaty. The handwriting was on the wall.

On December 8, Yeltsin met with the leaders of Byelorussia and Ukraine at a hunting lodge near Minsk. Legend has it that they made their bold decision in a bathhouse while well-fortified with liquid courage. On the next morning, they announced the Belavezha Accords: an agreement to dissolve the Soviet Union and create the Commonwealth of Independent States (CIS). This second coup against Gorbachev—this time from the left—was also completely illegal, but it triumphed. At first Gorbachev would not give them his resignation, lest he appear to confirm the legitimacy of their deed. But then, to give the document a touch of legality, the three men, Yeltsin, Kravchuk and Shushkevich, asked the Supreme Soviets of their republics to endorse their decision. When the Russian parliament quickly did so, the president of the Soviet Union gave up.

Gorbachev's downfall, and the fate of his country, was complete.

* * *

The nearly seven-year period between March 1985 and December 1991 is one of the most dramatic times in history. The world is a safer place and Russia is a more democratic society as a result of Gorbachev's leadership. He ended a war and averted new ones. He created multi-candidate secret elections, genuine legislatures, and civil liberties. And yet in the end, he could not fulfill his hopes.

I wish I knew of alternative tactics that would have succeeded, but I have to agree with the Moscow political analyst Lilia Shevtsova, who argues that nobody else could have done better. She wrote, "Gorbachev's failure to reform the USSR showed that it could not be reformed."[13]

His tactics were clear enough. He wanted to lead toward peace, democracy, and good governance, steering between BARKING DOGS who demanded that he go faster and DINOSAURS who wanted him to stop altogether. At the outset, he probably did not anticipate that his fellow TERMITES would ever consider him too conservative. Yet surprisingly, in the end, it was primarily their stampede to join the radical "democrats" that ended his presidency.

I am not the only observer who blames Gorbachev's downfall on his former non-dissident supporters. So does Vladislav Zubok in his book about "the last Russian intelligentsia," *Zhivago's Children*. His book's title refers to intellectual TERMITES working in the cultural sphere—artists, writers, musicians, and philosophers. They had been, he said, dedicated to the "centrality of culture and art in the social life of their people, and to the possibility of building a gentler society based on non-capitalist foundations."[14] In bitter disappointment they came to regard their old socialist idealism as unrealistic. Now they, who had been moral authorities in the Soviet Union, failed to support Gorbachev and, according to Zubok, were responsible for destroying the state he was reforming.[15] He writes,

The union between left-leaning intellectuals and the Gorbachev leadership began to disintegrate, and their mutual irritation grew. . . . These members of the
perestroika intelligentsia abandoned their onetime creed with a remarkable
ease. . . . In the course of 1990 the Moscow inter-regional group and thousands
of its followers began to leave the party and shift their allegiance and aspirations over to Gorbachev's rival, Boris Yeltsin. Yeltsin, guided by ambition and
iconoclastic populist instincts, had at first been seen by Sakharov and other intellectuals as a dangerous demagogue. In 1990, however, Yeltsin began to appear like the only leader who could grapple with the situation and at the same
time remain open to the ideas and advice of intellectuals. In the spring of 1991
he was elected, in the first free elections, as president of the Russian Federation, still subordinate to the Soviet Union and Soviet leader Gorbachev, but
thereafter increasingly autonomous. The more Gorbachev felt abandoned by the
intelligentsia and threatened by the forces of chaos, both national separatist and
economic, the more he remained hostage to the same party apparatus and to the
KGB he wanted to manage and control. Indecisive in every sphere, he antagonized the majority of Russians and only a few intellectuals and enlightened ap-
paratchiks remained his true admirers.[16]

I may never understand why TERMITES left Gorbachev. However, *Christian
Science Monitor* Moscow correspondent Fred Weir thinks he understands. He
explains it as simple greed. Although almost all of the party elite claimed that
they were pursuing democracy more avidly than Gorbachev, Weir maintains that
their objective was not democracy but capitalism, which they rarely acknowledged. Party officials had never been paid lavishly. Inequality in the Soviet Union was vastly less than in capitalist societies. The richest decile of households
received 4.5 as much income as the poorest decile in 1969. In the United States
and France, on the other hand, the decile ratio was 15.9.[17] But capitalism offered
possibilities for increasing the ratio.

The Soviet population as a whole did not favor the introduction of a free
market system; the majority preferred democratic socialism until the end.[18]
However, Party officials began to recognize that they were in an extremely favorable position to get rich as soon as capitalism could be introduced. Weir
states that the Party, state elite, and the urban intelligentsia had come to favor
capitalism by June 1991.[19]

I wanted to know more about Gorbachev's own motivations, so I visited
Alexander Likhotal seven months after the Soviet Union ended. He was still
Gorbachev's spokesman, but now in the Foundation instead of the Kremlin. I
have known Likhotal since 1986, when we both participated in founding a
UNESCO-funded peace university in Schlaining, Austria. In a meeting to plan
the first curriculum, the chairman had asked whether "class struggle" should be
one of the required topics. Likhotal said no. I was astonished. A Marxist scholar
had apparently become an ex-Marxist. This *was* change!

Thereafter Likhotal and I have stayed in touch occasionally. As Gorbachev's spokesman, he had made the official announcement on television that
the Soviet Union would end. Then he would go on to serve as one of Gorbachev's two closest aides in the years ahead, mainly in Geneva, where he is
president of Gorbachev's other organization, Green Cross International. But

when I visited him in 1992, it was the source of Mr. Gorbachev's political views that I asked about. He said,

> He wrote letters to his wife while he was just a low-level party functionary in Stavropol, and in these letters he puts very frankly his impressions of the stupidity of those who grasped power in the region—that it was impossible to deal with them. He felt that probably when he would become a secretary of the regional party, he could change things, but he found otherwise. He thought that as secretary of the Central Committee, he could change things, at least in agricultural affairs. And again, he produced new documents and it was impossible to get the agreement of members. Only when he was elected as general secretary of the party did he understand that he had received an opportunity to change everything. But he knew that it would take time and that he would have to maneuver a lot because the beast should be kept dreaming and not be awakened.
>
> He tried to do it smoothly, gradually, and people at a certain point supported these changes. He thought that probably this was a turning point, but in fact, from this point in time, the political landscape also had to be monitored. A lot of conflicts—national ethnic conflicts—were frozen in the totalitarian grip. When this grip loosened, they appeared. From this time on, he was fighting on both directions, with the right and with the left, just to keep this maneuvering on course. [Likhotal's hands undulate between right and left, while moving forward.] Once in an interview he was asked whether this was his mistake. He should be allied with the left, with progressive forces. We were in a car in the United States, on a road with sharp curves. He asked the driver, who posed this question, "Look, can you go just directly forward?" [We laugh.][20]

Gorbachev's tactics make perfectly logical sense: You stake out the common ground between the two extremes on your right and left and, while compromising whenever necessary, keep moving forward cautiously. Be progressive without "waking the beast." But unfortunately, this approach did not work as expected, for the two sides became more and more polarized. The common ground eroded from under his feet, leaving him no place to stand. Instead of being half-acceptable to both sides, he became hated by both sides. This outcome stands as a warning to other politicians.

And there *are* others. You may think of Kerensky when you analyze Gorbachev's tactics. I think instead of Barack Obama, whose political style is the same. He too intended to be "bi-partisan," to compromise, and to maintain consensus throughout the land. Instead, within months he came to be hated, not only by the Republicans but—especially!—by liberal Democrats who had so recently adored him. In a time of political polarization, a progressive politician evidently cannot succeed by taking a middle position. I wish it were otherwise.

The Beginning of Post-Soviet Russia

Suddenly it was the flag of Russia, not the Soviet Union, flying at the Kremlin. A triumphant Yeltsin moved into Gorbachev's office and started dismantling the Union. Surely he must not have expected the break-up to make life easier for ethnic Russians, a quarter of whom were suddenly living in the successor states of the Soviet Union, encountering hostility for staying loyal to Russia.

And Russia had other problems. Only half as populous as the late Soviet Union, it assumed all Soviet foreign debt[21] and the entire Soviet nuclear arsenal.

Also, it's expensive to break up a country. You have to set up new governmental structures and economic relations. This was especially a problem for the post-Soviet countries. Planners had taken little account of the cost and time delays involved in transportation. Freight rates had been kept ridiculously low and the Soviet Union was a nation of specialized "company towns"—industrial giants far apart from one another. Their enterprises were linked by vast interregional trade networks, with shipping distances as great as the international trades of Western nations.[22] Replacing these inter-dependencies with supply relations among new, internal enterprises would cost all the newly independent countries, including Russia, dearly.

But such concerns were hardly on Yeltsin's mind. He was exuberant and immediately launched capitalism.

* * *

And so began "shock therapy." Although Grigory Yavlinsky had been invited to work with Yegor Gaidar in creating economic reforms, their respective plans were incompatible so Gaidar was put in charge of everything, becoming the country's first prime minister. He was taking the advice of Harvard economists and the International Monetary Fund.

The first phase of shock therapy was the release of price controls in October 1991. During the final Soviet years most prices had been fixed and the shops had been empty. With the lifting of price controls, the producers were glad to offer their goods for inflated prices, so the shops soon became full, but hardly anyone could afford to buy their goods. Millions of Russians became destitute.

Privatization came next. A few thousand enterprises had already been privatized under Soviet laws, but between 1992–1994 many of Russia's productive assets were given to the citizens through a system of vouchers. Everyone, including children, received vouchers, which they could exchange for shares in formerly state-controlled enterprises. Some shares were given to employees, so as to keep from concentrating the ownership of productive property—yet that was the outcome anyway, for most people simply sold their vouchers or shares for a pittance. The managers of the firms quickly acquired ownership and, within a short period, a new class of wealthy capitalists emerged. Industrial output declined by half, and many companies could not pay their workers for months or even years. Corruption and crime became rampant.

In 1994–1995 the nearly bankrupt Russian government disposed of many of its remaining industries by auctioning off leases in a loans-for-shares scheme. These firms were unprofitable; the government had long been subsidizing them and would be better off without them. Moreover, Yeltsin needed money desperately at that point, for the budget was in deep deficit. However, the auctions were controlled by insiders and conducted without real competition, so that most big industries were sold for fire-sale prices—in some cases less than one percent of their real value.[23] This loan-for-shares scheme almost overnight made a few industrialists into immensely rich, influential "oligarchs."

The 1997 Asian financial crisis spilled over into Russia in 1998, causing a catastrophic collapse. The ruble and the price of oil and minerals dropped, and many people invested their capital abroad instead of in Russian businesses.

Not until Yeltsin's departure from office would these economic calamities give way to a period of recovery, from which the popularity of a new president, Vladimir Putin, would be the prime beneficiary.[24]

The transition to capitalism was more painful than Yeltsin's supporters expected. The question remains: Did it have to be such a tragedy? Might other policies have been easier? Not all Eastern European countries suffered so much during the transition—but they had not been communist for seventy years.

I asked Grigory Yavlinsky about it in 2008. After quitting Yeltsin's shock therapy project, Yavlinsky had continued as the leader of the liberal Yabloko party and had twice been a candidate for the presidency of Russia, coming in third each time. I like him and would vote for him if I could. Nevertheless, like others, he complained of the West's influence on Russia's transition. He said,

We had a big hope that the rest of the world would cooperate with us, and it didn't happen. We hoped that they would not come to give advice and money for wrong things. I'm talking about Russia in the post-Soviet period. For example, nobody would advise a government to liberalize prices when they had an all-monopolized economy. When you have such an economy, if you liberalize prices you have a 2,600 percent inflation. Nobody would give such advice!

I said, "Jeffrey Sachs did." Yavlinsky replied,

Yes, but it was not only Jeffrey Sachs. It was IMF. It was the American treasury who supported this line. It was not simply an academic exercise, no! It was a policy! But it was policy based on incompetent vision, and they knew that. Nevertheless, they did it. . . . It was an intention to bring Russia as far from the former Soviet Union as possible. They were still fighting.

I asked, "If you had got your 500-day program through, how would things have looked different now?" Yavlinsky replied,

We would have had no 2,600 percent inflation in 1992. I think we would have had no shooting from the tanks at the White House in 1993, and I think we would have had no voucher privatization. I think that we would have no economic collapse in 1998. And we would have had no criminal privatization. So I did not know how successful we would be but we could have avoided these things easily, simply by turning away from this super-radical approach.[25]

* * *

If the "democrats" who had supported Yeltsin expected him to usher in real democratic governance, they would soon learn otherwise. Whereas Gorbachev had tried to move forward between the right and left, while compromising enough to hold the country together, Yeltsin intended only to defeat all adversaries. Whereas Gorbachev had been pluralistic, allowing new parties without abolishing the CPSU, Yeltsin did abolish it and gave its buildings to organizations such as universities, led by democrats.

Yet there were still millions of devoted Communists in Russia and they had elected a parliament that was mainly DINOSAUR. From the beginning of Yeltsin's presidency the executive and legislative branches clashed, each seeking more power than the other, sometimes even in violation of the existing Constitution. This struggle went on for twenty months. Throughout 1992 Yeltsin fought the Supreme Soviet (the standing legislature) and the Congress of People's Deputies. The speaker of the Supreme Soviet, Ruslan Khasbulatov, opposed shock therapy. Neither man had a peaceable nature.

Their struggle begins. In December 1992, the parliament refuses to confirm Yeltsin's nominee for prime minister, so he schedules a referendum on a new Constitution and issues a decree giving himself full executive power until it meets. So the deputies try (but fail) to impeach him. Then he holds a conference to examine the proposed Constitution, but the parliament rejects its outcome and gives the Constitution-making authority back to the deputies.

Back and forth it goes. Yeltsin dissolves the Supreme Soviet and they void his decree, name a new president, Rutskoy, and impeach Yeltsin. He shuts off their phones, water, and electricity. Hundreds of armed men rush to aid parliament. Rutskoy tells the crowd to seize the mayor's office and the TV tower. Ministry of Interior troops meet the crowd and turn them back, killing 62.

Which side will the Russian army take? Hours pass while the generals debate, finally opting without conviction for Yeltsin. At daybreak, army tanks surround the White House and begin shelling it. By noon, soldiers enter the building. According to the police, 187 have died there and 437 are wounded, but I have heard other estimates of deaths as high as 2,000. We may never know.

Parliament and Yeltsin had both behaved abominably; it is hard to say which was worse. The democrats and former TERMITES overwhelmingly took Yeltsin's side;[26] he was still their man, though he had already given democracy a bad name and their morale would never recover. Even the governments of the U.S. and Europe did not criticize him. To have done so would have helped his Communist opponents—a position that old Cold Warriors still could not take.

Yeltsin's victory over parliament was conclusive, and he held a new referendum to approve his proposed Constitution. There would be a bicameral legislature, the lower house to be called the "State Duma." He could dissolve it and veto any bill passed by the Duma, which could over-ride his veto only by a two-thirds majority. Yeltsin was now truly the ruler of Russia.

* * *

Fyodor Burlatsky came to Toronto in 1996 and I had a chance to ask him about the new Constitution.[27] He was critical, saying,

> We have a parliament and a president who are elected, though maybe 90 percent of these officials used to belong to the Communist *nomenklatura*. Our president holds more power than the leader in any democratic society. He can even issue decrees that may be more important sources of law than what parliament does.

I asked, "But you were involved in writing the new Russian Constitution. Did you oppose all those structural arrangements at the time?" He replied,

Yes. After we finished our work a small group wrote many new articles and excluded the provisions for the State Duma to control the president and the government. According to the Constitution, the president proposes a candidate prime minister for the Duma's approval. The president can use this to push the Duma out, for if they refuse three times they must go out and a new election will take place.

It is not the Constitution, but Yeltsin's personal traits, that cause most of our problems. He has changed his team and his approach four times without worrying about anyone. He favored Gaidar so much at first that Gaidar believed that Yeltsin really loved him, but in the end was deeply disappointed. So were the last ministers whom Yeltsin sent from his cabinet, Kozyrev and Chubais.

And then there were his cruel decisions about Chechnya, which he took over all kinds of objections. And he has taken control of the TV programs. He likes authoritarian power. Gorbachev was a weak president, a polite president who listened to both sides and worried about many decisions. But this man Yeltsin is a real decision-maker. He likes to decide even though he understands nothing about what he is doing. During one year and a half he signed 3,000 decrees in addition to all his other responsibilities. He issued all kinds of decrees, including one about private ownership of land, and a decree against the Mafia, which allows people to be kept in jail for thirty days without permission from the court. The Constitution says that it can be done only for forty-eight hours, but that counts as nothing. Yeltsin's police use it, not only against the Mafia but against some individuals whom the people around Yeltsin dislike.

He has more power than even a general secretary, except, of course, Stalin. Brezhnev had a politburo with eighteen members who were elected on the same level as himself. All of them were powerful. But Yeltsin has an administration that he appoints personally.

That administration is a strange body because the Constitution doesn't say what its function is. It looks formally like the American administration but it doesn't include ministers. This one is just composed of bureaucrats—staff advisers. They work in the same building as the Central Committee of the Communist Party in the Old Square. There are about 2,000 to 3,000 persons working there—exactly as many as during Khrushchev's time when I was in the Central Committee. We had about 3,000 people, who prepared everything for us. But now nobody knows what these people are doing. They are divided into departments—economic department, international department, domestic department, propaganda department, and so on. However, they don't prepare decisions on these matters. Economic decisions usually come from Prime Minister Chernomyrdin's staff, and political decisions usually come from Yeltsin's advisers, so these people have nothing to do with these decisions.[28]

* * *

Separatism is a trap. If you endorse it for one region of a country, you'll lack coherent grounds for rejecting it when another group of people demand it. The people wanting independence know that their ethnic community dominates in the region that they want for their "national homeland." But invariably there are still other minorities within the region and if they cluster geographically, soon they too will want for their sub-region to secede.

And why not? There are no well-established international laws specifying the criteria for appraising a separatist group's claims. Moreover, acceptance of such claims is not a matter that sharply divides the Right from the Left. Most people are ambivalent about the subject, but peace activists and "democrats" do tend to be generous toward separatists.

I am not. I think that what people really need is democracy, not an ethnicity-based homeland. But specific democratic institutions must be developed to protect minorities. During the 1990s, separatist wars raged because no one knew what was fair and what rules for secession should be upheld. Many lives would have been spared if there had been well-established international laws to settle such disputes. And the problem continues, with tragedy generally resulting from secession. I wish a qualified organization would ask the International Court of Justice for an advisory opinion on the subject.[29]

Boris Yeltsin endorsed the break-up of the Soviet Union into independent republics. The fissiparous process did not stop there, and he had no consistent subsequent policies. He even had to address the issue that had caused Gorbachev such grief: creating a new "Union Treaty"—though now there was no Union, but only a single Russia with many different regions, each seeking more self-governance. He managed to put together a Federation Treaty that gave some "ethnic republics" greater autonomy than others. It gave the leaders of all regions formal representation in the upper house of the new parliament[30] and scheduled direct elections of regional governors.[31]

However, two of the eighty-eight federal subjects refused to accept this treaty: Tatarstan and the Republic of Chechnya. Both wanted independence. Yeltsin negotiated a solution with Tatarstan that granted it far more autonomy than would have been accepted in Switzerland, say, or the United States, but Chechnya rejected even those liberal terms.[32]

For a while Yeltsin left the matter unresolved. Then, in the summer of 1994, he undertook covert military operations, assisting the opponents of the Chechen leader, Djokhar Dudayev, to topple him. They almost succeed in November of that year. When the effort failed, the media exposed Russian participation, embarrassing the government. A DINOSAUR in Yeltsin's government, Deputy Premier Nikolai Yegorov, privately remarked that "we now need a small victorious war, as in Haiti. We must raise the president's rating."[33] This points to the motivation: to improve Yeltsin's sagging popularity.

So the president sent troops into Chechnya on December 11, 1994, for a war that he expected to be over within hours. It actually lasted until August 31, 1996.

* * *

The first Chechen War was immediately unpopular. Several generals resigned in protest against the use of the army against its own people. The troops were unprepared; some soldiers sabotaged their own equipment; others deserted.[34]

There were protests. For example, the Mothers of Soldiers[35] whom I had seen in Moscow at the END meeting in 1991 now became engaged protesters. In Toronto, I watched on TV as Maria Kirbasova, although crippled with arthritis, led soldiers' parents into Chechnya. These mothers famously ordered their conscripted sons to desert and come home with them immediately. (I heard that one colonel actually obeyed his mother.)

Another protester was a Japanese Buddhist monk, Junsei Terasawa. In the 1970s he had spent time meditating in the Himalayas, having a revelation that turned his whole life into peace activism. I used to see him at the head of every long peace march, chanting and banging on a drum that he carried everywhere. He had even managed to station himself in the garden of the Aga Khan's palace when Reagan and Gorbachev held their first summit in Geneva. It was January and as the two men sat down for their first fireside talk they could hear Junsei outside, drumming and praying for the success of the meeting. As he drummed, his 101-year-old teacher died in Japan.

Now he was in Chechnya, seeking to calm the fight and bring Russian soldiers home. As bombing began he was marching with thousands of Russian mothers, side by side with thousands of Chechen mothers. The Russian army blocked the way. (Terasawa had spent ten years in Russia training new Russian monks, but after his time in Chechnya, the government would cancel his visa.)[36]

The Russian soldiers wanted to quit the war but had no opportunity. Their misery did not make them gentler toward Chechens. Before the war was over, according to the Soldiers' Mothers, 14,000 of them were dead.[37] Perhaps 52,000 were wounded or sick, and about 3,000 more missing by 2005.[38] The Chechen count was even less certain, with up to 100,000 casualties, mostly civilians.[39]

* * *

Julia Kalinina, my friend and former assistant, had become a war correspondent. I worried about her, for ample reason, as her long letter made apparent:[40]

> I was lucky. I received a great journalistic opportunity: I was surrounded. I came to Grozny, the capital of Chechnya, spent a night there, and the next morning found I couldn't leave the area. The last road from Chernorechie (the southwest district of the city) was blocked by the federal troops. Soldiers were digging trenches in the fields. The teams of volunteer fighters who controlled this area of Grozny were encircled—and so was I.
>
> I couldn't even consider asking the soldiers to let me go home. They shot whenever they saw anything move. That morning four cars had been shot. Two wounded people escaped by crawling across the field to the woods. The others were still lying on the road. The Chechen detachment was alarmed. According to all rules of military science, eventually the federal forces were going to enter this area and take control.
>
> Apparently my confused face expressed my feelings. Nobody could look at me without laughing. "Why are you journalists always going where you don't need to be? For us it makes no difference. We are condemned men already. Either we win this war or die. But why did you come here?"
>
> Having mocked me for a while, they started to reassure me: "Don't worry. We'll break it. Or take you out some way." In the evening the heavy shelling

started. Two shells exploded in the yard of the headquarters building, so every-body rushed to the basement. I sat there in the first aid room with several Chechens and a seventeen-year-old girl who was supposed to be a nurse. She was absolutely helpless. I tried to help her. Five men were brought in, wounded by the shrapnel. Normally the wounded are transferred to hospitals in the villages but we were now surrounded, so such a trip was impossible. One of the wounded died, though he could have lived if somebody had extracted the shrapnel.

It was amazing how the Chechens discussed what to do with the wounded. They just couldn't believe that the Russians wouldn't let the bus with the wounded pass through. "But they are wounded! No armed person will go with them. How it can be, not to let a wounded man get medical help?" So naïve. But I've seen that they always treat wounded Russians.

In the kitchen the commanders held a meeting. They wanted to stay and fight, for they were sure the Russians could never capture the area if they stayed. The main argument against such a plan was that a lot of civilians, mostly Russian, were still living in the region—old men, women, and some women with children. Most of the fighters in the detachment were inhabitants of the area, so they knew their neighbors and didn't want to harm them. They had two options: to leave the area themselves or to force the inhabitants to leave.

One proposal was to gather the people and send them along the road to the Russian positions. I was supposed to lead the procession with a white flag and explain to the soldiers that we are all women and elders without any arms and that we just want to leave the area. My journalistic certificate would supposedly protect us from shooting. (I knew that the shooting would certainly start while we were far away, where nobody could see my identification card. And even if they noticed it, they wouldn't care about the press. That idea had been tested several times). Anyway I certainly agreed to play this honorable role, though the prospect of being shot was obvious. However, I was happy when the com-manders rejected the proposal, saying simultaneously that we would be shot.

By then it was late at night and there was no place to sleep except in the headquarters building. The shelling was so heavy that I doubted it was safe to sleep anywhere in the building except perhaps in the basement. The Chechens comforted me, saying that Russians are shelling the left side and we would sleep on the right side, so there was nothing to worry about.

At dawn the commander woke me, saying that his Chechen fighters would break through the encirclement today. Maybe they'd find a corridor. If not, they'd fight until they broke through. He said it would be better for me to stay in the area for a day or so until the Russian troops arrived. Then I could leave Grozny without risk. He took me to his neighbor, a woman of my age with two daughters, and went to order the breakthrough.

The Russians didn't come. Not in a day nor in a week.

While we drank our morning tea, my hostess Helen explained that she and the other inhabitants of Chernorechie who had stayed here didn't have relatives in the countryside who could take them in. They just didn't have any place to go from the war zone. Moreover, they didn't want to leave their apartments be-cause marauders would certainly start their job as soon as the region was cap-tured by Russian troops. I had always supposed that your life and your chil-dren's life would be more valuable than your apartment and furniture, but there was nothing to argue about. We both were surrounded and we had to think of how to survive.

The process of survival is simple. You need to eat, to drink, to sleep, and to avoid the shrapnel. That's all. There were no food stocks because nobody had been preparing for a blockade. For me it was evident that in a couple of weeks people would start to eat bark from the trees. Before I appeared, Helen had possessed one kilo of rice, a pack of tea, and two thousand rubles (half a dollar). My travel allowance saved the situation; we bought some potatoes and a jar of coffee, and we found a woman who was baking bread and selling it. She said that her flour stock was coming to an end but anyway we felt better for having a certain amount of food.

We were looking for food to the accompaniment of explosions and the buzz of planes. People explained to me that the Russians are not shelling here but somewhere else. And the plane isn't a bomber but only a reconnaissance aircraft. Helen showed me two little boys who recently had "collected pieces of their grandmother." During the shelling, the family had gone to the basement. The grandmother was kneading dough and didn't stop because the dough would be spoiled. A shell landed in the kitchen.

People spoke amazingly lightly of the shelling. At first I supposed that all of them were very brave in comparison to me. Later I understood that during these last months they had completely lost the feeling of danger. For example, during the night I jumped because of a loud explosion, but Helen explained that the thing hadn't fallen here but somewhere out there. And in the morning we found out that the shell had hit the neighbor's house.

To sleep during shelling—that's something that you have to learn to do. The massive shelling usually starts at 10 p.m. and continues until morning, so you can sleep only when you are so tired that you simply can't stay awake. People slept fully dressed, in case they had to jump up and run away. Children didn't sleep either. They sat with us until 2 a.m. playing cards by the light of a candle, drawing, and recording jokes on my tape recorder. For some reason Helen supposed that a shell doesn't break two walls, only one. So when the shelling was extremely loud, we forced the children to hide in the corridor between two rooms. There, in this "secure" place, they continued their night games.

To get water you need to go to a spring in an open zone that has been heavily shot up, so it's very risky. When it's quiet people go there as often as possible to collect huge amounts of water for their homes. Maybe you won't be able to go to the spring again for the next several days.

Two weeks before we were surrounded, a helicopter had thrown a bomb right into the crowd of civilians who were waiting their turn at the spring. Nine persons were killed immediately and seven of the wounded died later—mostly women and children. At that time the road was open. It was possible to transfer the wounded to the hospital. But now any injury is a catastrophe. Nobody will extract even the splinter of a shell. There is no surgeon in the area. But every day the number of wounded is increasing. If they don't get to the hospital, all of them are doomed.

The worst thing was that I couldn't inform my relatives that I was alive and staying in Chernorechie. During the first days after the fighters' departure the inhabitants sent several old men to the Russian positions to ask them politely to enter the area. The old men were severely beaten. One died. The chief of police made several unsuccessful attempts to contact the Russians. As soon as he appeared with his white flag, they started to shoot. We tried to send women there. Young women were excluded; the Chechens supposed that they would be raped. At last two old women agreed to try but the result was the same. The Russians shot and wounded one of them.

There had been no electricity for more than two months. No newspapers, no TV. At night I tried to get something on the radio but the endless flights of shells by the window agitated the air and it was impossible to catch a wave.

Actually I didn't know what news I was waiting for. There are no journalists in Chernorechie except me, so no one in the world could know what was going on there. Anyway it was silly to hope that the radio would say: Tomorrow Russian troops will stop shelling and enter Chernorechie.

Finally I caught a radio wave and learnt that Russian troops had suppressed the fighters' attempt to break through the encirclement. Good news except for the fact that the fighters had successfully left the area three days ago. I knew that better than anybody else.

The inhabitants were just sleepwalkers. They kept asking, "Why don't they enter? There are no fighters here!" They knew that the coming of Russians would bring the stress of permanent check-ups, arrests, maraudings, and murders. Still, they supposed that a horrible end is better than endless horror. They blamed everyone: Dudayev, Yeltsin, and the Russian army.

Don't the Russian troops know that the fighters have left? That means that they don't have any intelligence. Unbelievable! And suppose they know but don't enter anyway? Even more interesting. They are afraid that some fighters are still in the area and prefer just to appear to be fighting. For how long can that go on before the whole region dies of hunger and shrapnel wounds? It would be more humane to use air strikes. At least they would finish us off in a few days.

It was a deadlock. Either eliminate everybody or retreat. Those in the front line can't eliminate everybody. Those who give orders can't retreat. Russian citizens can't influence the situation because we know practically nothing about it—and don't want to know.

After one week the police chief found a corridor and helped a few of us go out. I brought one of Helen's children. We crawled 500 meters on our knees through the Russian lines, then walked four hours in the woods to reach safety. Back in Moscow, for three weeks I kept listening to the radio, which reported that "the federal troops continue to shell the southwestern regions of Grozny that still are under the control of Chechen fighters."

* * *

Still, Julia Kalinina remained a war correspondent and was soon back to reporting in the North Caucasus. On June 14, 1995, a group of Chechen fighters attacked the police station and other government offices in the Russian town of Budyannovsk, about seventy miles north of the Chechen border. They captured a hospital, taking hostage everyone inside and threatening to kill them unless the war ended. Julia was there and managed to get inside—for a few hours, she thought, but instead she stayed.

The hospital was under siege for four days and the Russians were throwing in grenades. About 160 buildings in the town were destroyed; estimates of the deaths vary from 129 to 415. Sergei Kovalev, then human rights adviser to Yeltsin, came and watched the hospital burning. Yeltsin was in Canada at a summit, but Prime Minister Chernomyrdin negotiated with the Chechen leader Shamil Basayev, agreeing to exchange hostages and to call a ceasefire in the war.

Basayev was allowed to take his fighters, plus a number of hostages, with him back to his stronghold in Chechnya. Julia was one of the sixteen journalists volunteering to make the trip as a hostage. After her return home the Russian government decorated her.

On August 31, 1996, General Alexander Lebed, Yeltsin's national security adviser, signed a peace accord with President Maskhadov of Chechnya. Both sides withdrew their troops from Grozny. The first war in Chechnya was over.

* * *

Military reforms had been overdue long before the war in Chechnya. The Mothers of Soldiers and even many military officers agreed that conscription was the source of most problems. They proposed for the military to be manned entirely by professionals. As Roger McDermott wrote,

> [T]he vast majority of Russians confirm that something must be done urgently about the army's ills, by which they mean its low level of combat readiness, dismal performance in Chechnya, poor funding and supply, criminality and corruption, *dedovshchina* (bullying), and broken system of conscription.[41]

Institutionalized bullying is the most egregious aspect of barracks life, which Joris van Bladel has described. He considers it a predictable response to a desperate situation. Young soldiers are forced to live together as inmates of what Erving Goffman called a "total institution," unable to pursue their personal needs, interests, or preferences. A new batch of conscripts are brought into the barracks every six months, needing guidance in this coarse, unfamiliar world. They encounter a cohort of slightly more experienced soldiers with whom it is necessary to maintain solidarity, voluntarily or not. Each *dedy* ("grandfather") becomes a patron, but also a bully, to a newcomer. The *Dedovshchina* system is an informal hierarchical structure among a group of soldiers that is primarily based on seniority. Here is an example:

> Yevgeny explained in an interview that he was obliged by the *dedy* to write to his mother asking her to send him money. As soon as the money arrived Yevgeny had to give it to the *dedy*. Had Yevgeny (and his mother) failed to obey this order, Yevgeny would have been beaten to death. Other witnesses recounted that category I soldiers systematically had to give up their meals to the older soldiers. Vitaly, for example, had to give his meal to a particular category IV soldier. When he complained to this soldier that he was hungry, he was beaten up and told to steal food in order to stay alive. Similar measures were taken by the *dedy* in order to obtain cigarettes and alcohol.[42]

Van Bladel interviewed the fathers of some soldiers who had done their service before 1968. They reported that the rule of elders had existed even then, but it was not as brutal or criminalized as in the 1990s. This suggests that the economic crisis in the 1990s had worsened the situation.[43] Some of these desperate soldiers even sold their own weapons during the war in Chechnya.

In 1996 during his second presidential campaign, Boris Yeltsin decreed that the military would become completely professional by 2000. Everyone knew the promise could not be fulfilled at that time, though it was highly desirable.

I asked several generals during the Yeltsin years about military reforms: What improvements were being made in military structure and doctrine? Their basic answer was: almost none. They said Yeltsin was no more attentive to military concerns than Gorbachev and had made no significant military reforms. General Mikhail Milshtein said,

> I am strongly for the professional army. We don't now have military forces. They are collapsing. . . . The problem would be solved only by having a professional army, part of conscripts and part of professionals.[44]

I also asked Major General Serebrenikov about military reforms, and he was frank to admit that it would entail unwelcome changes. He said,

> [Our] generals are second to none. But a majority of them are accustomed to old ways of organization. For example, the transition to the fully professional army grants more freedom to the soldiers and servicemen. These changes are perceived painfully by the generals. And my personal journey to my present ideas was painful. Finally I accepted the idea of the professional army. There is a strong psychological resistance, a longing for the past. The Soviet army had been an army based on conscription. It's hard to break this custom.
>
> A second issue is the control of the armed forces. In a totalitarian system power is focused in a single point. That's why the army can be used arbitrarily, even against its own people. The aim of military reform is to prevent the possibility for a dictator to use the armed forces against the people.

I asked, "Does this mean a change of rules, such as an oath to require soldiers to disobey orders under certain conditions?" Serebrenikov said,

> We are moving toward acceptance of this. Many commanders are suspicious of the idea, for they are afraid that many orders would not be obeyed. It has to be formulated as a duty of a serviceman not to fulfill a criminal order. A duty.[45]

Changes were taking place in military doctrine in the Yeltsin years. For example, "New Political Thinking," which had shaped military policies during the Gorbachev years, had vanished from conversations after the Cold War. I asked General Milshtein what had happened to the policy of "reasonable sufficiency."

He said, "First, you have to decide who's your enemy. Against whom is it reasonable? Who is our enemy now? Now it's all mixed up."

I asked him about current views of unilateral initiatives. He said,

> Military people are against this because the United States and NATO countries don't follow us, particularly in the nuclear field. We did a moratorium, but there was no moratorium on the other side. We should have done all these

things but we should have got something back. For our country, Gorbachev not only solved troubles but he added troubles to the ones we had. He is popular abroad but almost hated here.[46]

All the Russian generals whom I interviewed opposed nuclear weapons. Milshtein even resorted to the concept of "reasonable sufficiency" in explaining why. He said, "From my point of view, reasonable sufficiency in the nuclear field must be zero."

Another member of Generals for Peace, General Georgi Mikhailov, explained how the Russian military had turned against nuclear weapons.

There was a time when we and the Americans thought you can win a nuclear war. And then we had the Chernobyl catastrophe. Only one atomic plant and only one of four reactors at this plant burst and we received such casualties, such disasters over a big area! Not only military people but also the political guidance understood that we can have dozens of these Chernobyl [disasters] if there is not a nuclear but a simple conventional war. A single plane can come and destroy an atomic reactor near Leningrad and all this radiation would come. We'd have to evacuate millions of people. So if you use nuclear weapons then you will have not only no victory but no people to live in your country. This was one of the ideas in Gorbachev's "New Thinking." It came slowly to the heads of the military, but Chernobyl made this process quicker.[47]

I felt optimistic about the anti-nuclear predictions of the generals until I met civilian experts with different views. They included Sergei Karaganov and Sergei Rogov, Georgi Arbatov's successor as head of the USA/Canada Institute. In 1992 Rogov told me, "Nuclear weapons are going to remain the foundation of Russian security, in my view, and there is nothing defensive about them."[48] (He would repeat this prediction again as late as 2009, despite the agreement reached by Presidents Obama and Medvedev to reduce strategic nuclear weapons. He said, "Russia is lagging behind the USA in state-of-the-art high-precision conventional weaponry. It regards nuclear weapons as a means of deterring not only a nuclear war but also a large-scale conventional war.")[49]

Whether or not I like his predictions, Rogov is insightful. He said,

There has been no military reform. When the Russian Supreme Soviet was crushed in '93, what was defeated was not the Communist position toward reforms, but rather the legislature's ability to limit the power of the executive branch. The constitutional system we have had since 1993 has no checks and balances. Even on paper, control by the executive branch is nearly unlimited. The legislative branch has almost no authority; it cannot even control the purse. The government stopped performing its proper functions. Street crime has grown because the government cannot protect citizens. Bureaucracy has been given the right to supervise privatization without democratic control. Few bureaucrats can withstand this temptation, so corruption has reached enormous proportions. Organized crime moved into all economic spheres because the government is not enforcing the sanctity of contracts. . . .

In the Soviet time there was civilian control over the military (not democratic, but it was civilian: the Communist Party) but that mechanism was destroyed overnight. Nobody in the military is accountable.... The military didn't want to fight the civilians in Chechnya. They refused to fight in 1991 but later they were forced to shed the blood of their fellow citizens. It has psychologically harmed the Russian military, who don't want to think of themselves as an army that suppresses its own people.[50]

* * *

Yeltsin's approval ratings had dropped to low single-digits by 1996, when the next elections were held. In no democratic country would he have won a second term as president, but in Russia he did so easily. This was accomplished with considerable money from the oligarchs to whom he had given the country's enterprises, and with support from his friend Bill Clinton, as sociologist Dmitry Furman explained to me.

> In 1996, there were new, important elections—the second term of Yeltsin. These elections were absolutely fraudulent. Of course, not all Western governments supported Yeltsin. Nevertheless, in the headquarters of his campaign, there were American specialists. I don't think these specialists played a real, serious role; it was only symbolic support. But after this absolutely fraudulent election, there was no possibility of any rotation of power, of real choice. I think personally that there was no possibility of it from the very beginning, from 1991, but certainly after 1993 and 1996, Yeltsin had only one choice: to hold onto power or go to jail.[51]

The travesty prevailed by reminding everyone: If Yeltsin is defeated, Communists will take his post. Evidently, this argument was convincing.

Yeltsin's second term predictably prolonged the conditions of the first one: corruption, crime, and the population's declining longevity. The president was sick much of the time, incapacitated by heart attacks, quintuple bypass surgery, and apparent alcoholism.

Russia's relations with the West deteriorated during Yeltsin's second term, but he should not be blamed for it all. NATO offended Russians by expanding into the former Warsaw Treaty Organization and by bombing Belgrade and sending troops into Kosovo. (My own Russian friends refer to Serbs as "us.")

Chechnya had been virtually independent after the first Chechen War, but that had not ended the violence in the area. In the last months of Yeltsin's second term, a new war began. In August 1999 Basayev and Ibn al-Khattab, a mujahideen from Saudi Arabia, led about 2,000 insurgents into nearby Dagestan. Within weeks the Russians had reacted by killing several hundred militants and forcing the rest back into Chechnya.

In September, several apartment buildings and a mall were bombed in Moscow and other Russian towns, killing nearly 300 persons. Khattab first claimed, and then denied, responsibility for these bombings. For a while it seemed that Dagestani guerrillas had carried out the operations. But a far more sinister interpretation would emerge gradually that purported to explain, not only the second, but also the first, Chechen War.

About the first Chechen War, Julia had written to me early in 1995:

According to my sources in the Ministry of Defense, it was realistic to negotiate with Chechen leader Djokhar Dudayev—actually, to buy him somehow. He was capable of compromising. . . .

There are two main groups inside the Russian power structure now. The first one mainly consists of "power" people—Pavel Grachev, the minister of defense and Nikolai Yegorov, the minister of nations' affairs. The group is headed by a clerk, Aleksandr Korzhakov, head of the presidential guard. They also include the first prime minister Oleg Soskovetz, the secretary of the Russian Security Council, Oleg Lebov, the head of the President's Security Service, Aleksandr Barsukov, and the president's assistant, Viktor Ilyushin. These individuals are connected with each other by friendship or kinship and financial interests. They view Russia as a great empire that should be respected. They are not well educated. They were brought up to live in a socialist state and they want to return to that.

The other group includes Prime Minister Viktor Chernomyrdin, First Vice-Premier Anatoly Chubais, some ministers, lots of deputies, certainly former Prime Minister Yegor Gaidar, and many of President Yeltsin's counselors, such as Emil Pain. They are "reformers"—liberal, educated—and they see Russia's future in a world economy.

The question is, who is President Yeltsin? It looks as if he is more with the "power" people than the "reformers." The fact is, our president is a hard drinker. When he falls into such a period (which happens quite often now) only two people have access to his person (to the hand that signs the president's orders): Korzhakov and Ilyushin—both members of the "Party of War," as Gaidar calls them. During such periods the "violent" decisions win the competition. When the president wakes up or when something happens that demands his appearance, the "reformers" can win a slight revision of what was done.[52]

This account reminds me of Likhotal's prediction that Yeltsin's presidency might be taken over, while appearing to be the same government as before. Probably I did not take Julia's analysis seriously enough until I read a book by a writer who paid with his life for revealing too much.

* * *

Vladimir Putin was named prime minister in August 1999 and Yeltsin announced that he had chosen him as his successor. Then, on December 31, 1999 Yeltsin abruptly resigned, apologizing for his many failings. Putin became acting president. The public knew nothing about him except that he was a forty-seven-year-old former agent of the KGB (now called FSB) and a judo expert who had worked in East Germany.

Yet Putin would have to stand for election to the presidency within three months. Given the vast unpopularity of Yeltsin, the election of his chosen heir could not be taken for granted, especially since Moscow Mayor Yury Luzhkov and former Prime Minister Yevgeny Primakov would also run for the office.

But the leader of a nation at war could expect to be supported. Some apartment houses were blown up; Chechens were blamed; the public suddenly became ready to fight Chechens; and Putin won on the first ballot. This shocking theory of Putin's rise to power was offered in a 2007 book, *Blowing Up Russia*, by Alexander Litvinenko and Yuri Felshtinsky.[53] (Remember, I warned you that Russians believe theories of "provocation.") Litvinenko explained these events with a single theory in the foreword to the posthumously published book.

Litvinenko, a former FSB agent then living in London, was poisoned on November 1, 2006, and spoke by phone from his hospital bed to his co-author, who recounted his deathbed accusation in the foreword to their book. He knew, wrote Felshtinsky, that he had been poisoned but he believed that he had survived an assassination attempt.[54]

But on November 23, 2006, Alexander Litvinenko died. The book was full of shocking allegations against the FSB, the agency that succeeded the KGB.[55] I bought a copy in Paris and read it on the train, hiding its cover from the border guards as I entered Russia in 2008—a cover proclaiming that it is banned in Russia. I would not ordinarily have taken its charges seriously. Russians have too little trust in others, and I don't like to augment mistrust by spreading paranoid inferences. But somebody had killed this man for telling his story.

Litvinenko and Felshtinsky say Yeltsin fell into an FSB trap, finally relinquishing control of the state in return for promises of immunity from prosecution for his corrupt family. The leverage involved both Chechen Wars.

In 1992, says the book, the Chechen leader Djokhar Dudayev began paying multi-million dollar bribes to Korzhakov, Barsukov, and Soskovets, with the connivance of the Ministry of Defense, for Soviet weapons conveniently "left behind" in Chechnya. But as Moscow extorted more and more money, Dudayev started refusing to pay. He asked for a personal meeting with Yeltsin, but the three men refused to set it up without being paid in advance. Dudayev had compromising evidence against them, which he believed he could use as insurance against being arrested. He was mistaken. His blackmailing attempt failed and he never got a meeting with Yeltsin. Indeed, he had made himself into a dangerous threat who had to be removed. This was done, according to the book, by provoking the first war in Chechnya.[56]

Blowing Up Russia will never win a literary prize, but it was not meant to be light reading. I cannot summarize its endless details about murders and attempted murders—fully 318 pages naming victims, perpetrators and officials who cover up for them, along with biographical data, dates, hours and minutes of assassinations, street addresses, car license plate numbers, and other minutae about the social networks linking these people. This is the tedious investigative notebook of Litvinenko, a twenty-year veteran of the KGB. I read it like a detective, questioning the parts that didn't seem obvious. There were many.

The drama began on November 18, 1994, on a railroad track in Moscow, where a bomb went off prematurely, blowing up the track and the bomber himself. He was Captain Andrei Shchelenkov, who worked for an oil company called Lanakos, which was owned by a FSB agent named Maxim Lazovsky. Every employee of Lanakos was an agent a Russian counter-espionage agency.[57]

This is the kind of plot we find throughout the book: one FSB provocation after another. As a conspirator you perpetrate an act of apparent terrorism against Russia, so that you can accuse your enemies of doing it and justify going to war against them—which is what you really want but might be prevented from doing if the public were not enraged. In this instance, accusations against Chechens wouldn't hold water because of Captain Shchelenkov's clumsiness, but on most occasions, the plan worked. Four days after the botched bombing, Dudayev accused Russia of launching a war against Chechnya—though it had not actually begun yet. But on November 25, seven Russian helicopters fired rockets at the Grozny airport, starting the first Chechen War.

The second Chechen War began in much the same way, with FSB provocations in the form of apartment house explosions in Moscow and other cities, killing 300 persons. The book says the political goals of the bombings were to provoke Russia into war with Chechnya, and "to exploit the ensuing commotion to seize power in Russia at the forthcoming presidential elections in 2000."

But again, one such provocation failed. Alexei Kartofelnikov, a soccer team driver in Ryazan, spotted people carrying 50-kilogram sacks from a white Zhiguli car with license plates T534VT77RUS into the basement of a seventy-seven-flat apartment building at 14/16 Novosyolov Street during the night. (See what I mean about excessive details?) He called the cops, who arrived too late to catch the perpetrators. But they did dismantle the timer (set for 5:30 am), evacuated the building, hauled the sacks away, tested them, and declared them to contain the explosive hexogen. The building's inhabitants hopped around in the freezing wind all night, some of them barefooted.

By morning every radio and TV station in Russia was announcing that a terrorist bombing had been foiled in Ryazan. Putin praised the citizens for alertly preventing the disaster. The people of Ryazan would be avenged. Already the Russian military had started air strikes on the airport in Grozny. (Hmm. Would terrorists go there?)

Then the FSB had the sacks of hexogen brought to their own lab, where they claimed to have tested them and found them to contain only sugar.[58] (I wondered: Why say that? It was still plausible to accuse Chechens of terrorism—but only if the sacks really contained explosives.)

But soon a telephone operator recorded a suspicious call to Moscow: "Leave one at a time; there are patrols everywhere," said the voice at the other end. She reported the call and the suspicious telephone was monitored; it turned out to be one of the offices of the FSB in Moscow.

Following instructions, one terrorist probably made his way back to Moscow, but the other two stayed in Ryazan, in different safe apartments. The police were remarkably astute. A day later, they had managed to locate both suspects, but before arresting them, had phoned the top FSB man. At that point they were told not to arrest anyone since actually the whole thing was not really a serious terrorist action but a training exercise for the FSB!

This account was so absurd that a newspaper joked, according to the book:

> "The head of the FSB, Nikolai Patrushev, made the sensational announcement that the attempted bombing in Ryazan was nothing of the sort. It was an exercise.... The same day, Minister of the Interior Vladimir Rushailo congratulated his men on saving the building in Ryazan from certain destruction."

But in Ryazan, of course, no one was laughing. Obviously, even though Patrushev had forbidden it, the Ryazan UFSB went ahead and arrested the terrorists, considerably roughing them up in the process. Who was arrested where, how many there were of them, and what else the Ryazan UFSB officers found in those flats we shall probably never know. When they were arrested, the terrorists presented their "cover documents" and were detained until the arrival from Moscow of an officer of the central administration with documents which permitted him to take the FSB operatives, who had been tracked down so rapidly, back to Moscow with him. Beyond this point our investigation runs up against the old familiar "top secret" classification.[59]

The book's appendices include the transcript of a committee that sought to establish the truth about these matters. It had been convened by Sergei Kovalev, the venerated dissident who was at that time a member of parliament. Yet I could not determine from the transcript what the commission had concluded, so I went to see Mr. Kovalev. He said he had set up the inquiry himself, without being authorized. Yet, he cautioned me,

Probably this book is not very accurate and sometimes they have mistakes. Probably no one has enough proof to say that those houses were bombed by FSB. [Our] conclusion doesn't have any proof as well, because probably no civil committee can get their hands on that kind of proof. It was pretty predictable and they never hoped, in the beginning, that they could get any proof.

[Our committee] can't interview people under oath, you know. They can't get any kind of documents. They can ask for them but probably those are classified; they won't receive them. They can't even [warn] a person being interviewed by the committee that [his] words, if untrue, can be punishable. So in the end, they got what they hoped for. The whole committee was [meant] to see the reaction of power, presumably Putin and so on, not to get proof. . . .

Those bombings turned out to be a very powerful electoral factor for Putin. It would be very frightening to live in a country where power can do such things. The only way the power can deny such accusations is to hold its own clear, transparent investigation.[60]

It is impossible to separate the contents of the book from the circumstances surrounding its publication. Mr. Litvinenko had announced publicly that in November 1997 he had been ordered, as an FSB agent, to assassinate one of the Russian oligarchs,[61] Boris Berezhovsky, as well as given other illegal assignments. Shortly after saying this he was arrested on trumped-up charges and imprisoned in the FSB prison. Acquitted six months later, he was immediately arrested again for another criminal charge. It too was dismissed, and Litvinenko was released, promising not to leave the country. However, a third criminal case was launched so he did leave Russia, taking political asylum and then citizenship in Britain, where he worked for Mr. Berezhovsky.

But he was poisoned and was taken to hospital, where he died three weeks later. Autopsy revealed that he had ingested about 200 times the median lethal dose of polonium-210. Berezhovsky stated on BBC that on his deathbed, Litvinenko had accused another former FSB officer, Andrei Lugovoi, of poisoning him.[62] (Berezhovsky's own car had previously been bombed, killing his driver.

Litvinenko had been on the team investigating the event, which is when the two men became friends.)

About 95 percent of all the world's polonium-210 comes from a certain reactor in Russia. According to Oleg Gordievsky, a former KGB agent who had defected to England, the poisoners did not realize that equipment existed to detect traces left by polonium-210.[63] From their point of view it must have been a perfect poison (it does not set off airport alarms) but it actually became like the bread crumbs Hansel and Gretel left behind to retrace their steps: evidence of their presence wherever they had been with the polonium-210—on airplanes, hotel rooms, restaurant tables, even a teapot. Litvinenko had met Lugovoi four times, sometimes with other men, and soon Scotland Yard knew exactly where.

Litvinenko may have been the first human to die of polonium 210, and it was an agonizing way to go. American security expert Paul Joyal alleged on national television, "A message has been communicated to anyone who wants to speak out against the Kremlin. . . . If you do, no matter who you are, where you are, we will find you, and we will silence you, in the most horrible way possible."[64] Days later Joyal too was shot in the intestine and genitals at his home near Washington, D.C.[65]

In Russia, it would have been legal for President Putin to order the killing of Litvinenko or anyone else abroad. Earlier that year a new law had been adopted by the Russian Federation Council to formally permit the extra-judicial killings abroad of people Moscow considers "extremists." The president, alone and without consultation, is allowed to use the country's armed forces and special services to combat terrorism and extremism. The only proviso is that he must inform the Federation Council within five days, but he is not required to disclose other details about the operation. At the same time, other laws were amended to expand the definition of terrorism or extremism.[66]

Naturally, the British government did not regard this killing so permissively and asked for the extradition of Andrei Lugovoi on charges of murder. However, the Russian constitution prohibits extraditions,[67] and its government denied the request. Russian-British relations were spoiled by this contretemps; each side showed dismay by the traditional ritual of expelling diplomats.

Lugovoi held a news conference and accused MI6 (the British spy agency) of trying to recruit him. He blamed either MI6, Russian mafia, or Berezhovsky for the killing.[68] I watched an hour-long TV documentary about him, where he was lionized instead of shamed. Indeed, he was soon elected to parliament, where he enjoys immunity from extradition.

You ask: Why is this anecdote told in a book about the Russian quest for peace and democracy? I must regretfully acknowledge that it shows how few Russians are actually pursuing either peace or democracy.

* * *

Journalists' murders also show how precarious democracy and peace became in Putin's Russia. After all, in a democracy people must govern themselves, sometimes relying on the help of officials who are authorized to uphold their values and common interests. That requires that crucial information be available to inform every citizen's decisions. Thus freedom of the press is as essential as the right to free and fair competitive elections, and it needs to be secured in advance of the voting. By that standard, Russia is not progressing toward democracy.

Every dictatorship tries to control the flow of information, and there are many ways of doing so, not all of which involve murdering journalists. For example, few journalists have been killed in China and apparently none in North Korea, though in both countries there is less news criticizing the regime than in Russia.[69] China and North Korea control publications and broadcasting at the editorial level. Russia reverted to doing that too during Putin's presidency—a deplorable trend, though surely preferable to assassination, which nevertheless remains rampant.

I became aware of the dangers of Russian journalism only in 1994 when Dmitry Kholodov was murdered. My friend Julia Kalinina shared an office with him at *Moskovsky Komsomolets* newspaper. She happened to be out of the room when he opened the booby-trapped briefcase that killed him. This was vivid proof to me that reporting in Russia carries risks beyond any in Canada.

Various international organizations, such as the Committee to Protect Journalists, monitor the murders of journalists in Russia. They use varying counting schemes. The most informative is probably that of the International Federation of Journalists, which classifies such homicides according to the jobs of the media staff persons (e.g. whether a victim was a photographer, a driver, or a reporter) and the degree of certainty that the death was a homicide rather than, for example, being accidentally caught in crossfire. The important thing is to ascertain whether the reporter was killed to stop or retaliate for his or her work.

It is also essential to determine whether the murders have been investigated and whether they have led to prosecutions. In that regard, too, nothing seems to be improving. The International Federation of Journalists maintains an online database of murders and disappearances since 1993.[70] You can search it yourself. There are 322 such Russian cases.

The Committee to Protect Journalists has investigated in detail the deaths of seventeen journalists in Russia since 2000 who seem definitely to have died because of the work they were doing. Only one of those murders has led to partially successful prosecution.[71] The committee calls Russia one of the worst countries in the world and says it is getting no better at solving these cases. The reality is, journalists are murdered with impunity.

If freedom of the media comes to Russia, we will recognize it before the homicides of journalists cease; we will recognize it when politicians from opposition parties are invited to debate issues on television.

Grigory Yavlinsky made that point when we talked in 2008. Yabloko had begun as the leading liberal party, but no longer won enough votes to be represented in parliament because of being excluded from the mass media. He said,

> In my country there is no possibility of watching anything different on TV. In my country everyone must go one way. We have propaganda; we have no television. We have two or three free newspapers. We have no radio, no television, nothing. . . . Give me three years of consistent, honest, talking to my people—equal talk with the other candidates, without cutting anything out. And then you

qual talk with the other candidates, without cutting anything out. And then you will see the result. Certainly, if you held elections here tomorrow, you would have approximately what you have today. . . . Because you need three, four, five years of showing people the alternatives—you need a possibility of thinking, of analysis.[72]

Yavlinsky had just been to see Putin and I asked what he had said. He replied, "I said, 'You are just destroying independent people. You are not giving us a chance to speak. You want to operate the country through vertical power.' He said, '*I'm* destroying independent people? *Me*?'"

* * *

Some Russian friends will dislike this chapter, so harsh in its appraisal of both Yeltsin and Putin. The truth is, Putin has probably been the most popular ruler in the world throughout his term in office. Polls regularly show his approval levels at around 70 percent. In December 2007, his party, United Russia, won 64 percent of the popular vote in the State Duma election. Their nearest competitor, the Communist Party, won about 12 percent of votes.[73] What right have I, a foreigner, to complain when so many of Putin's own citizens are ardent supporters?

If I claim any such right, it is as a proponent of democracy. And nobody, whether friend or foe of Putin, calls him a democrat. President Medvedev may be. His speeches sound more democratic. But people rarely judge their government primarily in terms of its democratic legitimacy. Indeed, throughout history dictators have often enjoyed immense popularity; Bonaparte, Hitler, Stalin, Mao, Castro—even Genghis Khan—were in their prime adored by their own people. Popularity is a poor criterion for judging political leaders. What counts are their policies and how effectively they pursue them.

Putin's economic achievements seem spectacular—and the economy generally counts most with voters in every society. During his presidency the economy made real gains averaging 7 percent a year; it was the seventh largest economy in the world in purchasing power. Its GDP increased sixfold. Taxes are lower than in most European countries.[74]

Visitors to Moscow are dazzled. The city glitters. The shopping malls are as opulent as those anywhere else in the world. There are new statues, ATMs, and cathedrals. (I am easily impressed by gold domes.) The restaurants are especially remarkable, each decorated like the set for a historical movie, with waiters dressed in elaborate costumes. Everything costs two or three times as much as in Toronto, and middle-class people are jet-setters, flying around the world to ski slopes or tropical isles. So different from the drab Moscow of 1982!

Yet looks can deceive, and so can statistics. Most of this recovery can be attributed to petrodollars. Oil and gas account for 50 percent of Russia's budget revenues and 65 percent of its exports.[75] Russia's exports are primarily raw materials. The gap between rich and poor has grown immensely.

In 2008 Michael McFaul and Kathryn Stoner-Weiss published an important critique of Putin's policies.[76] They deny that the prosperity has resulted from its renewed authoritarianism. Indeed, "to the extent that Putin's centralization of power has had an influence on governance and economic growth at all, the effects have been negative. Whatever the apparent gains of Russia under Putin, the gains would have been greater if democracy had survived."

McFaul and Stoner-Weiss list Putin's anti-democratic changes: the "taming" of the free press and broadcasters; the increased control over regional governments; the weakening of parliament; the illegal imprisonment of Mikhail Khodorkovsky, previously Russia's richest man and the owner of the oil company Yukos; the harassment of politicized NGOs; the expulsion of foreign organizations supporting civil society.

For all its chaos, the Yeltsin government performed about as well as Putin's government, insist McFaul and Stoner-Weiss. The main claim of Putinism is that stability has been achieved, but the frequency of terrorist attacks in Russia increased under Putin. The murder rate increased, as did the deaths from fires. Public health did not improve, and even the percentage of GDP spent on health declined. Alcohol consumption per adults increased to 14.5 liters per adult—actually eighteen liters for males between twenty-five and fifty-four years old. The percentage of the population infected with HIV is highest of any country outside Africa. Since 1999, life expectancy of males has declined to fifty-nine years. As for corruption, Transparency International ranked Russia as 121st worst out of 163 countries—between the Philippines and Rwanda.

The 1998 financial collapse meant that the Russian government was essentially bankrupt. The recovery from that catastrophe did not begin with Putin, however, but rather with Prime Minister Yevgeny Primakov. Putin then implemented several reforms that had been proposed earlier under Yeltsin, including a flat income tax of 13 percent and a new legal code. But his real luck came from the rising world price of oil. McFaul and Stoner-Weiss conclude:

World energy and raw-material prices make sustained economic growth in Russia likely for the foreseeable future. But sustained autocratic rule will not contribute to this growth and, because of continued poor governance, is likely to serve as a drag on economic development in the long term.[77]

* * *

Yet fate does not doom Russians to permanent authoritarian rule. If Russians willingly (even gratefully) tolerate Putin's program, it is not because they demand it, but only because it seems a better deal than they have had before. If offered both prosperity and democracy—and I'm convinced that these are not incompatible—many would gladly accept.

We have focused attention on Russia's leaders and their policies, overlooking the changes within civil society. In the next chapter, we'll examine those changes arising "from below."

Notes

1. For example, see Jack F. Matlock Jr.'s comments on *Spies Without Cloaks*, by Amy Knight, in *New York Review of Books* 43, no. 20 (December 19, 1996); subsequent comments by Knight and Matlock, "The Gorbachev Factor, an Exchange," *New York Review of Books* 44, no. 5 (March 27, 1997) and Matlock and Archie Brown, "Gorbachev and the Coup: An Exchange," *New York Review of Books* 44, no. 11 (June 26, 1997).

2. Jack F. Matlock Jr., *Autopsy on an Empire: The American Ambassador's Account of the Collapse of the Soviet Union* (New York: Random House, 1995), 543.

3. Gorbachev, *Memoirs*, trans. Georges Peronansky and Tatjana Varsavsky (New York: Doubleday, 1995), 643.

4. Gorbachev, *Memoirs*, 632.

5. Alexander Likhotal, in discussion with the author, June 23, 1992, the Gorbachev Foundation, Moscow.

6. Gorbachev, *Memoirs*, 640.

7. Gorbachev, *Memoirs*, 641.

8. Pavel Palazchenko, *My Years with Gorbachev and Shevardnadze* (University Park, PA: Penn State University Press, 1997), 316.

9. Palazchenko, 316.

10. Palazchenko, 319.

11. Gorbachev, *Memoirs*, 646.

12. Palazchenko, 338.

13. Lilia Shevtsova, *Russia: Lost in Transition* (Washington, DC: Carnegie Endowment for International Peace, 2007), 325.

14. Vladislav Zubok, *Zhivago's Children: The Last Russian Intelligentsia* (Cambridge, MA: Belknap Press of Harvard University, 2009), 358.

15. See review of Zubok's book by Michael Scammel. "Writers in a Cage," *New York Review of Books* 57, no. 1 (January 14, 2010): 53–55.

16. Zubok, 350–51.

17. Fred Weir, *Russia's Path from Gorbachev to Putin: The Demise of the Soviet System and the New Russia*. Kindle edition, Jan 24, 2009, location 810–14.

18. Weir, Kindle location 3203–04.

19. Weir, Kindle location 3197–99.

20. Likhotal discussion 1992.

21. "Russia Pays Off USSR's Entire Debt," Pravda.ru. http://english.pravda.ru/russia/economics/22-08-2006/84038-paris-club-0 (accessed February 5, 2010).

22. Olga Medvedkov, *Soviet Urbanization* (London: Routledge, 1990), 145–47.

23. George W. Breslauer, *Gorbachev and Yeltsin as Leaders* (Cambridge, UK: Cambridge University Press, 2002), 186.

24. Konstantin Rozhov, "Russia Attracts Investors Despite its Image," BBC News, http://news.bbc.co.uk/2/hi/business/7096426.stm (accessed March 30, 2008).

25. Grigory Yavlinsky, "Grigory Yavlinsky: Moscow, June 2: Interview with Grigory Yavlinsky," by Metta Spencer, *Peace Magazine* 24, no. 4 (October–December 2008): 12.

26. Marina Peunova, "From Dissidents to Collaborators: The Resurgence and Demise of the Russian Critical Intelligentsia Since 1985," *Studies in East European Thought* 60, no. 3 (2008): 238.

27. For a somewhat less harsh appraisal of the constitution, see Viktor Sheinis, "The Constitution," in *Between Dictatorship and Democracy: Russian Post-Communist Political Reform*, ed. Michael McFaul, Nikolai Petrov, and Andrei Ryabov (Washington, DC: Carnegie Endowment for International Peace, 2004), 56–81.

28. Fyodor Burlatsky, "The Russian 'Democratura': Interview with Fyodor Burlatsky," by Metta Spencer, *Peace Magazine* 12, no. 3 (May–June 1996): 6.

29. One promising approach to such a project can be seen in a book by Rosalyn Higgins, which was written before she was appointed to the International Court of Justice. It is *Problems and Process: International Law and How We Use It.* (Oxford: Clarendon Press, 1994), esp. 111–128.

30. The 84 federal subjects of Russia, consisting of 21 republics, 47 oblasts, eight krais, two federal cities, five autonomous okrugs, and one autonomous oblast, each send two senators to the Council. As of January 2008, the total body of the Federation Council was 168 seats.

31. Breslauer, 171.

32. Breslauer, 196–97.

33. Breslauer (209) cites Valery Tishkov, *Ethnicity, Nationalism, and Conflict* (Oslo: International Peace Research Institute, 1997), 218.

34. Carlotta Gall and Thomas de Waal, *Chechnya: Calamity in the Caucasus* (New York University Press, 1998), 177–80.

35. Russian Research Center for Human Rights, "Union of the Committee of Soldiers' Mothers of Russia," http://humanrightshouse.org/Articles/5387.html (accessed March 12, 2010).

36. Junsei Terasawa, "That Peace Monk: Interview with Junsei Terasawa," by Metta Spencer, *Peace Magazine* 17, no. 3 (July–September 2001): 16–18.

37. Casualty figures provided by the Jamestown Foundation. http://www.cdi.org/russia/245-14.cfm (accessed January 9, 2010).

38. Global Security, "First Chechen War—1994-1996," *Global Security*, http://globalsecurity.org/military/world/war/chechnya1.htm (accessed January 22, 2010).

39. Pavel Feigenhauer, "The Russian Army in Chechnya," *Crimes of War*, http://crimesofwar.org/chechnya-mag/chech-felgenhauer.html (accessed January 12, 2010).

40. Julia Kalinina, "Under Siege: When They Shoot Toward the Right Side, Sleep on the Left Side," *Peace Magazine* 11, no. 4 (July–August 1995): 20.

41. Anne C. Aldis and Roger N. McDermott, eds. *Russian Military Reform, 1992–2002* (London: Frank Cass, 2003) Kindle location 1673.

42. Joris van Bladel, "Russian Soldiers in the Barracks: The Portrait of a Subculture," in *Russian Military Reform*, Aldis and McDermott, (Kindle edition), locations 1908–13 and 1946–51.

43. van Bladel, Kindle location 1998–2003.

44. General Mikhail Milshtein, in discussion with the author, June 1995, Moscow.

45. Major General Serebrenikov, in discussion with the author, June 1993, Moscow.

46. Milshtein discussion.

47. General Mikhailov, in discussion with the author, May 1993, Moscow.

48. Sergei Rogov, in discussion with the author, June 1992, Moscow.

49. Sergei Rogov, "Nuclear Strategy: What's at Stake," *Kommersant*, April 15, 2009.

50. Sergei Rogov, "Five Challenges for Russia," *Peace Magazine* 13, no. 5 (September–October 1997): 8–11.

51. Dmitry Furman, in discussion with the author, June 2008, Moscow.

52. Julia Kalinina, "What's Behind the Chechen War?" *Peace Magazine* 11, no. 2 (March–April 1995): 12–13.

53. Alexander Litvinenko and Yuri Felshtinsky, *Blowing up Russia: The Secret Plot to Bring Back KGB Terror* (London: Gibson Square, 2007).

54. Yury Felshtinsky, in foreword to *Blowing Up Russia.*

55. Litvinenko and Felshtinsky give the complicated denoument of the KGB and the various alternative agencies that were formed to take its place. See 14–16.

56. Litvinenko and Felshtinsky, 22–26.

57. Litvinenko and Felshtinsky, 23–24.

58. Litvinenko and Felshtinsky, 77–85.

59. Litvinenko and Felshtinsky, 99.

60. Sergei Kovalev, in discussion with the author, June 2008, Moscow.

61. Litvinenko and Felshstinsky, 317.

62. "Litvinenko Friend Breaks Silence," BBC News, Tuesday, February 6, 2007, http://news.bbc.co.uk/2/hi/uk_news/6333809.stm (accessed February 17, 2010).

63. Don Murray, "The Sadistic Killing of Alexander Litvinenko," CBC News, December 19, 2006, http://www.cbc.ca/news/reportsfromabroad/murray/20061210.html (accessed February 17, 2010).

64. Ann Curry, "Who Killed Alexander Litvinenko?," NBC Dateline, July 17, 2007, http://www.msnbc.msn.com/id17332541 (accessed February 19, 2010).

65. Demitri Sevastopulo, "Expert in Litvinenko Death is Shot," *Financial Times*, March 4, 2007, http://www.ft.com/cms/s/7af97578-c924-11db-9f7b-000b5df10621.html (accessed March 6, 2010).

66. Steven Eke, 27 November 2006, "Russia Law on Killing 'Extremists' Abroad," BBC News, November 29, 2006, http://news.bbc.co.uk/2/hi/europe/6188658.stm (accessed February 18, 2010).

67. Christian Lowe, "Russia Rejects UK's Extradition Request," Reuters, July 5, 2007, http://reuters.com/article/companyNewsAndPR/idUSL05367649246.html (accessed February 18, 2010).

68. "UK 'Behind Poisoning'," BBC News, May 31, 2007, http://news.bbc.co.uk/2/hi/europe/6706921.stm (accessed February 18, 2010).

69. Committee to Protect Journalists, "Killed in China since 1992," http://cpj.org/killed/asia/china/ (accessed April 15, 2010).

70. Journalists in Russia, 1993–2009: Deaths and Disappearances, an online database, http://journalists-in-russia.org (accessed April 15, 2010).

71. Anatomy of Injustice: The Unsolved Killings of Journalists in Russia, http://cpj.org/reports/ CPJ.Anatomy%20of%20Injustice.pdf (accessed April 15, 2010).

72. Yavlinsky, *Peace Magazine*, 11.

73. Election Preliminary Results for United Russia, December 4, 2007, http://www.rbc.ru/rbcfreenews.shtml?/20071204122205.shtml (accessed April 20, 2010).

74. Russian News and Information Agency RIA Novosti, "Russia's Economy under Vladimir Putin: Achievements and Failures," RAI Novosti, http://en.rian.ru/analysis/20080301/100381963.html (accessed April 20, 2010).

75. "Trouble in the Pipeline," *Economist*, May 8, 2008, http://www.economist.com/node/11332313 (accessed March 12, 2010).

76. Michael McFaul and Kathryn Stoner-Weiss, "The Myth of the Authoritarian Model: How Putin's Crackdown Holds Russia Back," *Foreign Affairs* 88, no. 1 (January–February 2008): 68–84.

77. This and the preceding passages are from McFaul and Stoner-Weiss.

Chapter 12: From Below and Sideways

TERMITES were democrats but not populists. They had never believed in change from below, much less tried to organize grassroots campaigns. However, in this chapter I want to explore the pursuit of democracy from below, with or without the aid of friends abroad.

Pro-democracy activists—BARKING DOGS—are bold risk-takers whose integrity I revere, but not all Russians share my opinion. I once asked Georgi Arbatov about Gorbachev's reforms and his answer was simple:

> It was a revolution from the top. A good thing, because we know what a revolution from below is—where it led France in the eighteenth century and where it led us. I don't believe much in revolution. I believe in evolution and reforms. In a country like ours that had a totalitarian past, the only chance to have change was from the top.[1]

On the other hand, I thought Gorbachev sounded ambivalent on the question. When recalling Stalinism, he'd repeat Solzhenitsyn's maxim: that everyone must take a stand against a would-be dictator and "make the ground burn under his feet." His "turn to the right" at the end of 1990 reflected not only the pressures within the CPSU, but also the disappointing lack of popular support throughout the country. He said he wanted to "switch on the process from below." Yet he didn't seem to try mobilizing people power.

In Moscow the BARKING DOGS, when finally joined by Yeltsin and Democratic Russia, did manage somewhat to "switch on the process from below" and bring crowds to the street—though not demanding well-thought-out reforms.

Not all countries change in the same way. Democracy often comes from below and, contrary to mainstream TERMITE opinion, usually is more successful and more durable than democracy conferred from above. Maria J. Stephan and Erica Chenoweth have studied transitions comparatively and report that "major nonviolent campaigns have achieved success 53 percent of the time, compared with 26 percent for violent resistance campaigns."[2]

In another study, Adrian Karatnycky and Peter Ackerman analyzed the sixty-seven cases of democratic transition that Freedom House monitored over a thirty-three-year period. Democratization has been surprisingly common; by

2005, the number of "free" states had increased from forty-three to ninety-nine, while the number of "not free" states had decreased from sixty-nine to forty-nine. Moreover, *how* a transition from authoritarianism occured affected its permanence. Civic resistance was a driving factor in over fifty of the sixty-seven transitions and benefited the prospects of the new democratic regimes. (Of those fifty countries, Freedom House had initially rated none as "free," twenty-five as "partly free," and twenty-five as "not free." Five years later, however, thirty-two of those countries were "free," fourteen were "partly free," and only four were "not free.")[3] People power is obviously the best approach.

That brings us to this painful question: Why did democratization fail to "switch on from below" in the Soviet Union? My answer: lack of social capital.

Why Hasn't Russia Democratized From Below?
Ludmilla Alexeyeva, the dissident co-founder of the Moscow Helsinki Group, was eighty when she welcomed me to her apartment in the Arbat in May 2008. Advising me not to expect much freedom in Russia very soon, she said,

> Many features in our characters were formed by our tragic history. Not all people, of course. With such a history as ours, we have a pretty good proportion of normal people, brave people. It should be much less. We decided to reach democracy. It's a heroic decision, I would say. And we will be a democratic country but we cannot do it so quickly. We cannot! Be more patient! . . . In fifteen years, I believe we will reach democracy. . . .
>
> In the Soviet Union, people couldn't do anything for themselves. Either the state did something for the people or it wasn't done at all. For example, I would like to have a good apartment. If the state didn't give it to me, I could not have it. It was impossible. We lived in such a way for three generations. And when the Soviet Union was crushed, we were like kids. We didn't know how to do anything. We had to learn to be grown-ups in a very cruel way because the state had forgotten about us. The state crushed our economy and our social system, and nobody helped people in this country. Those who couldn't learn to do things by themselves, those who couldn't pass the transition, they just died.[4]

Alexeyeva waits patiently in hope of democracy. She pins her hope on civil society, telling me,

> Of course, we now have bandit capitalism, though we have probably passed that stage. Being a historian, I can see that all the stages that took dozens of years, or centuries, in Europe and America, we are passing through in a few years. Now we have turned from bandit capitalism to state capitalism. Of course it's not democracy. But we will pass to other stages too, quickly. Believe me. Because . . . we have the development of civil society. . . .
>
> Even in our country, it is difficult to see because no TV, no mass media, shows it or writes about it. But this process is going on. For that reason, I never try to be a deputy or an official—never!—because this is the most important area where we should work to reach democracy: civil society. Even if we had an angel as a president, he could not organize democracy in this society if civil society is not ready for it.

I said she did not sound like a dissident anymore. She agreed, saying,

> I'm not a dissident now because we have a good Constitution and I support it.
> The dissidents are those who violate our Constitution. They are our officials,
> including our president. I don't know about our new president [Medvedev]
> yet. . . . I am a member of the Presidential Council for Human Rights. [The
> president] cannot tell me "Get out of my council." Why? It would be shameful.
> Everybody knows it is in the Constitution. I have a bigger moral weight, ac-
> cording to them. It is recognized even by state officials. Now I may call any-
> body. He doesn't do what I want him to do but he cannot refuse to speak with
> me. Instead, he says [she mocks Putin's simpering tone of voice] "Oh, Lud-
> milla Mikhailovna, it's so nice you called me," and so on. . . . Even *their* men-
> tality has changed. It means that our civil society has a chance to mature in
> time.

I asked why she was so confident that civil society organizations would
build social capital. She replied,

> Here's a good example. The Association of Car Owners was created three years
> ago to defend the right to drive cars from England or Japan with the steering
> wheel on the right side. We have a lot of those cars in the Far East, imported
> from Japan. The car owners won that right against the government, which
> wanted to abolish such cars. Then they won many other victories. Now, three
> years later, they are opposing the law that lets officials close the road so they
> can get through traffic easily or use special lights so they can drive on the op-
> posite side of the street. And this is political! They demand that citizens should
> be equal under the law. Maybe they don't even recognize that it's political, but
> they are demanding it. And now our social movements tell people to defend
> their own interests, combining with other people in the same situation. It's go-
> ing to move ahead very quickly.[5]

She was right. Not only government officials but even the business elite
were allowed to break the law and get away with it. But in February 2010 the
chauffeur driving a Lukoil executive veered into oncoming traffic to avoid a
jam, colliding with a small Citroën and killing two women, both gynecologists.
Initially the police covered up the cause of the crash, which however was witnessed, videotaped, and reported in the press.[6] A public scandal ensued, and
President Medvedev ordered an investigation. Change is coming!

Several times in the Putin and early Medvedev years I met intellectuals and
former dissidents who expressed the same hopeful attitude as Alexeyeva—patient waiting for the democracy that they believed would come, whether in ten
years or fifty. One was the eminent sociologist Dmitry Furman, whom I already
knew and liked. He was one of the few intellectuals who had not turned against
Gorbachev in 1990–91, and I respected him for that. In fact, he had published an
article after the August coup entitled, "Democracy Suffers From 'Democrats.'"[7]
He reminded me that most of the intelligentsia who had joined Yeltsin's side did
so because they believed he was giving them real democracy. When Russia then

became chaotic and criminalized, most Russians blamed it on democracy and concluded that they wanted no more of *that*. The sample was ample.

Furman was one of the Russians who "wait in hope" for democracy, but unlike Alexeyeva, who expected it to arrive in ten or fifteen years, his guess was twenty or thirty years. He said,

> In such a situation as Russia, the normal way to democracy is a color revolution, like Ukraine, like Georgia. It's not enough, but it's a necessary first step to democracy. But now it is impossible. For a color revolution you must have an opposition in parliament or somewhere near to parliament. You must have strong parties who can, for example, bring about a million people to Moscow squares. But now our demonstrations bring only about 100 people, not more – about the same as the dissidents in the Soviet period. So it is impossible now.[8]

Furman attributes this lagging impetus for change from below to Russia's authoritarian culture, connected to its Orthodox Christianity and Communism. Indeed, he had amused me in 1994 with his analysis of Russian political culture.

Furman and I had sat talking in the wide hallway outside Mr. Gorbachev's office in 1994. He had a cold, yet he gamely lectured into my tape recorder about surveys he had conducted in 1990 and 1991. With his hands he defined two opposite poles on the coffee table on either side of the tape recorder, calling one pole the atheist Communists and the other one the Orthodox Christians.

> The stronger the Orthodox beliefs or the atheistic beliefs, the more authoritarian are the political beliefs. Those who are democratic are here in between. People with amorphous, fuzzy religious consciousness are more democratic.

"That makes sense," I said as he pointed to the area between the two poles.

> Yes, but in Western countries, people here in this middle zone have a coherent, structured world view. It can be religious, humanistic, socialistic, but structured at the same time. This is the zone of social democracy or Christian democracy. In Italy or Germany you can find a person who is a sincere Catholic or socialist and at the same time democratic. But in our tradition, those are impossible. Our historical ideologies are Orthodoxy and Communism. Here, if a man is a strong believer, he is for the Czar and for Russian nationalism. If he is an atheist, he is a Communist.
>
> In our survey there was a strong correlation between belief in UFOs and a preference for Yeltsin over Gorbachev. In telepathy, in oriental cults, and the preference for Yeltsin. Very strong! New Age! But sympathy for Gorbachev and the Soviet Union were strong here at the poles, among the Orthodox and the atheist Communists. They were for the KGB, for a strong Russian empire.

I speculated, "The Orthodox and the Communist atheists preferred Gorbachev because he was the boss?" He nodded.

> Yes. To the Orthodox he represented the Czar, and to the atheists he represented the general secretary. But this atheistic part was diminishing very quickly. Two years before, they were 20 percent of the population. By 1990,

they were only five percent. The young people who are educated had moved here, into the New Age group. This is the zone of eclecticism, of entropy.

I frowned, "I don't understand why you use the word 'entropy' about the New Age." He replied,

Because it is not clear-cut convictions or coherent worldviews. A Russian man who is Zen Buddhist, for example, is just Zen Buddhist this month. Next month he will be Hassid, for example, or Hindu. The elements are labile, unstructured, and individual. It is like the Brownian motion of molecules, moving randomly. Entropy.

"This survey was conducted in when Gorbachev was still in office," I noted, asking: "Is this true of the Russian population today?" Furman shook his head.

No, not anymore. The Orthodox and atheists were for strong power. Now that Yeltsin is the President, he is the strong power, not Gorbachev. They were for Great Russia. Now Yeltsin is the symbol of Great Russia. This three-part system doesn't hold up anymore.[9]

I never found out which political leader the New Age Russians had turned to next, in their disappointment about Yeltsin.[10] But anyway I was more interested in the authoritarians—the people who yearned for a strict Czar or party leader. If Yeltsin had never fully satisfied their desires, Putin must have done so. And since over 70 percent of Russian voters strongly approve of Putin, it seems that authoritarianism is still powerful in the society.

Is there any cure for authoritarianism? If so, it is probably not indigenous to Russia. I recalled a past conversation with Alexander Likhotal at the Gorbachev Foundation in 1992. I had said, "Some people have told me that it was not just a revolution from the top because, had there not been a *readiness* in the society, then nobody at the top would have dared to try any of these changes. You don't think so?" Likhotal had replied,

No, I'm afraid the society still is not awakened. Probably there is some kind of fatigue or exhaustion after all these years, but at the same time it is not just communist ideology that produced this kind of society. It has historical roots. It's tradition. It's patriarchal society. It's linked to the confessional roots, to the religious consciousness of the society. Totalitarianism has never been imposed on this society from outside. It has always been, here in Russia, the result of the development of the society itself.

I said. "It's clear that this is not Poland. The Poles were ungovernable. If they hadn't been given more opportunity for political self-expression they just wouldn't have put up with it. That was not true here, it seems to me. But you say authoritarianism could have lasted a long time before any changes were made if Mr. Gorbachev himself had not. . . . But Likhotal interrupted, shaking his head,

I suppose Gorbachev could have gone smoothly in the traditional manner of the general secretary of the Communist Party, with unlimited powers. He could have served until he died and nothing would have changed. . . . When I was working in the Central Committee there was even a joke that the people working there would dig their own graves if the general secretary commanded it.[11]

If there is no local cure for authoritarian culture, you can never expect democracy to emerge from below. But how do you change a culture? Logically, the only remaining answer must be: *from outside*. And indeed, some Russians have looked to foreign influences to counteract the cultural weaknesses of their own society. The dissident leader Sergei Kovalev is one such man.

Sideways

I visited Kovalev twice, most recently at his Moscow apartment in 2008, shortly after visiting Alexeyeva. He had recently published an article in *The New York Review of Books* that sounded more pessimistic than Alexeyeva, but he claimed to be optimistic. I assumed that he credited Gorbachev's reforms from the top for Russia's move toward democracy, but he said, "It was from bottom up *and* from Gorbachev *and* from the side."

"The side? Oh, you mean foreign pressure," I said. "From the United States, Europe, and so on?" He replied,

It's a complex of all these things. Carter and Reagan played a big role in Russia's history. [Otherwise] dissidents—their pressure, their demands—could have been eliminated very easily. Gorbachev didn't move the country toward democracy. He moved it toward economic partnership with the West, to receive grants and credits from the West but it was he and the top of the Communist Party who would use this money, who would channel it, and not democracy, not the people.

Here Kovalev was expressing the typical BARKING DOG attitude toward Gorbachev, the TERMITE leader. I did not react, and he continued,

Dissidents, they had one last small tool, but it actually turned out to be the best one because it was the appeal toward popular opinion in the West. And in the West, popular opinion stimulated their leaders. Yes, the sideward pressure turned out to be very important. It shaped how things would go further. At first, that pressure was regarded by USSR public opinion as very good. People thought that soon there will be democracy. There will be freedom and that means that Communists will be eliminated and there will be freedom and sausage.

"And sausage?" I said, laughing. "Okay." Kovalev smiled and continued,

After that, people who called themselves democrats started the privatization process and the crowd in the street received the sausage but they didn't have any money to buy it. And at the same time, billions were raised by a few people. Where else have you seen a person start a business and then in three months he already counts his money by millions? Our oligarchs, the billion-aires, started at that time. Russian people don't like the rich. So I want to tell you about my second source of optimism. It is Western public opinion about Russia. It has been sleeping for some time but probably it will wake up.

Now there's not much Western interest in Russia. We are much more interested in the USA because we're connected tightly. Without us there wouldn't have been Saddam Hussein. Without the USSR playing the Cold War game there wouldn't be Palestinian terrorists, or al-Qaeda, or the Taliban. The USA competes with all the rest of the world, but we are the center of this competition. Saddam's regime, for example, was created in the antagonism toward the socialism that Russia spread.

"Okay, I won't argue with you," I said, "but where's the optimism in your comment?" Kovalev replied,

> Popular opinion will wake up again and the West will focus on Russia. People will begin thinking again about Russia as undemocratic and unfriendly. What I want is a small miracle—that with the help of the West, in Russia we will create a critical mass of people who understand that democracy is not about "liberté, égalité, fraternité," but about a boring procedure that's just supposed to happen. After this, any miracle—like a Charter 77 or something in East Europe—can happen. If that happens, then great possibilities open.
>
> Russia (actually with the Soviet system) infected the whole world with a bad germ called *realpolitik*. Nevertheless, the best minds of the twentieth century—Bertrand Russell, Albert Einstein, Sakharov—proposed a new political system. It's in the preamble to the United Nations Charter: the saying that law is above politics. No state observes that principle yet because there is a difference between professional and amateur politicians. I think Russia can be reformed with a critical mass of people who think that democracy is a boring procedure. Being amateurs, they can push us toward a new political thinking where law is above politics.

"Beautiful," I said. "But if you were his age [I point to my interpreter and guide, Ignat Kalinin, who was twenty-five years old] and you were a Russian wanting democracy, what would you do now?" Kovalev, who was then seventy-eight and had spent ten years in prison for his dissident activities, replied,

> I would have to get some experience as a propagandist and organizer, trying to create something like the Polish Workers' Defense Committee [KOR], which taught Solidarność to be a political movement. But then the power [government] would notice me and that would be the end of my biography. It would be easy to make it look like it was skinheads who shot me.[12]

So he *is* a pessimist, after all.

* * *

Kovalev and Furman seem to agree that Western influences have been decisive at times in determining the prospects of democracy in Russia. However, Kovalev did not argue, as had Furman, that a "color revolution" is a precondition for democratization. That's a crucial question. Putin's government (maybe Medvedev's too, but I'm not sure) fears that any empowerment of society from below will lead to a color revolution against their undemocratic regime.

That may not necessarily be so. In pointing to KOR and Solidarność as models for change, Kovalev is singling out an Eastern European country where democracy was won from below—but at a round table instead of in the street. Precisely because Solidarność was a civil society organization with such widespread popularity, the Jaruzelski regime held a fair election and turned power over to the democratic winners without a "color revolution." Of course, previous phases of Polish resistance had included martial law and a degree of violent repression, but Kovalev's choice of Poland as a model for Russia is indeed an optimistic vision of the future.

Sergei Kovalev still sees assassination as a risk for any activist. And Ludmilla Alexeyeva, at eighty-two feisty but frail, still joins pro-democracy confrontations. The riot police politely arrest but immediately release her. Nevertheless, both of these veteran BARKING DOGS can now envision democracy as evolving through the actions of civil society—at least if Russian activists have "sideways" support from abroad. Other civil society organizers also see the possibility of a gradual transition to democracy from below, and they all acknowledge the need for support "from the side."

* * *

So what kind of support can we offer them from the side? I'll suggest three forms of assistance: *providing resources*; *offering protection*; and *demonstrating alternatives*. There is no guarantee that any of these will work, but in the past they have sometimes helped.

Resources basically means money. Virtually all major organizations in Russia that champion democracy and human rights depend on funds from private or government-sponsored foundations abroad, such as Westminster, MacArthur, or the National Endowment for Democracy.[13] There are few sources of money for them inside the country—though until he was jailed and his holdings seized, Mikhail Khodorkovsky, the Yukos Oil oligarch, had been a generous donor.

After Ukraine's 2004 Orange Revolution, Putin's government reduced the flow of foreign funding to Russian civil society groups and applied other bureaucratic measures to limit their activities. In the next chapter I'll consider the implications of these restrictions, which especially hamper pro-democracy work.

Foreigners can occasionally offer *protection* to Russians, but only in minor ways. When I was visiting the Trust Group in the mid-1980s, they asked me and other Western peaceniks to publicize their cases whenever they were sent to prison camps for acts of public dissent. For example, when Olga Medvedkova was on trial, the embassies of Canada and other Western countries sent officials to witness and offer moral support. Later, women from the Greenham Common Peace Camp in Britain joined the Trust Group in postering around Moscow; they were not stopped for several hours because they included foreigners. Also, Amnesty International was not mistreated in the Soviet Union as much as other human rights organizations, probably because Amnesty is a famous transnational group and the publicity would have made the regime look bad.[14]

Such forms of protection are often used in some authoritarian states. For example, Nonviolent Peaceforce and Peace Brigades International are only two of the groups from the North providing "protective accompaniment" around the clock to union leaders, lawyers, or community organizers abroad who are threatened. Often would-be death squads feel inhibited about killing local democracy activists if this might also injure foreign visitors. So far as I know, no such accompaniment programs have been used in post-Soviet Russia, though the idea may have merit, especially for Russian journalists at risk. On the other hand, some foreign journalists have themselves been murdered in Russia, and even a few in the West, so this form of protection does not seem very promising.

Perhaps better is to confer international recognition, such as Nobel Prizes, on courageous Russians. In December 2009, The European Union awarded the Sakharov Prize to Ludmilla Alexeyeva, Sergei Kovalev, and Oleg Orlov on behalf of the human rights organization Memorial. During the ceremony in Strasbourg, the three distinguished BARKING DOGS called for a period of silence in memory of activists who had recently been slain in Chechnya. (Still, two weeks later Alexeyeva was arrested at a demonstration in Moscow, dressed as the female helper of Father Frost, the Russian incarnation of Santa Claus.[15] Her arrest may diminish the plausibility of honoring activists to protect their causes.)

Demonstrating alternatives is a third way for foreign democrats and peaceniks to assist Russian activists "from sideways"—and if I were a gambling woman, I would bet most on it. It already happens anyway to some extent because social action is "contagious." Activists just need to use it better.

Nineteenth century psychologists explained learning on the basis of trial-and-error attempts where the good and bad consequences induce people to repeat or avoid similar acts in the future. Thank heavens, other alert psychologists eventually noticed that we also learn from watching *other* people's mistakes and triumphs, thus sparing ourselves unnecessary trouble. Obviously, human beings do draw conclusions (rightly or wrongly) from observing the experiences of others. To be sure, we also learn from hot stoves, ideologies, and rule-books, but the power of "social learning" through empathy is under-estimated.

The mass media, including fictional enactments, teach powerful lessons. Indeed, the most effective way of persuading people to limit their family size is by broadcasting soap operas on radio or TV, mentioning birth control in the plots.[16]

In a visit with the Yabloko party leader, Grigory Yavlinsky, we were discussing how to change Russia's culture. I said, "I think you need television soap operas—TV or radio stories that go on for years about the same characters. The writers can create plots about social issues. They have an impact because the viewer forms an intense relationship with the characters over time."[17] Yavlinsky said,

> I understand. You would make a soap opera that would go parallel to the real politics, Your prime ministers are dealing with the most difficult issues in the world. What to do in Burma, what to do in China, what to do in Russia, what to do in America. How to speak to Sarkozy. It would be a soap opera in parallel with reality. It's a possibility. You are saying, this guy, Mr. Bush, was taking this decision, but *this* guy in our story, in the same situation, with the same

question, takes a different decision. First he goes to Schroeder, then he goes to Fischer, then he meets with his economists and convinces them that they should join with the United States, and not to start a war—and so on.

"You got it," I said. "There was one TV show that came close to that—*The West Wing*. It ran for eight years. Martin Sheen played a wonderful Democratic president, and most of the story was about his staff. Of course, they had their love affairs and their adventures. But every week, one of the three plots was about a political issue that was going on in reality." Yavlinsky said,

> That's exactly what I'm saying! . . . This would be a show about politics. That's how you would catch the people and show them different decisions.

I said, "It has to involve dramas that are emotional. Not just talking heads." Yavlinsky said,

> Exactly! I would be happy if you could help me to get it. But nothing that you have said is possible here in Russia. No way! Why? . . . This is an authoritarian system. The leaders would never, ever allow anything like that. By plan, they are entertaining the people by non-stop jokes, comedies, sex shows, and things that are just poisoning the minds.

"But they make trash in Hollywood too," I said. "It's a question of finding a producer who will make something better. . . . You say that you have to change public opinion and the political culture, and the only way I know to do that is to demonstrate examples in stories." Yavlinsky said,

> Let us make one satellite channel in Russian, which would be created in Canada—a real Russian channel, like Radio Liberty, made by normal people—not by enemies of this regime, . . . not a channel about the propaganda of America. It would be a news channel and political channel and television channel. I am willing to work with this twenty-four hours a day! I would leave the party and personally work for this. This is the conclusion of our discussion!

"It's a deal! I will look for a way to do it," I said. (To tell the truth, I have no idea how, but perhaps you do, dear reader.) Yavlinsky replied,

> Oh, I would be very happy. But you have experienced that life is very difficult here now. These are the friends of mine who died fighting for democracy in the last years. [He showed me a large colored paper with photos and short biographies of five people.] Simply fighting for democracy against corruption and things like that. They were killed. So I live in a very complicated time.

* * *

The year 1989 brought the most surprising series of events in modern history. Nobody expected Communist regimes to topple like dominoes. But that was the culminating phase of cultural changes that had been spreading around the world for years. Nor was 1989 the end of it. In 1991 Russia would have its own brief movement "from below." The whole process can be understood best as a chain reaction of social learning, passed on by further demonstrations to others. I owe much of my understanding of this process to Victor Sumsky, a political analyst at IMEMO who specializes in the Philippines.

Nonviolence as a Ripple
People imitate each other, spreading behavioral innovations onward, as a ripple spreads in a pond. Actions can be spread by strangers, even globally. This is obvious when we trace the ripple of nonviolent resistance in the 1980s, as I shall do throughout this chapter.

It's a long story. Let's begin it with a Filipino Jesuit priest and Gandhian, Ed Garcia, who became a major vector transmitting nonviolent methods. He had edited a collection of Gandhi's writings in Tagalog and formed an organization on nonviolent conflict in the 1970s.[18] After becoming a respected go-between in local disputes, Garcia began to travel the world. He spent about six years in Latin America studying liberation theology. Then he worked there for Amnesty International for three years.

In the late seventies and early eighties, Garcia began visiting nations that had brought down dictators, such as Portugal and Spain. Everywhere he studied local languages and compared experiences. In 1981 he stayed in a university dormitory in Krakow discussing Solidarność with the students. Before Aquino's assassination, he went home and became a moral leader, trying to bring together all the nonviolent forces.

In 1985 the Filipino nonviolent groups, led by a Catholic bishop, invited the Fellowship of Reconciliation to send trainers to Manila to prepare citizens for nonviolent resistance. The trainers included Hildegard and Jean Goss-Mayr and Richard Deats.[19] Shortly after they left, an extraordinary "people power" movement brought down the Marcos regime in February of 1986, within three days. [20]

Soviet officialdom was not impressed. At that time they insisted that it was the U.S. government that was in control, not the people in the street. According to this account, Marcos fell only because the Americans told him to quit. Five years later the Soviets would gain some understanding of the power of nonviolent resistance from the crowds at their own White House.

Indeed, Victor Sumsky has noted the striking resemblance between the Filipino movement and the actions that halted the coup in Moscow in August 1991.[21] The center of resistance was downtown in both cases. Ordinary citizens began to assemble near buildings that the opponents of the dictatorship were defending. The most active defenders were urban middle class citizens. On the second day the resisters became so numerous that only bloodshed could disperse them. Certain detachments of the military began to take the people's side, along with international public opinion. Officials negotiated and convinced the dictators to retreat. By the third day, it became obvious that they were finished.

There were also other similarities between the two resistance movements. Civilians surrounded tanks, giving food and flowers to soldiers and asking them not to shoot. The soldiers placed the flowers in the muzzles of their guns. Priests blessed both the White House supporters and the Filipino soldiers in Manila, and administered sacraments at the walls. A radio station helped coordinate the actions of the opposition. In both capitals there were grounds for fear, yet this emotion was overcome by the crowd's exuberance as rock music was played loudly and the defenders joked. Even the press conferences of the dictators were similar, with Yanayev and Marcos both having the same ominous, yet comical, effects. Sumsky insists that it is not by mere chance that these events seem similar. The stalwart defenders of the White House had learned from their predecessors in Manila and from other exemplars during the intervening years.

Garcia, for his part, had also learned while he was abroad. He knew the most dramatic leader of the late 1970s, Adolfo Perez de Esquivel, who had founded an organization, Servicio de la Paz y Justicia, that spread throughout Latin America, teaching people how to defend human rights nonviolently. Perez had organized the Mothers of the Disappeared in Buenos Aires. It was partly their unwavering presence as a group in the city square that brought down the dictatorial government of Argentina.[22] Soon the mothers of Guatemala also were standing in public, displaying photos of their own "disappeared" sons.

Garcia had gone from Latin America to Poland, where in 1976 KOR had formed. In 1980 Solidarność appeared, richly informed by Gandhism, despite the fact that books about Gandhi were forbidden by the Communist regime. Solidarność activists such as Adam Michnik and Jacek Kuron had a natural flair for innovation. Instead of fighting against the regime, they set up their own alternative social institutions, such as the "flying university," which offered courses in private apartments, and despite being regularly broken up by the police, resumed as prearranged, in another person's apartment. Solidarność even printed postage stamps that looked so good that for a while the post office delivered the letters on which they were affixed.

In 1981 the Polish government imposed martial law and jailed most Solidarność leaders, but the organization continued underground. It was joined by another offshoot group, Freedom and Peace, which comprised young people who were demanding the right of conscientious objection to military service. They did not call themselves "pacifists," since throughout the Slavic countries the term designated cowardly people who succumbed to coercion. The Poles were courageous but refused to injure others. (Konstanty Gebert told me that his first big assignment as a Solidarność activist was to locate some boys who had stolen dynamite from a government warehouse and persuade them to put it back where they had found it.)

While the campaign for conscientious objection was in full swing, Richard Attenborough's four-hour film *Gandhi* was released and influenced all the Poles who saw it. Young Czechoslovaks also saw it and were moved. Every year my "Negotiation and Nonviolence" classes watched it and became devoted to Satyagraha. In Chile, a union leader, Rodolfo Seguel saw it, led a day of protest against the dictatorship in May 1983, with Catholic support, and brought down the military dictator, General Pinochet. Seguel explained this achievement, noting parallels between Gandhi and the Polish movement.

I think it was the film *Gandhi*. It was shown in the public cinemas in 1983, when we began, and we all saw it at least twice. We had to, to really get it in

ourselves. . . . Both [Gandhi and Lech Wałęsa] took up struggles without violence that produced better results than armed confrontation.[23]

In September 1986 I spent two days with a Krakow priest who was responsible for about 900 high school-aged members of his parish. Father Josef Lucyszyn invited me to his meeting with about a dozen leaders of the youth organization "Light and Life." They sang a hymn to "Mary, Queen of Poland,"
and listened to my impromptu lecture on Gandhism. Father Lucyszyn told me
that whenever a young man reached the age of twenty-one, he held a private
conversation with him, explaining the duties of citizens to protect freedom. The
hero he held up as a model for the youths was the Polish bishop Vyshinsky, who
had been under house arrest for many years but who claimed that he was free
because of his commitment to nonviolent resistance. "There will be other periods like the Solidarność era," Father Lucyszyn assured me. "We will see to that.
Until recently I did not feel confident that the next time would be nonviolent.
However, since Mrs. Aquino came to power in the Philippines, I now believe
that our resistance will also remain nonviolent. My young people were deeply
moved by what they witnessed on television."

For their part, the Russians were watching the Poles on television. Polish
culture was far freer than anything available in Russia, and the Russians could
read Polish with very little instruction. There was a Polish bookstore on Gorky
Street in Moscow where ideas were imported on a large scale.

During this period Asians were also impressed by the Filipino "people
power" campaign. In Burma, a group of students carried out courageous nonviolent actions against the dictators. Somewhat later, South Korean students did
likewise, though with no immediate success in either country. And of course,
there would be Tiananmen Square.

Although the extraordinary events of 1989 were mostly spontaneous, this
was not entirely so. Nonviolence trainings had been going on around the world
without attracting much attention. During the early phase of the Intifada, a Palestinian Christian named Mubarak Awad was successfully organizing nonviolent resistance in the West Bank until the Israelis expelled him.[24]

In Massachusetts the most eminent scholar of nonviolence, Gene Sharp, had
created the Albert Einstein Institution for specialists studying the tactics and
strategy of nonviolent action.[25] I had first met Gene Sharp at a two-week workshop on nonviolence in Dubrovnik in 1983, where several other organizers also
taught, including one from India, one from the Philippines, two from the Middle
East, and two former aides of Martin Luther King. In 1990 Sasha Kalinin would
attend one of Gene's conferences in Boston and take home methods that he
would soon be able to use against the coup in Moscow.

Nonviolent resistance was happening. The mid-1980s was the peak of the
disarmament movement, and every day protesters were carrying out a "direct
action" someplace. American activists broke into nuclear submarines and missile sites and damaged as much as they could with crowbars or by pouring their
own blood onto weaponry. In Britain, people were acting from below at Greenham Common, Molesworth, and Cruisewatch.

In the Soviet Union, until about 1986, the only independent peace organization had been the Moscow Group for Trust. Whenever the Trustbuilders were imprisoned, activists in the West held demonstrations to publicize their plight. I organized a rally on the steps of the Ontario legislature in Toronto one winter day and luckily also had a chance to ask Prime Minister Pierre Trudeau to support my Russian friends. He did.

By 1987 it was possible for independent civil society groups to form freely in the Soviet Union, and thousands sprang up. In the Academy of Sciences an academic department was formed to study nonviolence; a philosopher named Guseinov organized an international conference and published the papers, especially promoting civilian-based defense. He invited Gene Sharp and the Fellowship of Reconciliation trainers to give nonviolence workshops. And the Russians watched the news in the year 1989 as the Polish Communist regime capitulated, holding a roundtable and enabling Solidarność to run in elections. On the day when those candidates won their astounding landslide election on one side of the world, Tiananmen Square was the center of attention on the other side.

Tragically, the Chinese students were untrained in nonviolent struggle. Gene Sharp had visited them only a few hours before the massacre. In an interview he told me later that they had not even realized the necessity of drinking water during a hunger strike. Instead of staying in the square, they could have switched tactics.[26] They could have "declared victory," dispersed, and turned to some other activity, such as organizing peasants. But they did not know.

Gene Sharp set about having some of his publications on nonviolence published in other languages. Years later, one of those booklets would be translated into Serbian and used to oust the authoritarian ruler Slobodan Milošević.

* * *

If the Tiananmen massacre stopped change in Beijing for decades to come, it had a different effect in Europe. Within weeks, dramatic new actions were taking place. One turning point occurred in Czechoslovakia. The singer and activist Joan Baez was on tour in Eastern Europe, eager to celebrate Solidarność's election victory with the joyous Poles. In Bratislava to participate in a traditional music festival, she invited Václav Havel, the writer Jan Urban, Sasha Vondra, and several other Chartists to the concert. Havel drove in from Prague, expecting to be arrested at any moment by the secret police who were following him. Baez and her assistant Martha Henderson stuffed him into their van among the guitars and ordered the technicians and musicians to go by taxi.

At the concert, Baez announced in Slovak, "I want to dedicate this next song to Charter 77, Independent Peace Association, and Peter Cibulka." (Cibulka was an activist whose trial was coming up soon in Brno.) The crowd went wild. Next Baez sang a duet with a Slovak man who was officially banned from all public performances. The police ordered the technicians to turn off the sound but they refused to do so until he had sung a verse or two. When the sound went off, Baez motioned to the crowd and continued singing *a cappella*. The crowd joined in, singing jubilantly.

The authorities had failed. The regime could no longer maintain the fiction that it was supported by the Czechoslovak people; everyone had seen for themselves that it was Havel and Charter 77 who were truly beloved.[27] This unquestionable fact empowered people, who would soon take matters into their own nonviolent hands and make what Havel called "our merry revolution." With this "sideways" help from a foreign friend, change "from below" was warming up.

The transition in Hungary was about as civilized as the Polish one. Already, since the death in 1988 of the party leader János Kádár, there had been a trend toward liberal policies: trade union pluralism, a revised constitution, and guarantees of freedom of association, assembly, and the press.

I was visiting Prague quite often in those years to participate in an East-West dialogue that gave rise to the Helsinki Citizens Assembly. We knew our meetings in Czechoslovakia might be broken up by the police, so we had a back-up plan to re-convene in Budapest, where communism was so lenient that we could gather with impunity.

In fact, this "Plan B" proved to be unnecessary. By October 1990, when our founding session took place in Prague, the Velvet Revolution had occurred. We were given the city's finest auditorium and addressed by the new Czechoslovak president, the dissident playwright Václav Havel. For these blessings we owe much to the Hungarians, who had simply opened their border to let people exit into Austria. Since the East Germans could freely go to Hungary, some 30,000 of them used Hungary as a route in September 1989 to flee to the West. Of course the East German party leader, Erich Honecker, was outraged.

* * *

For years there had been Monday-night peace prayer services in St. Nicholas Church in Leipzig, East Germany. In the spring of 1989 other protesters joined the group and began to parade around outside, chanting "We want out." By September there were several thousand marchers with candles, who were attacked by the police with dogs.[28] People expected a version of Tiananmen Square, but they knew what was happening in Poland and Hungary, and they were encouraged by the visit of Mikhail Gorbachev, who pointedly warned Honecker that "He who is too late is punished by life."

In October there were 300,000 protesters in Leipzig and instead of perpetrating a massacre, Honecker resigned. Then, on November 9, a mistaken announcement was issued that all East Germans could travel abroad without special permission. Thousands of people flooded through the Berlin Wall, in effect putting an end to the East German regime.

The other East Europeans were watching TV. The Bulgarians followed the East German example and ousted their leader Todor Zhivkov on exactly the day the Wall was breached. The Czechoslovak students already had been marching in Prague as often as possible, but always were beaten by the police. On November 17, a week after the Berlin Wall fell, they marched again and were beaten so badly that the other citizens were outraged and joined in the next protest. On November 20, more than 100,000 people filled Wenceslas Square, jingling their keys. This time, the police did not interfere. Václav Havel addressed the crowd. Within days, the Communist government simply surrendered control of the state to the Velvet Revolutionaries.[29]

In December it was the Romanians' turn. However, the Communist regime had been so intransigent that in this country alone, the transition turned lethal. Although Ceauşescu himself ordered the army to massacre the crowds—and there was violence at first—the soldiers began fraternizing with the protesters and the minister of defense shot himself instead of firing on the people. When Ceauşescu tried to speak to the crowd they turned on him. He fled, was captured, and after a perfunctory trial, was executed, along with his wife, on Christmas Day, 1989.[30]

The rest of Eastern Europe abandoned Communism later and with more difficulty. The Baltic states, Estonia, Latvia, and Lithuania, had unwillingly become absorbed into the Soviet Union. Gorbachev refused to tear the Union apart, but that happened anyway at the end of 1991. Initially the new independent states continued to be ruled by the same Party elites. Wars broke out in Moldavia and Tajikistan, and the violent breakup of Yugoslavia began in 1991.

Yet 1989 produced other success stories—even in faraway Mongolia, which had been controlled from Moscow. When Gorbachev removed Soviet troops from the country, some Mongol university students started demanding democracy and capitalism. The Communist regime was indulgent, even promising reforms in five years or so, but the students wanted faster action. They held hunger strikes, copying the Chinese students of Tiananmen Square, and organized strikes among workers. Unfortunately, drunken ruffians joined in their protest, stirring up local trouble. Nevertheless, within six months the lenient Communist government agreed to hold a free and fair election, which it then won. The nonviolent resistance movement from below was badly organized, lacking unity and discipline. However, learning from their electoral defeat, they formed a coalition and won the next election.[31] In 2010 Freedom House rates Mongolia as "Free."

Defeating the Coup against Gorbachev
Though they still have not organized politically from below, Russians did carry out a nonviolent struggle that successfully foiled the August coup in 1991. It began only hours after I left Moscow. Several of my friends, including Julia Kalinina, Alexander Kalinin, and Ruzanna Ilukhina, were involved in the drama. Here's Julia's letter to me.

> The question was when arrests would begin. I supposed that we had something like three hours, so we discussed if it were possible to hide the most evident compromising material. After a short discussion we decided that there was no sense hiding it because everything would be compromising. . . .
> The only way to resist was civil disobedience. However, during the day I had heard many conversations in the streets to the effect that the democrats had spoiled the country and at last we would have real order and food and CKChP (the coup plotters' acronym) promised to increase pensions and reduce prices. It seemed to me that most of the people were really glad to get rid of Gorbachev and of democrats, market relations, and national conflicts—all the problems of our last years. They wanted to live as they used to live. If so, civil

disobedience wouldn't be possible. People would be happy if they had an opportunity to buy cheap sausage and vodka and that would be enough for several years. I had no hopes concerning the future of my family. . . .

People were talking to soldiers, children were climbing on tanks. Soldiers looked peaceful. They were eating ice cream and responding to questions. . . . Later Sasha explained that the headquarters were changing sub-units as often as possible because the soldiers were being persuaded by the citizens. . . . Sasha found out that the soldiers had no idea what was happening. Some of them said they had been awakened in the morning and told that American troops had landed in Moscow that night, and that it was necessary to move to Moscow to protect Yeltsin. . . .

In the evening we went back to the White House. All the stairs and driveways to the building were blocked with high barricades and chains. They didn't let women go inside. These brave men said that women should go home or stay outside the terrace, which was stupid because crowds of unarmed women would be the most effective protection, much better than crowds of unarmed men. We managed to deceive them and got inside. Most of the people were organized in teams there. Every team had its task (such as to defend a particular entrance), and had gas masks. They were busy gathering stones, heavy sticks, and empty bottles to fill with gasoline. . . .

The defenders had great amounts of food because people, especially women, who couldn't stay for the whole night were bringing food. The most inconvenient thing was the absence of washrooms; maybe it was the main reason for them to refuse the women's help. . . .

We heard the first shots at 12:10, standing in a human chain on the parapet of the White House in the end of Kalinin Prospect. The tragedy happened just about 200 meters away but we couldn't see it. We only heard gunfire and saw the flashes. Most people didn't move from their place but some ran to take out food like rolls and cookies and ate it and offered food to each other and chewed feverishly. . . .

On the way home in the subway we saw rested, dressed-up people going to their offices. They had a fresh look and watched us, absolutely wet, dirty, and tired, with disapproval. . . .

There was no news about arrests but that didn't encourage me. I supposed that they would do everything later when the Soviet people and foreign countries got used to the new Soviet government. . . .

I heard an official report on the night's events: a group of criminals had attacked a peaceful tank so there were victims. Those extremists who were guilty would be found and punished. . . .

We went to distribute leaflets and I was absolutely sleepy. When we got home at 5:30 my father phoned and said, "They are finished." I switched on the radio and heard that exciting news and at last believed that everything was over. . . .

Assuredly, the defense was an example of nonviolent resistance, but I didn't see any signs of a theoretical basis to it. . . . Many people don't realize even now that the victory was ensured by the absence of arms, by the peaceful nature of the resistance. We still have to work on disseminating nonviolent ideas.[32]

Later I heard more about the coup days from Ruzanna Ilukhina, my Tolstoyan historian friend. She too had wanted to teach techniques of nonviolent resistance, using the famous 198 kinds of sanctions that Gene Sharp had listed.[33] Unfortunately, people in Moscow had no access to photocopiers in those days, so she improvised. She fed her poster through a fax machine again and again to duplicate it, then drove around in her car with a young woman who hopped out and stuck copies up in public places. These were soon torn down, so they started putting them up in women's washrooms, where they lasted longer.

* * *

I was troubled by Julia's statement that the White House had been defended successfully by people who had no idea why their own nonviolent tactics had worked. In 1995 I heard that the people in the ring of human flesh that surrounded the building had created a group called "the Living Ring."

We found the leader,[34] Victor M., a mild-mannered guy in his late forties. who told us that The Living Ring had formed immediately after the coup, declaring themselves a nonviolent organization for the defense of democracy. Immediately a sharp debate arose. Some wanted to create a national guard with weapons, while others wanted to create a purely nonviolent organization. They established contacts with foreign nonviolent organizations in the U.S., Canada, and Europe. At the time of the interview, they had 3,000 members and were holding a conference every year in memory of the August events. Victor said,

> One terrible consequence of the August defense was that several dozen defenders felt the fear of death. That's a drug. Afterward, they just couldn't stop.[35] They participated as volunteers in the wars in Moldova, Abkhazia, and even now in Chechnya. But mainly they joined the Cossacks.
>
> Why was nonviolence chosen in 1991? Most of those who gathered around the White House were representatives of the intelligentsia. There were 200 or 300 officers. Now we have 50 officers. People were without weapons. In the White House there were 5,000 machine guns, but we didn't distribute them to the people; 40 per cent were women.
>
> The other reason for nonviolence was that the soldiers who entered Moscow were not going to shoot. It was evident that they would not shoot so the resistance must also be nonviolent.
>
> On the very first day it was all spontaneous. People were disorganized but later they started to form groups. In every group a leader appeared. On Day Two the headquarters in the White House building organized detachments located just around the building. But mainly it was all self-organization.
>
> Some ex-military men were organizers. One was a specialist who delivered lectures on "war actions in the city." We leaned on his knowledge.
>
> Outside the building there were three circles of defense. As soon as a certain structure was created, it was immediately filled with volunteers. Partisan groups started to emerge but near the White House all the defense was controlled by headquarters.
>
> We issued instructions: Don't participate in any fighting. If they start to shoot, lie down. Don't block tank movements. But I think people wouldn't follow those instructions. Later some persons on their own initiative started making Molotov cocktails. Others brought weapons. There were probably 500 guns.

We have had lots of foreign guests who practice nonviolence. They provided us with useful literature, but the difference between our societies is so great that we can't use their experience. What suits them doesn't suit us. All these sit-down strikes and hunger strikes don't work here. What is important in our case is the careful organizing of meetings for protest.[36]

More Ripples

The ripples of social contagion continued in the 1990s. Nonviolent resistance movements kept emerging in the former Soviet zone well after Communism itself was gone, much to the annoyance of Vladimir Putin. Four such developments particularly irritated him and other Russians who claim a "zone of influence" over Yugoslavia, Georgia, Ukraine, and Kyrgyzstan.

* * *

Yugoslavia had been uniquely independent of the Soviet Union among Eastern European countries throughout the Cold War and had benefited by having the U.S. and Russia compete for its affections. In the long run, however, this privileged status was disadvantageous, for it meant that the Yugoslavs had been kept less informed about the problems of Communism than the citizens of the WTO countries. Russians and other Eastern Europeans had listened to Radio Free Europe, Radio Liberty, the Voice of America, and the BBC World Service. But according to Radio Free Europe's former chief, George Urban, the U.S. government had not broadcast his service into Yugoslavia, which he believes is one reason why it erupted into war at the end of the Cold War. As Urban argues,

Tito's Yugoslavia was a friendly state in Americans' eyes because it appeared to be a troublemaker for Moscow and a political pillar in the Balkan power game—never mind its unsavory domestic record. . . .
It was only a decade later, after three years of war and civil war and the breakup of Yugoslavia, that the board [of Radio Free Europe] and the U.S. government came to the same conclusion and agreed under the Radio's pressure [in 1993] to install a Radio Free Europe South Slavic Service.[37]

As elsewhere, when Communism lost its ideological influence, nationalism filled the gap; separatist demands rose in the republics, toward which Germany was particularly favorable. One after another, Slovenia, Croatia, and Bosnia-Herzegovina declared independence, each facing armed opposition from Serbia. President Slobodan Milošević seemed, on the other hand, to be trying to create a "Greater Serbia." Finally, in 1999, as Kosovo also descended further into violent conflict, NATO intervened, bombing Belgrade (over the objections of Russia) and setting up a regime in Kosovo that would become a sovereign state populated mainly by ethnic Albanians. The international affirmation of Kosovo's independence would be especially resented by Serbs and almost equally by Russians, who regard Serbs fraternally as a Slavic nation.[38]

Even before NATO intervened, democratic-minded Serbian students had already been preparing an opposition movement against President Milošević, who had already been charged by The Hague for war crimes. However, the bombing of Belgrade in 1999 so infuriated the population that it was impossible to oppose

the regime openly there until well after NATO's attack ended. Then these
youths, calling their movement "Otpor" (meaning "resistance"), began organizing with great effectiveness. With spray cans they decorated Serbia's cities with
their logo, a clenched fist, and distributed Serbian versions of Gene Sharp's
booklet on nonviolent sanctions. In 2000, when their membership had reached
40,000, they invited Colonel Robert Helvey, an associate of Gene Sharp, to train
their leaders at a Budapest hotel.[39]

On September 2000 there was an election, which evidently had been rigged.
Otpor summoned the whole population to surround the parliament buildings in
Belgrade on October 5. People came in droves—about 800,000 persons from all
over Serbia.[40] The army refused to support Milošević, who therefore had to meet
his opponent, Vojislav Koštunica, on October 7 and acknowledge defeat. He
would be turned over to the International Criminal Tribunal to stand trial but
would die in The Hague before the trial ended.

Otpor was celebrated internationally for its effective nonviolent campaign.
Some of the core members established in Belgrade the Center for Applied Nonviolent Action and Strategies (CANVAS), which teaches activists abroad how to
bring down a dictator.[41] Their staff helped plan the Rose Revolution in Georgia
and the Orange Revolution in Ukraine.

In February 2010 I interviewed Srdja Popović, the most prominent member
of CANVAS. He had just come from lecturing at the university, and was still
pumped up with enthusiasm.

I wanted to learn about their training of Russians, but Popović said he had
never been in Moscow and that CANVAS had never assisted any Russian or
Chinese movement. He said, "We never work anywhere that we are not invited.
I only went to Ukraine once—after the Orange Revolution, which worked with
people from my organization, CANVAS, but not with me."[42]

Popović described the principles CANVAS teaches in their workshops.
They begin by asking the group to formulate their "vision of tomorrow"—where
they want to be when the struggle is over. He said,

> The first day of our workshops we help people learn the tools. How to develop
> strategy. How to listen to the groups in society. How to talk to the farmers, to
> policemen, to women.
>   And after that comes the planning phase, which is to answer the question:
> How are we going to get there? The campaigns and tactics we are going to ap-
> ply. Usually the failure of a movement comes from not having spent enough
> time planning.
>   There are three principles. The first one is unity. . . . The second is plan-
> ning. The third is nonviolent discipline. The most powerful contaminant to
> nonviolent struggle is violence. One single act of violence can harm the reputa-
> tion of the movement.
>   The more people you attract to your side, the closer you are to victory—if
> you have unity. The only way to achieve unity is develop a vision of tomorrow
> that is wide enough for all groups to support.
>   Next, can you put the costs onto others? Otpor was clearly blackmailing
> the Serbian opposition. We built a movement that the people recognized as the
> most capable of opposing the regime. The international community recognized

us as the only movement that would never negotiate with Milošević. And we built a movement that could tell the opposition: The only way we'll support you is if you go together. If you don't go together, then you're working with Milošević—and we're going to attack you publicly. That was clear blackmail. Either you are with us or you are against us. And you cannot live by being against us because we are more popular than you are. We will go into the struggle with you only if you say: "We will argue *after* Milošević is gone."

I asked, "Does CANVAS participate in the groups you train?" Popović said,

We give them tools, skills. And we strongly oppose the idea that foreigners should get involved because that's a big contaminant to the struggle. The only way the struggle will be [effective] in any country in the world is if the locals are carrying it.

And that brings us to the sensitive issue of what foreign democratic governments should do to help democratic movements—and what they shouldn't do under any circumstances. They shouldn't interfere in politics. The last thing they should ever do is support the opposition parties. They should stay out of the political arena.

It took us a hell of effort to explain this to America. The big change came when Zoran Djinjić and I were in the U.S. in 2000. Zoran explained to them that only a united opposition should be funded and that they should refrain from picking any favorite opposition leader, including himself.

Second thing the internationals should avoid is public support. It took us a hell of a lot of work to stop people like Madeline Albright giving public statements because Madeline Albright was the person responsible for the bombing of Serbia. It harmed us domestically very much.

Then let's speak about the things that are effective, things they should do. In my opinion the most effective help to Serbia was helping the independent media. That support is very valuable because you are building the capability of the independent movement to communicate, you are raising the costs to the regime of committing human rights violations, and you are also developing the roots of democratic society. One of the reasons I strongly disagree with the criticism of the success of the Orange Revolution is the fact that they now have fair media in Ukraine. Quite fair, compared to what it was six years ago.

If Canada and the United States are standing for the value of democracy, free media, and human rights, these are things they are helping, and they cannot be accused of interfering because, by supporting independent media you are not supporting the opposition or the government. You are just supporting the right of the people to hear the truth.

* * *

The nonviolent resistance movements in the other post-Soviet states also were reactions to elections that the populace considered fraudulent. Georgia came next in November 2003. An organization of university students, Kmara ("Enough!"), led the protests, sponsored by a Georgian NGO, the Liberty Institute. Emulating their CANVAS friends in Serbia, Kmara used graffiti and street demonstrations, and trained election observers. Mikheil Saakashvili claimed to have defeated the incumbent president, former Soviet Foreign Minister Eduard Shevardnadze. Monitoring groups confirmed that opinion. Then, on November

23, Shevardnadze, being forced to meet with the opposition leaders, resigned, which sent 100,000 people into the streets to celebrate.[43]

Saakashvili was inaugurated in January, and his supporters soon won a parliamentary majority. This outcome greatly displeased the neighboring Putin government, as did Saakashvili's intemperate actions in 2008, which precipitated an actual invasion by the Russian army.

* * *

Next came Ukraine's Orange Revolution of 2004—a remarkably disciplined, well-planned nonviolent movement. The organizers had closely observed other "color revolutions," and sought foreign expertise. They astutely recognized that a nonviolent movement should not erupt as a spontaneous, expressive gesture, but requires extensive strategizing to undermine the "pillars of support" on which the existing regime depends.

The main pillars on which a government depends are its military and police force.[44] The Ukrainian movement, calling themselves "Pora," planned far in advance to win over these groups. They visited the wives and mothers of military officers, so that when the mass gathering finally took place in Independence Square, among the most conspicuous participants were members of the officers' families. Had there been any inclination to fire on the crowd, their presence might well have persuaded the commanders to defect.

But the military personnel themselves had already been won over, in large part. One retired officer, General Antonets, joined the movement early on and used his network of army relationships to contact and persuade other officers to support democracy.[45]

Pora recognized the importance of bringing large crowds to the streets quickly. They blocked the rear doors of buildings in Kiev to force protesters to fill the narrow streets. The protests lasted over three weeks, with people living in tents in the cold weather. Worried that the police might choose the middle of the night to attack the protesters, Pora arranged for a live TV camera to be transmitting twenty-four hours each day. As one Western diplomat said, the message was, "Come and get us, but if you are going to make us bleed, it will be 'live on CNN.'"[46]

The regime charged fifteen Pora members with terrorism, but they simply took this as an opportunity to communicate with police officers. In fact, Pora members had already visited police stations throughout Ukraine, giving flowers and letters to the policemen and asking them to abide by the law. Because these youths were so polite and disciplined, everyone was inclined to regard them favorably instead of as terrorists. They had even met with the city council and obtained the full cooperation of the Kiev police. (This outcome was more favorable than in Serbia, where police commanders who had openly declared their sympathies for Otpor were sacked.)[47]

Some of the Pora leaders expressed to me their concern about the role of foreign funders in the Orange Revolution. Although they had never been living on grants, they had alliances with Ukrainian NGOs who had existed for years on such grants. Also, Ukrainians were not as hostile to Western donors as the population of Serbia had been, since they had not been bombed or subjected to the scarcity caused by sanctions. A Toronto journalist, Mark MacKinnon, also reported substantial disquieting participation by foreigners in Ukrainian politics, especially by lavish and partisan funding.[48]

The Orange Revolution ended on a triumphant note, as the democratic candidate, Yushchenko, become president. Still, democracy can be a rocky road. Ukraine's many problems were not resolved and in the next election, in 2010, the candidate whom they had defeated, Yanukovich, won, satisfying especially the Russian-speaking Ukrainians. When I mentioned this to Srdja Popović, the Otpor leader, he replied,

> The Orange Revolution was not about pro-Russians or anti-Russians. It was about the right of the people to elect their government by free and fair elections. If they have gained free and fair elections, from my point of view I don't give a damn who is elected. That is not my job. My job is to change people's heads, so they understand that they have the power to change.

* * *

The Tulip Revolution in Kyrgyzstan was the next pro-democracy movement. It led to the overthrow of President Askar Akayev in early 2005. This too was an instance of cultural diffusion by exemplification, for the young protesters modeled their movement especially on Georgia. However, it was not an exemplary campaign for others to follow. The movement was far from united or disciplined. Shortly after the protests began, crowds resorted to violence. Although U.S. sources had been involved in funding the movement's communications technology,[49] the State Department and UN Secretary General Kofi Annan both urged the two sides to resolve their conflict through dialogue, not confrontation. In 2007, Freedom House gave Kyrgyzstan mediocre scores on democracy: 5 on political rights and 4 on civil rights, with an overall rating of "Partly Free."[50] In April 2010, a new movement ousted the Kyrgyz president, Kurmanbek Bakiyev, and over the next several months Kyrgyzstan was torn by ethnic riots which caused hundreds of deaths. In this case, the ripple of nonviolence had completely come to a tragic end.

* * *

Question: This book is about Russia, so why have I devoted so much space here to nonviolent pro-democracy campaigns in other former satellite states? After all, no resistance movement is likely to emerge in Russia in the near future. The election frauds in Russia are as grievous as those that brought enormous crowds of protesters to the squares of Belgrade, Tbilisi, Kiev, and Bishkek, but Russians merely shrug, complacent because of their new prosperity and stability.

I have two explanations. First, I believe everyone in the world should develop skill in nonviolent struggle. There are times when such an important conflict arises that even SHEEP become willing to sacrifice their lives to win. If that happens, and they know no alternative way of fighting, they will go to war. Nonviolence is an alternative way of struggling—one that offers real possibilities of winning, even if the opponent has military superiority. Knowing alternative ways of fighting is a great asset, especially in a society that is vulnerable to authoritarian rule, so as a peace studies professor, I always taught it. Democracies are less vulnerable than authoritarian regimes but everywhere the abuse of power is conceivable.

Second, the recent history of nonviolence shows that it is a "ripple" phenomenon. People get ideas from observing others, whom they imitate, thus "diffusing" the ideas to still others. We should analyze the lessons that people take from watching others, for their inferences may be right or wrong. I have included some tips here for would-be nonviolent revolutionaries. I am not advising you to attempt to oust your ruler, but if you do choose to do so, you should take the project as seriously as a general would when planning a military campaign. Successful nonviolence requires intelligent strategizing. It is not an amateur sport. Read Gene Sharp or Robert Helvey or Srjda Popović before you start.

If Russians ever do attempt a "color revolution," they are likely to emulate the others since 1989. However, many governments have learned how to block such pro-democracy movements, so new organizers must adjust too. Still, Russia is unlikely to experience a nonviolent pro-democracy campaign from below, for the reasons that Furman, Alexeyeva, and Kovalev mentioned.

The main promoters of such a future Russian attempt are a group of protesters called Oborona, who take Otpor as their model. The organization is nonhierarchical in structure, and was founded by Oleg Kozlovsky, who maintains an English-language blog.[51] I interviewed him by phone in March 2010, and was enthralled by the chirpy sounds of the tiny daughter on his lap. He had just returned from a meeting in the White House with President Obama, along with about twenty other human rights activists from different countries.

Oborona began in 2005 and now has members of various political persuasions who all want a democratic Russia. With branches in about a dozen cities, they use only nonviolent methods, varying from street protests to indoor activities for youth, to sharing ideas on the Internet. The problem that seemed to worry Oleg most was the government crackdown on the Internet, which began in 2007 and had been getting worse. One Oborona member had been under investigation for a year and a half, charged with "inciting hatred against social groups"—namely the police and FSB. He may face two years imprisonment.

Oleg told me about Madomed Yevloev, the owner of the most popular web site in Ingushetia, who had organized civil campaigns and gathered evidence of electoral fraud. At first the government sued him and blocked his web site, but he re-opened it in another place and was killed. Oleg said,

> He was arrested in the airport and killed by a police officer maybe an hour later. The official version is that it was an accidental shot in the head. The police officer. . . was sentenced to restriction of freedom. . . . [He] was the personal guard of the Ingush Republic President.

Even these cases have not stopped all the bloggers, but more of them are now trying to hide their identities. The ones who have been persecuted had blogged under their own names. Oleg said he could offhand name a dozen such cases, but "if I made a little search of my records, I think it would be at least 100 cases in the last three years."[52]

We talked about Obama's policies on human rights and democracy groups. When Presidents Medvedev and Obama met in 2009, they agreed to set up a commission to address civil society issues in both countries. As part of his campaign to "reset" a deteriorating relationship, Obama's administration has ceased criticizing Russia's human rights policies, as the preceding Bush administration regularly did. However, that cessation has antagonized Russian activists, who believe that it is unprincipled not to speak up against obvious abuses. At Obama's insistence, the commission retains the ability to keep the topic of human rights on the bilateral-relations agenda.[53]

Oleg knows and likes Obama's adviser on Russia and democracy, Michael McFaul, but is pessimistic about the new commission, which McFaul has been assigned to co-chair with Putin's adviser, Vladislav Surkov, who is one of the undemocratic, capitalist regime's hardliners—the new DINOSAURS. The trip to the White House had not encouraged Oleg, who told me,

> They want to separate the issues of human rights and democracy from issues of economy and national security. It's a mistake because the Russian government is just as interested in economic and trade or security issues as the U.S. government but is not at all interested in promoting democracy and human rights, so if you separate these two blocks of issues, you may have progress in trade or security but you will have no progress in human rights and democracy because you have no leverage. If this approach is not given up, then the administration of Obama won't bring anything good for Russian democracy.

Yuri Dzhibladze is the president of a Moscow organization called the Center for the Development of Democracy and Human Rights. He was a cardiologist who became so engaged in International Physicians for the Prevention of Nuclear War that eventually he decided to switch careers. Now he monitors Russia's legislation and government policies regarding human rights. Dzhibladze had been on the same junket to Washington as Oleg and shared his misgivings. Indeed, he published a statement afterward: "What I told President Obama." He had said,

> Many of us had urged the U.S. that arrogance, self-righteousness, and lecturing should give way to ability to listen, act respectfully, and build dialogue, even with unpleasant and difficult interlocutors. We acknowledge the value of this approach; we see how anti-Americanism has indeed started to decrease and how you have been able recently to secure new levels of cooperation with many governments in vitally important areas of military security, counterterrorism, nuclear non-proliferation, and trade.

Of course, a reader can sense the word "but" approaching. And indeed, Dzhibladze turns to complaining that the U.S. engagement strategy is not working, indeed that many Russian activists are feeling forgotten.

In the long run you must really be interested in these nations becoming demo-cratic; we know that democracies do not go to war with each other. Even when one speaks with others with respect and goodwill, it is important to base one's behavior on values and principles, to be consistent, to speak clearly, to call things by their real names, and to avoid pursuing engagement at any cost. We know that you are grappling with these dilemmas but we want you to hear that we are not happy with the way things are going on now.[54]

These are concerns that must be explored further in the final chapters, but now let's review the approaches taken by Russian civil society in 2010.

Civil Society's Democratic Missions
There is much to be said for Sergei Kovalev's version of democracy: that it is a "boring process that is just supposed to happen." Democracy should be routine and reliable. Whether it results in better decisions than a benevolent dictator would issue, it's inherently preferable because it gives people more control over their own lives and offers civilized ways of resolving conflicts. The ideal transi-tion for Russia would be a smooth, nonviolent shift toward democracy—from below and from "sideways." That's the goal of many civil society organizations.

However, new difficulties confronted the NGOs in the aftermath of the Or-ange Revolution, when the Russian government became rattled, expecting for-eign sources to help Russian protesters effect a "regime change" against them. To prevent that, in January 2006 President Putin signed into law a bill regulating non-governmental organizations. It requires those operating in Russia to register with the government, disclose their funding sources, and expect frequent state auditing. In March the state froze the accounts of the Open Russia Foundation, which was funded by Mikhail Khodorkovsky, the Yukos oligarch. Other phil-anthropic citizens also began finding it difficult to donate money.[55] The new law expanded state oversight on an estimated 300,000 Russian NGOs to keep them from spending foreign money on any political activities. It also enables courts to close NGOs down if they are involved in "extremist or unconstitutional" activ-ity. Actually, many of these groups perform needed social services for the population and are not involved in political activities, but the bureaucratic regu-lations encumber their effectiveness.[56]

I heard complaints from every NGO I interviewed, including Elena Grishina, a former journalist who runs an organization called the Center of In-dependent Information. She sends information out to civil society organizations throughout Russia and to selected journalists. She said that these groups are har-assed by bureaucrats and tax officials to such an extent that some have given up in despair. She explained,

> To register your organization, you have to go through ten or twenty different stops. You have to wake up at 6:00 am to go there and stand in line. There are small businesses that feed on this. Those people know how the system works so you can pay them money and they will process everything for you, bypassing the queue. It's either your money or your time.

I wanted to know about "GONGOs," the "Government-Organized NGOs" that are being created to compete with independent organizations. The main GONGO is the Public Chamber, which was set up in 2005 to oversee draft legislation and monitor government agencies, including parliament. I asked Yuri Dzhibladze about this institution, which most Russian NGOs seem to regard with great suspicion. He explained to me,

> Putin doesn't say that he is trying to destroy civil society. On the contrary, he says "We need non-governmental organizations. We support them." But they want to control and manage civil society, as they control government, the courts, and media. So they are quite happy with civil society organizations playing the role of assisting the state in this service-provision function. . . . And they create fake institutions that take over the role of real organizations. For example, the Public Chamber. . . . Two or three members are reasonable and real. Others are just there to block the access of real, independent activists and to create the impression that there is real civil society.[57]

I was troubled to learn that the Public Chamber is headed by Yevgeny Velikhov, the physicist who had done so much with Western scientists to overcome the nuclear arms race. I mentioned this to Yevgenia Issraelyan, a friend who works with civil society groups across Russia. She soothingly commented, "That doesn't mean that he has betrayed his principles."

And of course, there are two sides to the question, for not only may the government gain excessive influence over internal opposition movements but perhaps also foreign donors may do so. The United States has laws forbidding financial support to American politicians from abroad.[58] President Putin was correct when he stated in July 2005:

> I am categorically against the foreign financing of [NGOs'] political activities in Russia. . . We understand that he who pays the piper calls the tune. . . . Not a single self-respecting country will allow that, and neither shall we. . . . Let us solve our internal problems ourselves.[59]

Accordingly, the Russian government is seeking to counter foreign influence by providing funds itself to NGOs. I phoned Ida Kuklina in April 2010 to see how civil society was faring throughout Russia. Kuklina is an eminent scholar at IMEMO who for a number of years also has headed Mothers of Soldiers. She is also a member of the presidential council, advising the government on security matters and civil society. She said that in 2009 and 2010, the Russian government has been disbursing significant amounts of money to existing NGOs on a competitive basis, so as to reduce their involvement with foreign donors. But these grants are also limited to non-political projects.

Many other democratic countries also fund their societies' NGOs, albeit not for the purpose of constraining them politically. However, even in liberal democracies the recipients often wish they did not need to accept government money, lest civil society become dependent on the state. In such countries, the money is disbursed by "arms-length" organizations to avoid political favoritism.

Nevertheless, in Canada, where I live, there have been scandals lately when well-established church-based and liberal charities had their funding cancelled by the conservative government, raising questions as to whether civil society organizations are being kept on a leash. In Russia, groups are even more vulnerable to government control. Some of them would prefer foreign funding.

Evidently what is needed here is an international law to specify what kind of cross-border support is acceptable. The same rules should apply equally to all societies. Like Srdja Popović, for example, I believe it is improper to fund political parties or candidates abroad, but NGOs are a different matter.

Fortunately, I was happy to learn that certain international principles have already been established. Yuri Dzhibladze participated in formulating a document on the subject, "Defending Civil Society," with the World Movement for Democracy[60] and the International Center for Not-for-Profit Law. The report articulates principles protecting civil society. They include "the right of individuals to form and join NGOs; the right to operate to fulfill their legal purposes without state interference; the right to free expression and to communication with domestic and international partners; the right to seek and secure resources, including the cross-border transfer of funds; and the state's positive obligation to protect NGO rights."[61] This does not, however, specifically address the possibility that a foreign government or private donor might become involved in a campaign to effect "regime change." In this globalizing world, the process of democratization often crosses borders. The dilemma concerns how far to go in helping others to liberate themselves.

* * *

Despite the obstacles, civil society organizations have continued increasing in Russia, and obviously most of them are peaceful projects, not engaged primarily in political protest. I'll describe a few examples of the groups I heard about.

I joined a group of American students from Wittenberg University one morning in May 2008 at an old Moscow house, the headquarters of several human rights groups. We interviewed two men who work there, Slava Gamenyok and Lev Ponomarov. Gamenyok, a member of Yabloko Party, is organizing apartment owners. He reminded us that there had been no housing market during the Soviet days. (Some people could buy co-op apartments but if they sold them, they would only receive the original price, not any appreciation in value.)

In one district of Moscow dilapidated apartment buildings were going to be demolished, but the inhabitants did not want to move out. This was happening just when housing was being privatized; nowadays 80 percent of the Moscow population own their apartments. Some of these neighbors came together and formed associations to fight the demolition. They submitted about 2,000 complaints to the mayor's office and also proposed improved procedures for handling such complaints. They have fulfilled many of their goals and their association has taken over the maintenance of their buildings. (In the average Moscow apartment building, common spaces such as elevators are smelly and dirty because no one had been accountable to the residents for the upkeep.) Now the association is publishing a magazine for members and sometimes even organizes

social events for the residents. (I hope they learn mutual trust from all this socializing; most Muscovites hesitate to answer knocks at their doors, fearing that
some dangerous criminal may be on the other side.) Gamenyok said, "We think
we can awaken a sense of responsibility for home owner associations, and this
may encourage the formation of more democratic parties."[62] Good luck to him!

With the visitors from Wittenberg I also interviewed Lev Ponomarov, the
most prominent of the current human rights activists. He is a vigorous man in
his fifties who often leads political demonstrations. My friends had seen him on
TV two weeks before, being beaten in the street. Ponomarov's organization is
the largest human rights group in Russia, with branches in more than 100 locali-
ties. Since Putin came to power, he said that his group had been receiving requests from prisoners who allege that they were tortured. Also, the police regularly stop and check young people who are dressed "informally"—with Mohawk
haircuts, or nose rings in unusual places, or kids who appear to be skinheads.
Ponomarov said,

> On Saturday we held a workshop here to teach youth how to behave. When
> young people are detained they have no idea what rights they have—and they
> are probably right that they don't have any. Nevertheless, on paper they do.
> And if you follow those rules, you are creating a life for police that's a little
> more complex.[63]

George Hudson is one of the Wittenberg University professors with whom I
spent some days in Moscow. Since 2004 he has been studying civil society organizations in various regions of Russia—particularly in Moscow, Nizhny-
Novgorod, Samara, and Volgograd. His conclusions were more optimistic than
those I have already mentioned. Indeed, because of the growth of civil society
that he had witnessed, he expressed skepticism about Freedom House's abysmal
ratings of Russia's democratic development.

Hudson's papers describe several projects that civil society groups are carrying out from below. For example, in Samara there is an organization of wheel-
chair-bound invalids and also a Peace Foundation, which previously was the
Soviet Peace Foundation, but which operates independently today. Hudson recognizes a "mutual cooptation society" between the government and NGOs. The
state needs NGOs to offer social services, and NGOs need resources from the
government. Hence the independence of civil society from the state (or its
GONGOs) seems to be less than in most Western countries, but that fact does
not seem to worry Hudson.[64]

* * *

Now meet Andrei Kamenshikov, a forty-two-year-old activist who has been
working in the Caucasus for many years with an organization called Nonviolence International. He has lived in Moscow all his life, but his mother was
American so his accent sounds completely American. One day we met for lunch
and he introduced me to a Chechen colleague, Umar Khamzatovich. They were
addressing the violence that prevails in the Caucasus. As peace activists, they

distinguish between their cooperative approach and the protests of the human rights organizations, whom they respect but cannot emulate.

Mistrust runs deep between the Chechen public and the local police, as well as the local governments. Both Umar and Andrei are working to build trust there. For example, they provide the police with soccer balls and uniforms, which they can use to organize teams among the hostile youths. Also, the public does not know much about their own rights, so Umar and Andrei have made up brochures that list those rights. Andrei said,

> Rather than giving the booklet to them ourselves, we give it through the local police officer as a tool for developing trust. Usually when a police officer comes to your home, there's some problem. Maybe he will say that your son is in trouble, but when a policeman arrives with this useful brochure, it changes people's perception of him. Also, police officers took an oath to serve. Often they forget, so we printed posters to put on their office wall as a reminder.

Andrei and Umar keep local government officials informed about their projects and have encountered no difficulty because of the new laws governing civil society organizations. Human rights organizations more often run into trouble because of their more confrontational style.[65]

I think the aforementioned examples indicate that Russian civil society is flourishing, despite all the impediments, and is contributing to the society's well-being. No doubt these groups are building trust and social capital—at least when it comes to "bonding" effects.

On the other hand, there are few transnational groups, so the "bridging" effects are minimal. Russians need large-scale, popular, sustained dialogues among thousands of well-educated citizens throughout the country and, especially, with foreigners about serious matters.

The Second Political Typology

Finally, I'll update the changing Russian political orientations that I have been observing throughout the past 28 years. In 2010, my typology is still based on two crucial questions: whether one favors or opposes the existing state (now the Medvedev/Putin dyad) and whether one believes that political change in Russia will come from above, from below, or from below with help from abroad— "sideways."

	Favor existing state	Oppose existing state
Believe change comes from above	SHEEP (most Russians. Est.120 million are pro-Putin)	GIVE UP TRYING (defeated democrats. Est. 21 million)
Believe change comes from below	None	WAIT IN HOPE (optimistic democrats with long view. Est. 1 million)
Believe change comes from below, with help from outside	DINOSAURS (Putin and his team)	POLITICAL CHALLENGERS (risk-taking activists & new NGOs. Est. a few thousand.)

Figure 2. Russians' Attitudes and Civil Society, circa 2008–09

Most Russians remain SHEEP. Polls show at least 70 percent of the population accepting (if not enthusiastically endorsing) the current regime. These SHEEP are not indignant about electoral fraud, apparently believing that significant change can come only from above, not from protests in the streets.

However, a few people—DINOSAUR government officials primarily—seem actually to expect a color revolution from below, with the help of foreigners. Hence they are anxiously trying to keep grassroots activists from gaining power, especially those with support from Western democracies (notably Britain and the United States).

However, a substantial group of people (particularly the intelligentsia) still oppose the existing regime and fit into three categories. The most numerous are politically passive, having given up hope. Those people believe regretfully that change can come only from above. I call them the "GIVE UP TRYING" group. (I can't think of an animal to symbolize them. Maybe the opossum?) They include some people who were formerly committed activists but who feel that there is no prospect of being able to change the present situation toward democracy, human rights, and peace. One, for example, is Tair Tairov, the fearless Uzbek, who has given up activism and gone into collecting ancient textiles.

Among the regime's opponents another category seems strangely hopeful. They know that the present regime is far from democratic and they criticize its failings. However, they are patient, for they believe that Russia could not be a democracy yet "even if the president were an angel." Ludmilla Alexeyeva and Dmitry Furman belong in this group. While working cheerfully to make democracy possible, they also are prepared to wait for its inevitable arrival in some remote future. I call them the "WAIT IN HOPE" bunch.

There is also a third category of the regime's opponents who continue to criticize as fiercely as the old BARKING DOGS. I do not call them by that name, however, for the old BARKING DOGS believed that they would bring democracy to Russia strictly from below. These new POLITICAL CHALLENGERS believe that they also require assistance from other democrats and peace activists abroad. Sergei Kovalev is the prototype POLITICAL CHALLENGER. He is tough and resilient, but not as sanguine about the inevitability of victory as Alexeyeva.

There are still other defiant POLITICAL CHALLENGERS in Russia—both old and young ones. For example, Lev Ponomarov, Garry Kasparov, and Oleg Kozlovsky's Oborona movement all turn out courageously for "marches of dissent," expecting to be physically assaulted in the streets.

There are other more circumspect POLITICAL CHALLENGERS such as Yuri Dzhibladze and Grigory Yavlinsky who also work from below, mainly by building institutions and strengthening international laws rather than marching in the street.

Will they succeed? Can Russia become a democracy? Instead of glibly answering yes, I think we should take a hard, analytical look at the hideous alternative possibility: the restoration of totalitarian rule. No Russian can say with confidence that it cannot happen again. Yet foresight yields some power over fate. Let us foresee the worst.

Notes

1. Georgi Arbatov, in discussion with the author, July 1992, Moscow.

2. Maria J. Stephan and Erica Chenoweth, "Why Civil Resistance Works: The Strategic Logic of Nonviolent Conflict," *International Security* 33, no. 1 (Summer 2008): 8.

3. Adrian Karatnycky and Peter Ackerman, "How Freedom is Won: From Civic Resistance to Durable Democracy" (Washington, DC: Freedom House, 2005).

4. Ludmilla Alexeyeva, in discussion with the author, May 26, 2008, Moscow. Unfortunately, Muscovites have detected no discernable reduction, so far, in the use of special traffic privileges for VIPs.

5. Alexeyeva discussion.

6. Adam Newman, "Lukoil Executive in Car Crash Scandal," *Oil & Gas Next Generation,* http://www.cisoilgas.com/news/anatoly-barkov-car-crash-scandal (accessed March 10, 2010).

7. Dmitry Furman, "Democracy Suffers from 'Democrats'." *Moscow Times,* Nov. 13, 2001. Also see his "Imitation Democracies: The Post-Soviet Penumbra," *New Left Review* 54 (November-December 2008): 29–47.

8. Dmitry Furman, in discussion with the author, Moscow, 2008.

9. Furman, in discussion with the author, March 1994. He refers to an article published in *Voprosy Filosofia* 7 (1992).

10. Furman says that New Age religions were at least as popular in Russia as in California during that period. See also Anne Ferlat, "Neopaganism and New Age in Russia," *Folklore* 23, 40–48, http://www.folklore.ee/Folklore/vol23/newage.pdf (accessed March 9, 2010).

11. Alexander Likhotal, in discussion with the author, Gorbachev Foundation, 1992.

12. Sergei Kovalev, in discussion with the author, June 2008, Moscow.

13. Lev Ponomarov, in discussion with the author, May 2008, Moscow and Yuri Dzhibladze, in discussion with the author, June 2008.

14. Interview with Arkady Popov, Moscow, summer 1992.

15. "Soviet-Era Dissident Lyudmila Alexeyeva Detained by Moscow Police," The Legend of Pine Ridge, http://legendofpineridge.blogspot.com/2010/01/soviet-era-dissident-lyudmila-alexeyeva.html (accessed March 9, 2010).

16. William N. Ryerson, "The Effectiveness of Entertainment Mass Media in Changing Behavior," Population Media Center, http://www.populationmedia.org/wp-content/uploads/2008/02/effectiveness-of-entertainment-education-112706.pdf (accessed March 9, 2010). See also Arvind Singh and Everett M. Rogers, *Entertainment-Education: A Communication Strategy for Social Change* (Mahwah, NJ: Lawrence Erlbaum, 1999).

17. This is the argument of my book, *Two Aspirins and a Comedy: How Television Can Enhance Health and Society* (Boulder: Paradigm, 2006).

18. For this account of Garcia's influence I am indebted to Victor Sumsky, who recounted these events to me in 1992. For two of Garcia's books, see *The Filipino Quest: A Just and Lasting Peace* (Quezon City, Philippines: Claretian Publications, 1988) and *The Sovereign Quest: Freedom from Foreign Military Bases* (Quezon City, Philippines: Claretian Publications, 1988).

19. Richard L. Deats, *Marked for Life: The Story of Hildegard Goss Mayr (Leaders and Witnesses)* (Hyde Park, NY: New City Press, 2009).

20. Metta Spencer (interviewer) "Sharing nonviolence: an interview with Ed Garcia,*" Peace Magazine* 12, no. 3 (March–April 1996): 11.

21. Victor Sumsky, interviews and articles translated from Russian by Julia Kalinina.

22. Pérez Esquivel was awarded a Nobel Peace Prize for his efforts in 1980. I heard how this happened. Peace activists in Europe and North America were concerned because

he had been jailed and tortured, and there were concerns that the Argentine government would kill him. In order to protect him, they nominated him for a Nobel Peace Prize, hoping that the glare of publicity would make him too prominent to be killed easily. They were overjoyed and also surprised when he actually won.

23. Peter Ackerman and Jack Duvall, *A Force More Powerful: A Century of Nonviolent Conflict* (New York: St. Martin's, 2000), 291.

24. Mubarak Awad, "Nonviolence in the Holy Land," interview by Metta Spencer, Peace *Magazine* 4, no. 6 (December 1988): 5.

25. http://www.aeinstein.org/.

26. Gene Sharp and Mubarak Awad, "Killing the Pig to Frighten the Monkey," interview by Metta Spencer, *Peace Magazine* 5, no. 4 (August–September 1989): 16.

27. Martha Henderson, in discussion with the author, June 1994.

28. Ackerman and Duvall, 429.

29. Ackerman and Duvall, 435.

30. Ackerman and Duvall, 435–37.

31. Ackerman and Duvall, 439–49.

32. Julia Kalinina, "Mail from Moscow," *Peace Magazine* 7, no. 6 (November–December 1991): 14.

33. Gene Sharp, "The Methods of Nonviolent Action," *Peace Magazine,* http://peacemagazine.org/198.htm (accessed March 9, 2010).

34. I regret that I cannot identify Victor M. but I cannot locate him to ask permission.

35. For a discussion of war addiction, see Chris Hedges, *War is a Force That Gives us Meaning* (New York: Knopf Doubleday, 2003).

36. Victor M., in discussion with the author, February 1995, Moscow.

37. George Urban, *Radio Free Europe and the Pursuit of Democracy* (New Haven: Yale University Press, 1997), 153–54.

38. Metta Spencer, "Yugoslavia Timeline," in *The Lessons of Yugoslavia*, ed. Metta Spencer (London: Elsevier, 2000), 372.

39. Robert Helvey, *On Strategic Nonviolent Conflict: Thinking About the Fundamentals* (Boston: Albert Einstein Foundation, 2004).

40. The weekly magazine *Nedeljni Telegraf* estimated this number on Nov 1, 2000. The producers of *Bringing Down a Dictator,* dir. Steve York—a documentary film about this campaign—maintain a website at http://www.aforcemorepowerful.org/films/bdd/.

41. CANVAS maintains a website at http://www.canvasopedia.org/.

42. Srdja Popović, telephone discussion with the author, February 10, 2010.

43. Charles H. Fairbanks Jr., "Georgia's Rose Revolution." *Journal of Democracy* 15, no. 2 (2004): 110–124.

44. Anika Locke Binnendijk and Ivan Marović, "Power and Persuasion: Nonviolent Strategies to Influence State Security Forces in Serbia (2000) and Ukraine (2004)," *Communist and Post-Communist Studies* 39 (2006): 411–429. Also interviews with Anika Binnendijk, July 2008; Iryna Chupryna in Kiev, May 2008; Dmitro Potekhin in Kiev, May 2008; several conversations with Robert Helvey.

45. Binnendijk and Marović, 418.

46. Binnendijk and Marović, 415.

47. Binnendijk and Marović, 421.

48. Mark MacKinnon, *The New Cold War: Revolutions, Rigged Elections and Pipeline Politics in the Former Soviet Union* (Toronto: Random House, 2007).

49. "United States helped Kyrgyz pro-democracy programs," *Wikinews,* http://en.wikinews.org/wiki/United_States_helped_Kyrgyz_pro-democracy_programs (accessed March 5, 2010).

50. "Country Report: Kyrgyzstan (2007)," *Freedom House*, http://freedom-house.org/template.cfm?page=22&year=2007&country=7210.

51. "Oleg Kozlovsky's English weblog," http://olegkozlovsky.wordpress.com.

52. Interview with Oleg Kozlovsky by phone, Moscow March 2010.

53. Tatyana Stanovaya, "Civil Rights Defender Surkov," http://politcom.ru/9445.html (in Russian; accessed January 19, 2010).

54. Yuri Dzhibladze, "What I Told President Obama," *Huffington Post*, February 24, 2010, http://www.huffingtonpost.com/yuri-dzhibladze/what-i-told-president-oba_b_474646.html (accessed February 24, 2010).

55. Alexander Livshin and Richard Weitz, "Civil Society and Philanthropy Under Putin," *The International Journal of Not-for-Profit Law* 8, no. 3 (May 2006): 7–12.

56. Tom Parfitt, "Russia Clamps Down on Foreign Aid Organisations," *The Lancet* 366, no. 9502 (December 10, 2005): 1993.

57. Yuri Dzhibladze, in discussion with the author, June 2008, Moscow.

58. Jørgen Johansen, "External Financing of Opposition Movements," in *People Power: Unarmed Resistance and Global Solidarity* ed. Howard Clark (London: Pluto Press, 2009), 200.

59. President Putin's statement was reported by Reuters, 20 July 2005, as cited by Johansen, 199.

60. "World Movement for Democracy," http://www.wmd.org.

61. World Movement for Democracy, "Executive Summary," in World Movement for Democracy and International Center for Not-for-Profit Law, *Defending Civil Society*, (Washington, D.C.: National Endowment for Democracy, 2008): 3.

62. Slava Gamenyok, in discussion with the author, May 2008, Moscow.

63. Lev Ponomarov, in discussion with the author, May 2008, Moscow.

64. George E. Hudson, "System-Level and Contextual Factors as Determinants of the Effectiveness of Civil Groups in Russia," (paper, Wittenberg University, Springfield, OH, 2008).

65. Andrei Kamenshikov and Umar Khamzatovich, in discussion with the author, May 2008, Moscow. Also see an update on Kamenshikov's activities in an interview with Metta Spencer, "Rights and Conflicts in Russia: A Talk with Nonviolence International's Andrei Kamenshikov," *Peace Magazine* 26, no. 2 (April 2010): 8–11.

Chapter 13: Social Traps—Toward an Explanation of Totalitarianism

Question: If it is true, as Russian sociologist Yury Levada concluded, that as few as 10 percent of the Soviet people may ever have wholeheartedly favored Communism, how on earth did a series of dictators manage to dominate 100 percent of the Soviet population for seventy-odd years?

Answer: The Soviet people were caught in fiendish "social traps" that kept them uncertain what other people wanted, believed, or were willing to do. My purpose here is to describe some politically dangerous social traps so that people may recognize and avoid future instances of them.

I want to show that certain situations create and perpetuate totalitarianism. Instead of finding certain *types of people* who are born or bred to be totalitarian, I'll look for *totalitarian situations*. There are several stages in the creation of a society-wide totalitarian situation, and at each phase, a social trap is involved. A whole society does not find itself in an irreversible predicament until other traps have snapped shut on smaller groups. I cannot produce a full theory of totalitarianism, but any effort in this direction may help anticipate future cases and even forestall them.

A trap is any arrangement whereby one may unexpectedly find oneself or one's group facing unacceptable risks for doing what one wants to do or perhaps even saying what one thinks. One trap mechanism consists of an asymmetrical situation in which others have control over a powerful interest of one's own, but without there being a reciprocal kind of control.

Usually traps are created inadvertently, including most or all historic totalitarian repressions. However, we shouldn't assume that social traps are found only in conditions of political repression. Traps are an ordinary part of human experience, arising from such simple motives as the desire to conform rather than be humiliated by appearing deviant.

Almost everyone wants to be considered normal by those we respect, yet this motive can keep us from disclosing our true attitudes, thereby creating the conditions for a social trap to form.

The Illusion of Unanimity as a Social Trap

Many years ago psychologist Solomon Asch asked small groups of people to judge the length of pairs of lines and to answer this question aloud: "Which is longer, A or B?" The lines differed so much that any normal person could answer correctly. However, only the last person in each group was a genuine experimental subject. Unknown to him or her, all the other members were paid confederates who gave the wrong answer. By the time the last person's turn came, he or she would usually give the wrong answer too, simply to conform. However, if even one other person had given the correct answer, the true subject was far more likely to do so as well.[1]

Serious problems occur in real life if people hide their true judgments from others. Psychologist Irving Janis called such voluntary self-censorship "groupthink." He analyzed momentous situations in democratic societies when group pseudo-consensus actually led to a fiasco. These included the disastrous decision-making processes that resulted in the Korean War, the failed Bay of Pigs invasion, and the launch of the doomed *Challenger* space shuttle.[2] Because the decision-makers respected each other, those with private misgivings did not challenge the plans when the group appeared unanimous. "Groupthink" is the common tendency to try to sustain consensus and suppress dissent. It is a social trap that can be found in any type of society.

This social trap arises from a prevailing *illusion of unanimity*. One cannot know how many of the others share one's own doubts, and hence one hesitates to speak up with confidence. In a democratic setting, the illusion of unanimity usually involves "groupthink" and the protection of social cohesion. In a totalitarian setting the illusion of unanimity usually comes from the threat of punishment. Members of repressive societies stand to lose more than the approval of their peers for expressing dissent. They risk imprisonment, torture, or death.

Game theorists study the interactions over time of two or more persons, each one reaching decisions independently, but where the outcome depends partly on the other's decision. In such a situation one "strategizes"—reviews the various possibilities, as for example when two chess players or admirals analyze the situations that they and their opponent will create jointly. Game theory assumes that people calculate the probable rewards and costs of the options and choose the one that maximizes rewards and minimizes costs.

For example, consider the Eastern Europeans in 1989 who wanted to oust their Communist rulers. For them the enjoyment of human rights and democracy represented a "reward" for opposing the totalitarian rulers—but going to prison represented the possible "cost" of doing so. The "payoff" for a given course of action is the probable net reward (the expected reward minus the cost). If a high payoff seems likely, it is rational to perform the action, but if the payoff is low or negative, it is rational not to do so. "Payoff" must have been a gambler's term originally, but it can refer in game theory to any set of interests, including personal freedom.

Often the payoff for various possibilities will depend on how others behave. That is why people sometimes do things in a group that they would not do alone. Any single individual carrying a protest sign in public in the mid-1980s in Vilnius, Prague, East Berlin, or Moscow would have been arrested. However, the probability of this outcome diminishes if thousands of citizens protest together. The collective nature of the activity improves the payoff for each individual protester. The key to success is to recruit large numbers of others—yet in a totalitarian state, it is impossible to do so ahead of time without tipping off the police and having the plans blocked. Previously, tanks had quelled rebellions violently. In 1989, however, Gorbachev had made it plain that he would not intervene militarily. By announcing that fact, he reduced the probable cost of demonstrations and therefore increased the payoff. Crowds formed in one European capital after another; the citizens of the other countries heard radio reports describing the size of each rally, which enabled them to estimate the payoff for taking to the streets themselves. Night after night, larger crowds assembled, soldiers refused to shoot, and governments had to resign.

Thresholds and Dominoes
When the Communist regimes of Eastern Europe and the Soviet Union collapsed, about two years apart, virtually no pundits could claim to have predicted it. To explain why prediction was inherently impossible, the economist Timur Kuran has proposed a model of the "bandwagon" dynamic of those dramatic days.[3]

Suppose you and I live in a totalitarian state that we both secretly dislike, as do most of our countrymen. We know that no one alone can influence the regime and we are not eager to go to jail, lose our jobs, be expelled from university, tortured, or even reprimanded in a humiliating way for speaking out against the government. We must weigh each possibility.

Kuran suggests that in such decisions, we each estimate two different payoffs, which he calls "internal" and "external." The internal payoff consists of the dignity and self-respect that we can experience if we take a public stand against the government, or the shame we experience if we do not.

The external payoff is the overt penalty for taking such a public stand. It is determined by such factors as: How strong are our objections to the government's policies? How harshly are the secret police treating dissenters these days? How many of us are willing to "go public" simultaneously in opposing the regime?

Both the external and internal payoffs will differ from one person to the next. For any one individual they may also vary from one week to another, as the government's actions and other factors change. Your decision will be determined by comparing both payoffs. If the police become less harsh or if crowds of other protesters are in the streets, you may conclude that the *external* payoff for dissent has become more favorable. If you are outraged by some new offence by the rulers, your *internal* payoff for taking a public stand may increase.

Kuran says that for each one of us there is a threshold where both the inner and external payoffs become positive. Suppose, for example, that I think the cost of speaking out has declined to tolerable levels and, at the same time, I am coming to feel unbearably guilty for keeping silent. I may have reached my threshold—the moment when I will decide to stand up and be counted. Your threshold will probably differ from mine. Until we reach our thresholds, we continue to practice what Kuran calls "preference falsification." That is, we publicly pretend to agree with the Party. We lie.

In numbers there is strength. Nobody wants to be the only dissident in the country. Nobody even wants to be first to speak up, unless many others will follow. To act alone is dangerous. The support of others improves each person's external payoff.

But how many others have to be willing to join the opposition before our external payoff becomes positive and we reach our threshold? Again, that will vary. You may be willing to publicly oppose the government if 5 percent of the population does so too. My threshold may be higher; I may hold back until 30 percent of the population has openly declared their opposition. Your uncle's threshold may be very high; he will not breathe a word of criticism until 90 percent of the population has spoken out.

Kuran points out that "bandwagon" change takes place only when personal thresholds are distributed in a special way. Suppose, say, everyone is willing to be the second person but no one is willing to be the *first* to criticize the dictator in public. No demonstration would ever begin; everyone would continue "preference falsification" indefinitely. But one single person would be the "match that ignites the forest fire"—quite a powerful position to be in, if only she knew that it was so!

This was probably the case at Joan Baez's concert, but because she was a foreign celebrity, she could not be arrested. Her high payoff allowed her to start the bandwagon rolling. (And as a foreigner, my own high external payoff enabled me in Brezhnev's Moscow to say what TERMITES couldn't afford to utter—though I was not able to ignite a bandwagon reaction.)

Imagine another society of ten individuals (A through J) in which the distribution of thresholds resembles the proverbial row of dominoes. Hot-headed Mr. A is going to be the first person to speak up, whether anyone else does or not. Mrs. B is willing to back up anyone who protests, but will not take the initiative herself. Dr C is willing to speak up, but not earlier than as the third protester. Major D is willing to be the fourth. Principal E is willing to be the fifth. Reverend F is willing to speak out if half the people have already done so. Professor G will boldly take the podium to object to the government after 60 percent of the population has declared their opposition, becoming the seventh speaker. Mademoiselle H is not sure what she thinks about the government, but she does not want to be left out if something exciting is happening, so she will join in as the eighth protester. She will also drag along Lifeguard I, who will obligingly mumble something critical about the government as the ninth protester. Only Aunt J remains resolute to the end, refusing to speak a word of criticism against "The Great Leader," but by then the government has fallen anyway, toppled by the amazing outburst of 90 percent of the population.

Kuran's model depicts the conditions under which a dynamic for change can emerge. However, not all elements of his theory necessarily work as he supposes. Take, for example, the regime's harshness. Kuran assumes that when a government kills or imprisons protesters massively, it will successfully suppress the revolt by frightening others—raising the external cost and lowering the external payoff of political action. This is not necessarily so. Sometimes government violence prompts *more* instead of less action by the populace, especially if the violence is directed against unarmed, nonviolent protesters. One example from Czechoslovakia will illustrate.

In November 1989 several other Eastern European countries had already overturned their Communist regimes and the Czechs and Slovaks were feeling that their time had come. A demonstration was organized and the police not only allowed the march to take place but also even diverted it from a remote place into a main thoroughfare of Prague. Then something violent happened and a man fell to the pavement. His body was quickly covered by a blanket and the word went around that the police had killed a university student named Martin Šmíd. This violence prompted a much stronger response. New demonstrations now grew until, within a few days, the rulers simply resigned and left their government offices for the movement leaders to occupy. A citizens' inquiry was launched and established some curious facts. Apparently no one had been killed after all. Martin Šmíd was alive and well. The man under the blanket had been a secret police officer and he too was alive and well. Having discovered that much, the committee inexplicably disbanded without asking more.

The citizens of Prague all know this story and remain puzzled. Who organized the hoax? Some say that the CIA and KGB jointly planned this provocation so as to bring the Czechs to the streets in large numbers. Others say that the government staged it for exactly the opposite reason. Maybe the Communist regime intended to frighten people into silence. But violence can have paradoxical results. It is unpredictable whether it will silence or intensify the opposition.

* * *

Kuran's model explains why the 1989 revolutions spread so quickly and unexpectedly. However, notice that his model also explains the *failure* of revolutions to take off. It explains why totalitarianism usually persists. If the distribution of thresholds is not continuous, any uprising that is started will fail to spread because there are gaps in the row of dominoes.

Worse yet for the opposition, as Kuran points out, it is impossible to know the distribution of thresholds in a population. A dissident may sense that discontent has increased and the government is unpopular, but without knowing the *distribution* of thresholds, she cannot predict whether or not a mass movement can be ignited. With a slight gap in the "row of dominoes," the chain reaction would not be possible. This shows the extreme sensitivity of the population to slight variations in the distribution of thresholds.

The uncertainty as to the true distribution of thresholds works to the advantage of that ruler. Perhaps only rarely is the distribution right for starting a chain reaction. Moreover, even if the moment is right, no one may realize it, so the chance may be lost. That is why I have called this predicament a "social trap." It makes it very risky for an opposition group to take the lead in protesting.

In principle it should be possible to ascertain by anonymous opinion polls whether the distribution of thresholds is propitious. However, the regime may be able to block any such survey. Furthermore, people cannot be expected to answer abstract questions about their hypothetical "threshold levels." Finally, the population in a totalitarian state may not share their views with strangers at all. Prudent people engage in "preference falsification"—lying. But of course, it is their lying that is the source of their problem. As Alexander Solzhenitsyn pointed out, if everyone told the truth all the time, regardless of the cost, communist rule would break down immediately.[4] (Probably lots of other relationships, such as marriages, friendships, and businesses, would break down too.)

Also, we can question another of Kuran's notions—that each person's threshold is the point at which both payoffs become positive. That omits one category of people—fanatics or heroes. They choose to act even though they know it will cost them their lives. In such a case, the internal payoff must be very high indeed to offset a totally negative external payoff.

In the real world few people conform closely to Kuran's predictions. After all, specific relationships may matter as much as the size of a whole crowd. One may be profoundly influenced by the actions of particular acquaintances, yet utterly indifferent to others.

Nevertheless, Kuran's basic insight illumines the predicament so often described in the memoirs of Russian survivors of Stalin's purges, as they decided when to speak up and when to remain silent. And it raises a difficult issue: In totalitarian societies have people brought their difficulties on themselves by their own fear of speaking the truth?

Even to pose this question is unfair to those who spoke the truth and were punished. Still, it is true that bold dissidents, who were fewer than 1 percent of a totalitarian society's population,[5] blamed their society's plight on the conformity of all the others.[6] And the rest of the people held mixed feelings about the dissidents—admiring them, yet resenting them for demonstrating standards of behavior against which they, themselves, fell far short.[7] That resentment is one reason why TERMITES and most SHEEP never acknowledged the courage of BARKING DOGS.

Commitment, Intended and Unintended

The social trap outlined by Kuran is probably the best explanation for the *maintenance* of an established totalitarian society. However, we must explain not only how an existing totalitarian regime suppresses opposition but also how one comes into existence. Few people would intentionally create totalitarianism, yet such regimes have come into existence more than once. We need to examine the early phases of this process, especially the period when the inner circle coalesces and accepts a dictator.

In the Soviet case, the inner circle was the Bolshevik faction of the "Russian Social Democrats," as Marxists called themselves in the early days. The Bolsheviks would dominate the Soviet Union under Lenin's leadership and beyond. Other similar "vanguard" groups of fanatics are found in other totalitarian states—such as Nazi Germany and Maoist China—and a similar process must operate to bring them together. We can reconstruct some aspects of their interpersonal dynamics and learn from similar cases of non-political fringe groups.

* * *

It is one thing to show how hard it would have been to oust the Bolsheviks later and quite another thing to show how their movement originally attracted recruits and acquired power. Yet a theory of totalitarianism must explain both.

The most illuminating of the relevant social psychological studies was conducted by American psychologist Leon Festinger to explain the behavior of a doomsday cult called the "Seekers," who had formed around a spiritual leader, a Mrs. Keech. This charismatic housewife received word that their city would be destroyed by a flood, but that the Seekers would be rescued by flying saucers. Unable to avoid publicity, some members became socially stigmatized. Others spent their savings while awaiting doomsday, which passed uneventfully. Mrs. Keech then received a new message: God had been so impressed by the faith of the group that he had canceled the end of the world. After this anti-climax, instead of slinking away in embarrassment, the group stepped up their commitment, *sought out* the press, and tried to proselytize. Festinger had predicted this outcome in terms of "cognitive dissonance." According to this theory, people try to maintain general consistency among their beliefs, as well as between their beliefs and their observable behavior.

Cognitive dissonance is an uncomfortable state that seems to require some resolution. For example, if I believe that smoking harms health, but nevertheless I smoke, I can reduce the dissonance of these two cognitions either by quitting smoking or by avoiding news stories that remind me of the inconsistency between my actions and my beliefs.

The theory explains the Seekers' extra zeal *after* Mrs. Keech's prophecy had been disconfirmed. To reduce cognitive dissonance they tried to find new believers who would support their faith. Zeal is a predictable outcome of becoming involved with a cause that others do not find credible. It does not precede, but follows, disconfirmation, as understandable behavior in a social trap.

There are parallels between this process and a theory of commitment proposed by Howard Becker, which was based on game theory.[8] Since normal people tend to choose a course of action that maximizes their payoffs, we may try to influence others' actions by making one of their options more costly and another less costly. We may even do that to our *own* options by making "side bets" involving other interests of ours that were originally extraneous to the action. Thus if I seriously want to quit smoking, I may make a side bet to increase the cost of my own possible failure. For example, I may sign a legally binding pledge to donate my house and car to a charity if anyone ever sees me smoke again. Radically altering my payoff creates an irreversible commitment.

Becker points out that, while some commitments result from conscious decisions, others are "commitment by default." This may happen unintentionally, as for example when one paints oneself into a corner, or when one temporarily takes a disagreeable job with a pension that is not portable. When one is offered a more desirable job, the accrued pension may be too large to lose, so that one cannot afford to make the career change. *Any commitment arising from the unintended consequences of one's own actions is a social trap.* This is a common experience. If I invest more in a given line of activity than I can afford to lose, I am committed, whether I like it or not. Such investments need not be financial, of course. More often the investment at risk is one's reputation as a consistent person, entitled to feel pride, not humiliation.

Consider the case of George Lincoln Rockwell, who became the leader of the American Nazi Party and was finally assassinated. According to a woman who knew him as a young man, he used to enjoy shocking others, and would often make outrageous statements for sheer dramatic effect. He was always "on stage." At one point he went so far as to praise Hitler, expecting his statement to be taken for what it was: hyperbole. But his audience took him seriously, so he had to defend his position. The more he did so, the more he was stuck with his story, and bound to prove that he meant it. Gradually, his Nazi identity became so famous that he could not disavow it. He was "condemned to strut upon the stage" until he was finally shot down. Perhaps even jokingly, he had invested in something too costly to lose: his own public identity.[9] He stumbled into a trap of his own making.

I can recall many times when someone was "stuck with a story." A bluff, threat, or dare issued recklessly, but then challenged in public, may create a possibility of such painful humiliation that one will attempt to carry it off, despite terrible costs. There are also other types of verbal entanglements that the philosopher John Searle calls "speech acts"—utterances that create a new state of affairs that cannot be canceled with another equally simple utterance. Promises and oaths are examples. To say "I do" during a wedding is a speech act that cannot be reversed except through a legal action, perhaps requiring one to share his entire wealth with the unwanted spouse. Other speech acts also may be socially consequential, especially since shame is a feeling that people will go to great lengths to avoid.[10]

The Rockwell and Seekers cases can be explained both by Becker's theory of commitment as created by unwise side bets and by cognitive dissonance theory. This suggests that the two theories are alternative ways of describing the same human predicament: injudiciously putting one's own reputation for consistency at risk, and losing the gamble. In the hope of preserving a scrap of credibility, one then risks more and more, much as unwise investors must sometimes "throw good money after bad" so as not to lose their stakes. Eventually, they may lose even more anyway. This is how people sometimes are recruited to organizations that they would not have chosen independently to join—cults, terrorist groups, Nazi movements, extreme political parties, and other deviant communities.

This factor is often compounded by other types of "side bets" that may also be made unwittingly. For example, one may become peripherally involved in a deviant group before it is yet as radical as it will later become. One may nevertheless unexpectedly incur the full social penalties for belonging, such as ostracism, loss of employment, expulsion from university, or exile to Siberia. Such sanctions, in turn, spoil the conventional relationships that might moderate one's tendencies. Unwittingly committed to their new cause, such radicals are forced to depend more on each other, sometimes just while their group's teachings are becoming even more bizarre. Something of this sort probably befell a young Russian biology student named Ulyanov in 1886.

Alexander Ulyanov's Loose Talk

Alexander Ulyanov was a good student but socially immature, the son of an upwardly mobile, rather conservative[11] school inspector who had been elevated to the nobility. Apparently the young man became acquainted with a revolutionary group of students in St. Petersburg. The core group consisted of three: Lukashevich, Govorukhin, and Shevyrev. They were critical of Czar Alexander III. Little definite evidence exists about their early conversations, but there must have been some bravado, perhaps similar to George Lincoln Rockwell's initial Nazi pretensions. Someone must have professed admiration for terrorists and the others must have joined the chorus. Before long, the group must have made dangerous declarations to each other that, if exposed, would have incurred grave difficulties. They could justify this reckless talk only by solemnly professing their dedication to the Russian people, the *narod* to whose welfare the self-sacrificing terrorists of the day were committed. When the circle published a proclamation, Ulyanov was active in composing and distributing it. Having gone so far, it would be hard to explain why a privileged group of youths should not live up to their own rash words. Soon they had promised each other to collaborate in assassinating the Czar.

The responsibility fell on Ulyanov, as a competent young scientist, to manufacture the nitroglycerine. The would-be assassins assembled in Nevsky Prospect on March 1, 1887 to carry out their plans, but the secret police had heard of the scheme and arrested them. Shevyrev and Govorukhin, the original ringleaders, already had both fled, understandably preferring dishonor to the death penalty, leaving Alexander and Lukashevich in charge. Though all thirty-one members of the group were arrested, most of them wrote contrite letters from prison to the Czar begging for clemency, which was granted. Alexander's mother arrived in St. Petersburg and also wrote to the Czar, pointing out what a bright student her son was, as if that were a persuasive point. Allowed to visit Alexander, she implored him to beg for mercy. Instead, he proudly confessed to more crimes than he had probably committed. He explained, "Imagine, mama, that two men are confronting each other in a duel. One has already fired a shot at his opponent, the other one has not yet fired; and then the one who has already tried to kill his opponent turns to him with the request not to use his weapon. No, I cannot act in such a way."[12] He preferred to lose his life than to lose face. Shortly thereafter, he was hanged.

Alexander was the victim of a social trap, and his unreflective actions created other social traps that ensnared his mother and his siblings. Shame and loyalty combined to implicate the Ulyanov family, none of whom had previously been interested in such issues.[13]

His sister Anna, who had known nothing of his illegal activities, was immediately implicated. Arriving at his apartment while it was being searched, she was arrested and kept in prison until Sasha had been executed.[14] Anna and the rest of her family would all remain permanently stigmatized. After the execution, the whole town ostracized the family, who found it necessary to move away forever.

Despite (or probably because of) the shame, Alexander's family tried to defend his honor by adopting his political cause. His younger brother Volodya, who had never been interested in social issues, plunged into revolutionary literature. After being refused permission to go abroad to study, he read law independently and passed his examinations at St. Petersburg. Cut off from the usual channels of a conventional career, he soon became a true revolutionary and adopted the name that became famous, Vladimir Ilyich Lenin.

Lenin's commitment to revolution began almost instantaneously with the death of his older brother, whose sudden notoriety "stuck" his whole family with his story. As biographer Philip Pomper has suggested, and he "evidently felt that he had to try to be Alexander."[15]

My interpretation of Alexander's absurd social trap depends as much on Max Weber's method, *verstehen,* as on historical evidence, but it is consistent with the story that biographers have told. It also has much in common with the stories of several other revolutionaries in Lenin's circle who were recruited while living away from home among other youths. After a brush with the law, they were usually exiled to Siberia, into dependent relationships with other radicals. For example, Leon Trotsky became radicalized in secondary school under the influence of a group of youthful revolutionaries, with whom he lived in a scruffy commune.[16] Stalin began in much the same way, coming under the radical influence of fellow seminarians in Tbilisi.[17]

Marxists of that period were revolutionaries without being totalitarians. They were anti-authoritarian in ideology. Even Alexander Ulyanov, who was more a Narodnik (a populist) than a Marxist, claimed that only because free speech was prohibited had he found it necessary to resort to violence.

Probably people usually became Social Democrats by being compromised in the dynamics of "groupthink" and stuck with their stories in attempting to reduce cognitive dissonance and avoid shame. Even so, however, this theory does not explain their subsequent support for a totalitarian regime. Marxists were not inherently obedient toward dictators. Quite the contrary. To explain the next stage of the transition to authoritarian rule we must consider another group dynamic different from those we have just explored. We must explain how a dictator acquires his enormous power.

The Great Leader's Credit Rating

Dictators are like other politicians, only more so. Up to a certain critical stage, their methods of acquiring power are similar to those of democratic leaders. The acquisition of such power is best explained in Richard Neustadt's book, *Presidential Power,* which deals with American presidents. Neustadt shows that, however powerful a role the presidency is on paper, reality is very different. He quotes Harry Truman in 1952, sitting in the Oval Office and reflecting on what would happen if Eisenhower should win the coming election. "He'll sit here and he'll say, 'Do this! Do that!' *And nothing will happen.* Poor Ike."[18]

Truman was right. Presidential orders do not execute themselves. The president must build his support by accumulating a reputation based on a successful and well-publicized series of self-fulfilling prophecies.[19] So long as the leader is believed to be invincible, prudent subordinates will obey promptly. Power is like a credit rating, built up strategically by borrowing ever-increasing amounts of money and scrupulously repaying as agreed. Successful presidents start by tackling easy challenges and making their victories visible so they can move on to more difficult political fights.

In a democracy power, like beauty, is largely in the eye of the beholder. Indeed, the most important fights may be the ones that never take place at all because everyone knows who would win. Only fools take on hopeless causes and demonstrate their own weakness. Astute politicians try to limit their actions to fights they can win, for every visible loss or concession diminishes their reputation and encourages the opposition.

Until they become dictators, revolutionary leaders and führers have to observe these principles too. Each would-be "Great Leader" must cultivate support by bargaining and appealing to his followers' interests. During this pre-totalitarian period, there may be considerable give-and-take with others in the Party. Lenin skillfully bargained within the Party for several years, presenting himself as a team player. He did not show his true colors until the Second Party Congress of 1903, when he insisted on creating a hard, disciplined "vanguard party" to usher socialism to Russia. Breaking with the more pluralistic Mensheviks, he instituted the policy of "democratic centralism" which was authoritarian from the outset and soon abandoned all democratic pretensions. That was his crucial move toward totalitarianism.

* * *

The conformity characteristic of Janis's "groupthink" differs from that of the CPSU's inner circle during later repressive phases. In a democracy the penalty for dissent is social rejection—mild in comparison to totalitarian subjugation. Still, groupthink may be a precondition for more brutal dictatorial control. When a group is already enforcing consensus by informal pressures, only a small step is required to add terror to the penalties.

Lenin strengthened his power further in 1921, when he banned factions in the Bolshevik Party. His suppression of dissent created totalitarian conditions that would survive himself. Lenin was not entirely responsible for the prolonged cult that made him into the Soviet Union's saint after his death.[20] However, his banning of factions does mean that he was responsible for creating the worst period of dictatorship, which occurred in 1937, long after Stalin succeeded him.

There must exist a threshold—a period or a single event—when people look around at each other and see everyone else obeying on the basis of well-founded fear. *At this very moment, totalitarianism has arrived.* Each individual can sense how great has become the price of dissent, and no one dares speak freely anymore—hardly even to think. The social trap has sprung!

Nadezda Mandelstam has described that period in her book, *Hope Against Hope*. She was the widow of Osip Mandelstam, the greatest Russian poet of the century, whom Stalin exiled to Siberia and then murdered. Nadezha wrote,

> In the middle of the twenties, when the atmospheric pressure began to weigh more heavily on us—at critical periods it was heavier than lead—people all at once started to avoid each other. This could not be explained only by fear of informers and denunciation—we had not yet had time to get really scared of these. It was rather the onset of a kind of numbness, the first symptoms of lethargy. . . . [N]obody confided their doubts to their children: why condemn them to death? And then suppose the child talked in school and brought disaster to the whole family? And why tell it things it didn't need to know? Better it should live like everybody else. . . . So the children grew, swelling the ranks of the hypnotized.[21]

Sometimes a dictator tries to protect his own image, even while managing the transition to openly brutal methods. This can be accomplished, to some extent, by putting someone else in charge of the worst excesses of repression. Stalin did so by putting successive brutes, from Yagoda to Beria, into the role of masterminding the terror. Hitler had Rudolf Hess and Goebbels. Mao's equivalent monster was Kang Sheng.

Nothing is more confusing than asking people who had been in a totalitarian trap what they had really believed. Hardly anyone can explain it. One might suppose that people would know whether they were coerced into pretending to believe or whether they really did believe what they were told. This distinction was rarely clear to those who experienced repression. They had motives piled on top of different motives. Ideology was combined with terror, and for some people the one did not cancel out the other, but combined in a complex psychological fusion. It is not simple retrospectively to tease apart true beliefs and internalized ideology. Torture victims wrote "Long Live Stalin" on the walls with their own blood. Most people were believers at some level. People are truly persuaded by witnessing the unanimity of others—even when the others are saying that the shorter line is the longer one. The outcome may be the same, whether the unanimity results from terror or from groupthink.

* * *

I have suggested that two generic human problems lie at the motivational root of most social traps. The first is the universal need to appear consistent and credible to others. The other is the difficulty of coordinating mass opposition to the dictator while most people engage in "preference falsification." A transition into, and then out of, totalitarianism probably includes the following stages.

First, a few revolutionaries become compromised. Perhaps some of them are convinced fanatics from the outset, but most of them are probably trapped by their own reckless side bets. For each person, a basic motivation is to retain a reputation for cognitive consistency. Loss of it brings shame, an excruciating emotion.

Next in the evolution of a totalitarian system the leader emerges. At first he must behave much as do democratic political leaders—negotiating, bargaining, and building up his credibility by showing consistency and winning challenges. During this phase, the coterie of followers expect each other to conform; this is "groupthink."

At the next stage, the leader—the proto-dictator—must put himself beyond the challenge of ordinary debate and rationality. There are two aspects to this new pretension: (a) he must make a demonstration of ruthlessness sufficient to intimidate his rivals, and (b) he must establish his charisma by uttering profound statements that everyone accepts, even if they are nonsensical. The point is to prove that if anyone dissents, he will do so alone and will suffer for it. With this discovery comes the recognition that the Party, perhaps even the whole society, is in a new, seemingly permanent condition: totalitarianism. Now there are secret police around; now the neighbors and colleagues are spying. After this fear of speaking is established as permanent, the authority of the dictator can be transferred from one incumbent to another. In the Soviet case, totalitarianism continued with ups and downs for thirty-six years after the death of Stalin, reinforced from time to time with new repressions.

Such a system seems irreversible and is truly stable, for no one can determine the distribution of thresholds within the population—the extent of willingness to take open action or to speak against the regime.

Nevertheless, eventually those conditions begin to break down. Skepticism increases, possibly because the regime fails to produce the promised results. (For example, the Soviet failure to "bury" capitalism gradually became apparent.) The disillusionment may be articulated quietly by intellectuals and the costs and rewards of opposing the regime may be changing. During this phase if there is more contact with foreigners, additional strains are placed on the beliefs of the ordinary citizens. In the Soviet case, this came from contact with Western peace activists and access to foreign radio programming.

This may stimulate new resistance to the totalitarian regime, especially where it had never been adopted willingly, as was the case in Eastern European societies.

The Soviet citizens, on the other hand, could not blame their persecution on outsiders. For them, the collapse resulted in low morale, even though the dictatorial regime destroyed itself voluntarily from the top. When faith vanished, no new alternative doctrine took its place.

But there will be other stages. Wait in hope, Russia, for democracy is coming. Maybe.

Notes

1. Solomon Asch, *Social Psychology* (Englewood Cliffs, NJ: Prentice-Hall, 1952), 450–501.

2. Irving Lester Janis, *Victims of Groupthink: A Psychological Study of Policy Decisions and Fiascoes*, 2nd ed. (Boston: Houghton Mifflin, 1982).

3. Timur Kuran, "Now Out of Never: The Element of Surprise in the East European Revolution of 1989," in *Liberalization and Democratization: Change in the Soviet Union*

and Eastern Europe, ed. Nancy Bermeo, (Baltimore: Johns Hopkins University Press, 1991), 7–48.

4. Alexander Solzhenitsyn, "The Smatterers," in *From Under the Rubble,* trans. A. M. Brock et al. (Boston: Little, Brown, 1975), 275.

5. Ludmilla Alexeyeva and Paul Goldberg, *The Thaw Generation: Coming of Age in the Post-Stalinist Era* (Boston: Little, Brown, 1990).

6. Václav Havel, "The Power of the Powerless," in *The Power of the Powerless: Citizens Against the State in Central-Eastern Europe,* ed. John Keane and trans. Paul Wilson (Armonk, NY: M.E. Sharpe, 1985), 42.

7. Jirina Siklová, "Dilemmas of Transition: A View From Prague," *Peace Review* 4, no. 4 (Winter 1992): 24–28.

8. Howard S. Becker, "Notes on the Concept of Commitment," *American Journal of Sociology* 66, no. 1 (July 1960): 32–40.

9. The nature of this identity can be seen in an interview with Rockwell, *Alex Haley: The Playboy Interviews* (New York: Ballantine, 1993), 168–210.

10. This recognition of shame's central importance has also been discussed by Thomas J. Scheff in his book, *Bloody Revenge: Emotions, Nationalism, and War* (Boulder: Westview, 1994).

11. Nikolai Valentinov, *The Early Years of Lenin,* trans. Rolf Theen. (Ann Arbor: University of Michigan Press, 1969), 63; also Dmitri Volkogonov, *Lenin: A New Biography,* trans. and ed. Harold Shukman (New York: The Free Press, 1994), 13.

12. Valentinov, 101.

13. Valentinov, 77.

14. Leon Trotsky, *The Young Lenin,* trans. Max Eastman, ed. Maurice Friedberg. (Garden City, NY: Doubleday, 1972), 90.

15. Philip Pomper, *Lenin, Trotsky, and Stalin: The Intelligentsia and Power* (New York: Columbia University Press, 1990), 23.

16. Pomper, 105.

17. Pomper, 163, 165.

18. Richard E. Neustadt, *Presidential Power and the Modern Presidents: The Politics of Leadership from Roosevelt to Reagan* (New York: Free Press, 1990), 10.

19. Neustadt, 40.

20. Volkogonov, 1.

21. Nadezhda Mandelstam, *Hope Against Hope*, trans. Max Hayward (New York: Modern Library, 1999), 44–45.

Chapter 14: Quest? What Quest?

I hope that the title of this book is not false advertising, alluding as it does to a "quest" for peace and democracy. Perhaps you doubt that most Russians really want democracy, and that's a fair question. Unmistakably, however, they do want peace, perhaps even more than most other societies, because their lives have been so scarred by past wars. World War II took an estimated 26.6 million lives within the postwar Soviet boundaries.[1]

Initially my primary topic was the Cold War and the challenge of disarming nuclear weapons, and only to a lesser extent the defense of human rights. But the Cold War ended, whereas democracy in Russia has not progressed since the Soviet Union was dissolved. Nowadays no one expects war between Russia and any other major power (Georgia being a minor exception) and so over time, as with most other people, my attention shifted toward problems that seem more immediate—especially democracy.

But we must not lose sight of the other issue. Nuclear weapons are still an existential threat to humankind's future. Ordinary citizens are less worried about these weapons than they were during the Cold War, but complacency is absolutely unwarranted. Here we'll address them and also democracy.

Peace and Disarmament

There are several widespread misconceptions that need to be corrected. One is that the West won the Cold War by "containing" Communism and spending more on weapons than the Soviets could match, until finally Gorbachev "blinked."

I hope this book has helped dispel that myth. Neither side "won" the Cold War. Or perhaps both sides did, for it ended on terms that were favorable to the national interests of Western countries and the Soviet Union alike.[2] Moreover, Gorbachev was far ahead of the West in adopting such peaceable policies as common security, reasonable sufficiency, unilateral initiatives, and non-provocative defense. Although these ideas originated in the West, the United States government never even got round to considering them. Gorbachev was the leader; he liberated us all from the fiendish and exorbitant Cold War. For that the whole of humankind should thank him.

But he did not succeed in abolishing nuclear weapons throughout the world. That task remains our joint responsibility.

Another current misconception is the assumption that grave nuclear threats today are presented only by terrorists or "rogue states" that are trying to obtain nuclear arsenals for themselves. That is too optimistic a notion, for the existing arsenals of the Cold War superpowers remain enormous. They have multiplied over and over since the nuclear age began, and they still could be used by mistake, if not even by intent, with ghastly results.

The main effect of today's nuclear bombs, if exploded in cities, would be to ignite fires. The bomb that hit Hiroshima caused a firestorm covering about 12 km^2, but an average Russian warhead today would set about 225 km^2 ablaze. As of 2009 there were about 23,200 nuclear weapons on Earth, about 95 percent of which belonged to the U.S. and Russia. About 2,200 of them were mounted on some 900 missiles that could be launched within a few minutes, to reach their targets within twelve to thirty minutes. Once launched, they cannot be called back.

Nor is there at present any defense against them. A first-strike by a large number of missiles will destroy the missiles of the opponent while they are still on the launch pad. The only way to prevent this is to launch them before the incoming missiles can reach them and destroy them. Thus we have a situation called "launch-on-warning," whereby missiles are supposed to retaliate before any incoming missile arrives. They are meant to be launched as soon as signals warn that the other side has begun the war.

Unfortunately, false warnings are not unusual. It is entirely possible, therefore, for a nuclear war to begin as a result of human or technological errors. In such a case, the result would be enormous loss of life, as well as environmental devastation. In even a regional conflict, if nuclear weapons were exploded in cities, as much as five million tons of soot would be released. The result would be catastrophic climate change, for smoke would block out the sun and cause an ice age lasting several growing seasons. The resulting famine would kill most of the human population.[3]

Yet there is still hope. President Obama is committed to reducing nuclear weapons and eventually eliminating them from the planet, though he does not expect this to be completed soon. A follow-on treaty to the START agreement was signed by the United States and Russia in April 2010, modestly reducing the number of weapons but, more importantly, including new provisions for verification and more rigorous counting rules. Moreover, both countries have released reviews of their changing security policies. Russia's proposal seems mainly intended to shift decisive control away from NATO and toward institutions to which Russia and its Asian allies and neighbors belong.[4] Their document is not unrealistic or unreasonable, but it has received little attention in Europe.

Obama's nuclear policy review offered, as usual, a compromise aimed at satisfying both hawks and doves.[5] Without going so far as to promise No-First-Use of nuclear weapons, it does promise not to use them against countries that belong to the Nuclear Non-Proliferation Treaty and observe its conditions faithfully. Obama's resumption of work toward ratifying the Comprehensive Test

Ban Treaty has to proceed with an eye to winning votes in the Senate, and this constrains his personal inclination toward disarmament.

While the terms of the START follow-on treaty were being announced I phoned Pavel Podvig, a Russian-born specialist on American and Russian nuclear weaponry who now works at Stanford University, to discuss the prospects for further cuts in the future. He reminded me not to judge in terms of the number of nuclear weapons that are being reduced, for there is such a stupendous redundancy that they could be cut to a fraction of the existing arsenal, yet leave enough to end civilization. Moreover, he said,

> If you don't work on improving the basic relationship, there is no way you can negotiate [further] reductions. If you go to this with a Cold War, bean-counting approach, there will be mistrust. . . .
>
> I think it is a matter of engaging Russia, making sure that society in Russia in general does not see [a nuclear] confrontation with the West as something conceivable. And unless we go in that direction, unless we build relationships that do not include this confrontational element, there is no way that we could negotiate the nuclear forces down to zero or to any reasonably small number. I don't think there is a contradiction with democracy because the kind of things that I'm talking about, they will not happen unless Russia is more open and democratic.[6]

So again we are reminded that peace depends on democracy.

Democracy

We need not ask here whether democracy is the best form of government, since other authors, including recently Larry Diamond[7] and Michael McFaul,[8] already have provided convincing answers. To be sure, democratic governments make mistakes. Human wisdom is limited, even where governance is superb. Besides, every existing democratic state is a work in progress, always requiring improvement. For example, many Americans nowadays concede that the government in Washington is somehow "broken." As the journalist Thomas Friedman regularly points out with dismay, democratic America is paralyzed by political gridlock, whereas the authoritarian rulers of China can issue commands that are promptly fulfilled, to their competitive advantage.[9]

Nevertheless, freedom is better than slavery. That is the point that matters.

Besides, whether or not I am "my brother's keeper" I make us both safer by enabling him to live in a democracy. Established democratic states do not make war against other democratic states.[10] Thus democratization, when completed globally, will end international warfare. Surely that's another point that matters. Its corollary is this: The promotion of democracy is the promotion of peace.

But there's a catch—or actually two catches. First, a surprising number of citizens in liberal democracies now oppose any effort to promote democracy abroad. And, second, Russians don't much want it anyway.

What went wrong? Why did democracy promotion fail and create such a backlash? Unfortunately the United States bears primary responsibility for this debacle. Diplomacy is about relationships, but the improvement Gorbachev wrought between Russia and the West began deteriorating in some ways even before the Cold War ended in 1990. Russians' attitude toward democratic governance has been tainted by their well-founded case of anti-Americanism, which might easily have been avoided. I'll identify the worst mistakes that spoiled the relationship.

When Gorbachev allowed—even pressured—Eastern European countries to become independent, this posed a question about the future of NATO's dealings with those countries. In 2008 Jack Matlock, who had been the U.S. ambassador to the Kremlin, recalled that period, noting that President G. H. W. Bush had

> said, to some degree explicitly, "Let Eastern Europe go free. We will not take advantage of that. Que sera, sera! Let the Eastern Europeans decide."
>
> And it was in that framework that, a couple of months later in February of '90 . . . [Secretary of State James] Baker made the statement to Gorbachev that if united Germany was allowed to stay in NATO, there would be no extension of NATO's jurisdiction to the East. Not one inch!
>
> Now, Gorbachev never asked for a formal commitment. We would have been happy to give him one if it were legally possible. I don't know how you could legally bind future presidents on things like that. But the [point] that I want to make here is that, starting with Reagan but particularly with Bush, we tried to frame the relationship as one in which, if the Soviet Union liberalized and allowed East Europe and the other Communist countries to go democratic, we would not move in and use this against them. Also, although we had always favored the return of independence to the Baltic countries, we did not favor the breakup of the Soviet Union.[11]

But when the Warsaw Treaty Organization (WTO) was dissolved in 1991, three of its former members—Poland, Czechoslovakia, and Hungary—requested admission to NATO. In 1994, NATO offered them membership in a new organization, Partnership for Peace, which was designed as a consolation prize. But by 1996 President Clinton was speaking publicly about the prospect of offering the first-tier countries actual membership in NATO. This was the opening move in several changes. In 2003 Bulgaria, Estonia, Latvia, Lithuania, Romania, Slovakia (and Slovenia, which had not belonged to WTO) were admitted to the alliance. Other such admissions—notably Georgia and Ukraine—were still being considered even in 2010, greatly to the displeasure of Russia, where the whole affair is considered a broken promise and a military threat.

Most Russians feel that the U.S. disregarded their interests and concerns during the Yeltsin years, a time marked by chaos and financial ruination. Now that their country has become stronger again, they have no desire to emulate the Western democracies, which they now distrust and regard as enemies. If the Cold War is over, they ask, why was Russia not invited to join NATO, just as some of the former Soviet republics are now being offered membership? (My own question is somewhat different: If the Cold War is over, why didn't NATO dissolve itself at the same time as its counterpart, the WTO? If humankind needs a military force to protect people around the world, a UN peacekeeping force would be more legitimate than NATO.)

Another act of negligence that need not have happened was a financial one. Gorbachev was in dire financial straits in the spring of 1991, trying desperately to reform the Soviet economy. His allies Margaret Thatcher and Ronald Reagan were already out of office, but Thatcher came to Moscow, invited Ambassador Matlock to dinner, and asked him to intercede with Bush, saying, "We've got to help Mikhail. . . . History will not forgive us if we fail to rally to his support."[12] But although Matlock agreed with her, in the end he observed that President Bush

> did not seem willing to organize an international structure to help bring the So-
> viet Union into the world economy as a constructive partner. He lacked the vi-
> sion of how his leadership might shape the future and thus chose a reactive
> stance: waiting for Gorbachev to find the keys to reform for himself, he would
> from time to time mumble words of either encouragement or reproach, care-
> fully avoiding commitments to specific action.[13]

Had Gorbachev received bail-out help from the West, he would not have been vulnerable to the coups that ended his presidency and the life of the Soviet Union—calamities for him that the Western countries actually did not want but did little to prevent.

But it was President Clinton who committed some of the most egregious offenses against Russian democracy, though he considered himself a great friend of President Yeltsin. Indeed, one might even say that his friendship with Yeltsin *was* the most egregious offense against Russian democracy, for he stayed loyal to Yeltsin no matter how gravely he harmed his country. Everyone knew that the Russian president's rupture with the Soviet Union was an illegal coup, motivated by personal spite toward Gorbachev. Everyone knew that Yeltsin's regime was corrupt and increasingly autocratic. Everyone knew that he stole the 1996 presidential election. Everyone could watch Yeltsin's tanks shell his own parliament, killing scores of elected deputies and many others. Everyone knew that Yeltsin's new Russian constitution gave himself far too much power and the legislators far too little. Yet Clinton never criticized his friend Boris. Not surprisingly, the Russians concluded that Yeltsin and his team had been democrats, as they claimed to be, though they clearly ran the worst possible government. Who would want democracy if that is what it's like?

Russians still complain that the West approved of Yeltsin. In fact, a few Americans apparently did approve, though I personally never met one who said so. But then, my friends are mainly peace activists who, I can attest with affection, truly believe in democracy.

It was also Clinton who used NATO in 1999 to help Kosovo win its separatist fight against Serbia, again ignoring the objections of Russians, who consider the Serbs their Slavic kinfolk. Later, after much of the world had bestowed diplomatic recognition on the now-independent Kosovo, Russia would seize this as a precedent to use against American interests. In 2008 Putin carried out a military intervention against Georgia (which was not entirely unwarranted) and offered to recognize South Ossetia's independence on exactly the same principle as the U.S. had used in recognizing Kosovo's independence. What's sauce for the goose is sauce for the gander. Next time, the United States should work to establish an international law that they can live with if applied universally. They could, for example, ask the World Court for an advisory opinion about the circumstances under which separatists' claims should be recognized.

Also antagonizing to Russians were the "color revolutions" in former Soviet republics. After Georgia and Ukraine became sovereign states with the breakdown of the USSR, their citizens managed to oust crooked governments by means of nonviolent revolutions. Most Russians disliked those results, but what really upset them was the involvement of foreign governments in the process.

These unfriendly U.S./Russian interactions were matched by troubling military developments. The United States withdrew from the ABM Treaty in 2002 and proceeded developing a system of ballistic missile defense, even arranging to install bases around Russia's perimeter. President George W. Bush insisted that these were not designed to neutralize Russia's own missiles but instead to counter Iran's future missiles. Still, he rejected the sensible offer from President Putin to join in this effort and place the anti-missile installations in Azerbaijan or another country closer to Iran. President Obama later softened a bit, announcing his intention instead to put missile defense systems on ships in the Mediterranean. This prospect has not assuaged the anxiety of Russians who, after a century of turmoil, desire stability and calm above all else. President Medvedev has repeated Russia's offer to cooperate with the U.S. on missile defense, and this collaboration, if accepted, may improve their relationship.

The United States and its NATO partners bear much of the responsibility for the loss of momentum toward peace and democracy with Russia. For two decades, the U.S. considered itself the victor of the Cold War and treated Russia as a vanquished foe whose aspirations could be ignored. It is not surprising that Russians—the leadership and the populace alike—became hostile. Peace depends on trust, and if you want to be trusted, you have to be trustworthy—by keeping your word and telling the truth. The U.S., especially under Presidents Clinton and George W. Bush, violated Russias' trust and left them questioning the value of democracy. Even the "New Political Thinkers" were disillusioned.

Visitors to Moscow started noticing the downturn. Harvard political scientist Celeste Wallander noticed it just after Russians broke with the West over Chechnya and Kosovo. She wrote in 2001,

> In the past two years, I have participated in many meetings and conferences with leading figures of new thinking, and the chasm on Kosovo and Chechnya between Russian and U.S. scholars who are otherwise on the same intellectual wave-length is startling. It is as if we live in different worlds.
>
> One can still visit many of the new thinkers at the institutes that served as the incubators of revolutionary ideas in the late Soviet years. Where one used to visit offices bursting with big-name scholars, research assistants, and foreign visitors, however, one now finds quiet—and frequently empty—offices.[14]

I first noticed the same antipathy toward the United States and New Political Thinking in 1997 at an International Peace Bureau conference in Moscow. By then public opinion, even among Russian peace activists, had turned against the new thinkers—especially the chief one, Gorbachev himself. The Moscow organizers had not invited him to the meeting and had nothing good to say about him. Bruce Kent, who had headed the British peace group CND for many years, took the floor and gave a rousing speech to the Russian activists, reminding them of Gorbachev's extraordinary contributions to world peace. But it was, as Wallander said, "as if we lived in different worlds." And matters would get worse over the next decade, as most Americans came to reciprocate the mistrust, regarding President Putin as an authoritarian ruler who had squandered the opportunities that Gorbachev had created.

For his own part, Gorbachev had maintained an ambivalent but mainly positive attitude toward Putin throughout Putin's presidency. Only in 2010 did he begin to criticize the Russian regime seriously. He even said that authoritarian rule had been justified during Putin's first term, but that other approaches were needed now.

> There is a feeling that authorities fear civil society and want to control everything. . . . There will be no modernization if people stay aside as pawns again. There is only one recipe for them to feel as citizens and be citizens—it is democracy, law-governed state, open and honest dialogue between authorities and the people. Stabilization of the situation in the country cannot be the only and final aim.[15]

* * *

When Barack Obama took office, he pledged to "re-set" the U.S./Russia relationship. Diplomacy involves mainly the care and management of relationships, which Obama is trying to do. If Russians' dislike of democracy reflected only their anti-Americanism, then the prospect of recovery would seem favorable during Obama's presidency.

Still, the management of relationships involves a balancing performance when it comes to supporting both democracy and interactions with a regime that manifestly opposes democracy. President Putin announced early on that he wanted no liberal Western-style democracy but would create something called "managed democracy," by which he evidently means ordinary political repression. Putin is vastly better than Stalin—thank God!—but instead of becoming more democratic, Russia has become less so under his and Medvedev's rule.

You may recall that Freedom House rates all the countries of the world in terms of two dimensions of democracy: political rights and civil liberties. The scores on each dimension range from 1 to 7, where 7 is the worst. Each country is given a verbal rating too: as free, partially free, or not free. In 1996 Russia was considered partially free, scoring 4 on political rights and 5 in civil liberties. It has gone downhill since then, scoring 6 on political rights and 5 on civil liberties, with an overall status of "not free."[16]

This decline has not perturbed many Russian citizens, however, for democracy is currently not very important to them. For example, the Pew Research Center carried out a survey in 2009 on the importance attached to democratic institutions in eight post-Communist European countries. They combined six values (fair judiciary, multiparty elections, free media, free religion, free speech, and civilian control of the military) to form a single indicator of democracy and discovered that 66 percent of Hungarians considered these as very important. In descending order, the others were Bulgaria (60 percent), Czech Republic (52 percent), Poland (52 percent), and Ukraine (50 percent). But Russia was at the bottom of the list; only 39 percent considered these democratic features very important.[17]

What Russians generally want more are stability and prosperity. In a different 2009 study, some Russians were asked to choose between public order and democracy. Some 59 percent of the respondents agreed that "public order is more important even if some principles of democracy need to be violated and some personal freedoms need to be restricted."[18]

Early in 2010 I phoned Andrei Kamenshikov, the peace activist who works in the North Caucasus, and we talked about the attitudinal changes resulting from Russia's economic collapses—two crises in the 1990s. He said,

> Unfortunately, most people associate this with the term "democracy." For those who lost a lot during that period, democracy is not popular. People want stability, peace, and economic improvement. That has been happening over the past decade, so people don't care much if their democratic rights are seriously limited. Today, the results of elections are known well before they take place. Most people don't care.[19]

Nevertheless, a substantial number of Russians—especially among the young—do want to live in a country where they can criticize the government aloud and take initiative from below in addressing social issues. Some of them are brave pro-democracy activists, such as Oleg Kozlovsky, the leader of the Oborona movement mentioned in chapter 12, and Yury Dzhibladze. Both of these activists published expressions of their discontent with the level of support they are receiving from Washington. The backlash in the West against democracy promotion has cast doubt, even in the Left, as to the legitimacy of supporting the very people abroad whose democratic values we share.

Russian pro-democracy activists understand Obama's dilemma, of course. If you value peace you don't criticize your counterpart; if you value freedom you must speak up whenever it is threatened. If you want both, as Obama does, you're in a dilemma.

All peace and human rights workers are familiar with that dilemma. I faced it at Moscow peace conferences in the early 1980s. My own solution was to speak up, but with extreme politeness. That brought me into contact for the first time with TERMITES who thanked me for giving voice to their opinions, which they could not express in public. The KGB, however, did not hold me in the same generous regard. When I handed around some *Peace Magazines* containing a story about former Trustbuilders who had visited Toronto, they seized the copies and expelled me from Russia.[20]

Other people adopt different solutions to that dilemma, as I was reminded upon my return home. Two women friends came to see me and informed me that they were expelling me from a group in which I had been a founding member—the Toronto/Volgograd friendship society. They had heard of my expulsion from Moscow, which they imagined would jeopardize their warm contacts with Volgograd. (For the same reason, they had declined to sign a petition asking the Soviet Union to free Sakharov from house arrest.) They didn't realize how much the Volgograd TERMITES *wanted* them to speak up about human rights.

Nor did they realize that Toronto and Volgograd—indeed all of us, everywhere—are on a quest for both peace and democracy. That is the human journey. Bon voyage, Russia!

Notes

1. Michael Ellman, S. Maksudov, "Soviet Deaths in the Great Patriotic War: A Note," *Europe Asia Studies* 46, No. 4 (July 1994): 671.

2. Jack F. Matlock, lecture at the Kennan Institute (Woodrow Wilson Center) March 15, 2010, discussing his book, *Superpower Illusions: How Myths and False Ideologies Led America Astray and How to Return to Reality* (New Haven: Yale University Press, 2009).

3. Steven Starr, MT, "Climatic Effects of Nuclear War," *Peace Magazine* 25, no. 3 (July–September 2009): 6; and "Regional Nuclear War Could Devastate Global Climate," *Science Daily,* 11 December 2006.

4. Andrey S. Makarychev, "Russia and its New Security Architecture in Europe: A Critical Examination of the Concept," Centre for European Policy Studies, Working Document No. 310 (February 2009), http://ceps.be/ceps/download/1612 (accessed April 20, 2010).

5. Joshua Pollack, "What Obama's Nuclear Posture Review Accomplishes," *Bulletin of the Atomic Scientists* online edition, http://thebulletin.org/print/web-edition/columnists/joshua-pollack (accessed April 21, 2010).

6. Pavel Podvig, in telephone discussion with the author, March 26, 2010.

7. Larry Diamond, *The Spirit of Democracy* (New York: Times Books, 2008).

8. Michael McFaul, *Advancing Democracy Abroad: Why We Should and How We Can* (Lanham, MD: Rowman & Littlefield, 2010).

9. Thomas Friedman, *Hot, Flat, and Crowded* (New York: Farrar, Straus and Giroux, 2008).

10. There is an enormous body of research on the "democratic peace" relationship. See, for example, the bibliography of Paul Kuth and Todd L. Allee, *The Democratic Peace and Territorial Conflict in the Twentieth Century* (Cambridge: Cambridge University Press, 2002).

11. Jack F. Matlock, Jr. in a lecture to the American Association for the Advancement of Slavic Studies, November 20–23, 2008, Philadelphia.

12. Jack F. Matlock, Jr. *Autopsy on an Empire* (New York: Random House, 1995), 537.

13. Matlock, 539.

14. Celeste Wallander, "Lost and Found: Gorbachev's 'New Thinking,'" *The Washington Quarterly* 25, no. 1 (Winter 2002): 125.

15. "Gorbachev Says Democracy Backtracked in Russia," (Moscow: Itar-Tass, March 12, 2010).

16. http://freedomhouse.org/template.cfm?page=22&country=7689&year=2009 (accessed April 20, 2010).

17. *The Pulse of Europe 2009: 20 Years After the Fall of the Berlin Wall.* http://pewglobal.org/reports/pdf/267.pdf, accessed April 16, 2010. Cited by Dina Zisserman in her unpublished paper, "The Prospects for Democratization in Post-Putin Russia,"

presented to the Association for the Study of Nationalities, Columbia University, April 15, 2010.

18. "Chto takoie demokratiia I nuzhna li ona Rossii?," www.levada.ru/press/ 2010012105.html (accessed April 20, 2010). Cited by Zisserman, "The Prospects for Democratization".

19. Andrei Kamenshikov interview by Metta Spencer, "Rights and Conflict in Russia," *Peace Magazine* 26, no. 2 (April–June 2010): 10.

20. A fuller account of this expulsion can be found on this book's website at http://russianpeaceanddemocracy.com.

Chapter 15: Conclusion

So who was right? Does democracy come from above or below? You can still argue about it, since in Russia it hasn't come at all—or at least it hasn't stayed long. As of 2010, neither the TERMITES nor the BARKING DOGS can claim success. But let's review their statements from earlier chapters.

When I last asked, some TERMITES were adamant—Georgi Arbatov, for example, who insisted:

> It was a revolution from the top. A good thing, because we know what a revolution from below is—where it led France in the eighteenth century and where it led us. I don't believe much in revolution. I believe in evolution and reforms. In a country like ours that had a totalitarian past, the only chance to have change was from the top.[1]

On the other hand, empirical research shows that if democratization arises from below (from a grassroots nonviolent revolution) it has a better chance of lasting than if conferred from above by enlightened elite rulers.

That may be so, admit the unconvinced TERMITES, but it was not possible to organize a grassroots political movement in Russia, so if democracy was to come at all, it could only be from above.

But the debate has changed somewhat lately. The most astute remark I heard came from a former TERMITE, Sergei Kovalev, who described the reforms of the Gorbachev years this way: "It was from bottom up *and* from Gorbachev *and* from the side."

Of course, Kovalev was right. About half of this book constitutes evidence that foreigners contributed to the ideas that the reformers put into effect. Arbatov knows it better than anyone else, being the main conduit for foreign "New Thinking." And today, the pro-democracy activists in Russia, without exception, admit that they still require assistance from foreign supporters. Even the opponents of democracy believe that the best way of squelching it is to keep foreign donors and NGOs from functioning in Russia. Indeed, there seems to be consensus that Russia will not reach democracy without help from outside.

Unfortunately, that consensus was forming exactly when many Westerners were reaching a contradictory conclusion. In a "backlash" against George W.

Bush's readiness to effect "regime change" abroad, many citizens of democracies, even in the West and especially among left-of-center critics,[2] now regard
"democracy promotion" as illegitimate. It is urgent, therefore, that we resolve
this contradiction and determine what Westerners in liberal democracies can and
should do to support democratization elsewhere. Though Russia is the focus of
this book, our answer applies to every society where the state violates the rights
and freedoms of citizens. Should we help democratization, and if so, how? What
is our responsibility? And when should we, in the name of democracy itself,
refrain from attempting to influence political decisions in other nations?

The *desirability* of democratization is not in question—both for our own
sake (our democracy will always avoid wars against other democratic states) and
especially for *their* sake. Wishing them well, we naturally wish democracy for
them. But there are few recognized international principles to define the appro-
priateness of assisting nonviolent pro-democracy movements in other countries.

Actually, guidelines are more explicit when it comes to intervening *militarily* abroad. The United Nations has adopted as international law the "responsibility to protect" doctrine. If a state does not protect its own citizens but even
abuses them, then it forfeits sovereignty and the international community should
intervene on behalf of the mistreated people, even with military force as last
resort. Specific decisions about such interventions are difficult in certain cases,
but the general principle is now accepted.

But there is no such accepted principle guiding the assistance to, say, a
"color revolution" or even activists abroad who work to protect citizens' rights.
Apparently we have to work out ad hoc answers out for ourselves. President
Putin reacted against the color revolutions by outlawing any foreign funding of
civil society organizations with political agendas. He did not intend to be taken
unaware while civil resistance plots were being hatched against him. His crackdown has harmed Russian NGOs.

And the pro-democracy activists are counting on us. Sergei Kovalev said:

> What I want is a small miracle—that with the help of the West, in Russia we
> will create a critical mass of people who understand that democracy is not
> about "liberté, égalité, fraternité," but about a boring procedure that's just sup-
> posed to happen. After this, any miracle—like a Charter 77 or something in
> East Europe—can happen. If that happens, then great possibilities open.

But there are objections from all sides, including in Mikhail Gorbachev's
remarks about Ukraine's Orange Revolution. After noting that it was truly
Ukrainian in origin and support, Gorbachev said that there was "strong participation" by the U.S. embassy. He said,

> America has great experience interfering in the internal affairs of other States.
> If such things happened in America, I am convinced that they would immedi-
> ately put an end to outside interference.[3]

He was right. Toronto journalist Mark MacKinnon wrote a book about the
color revolutions in Serbia, Georgia, and Ukraine. He stated that the help pro-

vided by the Democratic and Republican parties' democracy-promoting organizations to "political parties in countries like Ukraine would have been illegal had a Ukrainian NGO been giving such aid to the Democrats or the Republicans."[4] Yet he did not see this criticism as grounds for condemning color revolutions. He admits that a question had been nagging him throughout his research:

> Were the Western-backed uprisings in Belgrade, Tbilisi, and Kiev a good thing? For the people of Serbia, Georgia, and Ukraine, the answer was yes. Life in 2006 in all three countries was freer and thus better than it had been under Milosevic, Shevardnadze and Kuchma . . . [T]he political sphere was unquestionably more open than it had been—people could complain freely, get useful information from their media, and pitch a tent in front of Parliament if they didn't like what was happening inside.[5]

Democratization is part of the current, historic globalization phenomenon. Influences no longer can be kept local by invoking the old Westphalian principle of national sovereignty. We need universalistic rules that would apply to American parties aiding political parties in Ukraine and equally to Ukrainians aiding the Democrats or Republicans. At a minimum, that rule would probably admonish governments and political parties against aiding foreign political parties or candidates for office. To do so would sabotage the democratic process.

During the Orange Revolution of 2003, the U.S. State Department is rumored to have donated $6.5 million, most of which paid for democratic *processes* rather than to support Pora as an organization. Moreover, Pora declared that the money they received from all foreign sources—governmental and private alike—was only a small fraction of the amount donated by Ukrainians inside the country. Government funding and other direct assistance probably should not cover any expenditures that would influence the outcome of a foreign election.

Many pro-democracy activists concur. The Otpor leader Srdja Popovic said that he opposes foreigners' involvement in any campaign to oust a dictatorship.

> The only way the struggle will be [effective] in any country in the world is if the locals are carrying it. . . . And that brings us to the sensitive issue of what foreign democratic governments should do to help democratic movements— and what they shouldn't do under any circumstances. They shouldn't interfere in politics. The last thing they should ever do is support the opposition parties. They should stay out of the political arena.

How to Promote Democracy Abroad

What, then, is left for us to do? How can we support democratization abroad? I have five proposals. *First, let's be modest.* Every democracy, including our own, has room for improvement. Admit that before offering advice to others. And admit that we cannot give democracy to them. They must take it for themselves.

Second, let's build trust through truth-telling. Much of Russians' distrust of democracy resulted from President Bill Clinton's reluctance to call Yeltsin's rule undemocratic. He tarred the good reputation of democracy itself.

Third, let's support international law. Let's base our agreements mainly on universal principles, rather than advancing our own country's interests. Thus societies should adopt common rules about, say, helping foreign civil society organizations or deciding whether a group has a right to secede from its present country. Fair rules are more likely to come from participating in multilateral institutions such as the United Nations than from bilateral negotiations.

Double standards are unfair. It is anti-democratic to let certain nations (e.g. Israel, India, and Pakistan) acquire nuclear weapons while denying others (e.g. North Korea and Iran) the same right. Instead of jockeying for power when negotiating, adherence to objective, rational standards yields friendlier, more trusting relations. Gorbachev calls many Western demands for human rights "hypocritical," since they are not applied even-handedly to all foreign countries. Thus, he notes, the U.S. chastises certain dictators while embracing others, on the reasoning that "they may be sons-of-bitches, but they are *our* sons-of-bitches."[6]

(He is right, but it is jarring to read a former TERMITE objecting to hypocrisy, a flaw that had been attributed to them in the old days. BARKING DOGS used to call TERMITES "whores"—careerists who bought promotions through the Party ranks by currying favor with DINOSAURS. However unfair, that allegation was understandable at the time. But slanging matches are particularly unfortunate when they involve accusations of being pragmatic and opportunistic on the one hand, or principled and ideological on the other hand. Everyone has to balance the two orientations and there is no perfect combination.)

Fourth, let's provide financial or material assistance for democratic processes and technological support, not specific outcomes. We already support civil society organizations and training in public opinion surveys, focus groups, political debates, exit polling, and electoral monitoring. All these are worthy approaches, but the line can be fuzzy between promoting democratic processes and manipulating the outcomes, so scrupulous care is required.[7] As Srdja Popović suggested in chapter 12,

> the most effective help to Serbia was helping the independent media. That support is very valuable because you are building the capability of the independent movement to communicate, you are raising the costs to the regime of committing human rights violations, and you are also developing the roots of democratic society. . . . [You] cannot be accused of interfering because, by supporting independent media you are not supporting the opposition or the government. You are just supporting the right of the people to hear the truth.

Russians over age forty all remember listening to the news from Radio Liberty and other overseas services, which were broadcast all over their country, spreading accurate information that the Brezhnev regime preferred to suppress. That approach is still useful in countries where the regime controls the media, but now there are additional possibilities. The Internet is already a superb means of communication, which even the most repressive regimes (such as China) do not completely shut down. Some computer labs in the West offer people help in outsmarting the censors.[8] Moreover, Oleg Kozlovsky's English language blog mentioned a good suggestion by Ethan Zuckerman of Harvard:

> When talking about how the new technologies changed democracy promotion, he said that now, instead of "parachuting receivers" to citizens of authoritarian countries you should be "parachuting transmitters." In other words, the new technologies empower people and give them more capacity to improve things from within. . . . [Foreign assistance] shouldn't be about building democracy from outside, but about bringing tools so that people can build democracy for themselves.[9]

Also, let's not overlook the power of fiction and drama. Hollywood influences global culture, but movies are less influential today than long-running TV stories about characters to whom the audience becomes attached. Television serials about intelligent, lovable people are ideal. I hope some organization will stimulate Russia's political culture from abroad by broadcasting long-running Russian-language "soap operas" about citizens in a well-functioning democracy.

This is not a new idea. Radio and TV serials are widely used in India, Latin America, and Africa to enlighten people about, say, health practices, deciding how many babies to have, and whether to send girls to school. Their powerful effects are not resented as propaganda because, as popular entertainment, these are shows that people voluntarily choose to watch. The same idea can be applied in Russian-language dramas about current social and political controversies.

Fifth, let's contribute to Russians' social capital by greatly expanding transnational civil society. This can be especially useful to Russia because of the unusually low levels of trust that prevail there. For example, a world-wide study asked respondents whether they believed that "most people can be trusted"; 35 percent of the Russians and 74 percent of the Danes believed so.[10] Vladimir Shlapentokh has compared the average Russian to Stalin, who was totally paranoid. He writes,

> Today the average Russian, with his or her distrust in almost everything, resembles somewhat the old leader, although their distrust, unlike Stalin's, is mostly rational. A climate of mutual distrust dominates Russian life at all strata. Describing the mood in the country in March 2005, one of the most prominent and respected Russian journalists, Yulia Kalinina, wrote in *Moskovskii Komsomolets*, a popular newspaper, about "the moral degradation" of society, suggesting that people take for granted the fact that "lying and deception has become a norm of life." . . . As the major subjects of mistrust and the champions of deception, Kalinina names the state and "politicians, deputies, the government, and the Kremlin aristocracy." The gloomy picture limned in *Moskovskii Komsomolets* has been supported publicly by politicians, businesspeople, and journalists of all political colors as well as by foreign observers. . . .
>
> Today Russia is a country, much more than any other, that mistrusts almost all social institutions in the country and political institutions in the first place. There is no one institution that can garner more than 40–50 percent of the nation's trust. Most political institutions enjoy a confidence level of only 10 to 30 percent and some even lower. . . . Of all sixty-six countries included in

[the World Values Survey] on the satisfaction with democracy, Russia was in last place.[11]

A deficiency of trust in public institutions impairs the state and the economy. Indeed, Francis Fukuyama has depicted trust as the main factor determining a country's economic development.[12] Low levels of trust means that people are unlikely to cooperate with the state. Shlapentokh opines that by 2005, the Kremlin no longer could rely on the support of the masses in any of its endeavors. For example, people try to keep their children out of the army, and do not expect the police to catch criminals. "In the case of necessity—for instance, to collect on the debts of their clients—they address their concerns not to the police, but to criminals as more efficient operators."[13]

Low levels of trust mean that people are apt to falsify their own preferences, preventing assessment of the group's readiness to oppose a ruler. It may be impossible to mobilize them in defense of their own values. Hence low levels of trust—deficient social capital—make totalitarian rule more likely. Totalitarianism in turn further reduces social capital. Causally, this is a vicious spiral.[14]

There is even such a thing as "negative social capital." This occurs when secret, illegal networks develop as a defense against the state. Such groups always arise in communist societies, for goods and services are supplied without much attention to demand. Also, firms are required to produce, whether or not the required inputs are available, so the managers often resort to unauthorized sources. Such "gray" social networks may continue existing years later, interfering with the development of above-board businesses. Corruption is another manifestation of negative social capital.

There is one way in which we outsiders can help and at the same time gain social capital ourselves—by sustained transnational interactions with Russians. Fortunately, inexpensive technologies now enable us to so.

Cultural exchange programs are the ideal, but expensive, way of building transnational civil society. However, there are cheaper ways—notably video-conferencing. Almost all young Russians now study English and/or own a computer with a video camera. The United States and Russia have established a commission to support civil society. I propose that every year the new commission organize about 1,000 groups of people aged twenty to thirty-five to meet by video-conference links once or twice a month for a year. Each group should be made up of, say, four Russians and four Americans who agree to sustain a regular discussion on some topic of mutual interest in English or Russian. This can be organized for about one million dollars per year—without interfering with any nation's sovereignty.

Some of the groups will tackle serious global problems, while others may choose lifestyle topics such as dog training, biochar farming, ethnic cuisines, Persian art, or geo-engineering. There will be four Russians, sitting in front of a computer in Volgograd, St. Petersburg, or Novosibirsk, watching and talking for an hour with four Americans in front of a computer in Memphis, Minneapolis, or Santa Fe. After one year, 8,000 people will have several good friends in the other country. The key to success is to have the conversation be sustained over many meetings. This is an affordable way to build transnational civil society and trust. I'm proposing it to Michael McFaul, who co-chairs the commission on civil society from the White House. You may want to second the motion.

The Gandhian Gorbachev
Syllogism: Every TERMITE I had ever met seemed wary of populist movements, protesters, and color revolutions. Mr. Gorbachev was the Master TERMITE. Hence Mr. Gorbachev must be opposed to, or at least dubious about, such political movements. It stood to reason.

But it occurred to me that I had never actually heard or read any explicit statement of his to that effect, so I'd better verify my assumption.

Come to think of it, the evidence was ambiguous. It was clear enough that he believes in democracy. For example, in their book, *Conversations with Gorbachev*, he and Zdeněk Mlynář discuss their lives and political views at great length, and both of them express the unswerving conviction that socialism requires true democracy. They talk about democracy all the time.

Moreover, Mr. Gorbachev states twice there that he believes that reforms had to start from the top. For example, he says:

> I am convinced that in the countries of "actually existing socialism" any attempts to begin reform and make change *from below* were doomed to failure. The system had the capacity to suppress such attempts and to effectively combat them. For that reason it was only possible and necessary to begin from the top down.[15]

Yet there is evidence that Gorbachev also recognizes the importance of having political support from below. He refers to a period in late 1987, saying,

> [W]ithin the new leadership of the country we came to the conclusion that the same fate that had befallen Khrushchev awaited us if the efforts made from above were not reinforced by support from below. Political reform was placed on the order of the day.[16]

What kind of "support from below" does he have in mind? And what about "opposition from below"? What would he think of a color revolution in Russia? (Apart from predicting that it would fail.) He never says. He had warned the rulers of all the Eastern European countries that he would not defend them against uprisings, as previous general secretaries had done, and he seems proud of having refrained from taking sides in their internal conflicts. He says, "nowhere did we try to give a push from the outside to the internal processes: that would have been a return to the old practices."[17] Likewise, recalling his trip to Havana, he says he had reassured Castro that Cuba did not have to follow Russia's example by introducing reforms.

A disagreement about Gorbachev's studied neutrality arouses the only strong dispute in his book with Mlynář. It concerns his visit to Prague in 1987. Angrily recalling how Gorbachev had said nothing sympathetic about the tragic Prague Spring of twenty years before, Mlynář says, "We expected that in some way you would make it understood that you sympathized with the Prague Spring. After all, those actually were your real sympathies."

How did Mlynář know that those were Gorbachev's real sympathies? He hadn't said so in the book. His inhibited way of discussing this grassroots movement did not jibe with some remarks of Pavel Palazhchenko's that I recalled.

* * *

Pavel Palazhchenko is Mr. Gorbachev's interpreter and the director of the Gorbachev Foundation; he sees Gorbachev almost every day. Alexander Likhotal is President of Green Cross International and also is in frequent contact with its founder. If I address questions to Mr. Gorbachev, it is through one of them, and so I wrote an e-mail to Mr. Palazhchenko, part of which follows here:

> You may recall that you and I talked for about an hour in June 2008 and you said something that surprised me. I'm not sure whether it was your own opinion or also that of Mr. Gorbachev. We were discussing grassroots nonviolent movements such as Solidarność and the Orange Revolution. I expressed admiration for Gandhi, and you seemed to share my high opinion of nonviolent "people power." You said that Ukraine was none the worse for its Orange Revolution. It had not been my impression that Mr. Gorbachev had much faith in that method of political change, and I would like to ask his opinion about such approaches. Alexander also seemed to think that I have not understood Mr. Gorbachev's attitude in that regard. Of course, I don't want to make such a serious error in my book.
>
> Research at Freedom House has shown that in countries that have democratized during the past thirty-three years, civic resistance was a driving factor in over fifty of the sixty-seven transitions. Moreover, those were more likely still to be democracies five years later than were countries that democratized "from above."
>
> Can you please ask Mr. Gorbachev to express his opinion about the circumstances (if any) under which democratization "from below" via civic resistance should be encouraged?

To this query, Mr. Palazhchenko replied,

> I can confirm that you understood me correctly. President Gorbachev thinks very highly of grassroots movements and his view is that movements from below are indispensable for real change to happen and to take root. He has spoken very highly on many occasions of Gandhi, of Solidarność in Poland and of velvet revolutions in Central and Eastern Europe. In the Soviet Union change had to be initiated from the top but as he has said many times the goal was to "awaken the people" and "people's creativity" rather than conduct the whole process from above. As for "civic resistance" he has not used this term.
>
> I could try to put together some quotations and remarks from his recent speeches and interviews that express his position on this subject. . .

How could I have been so mistaken about such an important matter? For twenty-five years I have followed Mr. Gorbachev's every comment. But imagine! All along he had been hoping for the Russian people to become actively engaged in the political causes that he initiated—and I had not realized it. Suddenly I had an image of Gorbachev dressed in a homespun dhoti, leading throngs of followers to the sea to make salt.

Separately Mr. Likhotal and Mr. Palazhchenko had corrected my misconceptions in the same way, by insisting that Mr. Gorbachev encourages grassroots social movements. I am grateful to them for clarifying his thoughts on this vital matter. Those two men probably know him as well as anyone else in the world, so I am sure they are right and I have been wrong.

Except regarding publicity. I feel sure that Mr. Gorbachev's statements on this issue were not as widely publicized as they assume. I would have read them.

Or would I? Perhaps other scholars and activists *are* familiar with this aspect of Gorbachev's political orientation. Perhaps I have read the wrong things.

To check on this possibility, I e-mailed six activists and journalists who had been organizers of color revolutions or who reported on them. I also posted a query about it on Twitter and Facebook. Nobody can recall having heard the loquacious Mr. Gorbachev express an opinion—favorable or unfavorable—about a nonviolent campaign. (Yes, he did criticize the U.S. for meddling in the Ukrainian movement, but without saying whether he admired the events.)

This puzzled me until I concocted a theory. It is based on the principle that people prefer narratives that are internally consistent.

Let's say that Gorbachev had to start his change from the top, but wanted it to come alive from below. He wanted to lead an enthusiastic society of political activists liberating themselves from totalitarianism. He wanted to be a charismatic Gandhi, a Martin Luther King, a Lech Wałęsa, or at least a César Chávez.

Instead, as we learned in chapter 12, people perceived him as the Czar. He was the head of the government, which Russians think of as the Czar—the supreme authority figure. A grassroots movement ordinarily *opposes* established authority. The activists are rebelling *against* something; they are demanding change. Their leader has to fit the role, but a Czar does not.

There have been very few cases when a leader has come to power in the normal way and, while retaining a high post, has also become leader of a grassroots movement. Hugo Chávez is trying to do that now, but I can think of no other instances.

Except one: The Prague Spring! In a normal way, Alexander Dubček, Zdeněk Mlynář, and the other Communist reformers came to power and began some brilliant innovations. They were not the opposition, but instead formed the government. Yet the whole populace became intensely enthusiastic supporters. They "switched on from below." It was Russia that stopped the Czechoslovak reforms. Then Gorbachev was sent to Prague as a representative of the regime that suppressed his best friend's political movement. He could not apologize.

Yet, just as Lenin had felt impelled to complete his brother's project, Gorbachev felt impelled to fulfill Mlynář's project. He would lead a Moscow Spring just like the one in Prague. But *his* Spring would not be crushed. That would be his redemption for abandoning his friend. I wish he had succeeded.

316

Chapter 15

* * *

As a young man, the writer Alexander Herzen went to the Sparrow Hills over-looking Moscow with a friend and took an oath to devote his life to opposing absolutism. More than a century later, young Mikhail Gorbachev also took an oath there: to devote his life to opposing totalitarianism.

He kept his oath. Russia is a better place for it and so is the world. With fuller support, he might even have fully succeeded.

But he did well. Russia is not totalitarian and we've had no World War III.

Thank you, Mikhail Sergeyevich.

Notes

1. Georgy Arbatov, in discussion with the author, July 1992, Moscow.
2. Howard Clark names several left-wing critics who argue against promoting de-mocracy abroad, in *People Power: Unarmed Resistance and Global Security* ed. Howard Clark (London: Pluto Press, 2009), 195.
3. Mikhail Gorbachev, *Izvestia*, June 26, 2006. http://www.izvestia.ru/news/11/news 109658/index.html (accessed April 27, 2010).
4. Mark MacKinnon, *The New Cold War: Revolutions, Rigged Elections and Pipe-line Politics in the Former Soviet Union* (Toronto: Random House, 2007), 274.
5. MacKinnon, 273–74.
6. Gorbachev, *Izvestia*.
7. Andrew Wilson, *Ukraine's Orange Revolution* (New Haven: Yale University Press, 2005), 189, cited by Jørgen Johansen, "External Financing of Opposition Move-ments," in *People Power*, ed. Howard Clark, 205.
8. The Citizen Lab at University of Toronto is a pioneer in this area; see http://www.citizenlab.org/.
9. http://olegkozlovsky.wordpress.com/ (accessed April 20, 2010).
10. Lene Hjollund, Marti Paldam, and Gert Tinggaard Svendsen, "Social Capital in Russia and Denmark: A Comparative Study," unpublished paper, Department of Eco-nomics, Aarhus University, Denmark, 2001, http://www.umar.gov.si/fileadmin/ user_up load/konference/06/17_paldam.pdf (accessed April 20, 2010).
11. Vladimir Shlapentokh, "Trust in Public Institutions in Russia: The Lowest in the World," *Communist and Post-Communist Studies* 39 (2006): 154–57.
12. Francis Fukuyama, *Trust: The Social Virtues and the Creation of Prosperity* (London: Penguin, 1996).
13. Shlapentokh, 168.
14. Hjollund, Paldam and Svendsen, 4.
15. Mikhail Gorbachev and Zdeněk Mlynář, *Conversations with Gorbachev: On Perestroika, The Prague Spring, and the Crossroads of Socialism*, trans. George Shriver (New York: Columbia University Press, 2002), 96.
16. Gorbachev and Mlynář, 58.
17. Gorbachev and Mlynář, 88.

Acknowledgments

This is the best part of writing a book. The last thing you do is thank the people who helped make it possible. It's a great feeling. Psychologists studying human happiness say that the best emotion is gratitude, and that to savor it you should send thank-you notes. But my list would be endless—especially for a book that started twenty-eight years ago. Making this list brought to mind hundreds of people who contributed in various ways. I thought of the people who had helped me every day: especially my indispensable current assistant, Ken Simons (one of the smartest people I know) and his fine predecessor, Lisa Ferguson. I thought of friends in Russia with whom I lived for months at a time, who interpreted for me and made my appointments: Alexander Kalinin, Julia Kalinina, and their son Ignat, who was about eight when we met but has become my Moscow assistant. I thought of my son, Jonathan Spencer, my best editor. After I am satisfied with a draft I give it to him and he makes me start over. And I thought of a kind woman in the Warsaw train station who helped me when my suitcase fell apart.

I thank friends who read parts of it and gave their comments (John Bacher, Arlie Hochschild, Nancy Howell, Joanna Santa Barbara). I thank others who shared their ideas or tapes of their own interviews with me: Gwynne Dyer, for example. And Lindsay Mattison, who gave me the home phone numbers of top Soviet officials. Yet I know I'll forget dozens and I'm sorry. Thanks to Helju Bennett, Max Bergholz, Fyodor Burlatsky, James Bush, Robert De Gendt, Yury Djachenko, Ivan Fiala, George Hudson, Yevgenia Issraelyan, Yegor Kuznetsov, Alexander Likhotal, Mac Makarchuk, Scott Marentette, Olga Medvedkov, Yuri Medvedkov, Pavel Palazhchenko, Sergei Plekhanov, Maria Pokacheva, Mikhail Schuman, Lev Semeiko, and Victor Sumsky.

Most of all I thank the generous, fascinating, mainly historic figures who let me interview them, often repeatedly. This work has been both the most engrossing project of my life and the most fun. What a privilege! These interviews and conversations gave me enough material for twenty books. On the next page I will name most informants from Russia and other Eastern European countries, though I have an even longer list of Western interviewees who have also contributed their insights. All errors are my own fault. Thank you all!

Agrachev, Dimitri
Alexeyeva, Ludmilla
Andreyev, Sergei
Andreyeva, Yevgenia
Arbatov, Georgy
Bagramov, Leon
Bashkirova, Elena
Bayandour, Anahit
Blagovolin, Sergei
Bobroshova, Alice
Borovik, Genrikh
Bulgakov, Viktor
Burlatsky, Fyodor
Chagodaeva, Marie
Chupryna, Iryna
Císař, Čestmír
Davidov, Gen.
Deliusin, Lev
Dienstbier, Jiří
Dzhibladze, Yuri
Ettinger, Jacob
Falin, Valentin
Ferenčáková, Dana
Fiala, Ivan
Furman, Dmitry
Gamenyok, Slava
Gerasimov, Gennady
Gladkov, Peter
Goldansky, Vitaly
Goldstücker, Eduard
Gredelj, Stjepan
Grigoriants, Sergei
Grishina, Elena
Hajek, Miloš
Holzer, Maria
Ilukhina, Ruzanna
Issraelyan, Yevgenia
Ivanenko, Vladimir
Kalinin, Alexander
Kalinin, Ignat
Kalinina, Julia
Kamenshikov, Andrei
Karaganov, Sergei
Kasaev, Alan
Kasutin, Vladimir
Kavan, Jan
Kazaryan, Rafael
Khamzatovich, Umar
Khodareva, Ailita
Khoros, Vladimir

Khramov, Nikolai
Khramovo, Nikolai
Kirbasova, Maria
Kislov, Alexander
Kolbasev, Alexander
Kornilov, Vladislav
Kortunov, Andrei
Kovalev, Sergei
Kozlovsky, Oleg
Krasin, Yury
Krasnorutsky, Jana
Krasnorutsky, Yuri
Kuklina, Ida
Kuznetsov, Nikolai
Kuznetsov, Yegor
Langer, Alexander
Lashiver, Asya
Lebedev, Mikhail
Libergal, Grigory
Likhotal, Alexander
Loginov, ___
Lokshin, Grigory
Lopatin, Vladimir
Malikov, Viktor
Malisheva, Yulia
Maltsev, Yuri
Maslennikov, Nikita
Mazkova, Tatiana
Medvedkov, Yuri
Medvedkova, Olga
Melville, Andrei
Mikhailov, Col. Gen.
Milshtein, Gen. A.
Nikitin, Alexander
Nikitin, Sergei
Novodvorskaya, Valeria
Obushenkov, ___
Oreshene, Boris
Orlov, Andrei
Orlov, Yuri
Pain, Emil
Palazhchenko, Pavel
Palous, Martin
Panov, Anatoly
Pavlova, Tatiana
Pavlovna-Silvanskaya, M.
Petrov, Andrei
Petrovsky, Vladimir
Plekhanov, Sergei
Podvig, Pavel

Pokachev, Konstantin
Ponamarov, Lev
Popov, Arkady
Popov, Nikolai
Popović, Srdja
Potekhin, Dmitro
Povolofsky, Alexander
Pozharskiy, ___
Puiu, Rodica
Rashkovsky, Yevgeny
Rogov, Sergei
Rubinin, Pavel E.
Rugova, Ibrahim
Rusakova, Elena
Rybakov, Vselovod
Šabata, Jaroslav
Saganov, ___
Said, Zaki
Sckundin, Mark
Semeiko, Alla
Semeiko, Lev
Serebrenikov, Gen.
Shakhnazarov, Georgi
Sheinis, Victor
Shevardnadze, Eduard
Silhan, Venek
Simonia, Nodari
Skripnikov, Sergei
Skvirsky, Yuri
Slavik, Vaclav
Smirniagin, L.V.
Smirnov, Andrei
Smirnov, William
Stepanov, Timur
Sukhodrev, Viktor
Sumsky, Viktor
Tairov, Tair
Terasawa, Junsei
Trojan, Václav
Urban, Jan
Velikhov, Yevgeny
Vendina, Olga
Yavlinsky, Grigory
Žagar, Mitja
Zavkaev, ___
Zmilyakova, ___
Zukal, Rudolf

Bibliography

Ackerman, Peter, and Jack Duvall. *A Force More Powerful: A Century of Nonviolent Conflict*. New York: St. Martin's, 2000.

Aganbegyan, Abel. *Inside Perestroika: The Future of the Soviet Economy*. New York: Harper and Row, 1980.

Akhapkin, Yuri, comp. *First Decrees of Soviet Power*. London: Lawrence and Wishart, 1970.

Aldis, Anne C., and Roger N. McDermott, eds. *Russian Military Reform, 1992-2002*. Kindle edition.

Alexeyeva, Ludmilla. *Soviet Dissent*. Translated by Carol Pearce and John Glad. Middletown, CT: Wesleyan University Press, 1985.

Alexeyeva, Ludmilla, and Paul Goldberg. *The Thaw Generation: Coming of Age in the Post Stalin Era*. Boston: Little, Brown, 1990.

Arbatov, Georgi. "How Much Defense is Enough?" *International Affairs*, no. 4 (Autumn 1989).

———. *The System: An Insider's Life in Soviet Politics*. New York: Times Books, 1992.

Asch, Solomon. *Social Psychology*. Englewood Cliffs, NJ: Prentice-Hall, 1952.

Azbel, Mark Yakovlevich. *Refusenik: Trapped in the Soviet Union*. Edited by Grace Pierce Forbes. Boston: Houghton Mifflin, 1981.

Bacher, John. *Petrotyranny*. Toronto: Science for Peace and Dundurn Press, 2000.

Baev, P., Sergei Karaganov et al. *Tactical Nuclear Weapons in Europe*. Moscow: APN, 1990.

Becker, Howard S. "Notes on the Concept of Commitment." *American Journal of Sociology* 66, no. 1 (July 1960): 32-40.

Benn, David Wedgwood. *Persuasion and Soviet Politics*. New York: Blackwell, 1989.

Blick, Robin. *The Seeds of Evil: Lenin and the Origins of Bolshevik Elitism*. London: Ferrington, 1993.

Bloch, Sidney, and Peter Reddaway. *Soviet Psychiatric Abuse: The Shadow Over World Psychiatry*. Boulder: Westview Press, 1985.

Bolling, Landrum R. "The Dartmouth Conference: Subjective Reflections" in *Private Diplomacy with the Soviet Union*, edited by David D. Newsom. Lanham, MD: University Press of America, 1987.

Boserup, Anders, Robert Neild, Frank von Hippel, and Albrecht von Mueller. "Letter of October 10, 1987." *FAS Public Interest Report* 41, no. 2 (February 1988).

Breslauer, George W. *Gorbachev and Yeltsin as Leaders*. Cambridge: Cambridge University Press, 2002.

Brown, Archie. *The Gorbachev Factor*. New York: Oxford University Press, 1996.

Brown, Julie V. "Revolution and Psychosis: The Mixing of Science and Politics in Russian Psychiatric Medicine, 1905–13." *The Russian Review* 46 (1987): 283-302.

Bukovsky, Vladimir, and Semyon Gluzman. "A Dissident's Guide to Psychiatry." *A Chronicle of Human Rights in the USSR* 13 (1975): 31-57.

Bulletin of the Atomic Scientists, various articles and authors.

Burlatsky, Fyodor. "Democratization is a Long March." In *Voices of Glasnost: Interviews with Gorbachev's Reformers*, edited by Stephen Cohen and Katrina vanden Heuvel. New York: Norton, 1989.

Carrillo, Santiago. *Eurocommunism and the State*. Translated by Nan Green and A. M. Elliott. Westport, CT: Lawrence Hill, 1978.

Carter, Ashton B., and David N. Schwartz, eds. *Ballistic Missile Defense*. Washington DC: Brookings Institution, 1984.

Cohen, Stephen F. *Soviet Fates and Lost Alternatives: From Stalinism to the New Cold War*. New York: Columbia University Press, 2009.

Committee to Protect Journalists. "2 Journalists Killed in China since 1992/Motive Confirmed." Committee to Protect Journalists. http:/cpj.org/killed/asia/china/

———. *Anatomy of Injustice: The Unsolved Killings of Journalists in Russia*. Committee to Protect Journalists. http://cpj.org/reports/CPJ.Anatomy%20of%20Injustice.pdf (accessed Sept. 28 2009).

Cortright, David. *Peace Works: The Citizen's Role in Ending the Cold* War. Boulder: Westview, 1993.

"Country Report: Kyrgyzstan (2007)." *Freedom House*. http://freedomhouse.org/template.cfm? page=22&year=2007&country=7210

Cousins, Norman. *The Improbable Triumvirate: John F. Kennedy, Pope John, Nikita Khrushchev*. New York: Norton, 1972.

Dahl, Robert. *Who Governs? Democracy and Power in an American City*. New Haven: Yale University Press, 1961.

Deats, Richard L. *Marked for Life: The Story of Hildegard Goss Mayr (Leaders and Witnesses)*. Hyde Park, NY: New City Press, 2009.

Diamond, Larry. *The Spirit of Democracy*. New York: Times Books, 2008.

Dobson, Miriam. *Khrushchev's Cold Summer: Gulag Returnees, Crime, and the Fate of Reform After Stalin*. Ithaca: Cornell University Press, 2009.

Doder, Dusko, and Louise Branson. *Heretic in the Kremlin*. New York: Penguin, 1991.

Dragsdahl, Jorgen. "How Peace Research Has Reshaped the European Arms Dialogue." in *Peace Research in Europe, Annual Review of Peace Activism, 1989*, edited by John Tirman, 39–45. Washington, DC: Winston Foundation for World Peace, 1989.

Dubček, Alexander. *Hope Dies Last: The Autobiography of Alexander Dubček*. Edited and translated by Jiri Hochman. New York: Kodansha International, 1993.

Dudintsev, Vladimir. *Not by Bread Alone*. Translated by Edith Bone. London: Hutchinson, 1957.

Dzhibladze, Yuri. "What I Told President Obama." Huffington Post, February 24, 2010. http://www.huffingtonpost.com/yuri-dzhibladze/what-i-told-president-oba_b474646.html (accessed February 24, 2010).

Ellman, Michael, and S. Maksudov. "Soviet Deaths in the Great Patriotic War: A Note," *Europe- Asia Studies* 46, no. 4 (July 1994): 671-81.

English, Robert D. *Russia and the Idea of the West: Gorbachev, Intellectuals & the End of the Cold War*. New York: Columbia University Press, 2000.

Etzioni, Amitai. "The Kennedy Experiment" *Western Political Quarterly* 20, no. 2 (June 1967): 361-80.

Evangelista, Matthew. *Unarmed Forces*. Ithaca: Cornell University Press, 1999.
Fairbanks, Charles H., Jr. "Georgia's Rose Revolution." *Journal of Democracy* 15, no. 2 (April 2004): 110–24.
———. "The Nature of the Beast." *The National Interest*, no. 31 (Spring 1993): 46-57.
Faraone, Stephen. "Psychiatry and Political Repression in the Soviet Union." *The American Psychologist* 37, no. 10 (1982): 1105-12.
Feigenhauer, Pavel. "The Russian Army in Chechnya." *Crimes of War*, April 18, 2003. www.crimesofwar.org/chechnya-mag/chech-felgenhauer.html (accessed January 12, 2010).
Feld, Bernard. "Artsimovich and the Pugwash Movement." In *Reminiscences about Academician Lev Artsimovich*, edited by B. B. Kadomtsev et al. Moscow: Nauka, 1986.
Ferlat, Anne. "Neopaganism and New Age in Russia." *Folklore* 23: 40-48. www.folklore.ee/ Folklore/vol23/newage.pdf (accessed March 9, 2010).
Fischer, Dietrich. *Preventing War in the Nuclear Age*. Totowa, NJ: Rowman and Allanheld, 1984.
Florida, Richard. *Cities and the Creative Class*. New York: Routledge, 2005.
Friedman, Thomas. *Hot, Flat, and Crowded*. New York: Farrar, Straus and Giroux, 2008.
Fukuyama, Francis. *Trust: The Social Virtues and the Creation of Prosperity*. London: Penguin, 1996.
Furman, Dmitry. "Democracy Suffers from 'Democrats.'" *Moscow Times*, Nov. 13, 2001.
———. "Imitation Democracies: The Post-Soviet Penumbra," *New Left Review* 54 (November- December 2008): 29–47.
Gall, Carlotta, and Thomas de Waal. *Chechnya: Calamity in the Caucasus*. New York: New York University Press, 1998.
Garcia, Ed. "Sharing nonviolence: an interview with Ed Garcia." By Metta Spencer. *Peace Magazine* 12, no. 2 (March-April 1996): 11-14.
———. *The Filipino Quest: A Just and Lasting Peace*. Quezon City, Philippines: Claretian Publications, 1988.
———. *The Sovereign Quest: Freedom from Foreign Military Bases*. Quezon City, Philippines: Claretian Publications, 1988.
Garthoff, Raymond. "BMD and East West Relations." In *Ballistic Missile Defense*, edited by Ashton B. Carter and David N. Schwartz. Washington DC: Brookings Institution, 1984.
Gates, Robert M. *From the Shadows: The Ultimate Insider's Story of Five Presidents and How They Won the Cold War*. New York: Simon and Schuster, 1996.
Gerasimov, Gennady. Interview. *Good Morning America*. October 25, 1989.
———. *Keep Space Weapon-Free*. Moscow: Novosti, 1984.
———. "The First-Strike Theory." *International Affairs* (Moscow) no. 3 (1965): 39–45.
Gluzman, Semyon F. "Abuse of Psychiatry: Analysis of the Guilt of Medical Personnel." *Journal of Medical Ethics* 17, no. 4 (1991): 19-20.
Goldman, Marshall. *Gorbachev's Challenge: Economic Reform in the Age of High Technology*. New York: Norton, 1987.
———. *What Went Wrong with Perestroika?* New York: Norton, 1991.
Gorbachev, Mikhail. *Memoirs*. Translated by Georges Peronansky and Tatjana Varsavsky. New York: Doubleday, 1995.
———. *On My Country and the World*. New York: Columbia University Press, 1999.
———. *Perestroika: New Thinking for Our Country and the World*. New rev. ed. London: Collins, 1987.

Gorbachev, Mikhail, and Zdeněk Mlynář. *Conversations with Gorbachev: On Perestroika, the Prague Spring, and the Crossroads of Socialism.* Translated by George Shriver. New York: Columbia University Press, 2002.

Gorbachev, Raisa. *I Hope: Reminiscences and Reflections.* Translated by David Floyd. New York: HarperCollins, 1991.

Grant, Jonathan. "The Socialist Construction of Philately in the Early Soviet Era." *Comparative Studies in Society and History* 37, no. 3 (1995): 483–94.

Grudzinska Gross, Irina, ed. *Letters from Freedom: Post-Cold War Realities and Perspectives.* Berkeley: University of California Press, 1998.

Havel, Václav. "The Power of the Powerless." In *The Power of the Powerless: Citizens Against the State in Central-Eastern Europe,* edited by John Keane and translated by Paul Wilson. Armonk, NY: M.E. Sharpe, 1985.

———. "The Strange Epoch of Post-Communism: A Conversation with Václav Havel." by Adam Michnik. *Letters from Freedom: Post-Cold War Realities and Perspectives,* edited by Irena Grudzinska Gross. Berkeley: University of California Press, 1998.

Hedges, Chris. *War is a Force That Gives Us Meaning.* New York: Knopf Doubleday, 2003.

Helsinki Watch. *Nyeformaly: Civil Society in the USSR.* New York: Helsinki Watch, 1990.

Helvey, Robert L. *On Strategic Nonviolent Conflict: Thinking about the Fundamentals.* Boston: The Albert Einstein Foundation, 2004.

Higgins, Rosalyn. *Problems and Process: International Law and How We Use It.* Oxford: Clarendon Press, 1994.

Hjollund, Lene, Marti Paldam, and Gert Tinggaard Svendsen. "Social Capital in Russia and Denmark: A Comparative Study." Paper, Department of Economics, Aarhus University, Denmark, 2001.

Hoffman, Eva. *Exit into History: A Journey Through the New Eastern Europe.* New York: Penguin, 1993.

Hough, Jerry. "Debates About the Postwar World." In *The Impact of World War II on the Soviet Union,* edited by Susan J. Linz. Totowa, NJ: Rowman and Allenheld, 1985.

———. *Democratization and Revolution in the USSR, 1985-91.* Washington, Brookings Institution, 1997.

Howard, Marc Morje. "Postcommunist Civil Society in Comparative Perspective." *Demokratizatsiya* 10, no. 3 (Summer 2002): 285-306.

Hudson, George E. "System-Level and Contextual Factors as Determinants of the Effectiveness of Civil Groups in Russia." Paper, Wittenberg University, Springfield, OH, 2008.

Inkeles, Alex, and Raymond Bauer. *The Soviet Citizen.* Cambridge: Harvard University Press, 1959.

Janis, Irving Lester. *Victims of Groupthink: A Psychological Study of Policy Decisions and Fiascoes.* 2nd ed. Boston: Houghton Mifflin, 1982.

Johansen, Jørgen. "External Financing of Opposition Movements." In *People Power: Unarmed Resistance and Global Solidarity,* edited by Howard Clark. New York: Pluto Press, 2009.

Journalists in Russia, 1993-2009: Deaths and Disappearances, Online database, journalists-in-russia.org.

Kadomtsev, B. B., et al. *Reminiscences about Academician Lev Artsimovich.* Moscow: Nauka, 1986.

Kagarlitsky, Boris. *The Thinking Reed: Intellectuals and the Soviet State from 1917 to the Present.* Translated by Brian Pearce. London: Verso, 1988.

Kalugin, Oleg. *The First Directorate: My 32 Years in Intelligence and Espionage Against the West.* With Fen Montaigne. New York: St. Martin's, 1994.

Kapitza, Peter. "The Paramount Task." *New Times* no. 39 (Sept. 1956): 10-11.

Karatnycky, Adrian, and Peter Ackerman. *How Freedom is Won: From Civic Resistance to Durable Democracy.* Washington, DC: Freedom House 2005.

Karpinsky, Len. "The Autobiography of a 'Half-Dissident.'" In *Voices of Glasnost: Interviews with Gorbachev's Reformers,* edited by Stephen F. Cohen and Katrina vanden Heuvel. New York: Norton, 1989.

Keohane, Robert O., and Joseph S. Nye, Jr., eds. *Transnational Relations and World Politics.* Cambridge: Harvard University Press 1972.

Knight, Amy. *Beria: Stalin's First Lieutenant.* Princeton: Princeton University Press, 1993.

Korbonski, Andrzej. "Poland." In *Communism in Eastern Europe.* 2nd ed. Edited by Teresa Rakowska-Harmstone. Bloomington: Indiana University Press, 1984.

Kort, Michael. *The Soviet Colossus: History and Aftermath.* Armonk, NY: M.E. Sharpe, 2001.

Kotkin, Stephen. *Uncivil Society: 1989 and the Implosion of the Communist Establishment.* Kindle edition.

Kovrig, Bennett. "Hungary." In *Communism in Eastern Europe,* edited by Teresa Rakowska- Harmstone. 2nd. ed. Bloomington: Indiana University Press, 1984.

Kramer, Mark. "The Collapse of East European Communism and the Repercussions within the Soviet Union (Part I)." *Journal of Cold War Studies* vol. 5, no. 4 (Fall 2003): 178-256.

——— "The Opening of the Berlin Wall: A Twenty-Year Retrospective." Carnegie Council, http://www.cceia.org/resources/ethics_online/0039.html (accessed March 28, 2010).

Khrushchev, Nikita Sergeevich. *Khrushchev Remembers.* With an introduction, commentary, and notes by Edward Crankshaw. Translated and edited by Strobe Talbott. (Boston: Little Brown, 1970).

Kuran, Timur. "Now Out of Never: The Element of Surprise in the East European Revolution of 1989." In *Liberalization and Democratization: Change in the Soviet Union and Eastern Europe,* edited by Nancy Bermeo. Baltimore: Johns Hopkins University Press, 1991.

Kuth, Paul, and Todd L. Allee. *The Democratic Peace and Territorial Conflict in the Twentieth Century.* Cambridge: Cambridge University Press, 2002.

Kuusinen, Otto. *Fundamentals of Marxism-Leninism, Manual.* Translated and edited by Clemens Dutt. 2nd ed. Moscow: Progress Publishers, 1964.

Lecerf, Yves, and Edward Parker. *The Chernobyl Affair.* Paris: Presses Universitaires de France, 1987.

Levada, Yury. "The Disappearing Model? Homo Sovieticus: The Preliminary Results." *Znamya,* no. 6 (1992): 203-4.

Linz, Susan J., ed. *The Impact of World War II on the Soviet Union.* Totowa, NJ: Rowman and Allenheld, 1985.

Litvinenko, Alexander, and Yuri Felshtinsky. *Blowing up Russia: The Secret Plot to Bring Back KGB Terror.* Translated by Geoffrey Andrews and Co. London: Gibson Square, 2007.

Livshin, Alexander, and Richard Weitz. "Civil Society and Philanthropy Under Putin." *The International Journal of Not-for-Profit Law* 8, no. 3 (May 2006): 7-12.

Locke Binnendijk, Anika, and Ivan Marovic. "Power and Persuasion: Nonviolent Strategies to Influence State Security Forces in Serbia (2000) and Ukraine (2004)." *Communist and Post-Communist Studies* 39 (2006): 411–429.

MacKinnon, Mark. *The New Cold War: Revolutions, Rigged Elections and Pipeline Politics in the Former Soviet Union*. Toronto: Random House, 2007.

Makarychev, Andrey S. "Russia and its New Security Architecture in Europe: A Critical Examination of the Concept." Center for European Policy Studies. Working Document No. 310, February 2009. http://ceps.be/ceps/download/1612 (accessed April 20, 2010).

Mandelstam, Nadezhda. *Hope Against Hope*. Translated by Max Hayward. New York: Modern Library, 1999.

Marx, Karl, and Friedrich Engels. *Collected Works*. Translated by Emile Burns and Clemens Dutt. Edited by Tatyana Chikileva. Vol. 1. New York: International Publishers, 1975.

———. *Collected Works*. Translated by Emile Burns and Clemens Dutt. Edited by Tatyana Chikileva. Vol. 20. New York: International Publishers, 1985.

———. *The German Ideology*. Edited and translated by C. J. Arthur. New York: International Publishers. 1970.

Matlock, Jack F., Jr. *Autopsy on an Empire: The American Ambassador's Account of the Collapse of the Soviet Union*. New York: Random House, 1995.

———. Lecture, American Association for the Advancement of Slavic Studies, Philadelphia, PA, November 20-23, 2008.

———. Lecture, Kennan Institute, Woodrow Wilson International Center for Scholars, Washington, DC, March 15, 2010.

———. *Superpower Illusions: How Myths and False Ideologies Led America Astray and How to Return to Reality*. New Haven: Yale University Press, 2009.

McFaul, Michael. *Advancing Democracy Abroad: Why We Should and How We Can*. Lanham, MD: Rowman and Littlefield, 2010.

McFaul, Michael, and Kathryn Stoner-Weiss. "The Myth of the Authoritarian Model: How Putin's Crackdown Holds Russia Back." *Foreign Affairs* 88, no. 1 (January-February 2008): 68-84.

McFaul, Michael, Nikolai Petrov, and Andrei Ryabov. *Between Dictatorship and Democracy: Russian Post-Communist Political Reform*. Washington, DC: Carnegie Endowment for International Peace, 2004.

Medvedev, Zhores. *Gorbachev*. New York: W.W. Norton, 1987.

Medvedkov, Olga. *Soviet Urbanization*. London: Routledge, 1990.

Millar, James R. "History, Method, and the Problem of Bias." In *Politics, Work, and Daily Life in the USSR*, edited by James R. Millar. Cambridge: Cambridge University Press, 1987.

———. ed. *Politics, Work, and Daily Life in the USSR*. Cambridge: Cambridge University Press, 1987.

Neild, Robert R. *An Essay on Strategy as it Affects the Achievement of Peace in a Nuclear Setting*. Basingstoke: Macmillan, 1990.

Neustadt, Richard E. *Presidential Power and the Modern Presidents: The Politics of Leadership from Roosevelt to Reagan*. New York: Free Press, 1990.

Newsom, David D. *Private Diplomacy with the Soviet Union*. Lanham, MD: University Press of America, 1987.

New York Review of Books, various articles and authors.

Oberdorfer, Don. *The Turn: From the Cold War to a New Era*. New York: Simon and Schuster, 1991.

Osgood, Charles Egerton. *An Alternative to War or Surrender*. Urbana: University of Illinois Press, 1962.

Palazchenko, Pavel. *My Years with Gorbachev and Shevardnadze: The Memoir of a Soviet Interpreter*. University Park, PA: Penn State University Press, 1997.

Peace Magazine, various articles and authors.

Peierls, Rudolf. *Bird of Passage: Recollections of a Physicist*. Princeton: Princeton University Press, 1985.

Peunova, Marina. "From Dissidents to Collaborators: The Resurgence and Demise of the Russian Critical Intelligentsia Since 1985." *Studies in East European Thought* 60, no. 3 (2008): 231-50.

Pomper, Philip. *Lenin, Trotsky, and Stalin: The Intelligentsia and Power* (New York: Columbia University Press, 1990.

Popov, Nikolai. *The People of Russia at the Crossroads*. Syracuse, NY: Syracuse University Press, 1994.

Pribylovskii, Vladimir. *Dictionary of Political Parties and Organizations in Russia*. Edited by Dauphine Sloan and Sarah Helmstadter. Washington, DC: Center for Strategic and International Studies, 1992.

Putnam, Robert D. *Bowling Alone*. New York: Simon and Schuster, 2000.

Putnam, Robert D., Robert Leonardi, and Raffaella Y. Nanetti. *Making Democracy Work: Civic Traditions in Modern Italy*. Princeton: Princeton University Press, 1994.

Rakowska-Harmstone, Teresa. *Communism in Eastern Europe*. 2nd. ed. Bloomington: Indiana University Press, 1984.

Reddaway, Peter. "Soviet Psychiatry: An End to Political Abuse?" *Survey* 29 (October 1988).

Richmond, Yale. *Cultural Exchange and the Cold War: Raising the Iron Curtain*. University Park, PA: Pennsylvania State University Press, 2003).

Rogov, Sergei. "Nuclear Strategy: What's at Stake." *Kommersant*, April 15, 2009.

Rotblat, Joseph. *Pugwash—the First Ten Years: History of the Conferences of Science and World Affairs*. London: Heinemann, 1967.

———. *Scientists in the Quest for Peace: A History of the Pugwash Conferences*. Cambridge: MIT Press, 1972.

Roxburgh, Angus. *The Second Russian Revolution: The Struggle for Power in the Kremlin*. New York: Pharos Books, 1992.

Rozman, Gilbert. *A Mirror For Socialism: Soviet Criticisms of China*. Princeton: Princeton University Press, 1985.

Russian Research Center for Human Rights. "Union of the Committees of Soldiers' Mothers of Russia." http://humanrightshouse.org/Articles/5387.html

Ryan, Michael. "Life Expectancy and Mortality Data from the Soviet Union." *British Medical Journal* 296 (May 28, 1988).

Sagdeev, Roald Z. *The Making of a Soviet Scientist: My Adventures in Nuclear Fusion and Space From Stalin to Star Wars*. New York: Wiley, 1994.

Sakharov, Andrei. *Memoirs*. New York: Vintage, 1992.

———. *Reflections on Progress, Peaceful Coexistence, and Intellectual Freedom*. New York: Norton, 1968.

Scammel, Michael. "Writers in a Cage." Review of *Zhivago's Children: The Last Russian Intelligentsia*, by Vladislav Zubok. *New York Review of Books* 57, no. 1 (January 14, 2010): 53-55.

Scheff, Thomas J. *Bloody Revenge: Emotions, Nationalism, and War* (Boulder: Westview, 1994).

Schrag, Philip G. *Global Action: Nuclear Test Ban Diplomacy at the End of the Cold War*. Boulder: Westview, 1992.

————. *Listening for the Bomb: A Study in Nuclear Arms Control Verification Policy*. Boulder: Westview Press, 1989.

Sheehy, Gail. *The Man Who Changed the World: The Lives of Mikhail S. Gorbachev*. New York: HarperCollins, 1990.

Sheinis, Viktor. "The Constitution." In *Between Dictatorship and Democracy: Russian Post-Communist Political Reform*, edited by Michael McFaul, Nikolai Petrov, and Andrei Ryabov. 56-81. Washington, DC: Carnegie Endowment for International Peace, 2004.

Shenfield, Stephen. "The USSR: Viktor Girshfeld and the Concept of 'Sufficient Defence.'" *ADIU Report* 6, no. 1 (January–February 1984).

Shevtsova, Lilia. *Russia: Lost in Transition*. Washington, DC: Carnegie Endowment for International Peace, 2007.

Shlapentokh, Vladimir. "Trust in Public Institutions in Russia: The Lowest in the World." *Communist and Post-Communist Studies* 39, no. 2 (June 2006): 153–174.

Siklová, Jirina. "Dilemmas of Transition: A View From Prague." *Peace Review* 4, no. 4 (Winter 1992): 24-28.

Silver, Brian D. "Political Beliefs of the Soviet Citizen." In *Politics, Work, and Daily Life*, edited by James R. Millar. Cambridge: Cambridge University Press, 1987.

Singh, Arvind, and Everett M. Rogers. *Entertainment-Education: A Communication Strategy for Social Change*. Mahwah, NJ: Lawrence Erlbaum, 1999.

Skilling, H. Gordon. *Communism National and International: Eastern Europe After Stalin*. Toronto: University of Toronto Press, 1984.

Solzhenitsyn, Aleksandr. *The Oak and the Calf*. New York: Harper and Row, 1980.

————. "The Smatterers." *From Under the Rubble*, translated by A. M. Brock et al. Boston: Little, Brown, 1975.

Spencer, Metta. "Politics beyond Turf: Grass-roots Democracy in the Helsinki Process." *Bulletin of Peace Proposals* 22, no. 4 (1991): 427–435.

————. *Two Aspirins and a Comedy: How Television Can Enhance Health and Society*. Boulder, CO: Paradigm, 2006.

————. "Yugoslavia Timeline." *The Lessons of Yugoslavia*. Edited by Metta Spencer. London: Elsevier, 2000.

Spencer, Metta, ed. *Separatism: Democracy and Disintegration*. Lanham, MD: Rowman and Littlefield, 1998.

Stephan, Maria J., and Erica Chenoweth. "Why Civil Resistance Works: The Strategic Logic of Nonviolent Conflict." *International Security* 33, no. 1 (Summer 2008): 7-44.

Stewart, Philip D. "Informal Diplomacy: The Dartmouth Conference" In *Private Diplomacy with the Soviet Union*, edited by David D. Newsom. Lanham, MD: University Press of America, 1987.

Stockman, David. *The Triumph of Politics: How the Reagan Revolution Failed*. New York: Harper and Row, 1986.

Stone, Jeremy J. *Every Man Should Try: Adventures of a Public Interest Activist*. New York: Public Affairs, 1999.

Talbott, Strobe. *The Master of* the Game. New York: Vintage, 1988.

Teague, Elizabeth. *Solidarity and the Soviet Worker: The Impact of the Polish Events of 1980 on Soviet Internal Politics*. London: Croom Helm, 1988.

Teggart, Frederick J. *The Processes of History*. New Haven: Yale University Press, 1918.

Tishkov, Valery. *Ethnicity, Nationalism, and Conflict*. Oslo: International Peace Research Institute, 1997.

Trotsky, Leon. *The Young Lenin*. Translated by Max Eastman. Edited by Maurice Friedberg. Garden City, NY: Doubleday, 1972.

United States Department of Defense. *The Pentagon Papers: The Defense Department History of United States Decisionmaking on Vietnam*. The Senator Gravel ed. 5 vols. Boston: Beacon Press, 1971–72.

Urban, George. *Radio Free Europe and the Pursuit of Democracy*. New Haven: Yale University Press, 1997.

Valentinov, Nikolai. *The Early Years of Lenin*. Translated by Rolf Theen. Ann Arbor: University of Michigan Press, 1969.

van Bladel, Joris. "Russian Soldiers in the Barracks: The Portrait of a Subculture." In *Russian Military Reform*, edited by Anne C. Aldis and Roger N. McDermott. Kindle edition.

Velikhov, Yevgeny. "Chernobyl Remains on Our Mind: Interview with Yevgeny Velikhov." By Stephen F. Cohen and Katrina vanden Heuvel. Translated by Nina Bouis, et al. In *Voices of Glasnost: Conversations with Gorbachev's Reformers*, edited by Stephen F. Cohen and Katrina vanden Heuvel. 157-73. New York: Norton, 1989.

Volkogonov, Dmitri. *Lenin: A New Biography*. Translated and edited Harold Shukman. New York: The Free Press, 1994.

von Hippel, Frank, ed. *Citizen Scientist*. New York: Simon and Schuster, 1991.

———. "Nongovernmental Arms Control Research: The New Soviet Connection." *Citizen Scientist*. Edited by Frank von Hippel. New York: Simon and Schuster, 1991.

von Hippel, Frank, and Roald Z. Sagdeev, eds. *Reversing the Arms Race: How to Achieve and Verify Deep Reductions in the Nuclear Arsenals*. New York: Gordon and Breach, 1990.

von Hippel, Frank, David H. Albright, and Barbara G. Levi. "Fissile Weapons Materials." *Citizen Scientist*. Edited by Frank von Hippel. 105-116. New York: Simon and Schuster, 1991.

Wallander, Celeste. "Lost and Found: Gorbachev's 'New Thinking.'" *Washington Quarterly* 25, no. 1 (Winter 2001): 117-129.

Warner, Gale. *Invisible Threads: Independent Soviets Working for Global Awareness and Social Transformation*. Washington, DC: Seven Locks Press, 1991.

Warner, Gale, and Michael Shuman. *Citizen Diplomats: Pathfinders in Soviet-American Relations—And How You Can Join Them*. New York: Continuum, 1987.

Weir, Fred. *Russia's Path from Gorbachev to Putin: The Demise of the Soviet System and the New Russia*. Kindle edition.

Wilson, Andrew. *Ukraine's Orange Revolution*. New Haven: Yale University Press, 2005.

Zaslavskaia, Tat'iana. *A Voice of Reform*. Armonk, NY: M.E. Sharpe, 1989.

Zhurkin, Vitaly, Sergei Karaganov, and Andrei Kortunov. "Old and New Challenges to Security." *Kommunist*, no. 1 (January 1988): 42-50.

———. *Reasonable Sufficiency and New Political Thinking*. Moscow: Nauka, 1989.

Zinoviev, Alexander. *Homo Sovieticus*. Translated by Charles Janson. London: Gollancz, 1985.

Zisserman, Dina. "The Prospects for Democratization in Post-Putin Russia." Paper, Association for the Study of Nationalities, Columbia University, New York, NY, April 15, 2010.

Zubok, Vladislav. *Zhivago's Children: The Last Russian Intelligentsia*. Cambridge, MA: Belknap Press of Harvard University, 2009.

RussianPeaceAndDemocracy.com

Metta Spencer has created a website with a wide range of supplementary and source material on the events described in this book.

The site at **www.RussianPeaceAndDemocracy.com** features:

- hundreds of her interviews with both Eastern and Western informants—as unedited transcripts and/or voice recordings;
- other background essays (some of which were originally written as chapters in the book, but which were omitted to keep the length manageable);
- a photo gallery (invaluable for readers who want to put faces to many of the names mentioned in the book);
- biographical information and updates on many of her informants;
- a links page, including published articles and interviews about her informants and news about Russian politics and culture;
- notes and itineraries of some of Metta's visits to the people whose stories are told in the book.

Index

Breinigsville, PA USA
07 December 2010
250778BV00003B/2/P

9 780739 144725